Praise, Praise, Praise For Dr. Ruth

Dr. Ruth's Encyclopedia of Sex:

Sex and the single CD

"Her buoyant personality puts forth a provocative message without a hint of prurience. Dr. Ruth loves what she does, and wants to help you enjoy sex to the fullest. . . . Its objective noninflammatory treatment of a sensitive subject gives the program credence and substance. Dr. Ruth, nonthreatening as well as nonpolitical, has become a natural and obvious master of this modern medium." — *Multimedia World.*

CD-ROM Report

"Human sexuality maven Ruth Westheimer has earned a huge following by delivering straight facts about impotence, birth control and safer sex, and presenting them in the palatable (and often humorous) patois of a Jewish grandmother. . . . this is one encyclopedia that will provide reference and entertainment for children and adults alike." — *Newmedia,* Awesome Award, April 1995

All You Need to Know without The Heavy Breathing

"Dr. Ruth Westheimer is the Stealth fighter of sex education. This tiny woman . . . knows how to talk about important sexual issues without triggering fear or embarrassment among the readers of her books and newspaper columns, listeners to her radio talk show and viewers of her frequent television appearances. . . . Dr. Ruth talks in simple sentences that even pre-adolescents will understand and delves into the most intimate subjects without ever becoming prurient." — *San Jose Mercury News,* January 29, 1995

Multimedia Reviews

". . . [T]his guide reaches out to people of all ages. . . . Dr. Ruth Westheimer says here that she wants to boost 'sexual literacy'; as in her television shows and books, she sets about her mission with no-nonsense good cheer. . . Health and happiness, not sexual refinements, are the prevailing concerns, and this comfortable presentation is likely to promote both." — *Publishers Weekly,* March 27, 1995

Everything You Ever Wanted to Know . . .

". . . [I]f you're interested in becoming more educated, 'sexually speaking,' this is a disc you can get excited about." — *Computer Life,* April 1995

CD-Roms Worth Having

"Its star is Ruth Westheimer, the diminutive figure who nonchalantly describes every known sexual practice and proclivity with the same sweet tone your grandma might have used to ask you to pass the dinner rolls. . . . All are presented with a light touch, even when the topics are quite serious. 'Click around! that you can do without a condom,' the doctor cheerfully advises." — *Wall Street Journal,* April 13, 1995.

The Author

"Her energy level is higher than that of a charged particle." — *People Magazine,* 1985.

"America's star sexologist . . ."— *TV Guide.*

"If height were measured in courage, determination and hard work, this little lady would be 10 feet tall." — *Newsday,* 1987.

"Her name and the distinctive thrill of her voice have become inextricably linked with the subject of sex." — *New York Times,* 1992.

"Her manner is down-to-earth and reassuring . . . she tries to make people feel better, value themselves, trust their instincts . . ." — *Ladies Home Journal,* 1986.

"She can seemingly say things on the air that no one else can. This could be because she is short and sweet and takes her subject seriously . . ." — *New York Times,* 1985.

"Dr. Ruth writes the way she talks — enthusiastically, nonjudgementally and informatively . . ."— Booklist, 1994.

"Her image is synonymous with sex . . ." — *Time, 1987.*

 ™

References for the Rest of Us

BUSINESS AND GENERAL REFERENCE BOOK SERIES FROM IDG

Do you find that traditional reference books are overloaded with technical details and advice you'll never use? Do you postpone important life decisions because you just don't want to deal with them? Then our *...For Dummies*™ business and general reference book series is for you.

... For Dummies business and general reference books are written for those frustrated and hard-working souls who know they aren't dumb, but find that the myriad of personal and business issues and the accompanying horror stories make them feel helpless. *...For Dummies* books use a lighthearted approach, a down-to-earth style, and even cartoons and humorous icons to diffuse fears and build confidence. Lighthearted but not lightweight, these books are perfect survival guides to solve your everyday personal and business problems.

> **"More than a publishing phenomenon, 'Dummies' is a sign of the times."**
> — The New York Times

> **"A world of detailed and authoritative information is packed into them..."**
> — U.S. News and World Report

> **"... you won't go wrong buying them."**
> — Walter Mossberg, Wall Street Journal, on IDG's ...For Dummies™ books

Already, hundreds of thousands of satisfied readers agree. They have made *...For Dummies* the #1 introductory level computer book series and a best-selling business book series. They have written asking for more. So if you're looking for the best and easiest way to learn about business and other general reference topics, look to *...For Dummies* to give you a helping hand.

IDG BOOKS WORLDWIDE

SEX FOR DUMMIES™

by Dr. Ruth K. Westheimer

IDG Books Worldwide, Inc.
An International Data Group Company

Foster City, CA ♦ Chicago, IL ♦ Indianapolis, IN ♦ Braintree, MA ♦ Dallas, TX

Sex For Dummies™

Published by
IDG Books Worldwide, Inc.
An International Data Group Company
919 E. Hillsdale Blvd.
Suite 400
Foster City, CA 94404

Text copyright © 1995 by Dr. Ruth K. Westheimer. Medical art copyright © 1995 by IDG Books Worldwide, Inc. All rights reserved. No part of this book may be reproduced or transmitted in any form, by any means (electronic, photocopying, recording, or otherwise) without the prior written permission of the publisher.

Library of Congress Catalog Card No.: 95-78778

ISBN: 1-56884-384-4

Printed in the United States of America

10 9 8 7 6 5 4 3 2 1

1I/RY/QY/ZU

Distributed in the United States by IDG Books Worldwide, Inc.

Distributed by Macmillan Canada for Canada; by Computer and Technical Books for the Caribbean Basin; by Contemporanea de Ediciones for Venezuela; by Distribuidora Cuspide for Argentina; by CITEC for Brazil; by Ediciones ZETA S.C.R. Ltda. for Peru; by Editorial Limusa SA for Mexico; by Transworld Publishers Limited in the United Kingdom and Europe; by Al-Maiman Publishers & Distributors for Saudi Arabia; by Simron Pty. Ltd. for South Africa; by IDG Communications (HK) Ltd. for Hong Kong; by Toppan Company Ltd. for Japan; by Addison Wesley Publishing Company for Korea; by Longman Singapore Publishers Ltd. for Singapore, Malaysia, Thailand, and Indonesia; by Unalis Corporation for Taiwan; by WS Computer Publishing Company, Inc. for the Philippines; by WoodsLane Pty. Ltd. for Australia; by WoodsLane Enterprises Ltd. for New Zealand.

For general information on IDG Books Worldwide's books in the U.S., please call our Consumer Customer Service department at 800-762-2974. For reseller information, including discounts and premium sales, please call our Reseller Customer Service department at 800-434-3422.

For information on where to purchase IDG Books Worldwide's books outside the U.S., contact IDG Books Worldwide at 415-655-3021 or fax 415-655-3295.

For information on translations, contact Marc Jeffrey Mikulich, Director, Foreign & Subsidiary Rights, at IDG Books Worldwide, 415-655-3018 or fax 415-655-3295.

For sales inquiries and special prices for bulk quantities, write to the address above or call IDG Books Worldwide at 415-655-3200.

For information on using IDG Books Worldwide's books in the classroom, or ordering examination copies, contact Jim Kelly at 800-434-2086.

For authorization to photocopy items for corporate, personal, or educational use, please contact Copyright Clearance Center, 222 Rosewood Drive, Danvers, MA 01923, or fax 508-750-4470.

All opinions expressed in this book are solely those of the author and not necessarily those of IDG Books Worldwide, Inc., or its employees.

Limit of Liability/Disclaimer of Warranty: The author and publisher have used their best efforts in preparing this book. IDG Books Worldwide, Inc., and the author make no representation or warranties with respect to the accuracy or completeness of the contents of this book and specifically disclaim any implied warranties of merchantability or fitness for any particular purpose and shall in no event be liable for any loss of profit or any other commercial damage, including but not limited to special, incidental, consequential, or other damages.

Trademarks: All brand names and product names used in this book are trademarks, registered trademarks, or trade names of their respective holders. IDG Books Worldwide is not associated with any product or vendor mentioned in this book.

 is a trademark under exclusive license to IDG Books Worldwide, Inc., from International Data Group, Inc.

About the Author

Dr. Ruth K. Westheimer

Dr. Ruth K. Westheimer is a psychosexual therapist who helped pioneer the field of media psychology with her radio program, *Sexually Speaking*, which first aired in New York in 1980. Within a few years, she had built a communications network to distribute her expertise that included television, books, newspapers, games, calendars, home video, and computer software.

Dr. Westheimer received her Master's Degree in Sociology from the Graduate Faculty of the New School of Social Research and her Doctorate of Education (Ed.D) in the Interdisciplinary Study of the Family from Columbia University Teacher's College. Working at Planned Parenthood prompted her to further her education in human sexuality by studying under Dr. Helen Singer Kaplan at New York Hospital-Cornell University Medical Center. She later participated in the program for five years as an Adjunct Associate Professor. She has also taught at Lehman College, Brooklyn College, Adelphi University, Columbia University, and West Point. She is currently an Adjunct Professor at New York University.

Dr. Westheimer is a Fellow of New York Academy of Medicine, leads regular seminars for residents and interns in pediatrics on adolescent sexuality at Brookdale Hospital, and has her own private practice in New York. She frequently lectures around the world, including at universities, and has twice been named "College Lecturer of the Year."

Sex For Dummies is Dr. Westheimer's twelfth book. The others include: *Dr. Ruth's Encyclopedia of Sex* (which has been released on CD-ROM), *The Art of Arousal, Dr. Ruth Talks to Kids,* and *Dr. Ruth's Guide for Safer Sex.*

ABOUT IDG BOOKS WORLDWIDE

VIII
WINNER
Eighth Annual
Computer Press
Awards ⮕ 1992

IX
WINNER
Ninth Annual
Computer Press
Awards ⮕ 1993

IDG BOOKS WORLDWIDE

Welcome to the world of IDG Books Worldwide.

IDG Books Worldwide, Inc., is a subsidiary of International Data Group, the world's largest publisher of computer-related information and the leading global provider of information services on information technology. IDG was founded more than 25 years ago and now employs more than 7,500 people worldwide. IDG publishes more than 235 computer publications in 67 countries (see listing below). More than 60 million people read one or more IDG publications each month.

Launched in 1990, IDG Books Worldwide is today the #1 publisher of best-selling computer books in the United States. We are proud to have received 8 awards from the Computer Press Association in recognition of editorial excellence, and our best-selling ...For Dummies™ series has more than 17 million copies in print with translations in 25 languages. IDG Books Worldwide, through a recent joint venture with IDG's Hi-Tech Beijing, became the first U.S. publisher to publish a computer book in the People's Republic of China. In record time, IDG Books Worldwide has become the first choice for millions of readers around the world who want to learn how to better manage their businesses.

Our mission is simple: Every one of our books is designed to bring extra value and skill-building instructions to the reader. Our books are written by experts who understand and care about our readers. The knowledge base of our editorial staff comes from years of experience in publishing, education, and journalism — experience which we use to produce books for the '90s. In short, we care about books, so we attract the best people. We devote special attention to details such as audience, interior design, use of icons, and illustrations. And because we use an efficient process of authoring, editing, and desktop publishing our books electronically, we can spend more time ensuring superior content and spend less time on the technicalities of making books.

You can count on our commitment to deliver high-quality books at competitive prices on topics consumers want to read about. At IDG Books Worldwide, we value quality, and we have been delivering quality for more than 25 years. You'll find no better book on a subject than an IDG book.

John J. Kilcullen

John Kilcullen
President and CEO
IDG Books Worldwide, Inc.

IDG Books Worldwide, Inc., is a subsidiary of International Data Group, the world's largest publisher of computer-related information and the leading global provider of information services on information technology. International Data Group publishes over 235 computer publications in 67 countries. More than sixty million people read one or more International Data Group publications each month. The officers are Patrick J. McGovern, Founder and Board Chairman; Kelly Conlin, President; Jim Casella, Chief Operating Officer. International Data Group's publications include: **ARGENTINA'S** Computerworld Argentina, Infoworld Argentina; **AUSTRALIA'S** Computerworld Australia, Computer Living, Australian PC World, Australian Macworld, Network World, Mobile Business Australia, Publish!, Reseller, IDG Sources; **AUSTRIA'S** Computerwelt Oesterreich, PC Test; **BELGIUM'S** Data News (CW); **BOLIVIA'S** Computerworld; **BRAZIL'S** Computerworld, Connections, Game Power, Mundo Unix, PC World, Publish, Super Game; **BULGARIA'S** Computerworld Bulgaria, PC & Mac World Bulgaria, Network World Bulgaria; **CANADA'S** CIO Canada, Computerworld Canada, InfoCanada, Network World Canada, Reseller; **CHILE'S** Computerworld Chile, Informatica; **COLOMBIA'S** Computerworld Colombia, PC World; **COSTA RICA'S** PC World; **CZECH REPUBLIC'S** Computerworld, Elektronika, PC World; **DENMARK'S** Communications World, Computerworld Danmark, Computerworld Focus, Macintosh Produktkatalog, Macworld Danmark, PC World Danmark, PC Produktguide, Tech World, Windows World; **ECUADOR'S** PC World Ecuador; **EGYPT'S** Computerworld (CW) Middle East, PC World Middle East; **FINLAND'S** MikroPC, Tietoviikko, Tietoverkko; **FRANCE'S** Distributique, GOLDEN MAC, InfoPC, Le Guide du Monde Informatique, Le Monde Informatique, Telecoms & Reseaux; **GERMANY'S** Computerwoche, Computerwoche Focus, Computerwoche Extra, Electronic Entertainment, Gamepro, Information Management, Macwelt, Netzwelt, PC Welt, Publish, Publish; **GREECE'S** Publish & Macworld; **HONG KONG'S** Computerworld Hong Kong, PC World Hong Kong; **HUNGARY'S** Computerworld SZT, PC World; **INDIA'S** Computers & Communications; **INDONESIA'S** Info Komputer; **IRELAND'S** ComputerScope; **ISRAEL'S** Beyond Windows, Computerworld Israel, Multimedia, PC World Israel; **ITALY'S** Computerworld Italia, Lotus Magazine, Macworld Italia, Networking Italia, PC Shopping Italy, PC World Italia; **JAPAN'S** Computerworld Today, Information Systems World, Macworld Japan, Nikkei Personal Computing, SunWorld Japan, Windows World; **KENYA'S** East African Computer News; **KOREA'S** Computerworld Korea, Macworld Korea, PC World Korea; **LATIN AMERICA'S** GamePro; **MALAYSIA'S** Computerworld Malaysia, PC World Malaysia; **MEXICO'S** Compu Edicion, Compu Manufactura, Computacion/Punto de Venta, Computerworld Mexico, MacWorld, Mundo Unix, PC World, Windows; **THE NETHERLANDS'** Computer! Totaal, Computable (CW), LAN Magazine, Lotus Magazine, MacWorld; **NEW ZEALAND'S** Computer Buyer, Computerworld New Zealand, Network World, New Zealand PC World; **NIGERIA'S** PC World Africa; **NORWAY'S** Computerworld Norge, Lotusworld Norge, Macworld Norge, Maxi Data, Networld, PC World Ekspress, PC World Nettverk, PC World Norge, PC World's Produktguide, Publish& Multimedia World, Student Data, Unix World, Windowsworld; **PAKISTAN'S** PC World Pakistan; **PANAMA'S** PC World Panama; **PERU'S** Computerworld Peru, PC World; **PEOPLE'S REPUBLIC OF CHINA'S** China Computerworld, China Infoworld, China PC Info Magazine, Computer Fan, PC World China, Electronics International, Electronics Today/Multimedia World, Electronic Product World, China Network World, Software World Magazine, Telecom Product World; **PHILIPPINES'** Computerworld Philippines, PC Digest (PCW); **POLAND'S** Computerworld Poland, Computerworld Special Report, Networld, PC World/Komputer, Sunworld; **PORTUGAL'S** Cerebro/PC World, Correio Informatico/Computerworld, MacIn; **ROMANIA'S** Computerworld, PC World, Telecom Romania; **RUSSIA'S** Computerworld-Moscow, Mir - PK (PCW), Sety (Networks); **SINGAPORE'S** Computerworld Southeast Asia, PC World Singapore; **SLOVENIA'S** Monitor Magazine; **SOUTH AFRICA'S** Computer Mail (CIO),Computing S.A.,Network World S.A., Software World; **SPAIN'S** Advanced Systems, Amiga World, Computerworld Espana, Communicaciones World, Macworld Espana, NeXTWORLD, Super Juegos Magazine (GamePro), PC World Espana, Publish; **SWEDEN'S** Attack, ComputerSweden, Corporate Computing, Macworld, Mikrodatorn, Natverk & Kommunikation, PC World, CAP & Design, Datalngenjoren, Maxi Data,Windows World; **SWITZERLAND'S** Computerworld Schweiz, Macworld Schweiz, PC Tip; **TAIWAN'S** Computerworld Taiwan, PC World Taiwan; **THAILAND'S** Thai Computerworld; **TURKEY'S** Computerworld Monitor, Macworld Turkiye, PC World Turkiye; **UKRAINE'S** Computerworld, Computers+Software Magazine; **UNITED KINGDOM'S** Computing /Computerworld, Connexion/Network World, Lotus Magazine, Macworld, Open Computing/Sunworld; **UNITED STATES'** Advanced Systems, AmigaWorld, Cable in the Classroom, CD Review, CIO, Computerworld, Computerworld Client/Server Journal, Digital Video, DOS World, Electronic Entertainment Magazine (E2), Federal Computer Week, Game Hits, GamePro, IDG Books Worldwide, Infoworld, Laser Event, Macworld, Maximize, Multimedia World, Network World, PC Letter, PC World, Publish, SWATPro, Video Event; **URUGUAY'S** PC World Uruguay; **VENEZUELA'S** Computerworld Venezuela, PC World; **VIETNAM'S** PC World Vietnam.

05/17/95

Dedication

"The reticent do not learn; the hot-tempered do not teach."

Chapters of the Fathers 2.6

I dedicate this book to my parents, grandparents, uncles, and aunts who perished in concentration camps during World War II.

The set of values, the joie de vivre, and the positive outlook they instilled in me live on in my life and in the new family I have created to carry on their traditions: My husband Fred, daughter Miriam Westheimer, Ed.D., her husband Joel Einleger, M.B.A., my son Joel Westheimer, Ph.D., and the "best grandson" in the whole world, Ari Einleger.

Acknowledgments

In addition to the individuals mentioned here, I have a long list of friends, relatives, colleagues, clients, listeners, readers, and viewers to thank for their encouragement and constructive criticism. They all have helped me in my endeavors. I wish I could thank all of you by name.

I am grateful and appreciate the tremendous contribution in writing this book made by Pierre Lehu. Pierre and I are now entering our 14th year of working together — he is the best "Minister of Communications" anybody could wish for. So a special toast to Pierre and to many more years of cooperation.

To the IDG staff: what a terrific, hard working, competent, and expert group you are to work with! First of all, Kathy Welton, who "conceived" the idea and went chasing after me; Kathy Cox, our superb project editor; Shannon Ross, our talented copy editor; John Kilcullen, Milissa Koloski, Stephanie Britt, Diane Steele, Kathy Day, Stacy Collins, Sarah Kennedy, Mary Bednarek, Mike Kelly, Valery Bourke, Chris Collins, Kathie Schnorr, Dwight Ramsey, Rob Springer, Melissa Buddendeck, Kathleen Prata, and Sharon Hilgenberg. Thanks also to Dr. Michael Rosenberg and Dr. Diane Brashear for their professional reading of this manuscript, to Jeff Leopold, and to the reviewers, especially Karen Raridan and Jay Bastian.

To Pierre Lehu's family, his wife Joanne Lehu, Esq., his son Peter, and daughter Gabrielle; Helen Singer Kaplan, M.D., Ph. D., who has given her best in training me as a sex therapist; Marty Englisher, Ellen Goldberg, Al Kaplan, Steve Kaplan, Richard Kendall, Rabbi Leonard Kravitz, Marga and Bill Kunreuther, Rabbi William Lebeau, Marsha Lebby, Rabbi Robert Lehman, Lou Lieberman, Ph.D., and Mary Cuadrado, John Lollos, Jonathan Mark, Dale Ordes, Fred Rosenberg, Cliff Rubin, Joseph Seminara, Esq., Amir Shaviv, Ben Yagoda — lots of thanks and good wishes to all!

(The Publisher would like to give special thanks to Patrick J. McGovern and Bill Murphy, without whom this book would not have been possible.)

Credits

Senior Vice President and Group Publisher
Milissa Koloski

Vice President and Publisher
Kathleen A. Welton

Executive Editor
Sarah Kennedy

Managing Editor
Stephanie Britt

Brand Manager
Stacy S. Collins

Executive Assistant
Jamie Klobuchar

Editorial Assistants
Stacey Holden Prince
Kevin Spencer

Acquisitions Assistant
Suki Gear

Production Director
Beth Jenkins

Supervisor of Project Coordination
Cindy L. Phipps

Supervisor of Page Layout
Kathie Schnorr

Pre-Press Coordinator
Steve Peake

Associate Pre-Press Coordinator
Tony Augsburger

Media/Archive Coordinator
Paul Belcastro

Project Editor
Kathleen M. Cox

Copy Editor
Shannon Ross

Peer Reviewers
Michael Rosenberg, M.D., M.P.H.
Diane L. Brashear, Ph.D.

Project Coordinator
Valery Bourke

Production Staff
Patricia R. Reynolds
Melissa Buddendeck
Robert Springer
Dwight Ramsey
Theresa Sánchez-Baker
Chris H. Collins
Angie Hunckler
Drew Moore
Brian Noble

Proofreader
Kathleen Prata

Indexer
Sharon Hilgenberg

Book Design
University Graphics

Cover Design
Kavish + Kavish

Medical Drawings
Christopher Brown,
Medical Illustrations Department,
Indiana University School of Medicine

Contents at a Glance

Cartoons at a Glance

By Rich Tennant

The 5th Wave — By Rich Tennant

"It's an agreement Arthur and I made—he agrees to stay home from the gym 2 nights a week, and I guarantee that he'll still burn over 300 calories each night."

Page 120

The 5th Wave — By Rich Tennant

"MOM AND DAD GET LIKE THIS EVERYTIME THEY WATCH BACK-TO-BACK EPISODES OF 'THE LOVE BOAT'."

Page 226

The 5th Wave — By Rich Tennant

"JUST TO SPICE THINGS UP, I THOUGHT I'D WEAR THE FRENCH TICKLER INSIDE OUT THIS TIME TO ADD TO MY EXCITEMENT."

Page 207

The 5th Wave — By Rich Tennant

"THEY'RE A VERY PROGRESSIVE COMPANY—IT COMES WITH MATCHING COLORED CONDOMS."

Page 269

The 5th Wave — By Rich Tennant

"Oh, wait a minute Arthur! When I said I'd only have safe sex with you, this isn't what I meant!"

Page 343

The 5th Wave — By Rich Tennant

SUDDENLY LINDA FOUND HERSELF MYSTERIOUSLY DRAWN TO THE STRANGER ON HER TRAIN THAT DAY.

DOO DA
DOO DA

Page 57

The 5th Wave — By Rich Tennant

"I KNOW WHAT A ROMANTIC GETAWAY IS. IT'S WHEN MY PARENTS TELL ME TO GET AWAY FROM THE HOUSE FOR A FEW HOURS."

Page 140

The 5th Wave — By Rich Tennant

"We met on the Internet and I absolutely fell in looove with his syntax."

Page 261

The 5th Wave — By Rich Tennant

"NOW THAT WOULD SHOW HOW IMPORTANT IT IS TO DISTINGUISH 'FERTILIZER PRACTICES' FROM 'FERTILITY PRACTICES' WHEN DOWNLOADING A VIDEO FILE FROM THE INTERNET."

Page 16

The 5th Wave — By Rich Tennant

"IF WE ARE GOING TO DO THIS, CAN I ASK THAT WE NOT DO IT IN THE ROOM WHERE YOU KEEP YOUR PIRANHA COLLECTION?"

Page 141

Table of Contents

From the desk of Dr. Ruth

Dear Reader,

I have to start by saying that, when I was first asked to do a book called *Sex For Dummies*, I wasn't thrilled with the idea. Even though for years I've been saying that we must eradicate sexual illiteracy — a phrase that I thought appropriate for a college professor like myself to use — writing a book for people who considered themselves to be sexual dummies just didn't sit right with me.

But then I began to think

- ✔ of the tremendous number of unintended pregnancies we have each year in America (of which more than one million are teenage pregnancies)

- ✔ of all the women who do not have orgasms and think that they can do nothing about it

- ✔ of all the men who are premature ejaculators and who think that they have an uncorrectable physical problem instead of a learning disability

- ✔ of all the couples who expect so much from sex but who don't know the importance of foreplay and who neglect afterplay

And so, you know what?

I decided that there are a lot of people having trouble mastering the sexual basics who need a book that clearly addresses the root of the problem.

Once I came to that realization, something else dawned on me. I've written many books about sex, and the bookstores are filled with other books on the subject — as are magazines and television shows — yet the message still doesn't get across correctly. "Why is that?" I asked myself. The research has been done. Good sex can be available to everybody. So why do so many people go without having truly pleasurable sex?

I think that many people have trouble sorting through the mass of sexual information and sexual imagery that they get each day. Much of this information is not clear, and some of it is contradictory. In the face of this, many of you begin to think of yourselves as sexual dummies of the 1990s — caught between conflicting sexual views — or at least as people not capable of performing up to par.

Now a lot of people had given up on learning to use a computer, something that I think is a lot more complex than sex. Many people were afraid to buy a book about Windows or DOS because they thought they wouldn't understand it. Then along came the *...For Dummies* series, which stuck with the basics and used everyday words with a frank, humorous style, and those same people — you may be among them — have now become computer whizzes. So I decided if other writers can do it for computers, I know that I can do it for the subject I know best — sex.

So here I am with *Sex For Dummies* — a book made for those of you who want great sex in the 1990s, but who may have had difficulties getting it "right." You can get it right. Just keep on reading.

Dr. Ruth K. Westheimer

P.S. IDG Books Worldwide has generously agreed to donate a portion of the profits from the sales of *Sex For Dummies* to designated charities.

Introduction

● ●

*T*he main problems that we have in dealing with human sexuality most often come directly from ignorance — both the not-knowing kind and the not-caring kind.

You would think that after "doing it" for thousands of years, we all would have found a simple and effective system for passing on vital sexual information from generation to generation. But sadly, here we are, near the 21st century, and we adults continue to do a lousy job of educating ourselves and our young people about sex.

Part of the reason is that, in American culture, we're often embarrassed to talk about sex, especially when it comes to talking with our own flesh and blood (who wouldn't even be here without it).

As parents, many of us avoid the subject entirely. Often, even when we do work up the courage to have a heart-to-heart talk with "the kids," we don't do much more than pass on the bare-bones basics: concentrating on how to avoid pregnancy and scaring kids with the threat of sexually transmitted diseases.

These issues are certainly important points to cover. But what about issues of good sexual functioning, such as how to have an orgasm, or how to be the best lover possible? Is that ever on the agenda? After listening to the couples who come to see me in therapy, I don't believe these topics are talked about in the vast majority of families.

Direct from the Playground

So where did most of you learn about sex? You learned a little bit from your parents and a little bit at school. But because much of this information was passed on before you were really ready to use it, it may not have meant all that much to you, and so it didn't totally sink in. Later on, if you had another class, you probably felt the need to act blasé, as if you knew it all, and you may not have bothered to listen.

It's this Catch 22 that makes having good sex so difficult — you get the information before you need it, and you forget about it by the time you do need it. Or you get it so confused that it's not helpful to you.

Our children are the same way. Often, despite our best efforts as parents, kids are more likely to pay attention to what they hear on the street or in the locker room or at a pajama party. How much of this information is accurate is anybody's guess.

But even though some of this information is true, because it does not match the sexual myths that are also out there, the new information only leads to more confusion. And when you're confused, don't you often end up not paying attention to anything you've heard — preferring to trust your instincts?

Unfortunately, in sexual matters, trusting your instincts can often lead to problems.

In the end, you let trial and error become the teacher of last resort. And when that happens, not unexpectedly, you can often make serious mistakes — such as becoming pregnant when you don't intend to be, or catching a sexually transmitted disease, or, at the very least, having a less-than-satisfactory sex life, or going through your entire life never having terrific sex.

In the 1990s, and even more so in the 21st century, this process of misinformation and confusion cannot continue. In the past, we had rules in place to guide us so that, even if we didn't understand human sexuality all that well, as long as we followed the rules and got married before having sex, we couldn't stray too far.

But over the past 30 years, these rules have begun to disintegrate badly. Some people would say the results — millions of unintended pregnancies, millions of single parents, vast numbers of people with sexually transmitted diseases — were predictable.

Marriage, Morality, and Sexual Safety

Let me say something about my philosophy at this point.

- I am old-fashioned and a square.
- I believe in God, I believe in marriage, and I believe in morality.

But, because I cannot dictate to you how you should live your life,

- I believe that I must give you the tools with which to conduct yourself as safely as possible.

That's why I believe in giving you information so that, even if you do have premarital sex, at least you have a better chance of not causing unintended pregnancies and not catching a sexually transmitted disease.

Do I encourage people to develop a relationship before they engage in sex with another person? Absolutely. And I'll say it again and again throughout this book.

But even if you're having a one-night stand that I don't approve of, I still want you to wake up the next morning healthy and safe. And I look at this book as an important tool in reaching you and others of all ages to help you discover more useful information on this important subject.

About This Book

Sex For Dummies is intended to give you a start on a healthy approach to sexuality. It follows the *...For Dummies* ™ format that has proven so successful for computer and business topics. Important information is highlighted with little pictures, called icons, lurking in the margins. Here's what the ones used in this book signify.

Tip — This icon alerts you to a useful tidbit of information.

In The Mood — You'll find this icon next to ideas that help you create a romantic aura.

Hot Stuff — This icon points out tips to enhance sexual pleasure (so you won't have to put sticky tabs on the pages).

Mainly For Men — This icon is the "men's locker room" stuff that guys especially need to know.

Mainly For Women — This icon highlights "girls' night out" stuff that women need to know.

Case Study — This icon points out stories from therapy sessions or likely scenarios involving individuals and couples that can help you cope with similar situations. The names used are not those of real couples, and the situations described are composites derived from various therapy sessions.

Dr. Ruth Says — This icon points to practical advice and my personal thoughts on today's sexual dilemmas.

Food For Thought — This icon highlights information that may make a difference in what you think or believe.

Clinical Info — You'll see this icon next to medical descriptions of your anatomy or physical conditions.

Sexual Myth — This icon highlights some of the things you may think you know about sex that are false or misleading.

Caution — This icon tells you when to look before you leap to stay clear of pitfalls to your relationships.

Warning — This icon signals behaviors that could cause trouble, either for you or someone else.

Starting Now

Whether you consider yourself a Don Juan, a Lady Chatterly, or a sexual novice, the first piece of advice I have for you is that everybody can become a better lover given the proper instruction. And since we are all sexual beings, whether we like it or not, why not get the most out of the pleasures our bodies are capable of giving us? So relax and read on. I guarantee that, by the end of this book, you can take the dunce cap that you may be wearing off your head and perhaps replace it with a condom somewhere else!

Part I
Back to Basics

The 5th Wave   **By Rich Tennant**

"REMEMBER, THIS IS JUST A GUIDE. FEEL FREE TO IMPROVISE AND DON'T FORGET TO READ THE PILLOW CASES—MOST OF THE FOREPLAY IS OUTLINED ON THEM."

In this part...

*I*n this part I give you basic information which you need to master in order to fully enjoy good sex. And just because you're not a virgin, don't think that you can skip over this section. No matter how much experience you may have in the bedroom, to become a great lover you still need to spend some time in the classroom. Sexual illiteracy is often the cause of sexual problems, so that what you don't know may end up being a lot more important to your enjoying good sexual functioning than what you do know.

Chapter 1

In the Beginning: Making a Baby

....

In This Chapter

▶ Taking the sex quiz

▶ Unlearning the pregnancy myths

▶ Making babies

....

*T*he English language is a rich one because we have borrowed heavily from so many different tongues. As a result, we use a variety of words to describe the same thing — especially if that thing involves sex (some of these words, I'm sure that you are familiar with, but being polite I won't mention them). But it never ceases to amaze me how often people who engage in the act of sexual intercourse forget that what they're doing is directly related to procreation, propagation, continuing the species, conception, pregnancy, MAKING BABIES!

Some unlucky couples must go through a great deal of trouble in order to have a family, and some can't manage to do it on their own at all. But, for most people, the process is relatively easy — at least until the baby actually arrives. The man only has to place his erect penis into the woman's vagina and ejaculate. A baby may not result the first time — though it could — but eventually one of the man's sperm will unite with the woman's egg, and, voilá, a baby is conceived.

The fact that baby-making is so easy is the reason that many women find themselves pregnant even though they don't intend to be. So here's my first of many tips:

If you absolutely, positively don't want to make a baby, then don't have sexual intercourse — be abstinent.

Yes, I know there are ways of preventing pregnancy from occurring. I talk about them in Chapter 7. But none of these methods is foolproof. Believe it or not, in at least one recorded case, the man had a vasectomy, the woman had her tubes tied, and she still became pregnant. So remember, *the only method that works 100 percent of the time is abstinence.*

Ignorance Isn't Bliss

Now I'm pretty sure that most of you reading this book are not abstinent — at least not voluntarily — and that you bought this book to discover how to become better lovers, not to find out how to become parents. And, anyway, you probably think you know all there is to know about the process of making babies, so you're tempted to skip this chapter.

Before you give in to temptation, try this little quiz:

> Q. 1 How many sperm are manufactured in the testicles?
>
> A. 5,000 a day; B. 50 a minute; C. 5 million a year; D. 50,000 a minute
>
> Q. 2 After a woman has ovulated, the egg remains fertile for approximately:
>
> A. 12 hours; B. 24 hours; C. three days; D. one week
>
> Q. 3 The sperm and the egg usually meet:
>
> A. at the entrance to the fallopian tubes; B. inside the fallopian tubes; C. in the uterus; D. in the vagina

The answers are: D, C, and B.

Unless your wild guesses were lucky ones, I'm willing to bet that you didn't know the answers to these three questions. I'm also willing to bet that there are other parts of the process that are unfamiliar to you. And don't argue. Yes, you do need to know what making babies is all about.

"But Dr. Ruth," I can hear you asking, "will knowing all the details about the birds and the bees really help my sexual functioning? After all, I don't know how my car works, but it still gets me around."

Good question. And the best way that I can answer it is by giving you some examples of cases I see in my private practice that stem directly from ignorance.

First are the men and women who make appointments to see me because they don't enjoy having sexual intercourse, and their problem turns out to be an underlying fear that the woman may become pregnant. Even if they know about contraception, or think they know, deep down inside they have misgivings. Their concern that having sexual intercourse will cause the woman to become pregnant affects their enjoyment of sex. Let me illustrate:

Kenny and Vera

Kenny and Vera had been living together for several years, and their sex life was fine. Before they were married, they used condoms, but after they got married, Vera began to use a diaphragm. Right away, their sex life began to deteriorate. At the time they came to see me, both Kenny and Vera thought that their sexual problems had something to do with the fact that they had gotten married.

But, after speaking with the two of them separately, I guessed what the problem might be. I explained it to them so that they'd realize what was happening. Even though Kenny knew that Vera was using a diaphragm, he did not have the same sense of assurance that he'd had with condoms. He could no longer see the birth control device, and he had nothing to do with putting it there.

I suggested that, instead of Vera inserting the diaphragm by herself in the bathroom, Kenny insert the diaphragm with her as part of foreplay. Seeing the diaphragm placed inside of Vera restored Kenny's confidence that having sex with his new bride wasn't going to make her pregnant, and their sex life returned to normal.

In another example from my practice, some men believe that, because cavemen had to reach their orgasms quickly in order to impregnate their women before some wild animal got to them (and no one knows for sure whether that is true or not), premature ejaculation has been encoded into their genes. These men think that they can't do anything about being premature ejaculators. That presumption, of course, is a myth. Premature ejaculation is a learning disability, not a physical problem. Once a man understands this, he is usually ready to do something positive about it. (I discuss the treatment of this sexual problem in Chapter 22.)

Some Myths about Making Babies

Myths about things like premature ejaculation get in the way of terrific sex, but myths about making babies have also caused people a great deal of hardship.

- ✔ It's a myth that a woman can't get pregnant the first time she has intercourse. (She can.)
- ✔ It's a myth that a woman can't get pregnant if she "does it" standing up. (She can.)

> ✔ It's a myth that douching with a soft drink or vinegar after intercourse prevents pregnancy. (It doesn't.)
>
> ✔ And then there's the one myth that has caused more unintended pregnancies than all of the others combined: the myth that, if a man pulls his penis out of the woman's vagina before he ejaculates (the "withdrawal" method), she can't get pregnant. (She most definitely can! You can find out more about this myth in Chapter 7.)

Even if you've never fallen for any of these tall tales, you may have picked up some other myths along the way. Just to be safe, I recommend that you start right from the very beginning — the process of making a baby — to be absolutely sure that you've got your facts straight.

Making a Baby

The process of making a baby has been the same since Adam and Eve discovered sex: A sperm from the man must meet an egg inside of the woman (test tube babies notwithstanding). When the sperm and the egg unite, the egg becomes *fertilized*.

Both the sperm and the egg are very special cells; they have only half of the genetic material (chromosomes) that other cells have. All cells need chromosomes to provide the instructions on how to divide and create an individual.

By combining the chromosomes from both the sperm and the egg into one entity, called a *zygote*, the process of fertilization mixes the genes of both partners together. As a result, instead of an identical copy of one of the parents (a clone), fertilization creates a unique individual that shares features of both parents. So now you know that the reason you got your father's nose and your mother's feet is that, at least once in their lives, your parents mingled their genetic material.

Setting the stage

Female humans are different from nearly all the rest of their sex in the animal kingdom because, rather than being interested in sexual intercourse only when they are able to conceive (that is, when they are *in heat)*, women can be interested in sexual intercourse at any time (provided they don't have a headache). Despite this difference, female humans do share the trait with other female mammals that enables them to make a baby, or *conceive*, only at certain times — in most cases, from one to three days a month.

Don't think that, just because a woman is only fertile a few days a month, those are the only days that unprotected sexual intercourse can make her pregnant. It's a lot more complicated than that, as I explain in Chapter 7.

Unlike a man, who continually makes sperm (more than 26 trillion a year!), a woman is born with all of her eggs already inside her. These eggs — about 200,000 of them — reside in a woman's two *ovaries* (see Figure 1-1). About every 28 days, one of the eggs is released from a fluid-filled sac, called a *follicle,* in the ovary. When an egg is released, many women can feel a dull ache, known as *mittelschmerz,* in the area around the ovary.

Figure 1-1:
The egg begins an incredible journey in search of a sperm to produce a child. No wonder sex has been called "making whoopie"!

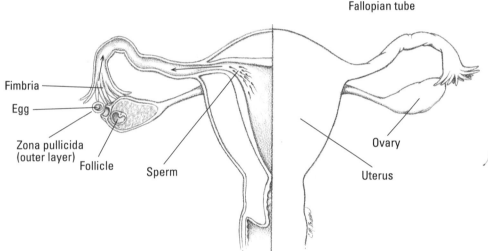

Fallopian tube

Fimbria

Egg

Zona pullicida (outer layer)

Follicle

Sperm

Ovary

Uterus

Becoming aware of when mittelschmerz occurs is a good point of reference for anyone practicing natural family planning. I talk more about family planning in Chapter 7.

Getting the egg and sperm together

Everyone's talking about what happened last night at Club Fallopian. Mr. Sperm bumped into Ms. Egg, and now they're really stuck on each other!

Just as people have to meet each other before they can form a relationship, the process of fertilization can't begin until a sperm gets up into the fallopian tubes and meets the egg. This introduction takes place as a result of *sexual intercourse,* which is defined as a man placing his penis in a woman's vagina. When the man has an orgasm, he releases millions of sperm into the woman's upper vagina. These sperm swim right up through the entrance to the uterus, called the *cervix,* through the uterus itself, and then into the fallopian tubes — each one hunting for an egg. And if an egg happens to be floating along, the fastest sperm is the one that takes the prize.

Here are two very important points about sperm which you should always keep in mind:

- Sperm can live from two to five days inside a woman after being ejaculated by the man. This means that, although the egg may have only a short time during which it can be fertilized (see the Sex Quiz earlier in this chapter), sperm that were deposited in the woman up to a week ahead of time could fertilize the egg and cause pregnancy.

- Even before a man ejaculates, his penis gives off some liquid (called *Cowper's fluid,* because it comes from the Cowper's gland), which serves as a lubricant to help the sperm go up the shaft of the penis. Inside Cowper's fluid are thousands of sperm. Although that's fewer than the millions of sperm that are in the ejaculate, how many does it take to make a woman pregnant? One fast one.

Because of Cowper's fluid, a man deposits sperm inside a woman's vagina before he has an orgasm. That's why the pull-out, or withdrawal, method does not work as a means of preventing pregnancy.

Going for a ride

Little finger-like appendages called *fimbria* lead the egg into the *fallopian tube,* through which it makes its way down into the *uterus.* If, during this trip, the egg encounters some male sperm swimming along, then the first sperm to reach the egg and penetrate the hard outer shell, called the *zona pellucida,* will enter the egg and begin the life-creating process called *fertilization.*

A fertilized egg continues down the fallopian tube on a journey that takes about three days. During the first 30 hours, the chromosomes of the egg and the sperm merge, and the cells begin to divide. This new entity is now called an *embryo.* When the embryo finishes its journey and enters the uterus (see Figure 1-2), it is nourished by uterine secretions, and the cells inside it continue to divide, causing the embryo to continue to grow. Approximately six days after it has been fertilized, the egg "hatches," emerging from its hard shell and then burrowing its way into the uterine wall, or *endometrium.*

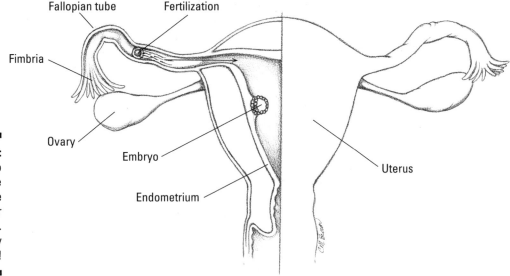

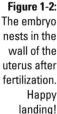

Figure 1-2:
The embryo
nests in the
wall of the
uterus after
fertilization.
Happy
landing!

The embryo releases a hormone called hCG; when the hCG reaches the mother's bloodstream, it signals that she is pregnant and causes the ovaries to continue producing the hormones, estrogen and progesterone, that are necessary to maintain the pregnancy.

If the egg is not fertilized, it passes through the uterus. About two weeks later, the uterus sheds its lining, the *endometrium*, in a process called *menstruation*. A new lining then begins to grow, ready to receive a fertilized egg the next month.

Giving birth

After an embryo burrows its way into the endometrium, it continues to grow until it reaches a point where it has a human shape and all its organs — a process that takes about 12 weeks. At this point, the embryo is renamed a *fetus*.

The fetus continues to grow inside the uterus until approximately nine months after the egg was first fertilized. Then, in a process we call *giving birth,* a fully formed baby comes out of the uterus and through the vagina (unless there's a reason to remove the baby surgically, which is called a cesarean section, or c-section) into the world.

So an important possible consequence of sexual intercourse is the making of a baby that will be born nine months later. Of course, giving birth to a baby is only the beginning of providing the care a child requires. Having a child is a very big responsibility, not one to be taken lightly, and certainly not one to be ignored when having sexual intercourse.

Making babies makes good sex too

One more thing about sexual intercourse and its pleasures: As great a feeling as you get when having an orgasm from sexual intercourse, I think that most couples will tell you that the intercourse they had when they were trying to make a baby was even more pleasurable. There's an extra kick that comes from knowing that the possible result of this union between two people who love each other is another little human being.

"NOW THAT WOULD SHOW HOW IMPORTANT IT IS TO DISTINGUISH 'FERTILIZER PRACTICES' FROM 'FERTILITY PRACTICES' WHEN DOWNLOADING A VIDEO FILE FROM THE INTERNET."

Chapter 2

It's a Male Thing

Sexual intercourse occurs whenever a man puts his penis into a woman's vagina. When the penis is in its normal, flaccid state, this feat is difficult (though not impossible) for a man to accomplish. However, when the penis becomes erect and hard, most men learn quite quickly the technique of inserting the penis into the vagina — sometimes too quickly (for more about that, see Chapter 11). This chapter is all about how and why a man gets an erection.

The Penis: Inside and Out

How a man gets an erection is relatively, ahem, straightforward. But to understand it, you need to examine a man's basic apparatus: his penis.

The three sponges (not Larry, Curly, and Moe)

Basically, a penis is composed of three structures (see Figure 2-1) which are made of a sponge-like material that can fill with blood.

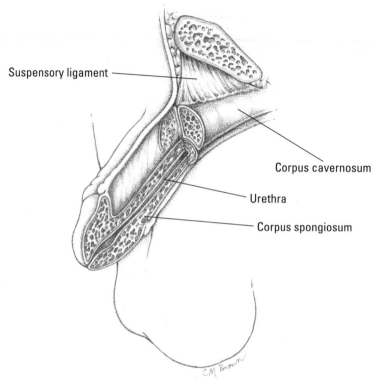

Suspensory ligament

Corpus cavernosum

Urethra

Corpus spongiosum

Figure 2-1:
The penis:
not as
simple as it
looks!

- ✔ The two *corpus cavernosa* contain the central arteries and lie on the top half of the penis. They are cylindrical tubes and are larger than the other spongy structure.

- ✔ The *corpus spongiosum*, which is under the two *corpus cavernosa* and which surrounds the *urethra*, is the pipeline for both urine and sperm.

When a man becomes excited — and I'm not talking about watching his team score the winning touchdown here — the nerves surrounding his penis become active, causing the muscles around the arteries to relax and more blood to flow into the penis. This additional blood is then absorbed by the sponge-like material, making the penis stiff and hard, or *erect.* This erection tightens the veins so that the blood cannot leave the penis, enabling the penis to remain erect.

At the base of the penis, the two corpus cavernosa split to form a Y, where the two ends are connected to the pubic bone. This ligament controls the angle of the erect penis. I get many questions from men, each asking me if there is something wrong with him because the angle of his erect penis is not straight out, parallel to the floor. I tell all of them not to go hanging any weights in an effort to change the angle, because there is nothing to worry about!

Penises become erect at all different angles — and the angle doesn't have any effect on the way the penis performs. As a man gets older, the ligament at the base of his penis stretches, and the angle changes. This is why a man of 70 may have an erection that points downward instead of upward, the way a young man's erection does.

At the head of the class: the glans

The head of the penis, called the *glans,* is shaped like a cone (see Figure 2-2). The opening of the glans is called the *meatus,* and at the base of the glans is a crown-like structure called the *corona.*

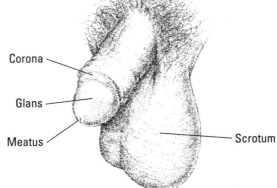

Figure 2-2:
The glans brings it all to a head.

Corona

Glans

Meatus

Scrotum

The glans serves several purposes:

✔ The glans is a little thicker than the rest of the penis, particularly around the corona. This extra thickness serves as a seal to keep the ejaculated semen inside the vagina, near the cervix, after an orgasm. This is nature's way of making sure that the chances for fertilization are high.

✔ The glans also creates extra friction, which, in this case, produces "good vibrations" that help promote ejaculation.

✔ Men aren't the only ones who benefit from the glans. With all the thrusting of the penis inside the vagina that goes on during intercourse, the woman's cervix might get damaged if it weren't for the glans, which acts as a shock absorber.

For all you ladies, I suggest that the next time you see your lover's glans you give it the proper thank you it deserves. I leave the choice of how to do this up to you.

The foreskin: a real cover-up

At birth, the glans is covered by the foreskin, a sheath of skin that opens at the top. In an infant, this opening is very tight and usually cannot be pulled back (or *retracted,* to use the medical term). Usually, the foreskin loosens up as the baby grows older. When a male has an erection, the foreskin pulls back entirely to fully reveal the glans. The skin of the glans is very sensitive, and the purpose of the foreskin is to protect it.

In the Jewish and Muslim cultures, the foreskin is always surgically removed in a procedure called *circumcision.* Circumcision has also become popular in many Western societies because the penis is easier to keep clean without the foreskin. Because of today's better hygiene, some parents and physicians believe that circumcision is no longer necessary, although the debate is not entirely over.

Small glands underneath the foreskin release a cottage-cheese-like substance called *smegma.* In an uncircumcised man, this smegma can build up and lead to infections and, sometimes, even more serious diseases. An uncircumcised man should always take special precautions when bathing to pull back the foreskin and clean carefully around the glans.

If you happen to be bathing with a friend, pulling back the foreskin might be a pleasurable task to assign to your partner. Some women, who've seen the piles of dirty laundry stuffed into a corner of a bachelor's apartment, have general doubts about the personal hygiene of the average male. This can be one reason why they avoid performing oral sex. If oral sex is something that you would like, and your partner has been hesitant about doing it, having your partner make sure that your penis is absolutely clean might be one way of changing her mind. Even if it doesn't change her mind, at least you'll have a very clean penis.

Circumcision and sexual performance

Because the skin of the glans of a circumcised male grows tougher and less sensitive than that of an uncircumcised male, people often wonder whether circumcision affects sexual performance.

Some men who aren't circumcised believe that, because their skin is more sensitive, they are more likely to have premature ejaculation. I've even been asked by adult men whether they should be circumcised to cure them of this problem. (Since premature ejaculation is a learning disability that you can overcome, see Chapter 22, I don't recommend having this surgery performed later in life.)

I also get asked by men who have been circumcised whether there is a way of replacing their foreskin. These men feel that, because the skin of the glans has been toughened, they are missing out on certain pleasures. I tell them that, as long as they are having orgasms, this is not something that they should be worrying about.

Size and sexual performance

Of course, when considering the penis, what concerns a great many men the most is the size of their sexual organ. They think that bigger is better.

Because men are more likely to get turned on by what they see, physical appearance is very important to them. That's why men are so concerned about penis size — just as they are concerned about the size of women's breasts. To men, the more there is of a body part that attracts them, the better. (Sadly, thighs, which all women seem able to enlarge with ease, no longer fall into this category. Where is Rubens, who painted such magnificent, voluptuous nude women, now when we need him?)

Now, if men were to ask women how they feel about penis size, they'd get another story. Some women are actually frightened by very big penises, and many women just don't attach very much importance to the issue. But these men who are all hung up about the size of their penises can't seem to get it straight — and, since many of them are also stubborn, it's a difficult job convincing them otherwise.

Although there's no denying that men have different-sized penises, does the size of the penis make any difference where it really counts — inside the woman's vagina? In most cases, the answer is a very big no — the size of the penis makes no difference inside a woman's vagina.

MAINLY FOR MEN

Measuring Up

There are different ways to measure a penis, and a man usually chooses the method that makes his penis seem the biggest. Although the basic penis measurements are length and circumference, in what mood the penis happens to be at the moment you pull out that tape measure is the key.

Even if two flaccid penises look about the same size, they may be very different in size when they become erect. (And even an individual man may have different-sized erections depending on how aroused he is.) In the locker room, it's the man with the biggest flaccid penis who feels the most cocky; but the real proving ground is in the bedroom.

One of the reasons that you may think that your penis is too small is the way you look at it. (And no, I'm not going to suggest that you put on rose-colored glasses.) Most of the time, you're looking down at your penis, and when you do that your eyes play a trick on you called foreshortening, the result of which is that your penis looks smaller than it appears to someone else looking at it. To get *that* perspective, simply stand in front of a full-length mirror and take in that view. If you've never done this before, I think you'll be surprised. Have a look both before and after you have an erection, and, especially in the latter case, I'm sure your ego is going to get a nice boost.

The vagina is elastic; it has to be in order to allow babies to be born vaginally. So a woman's vagina can accommodate a big or a small penis. Because most of a woman's nerve endings are concentrated at the entrance to the vagina, the sensations that a bigger penis may cause aren't all that different to her from those caused by a smaller penis.

Obviously, if a man has a minuscule penis, a woman may not feel it very much, and that is a slight problem. But, as you see in Chapter 13, most women need direct clitoral stimulation in order to achieve an orgasm. Because no penis can do that trick while performing intercourse, the issue of size becomes even less important.

Men ask me all the time if there isn't some way of making their penises bigger. I know of only one way to do this, and I'm only passing it on because it actually also promotes good health. Although most of the penis is visible, part of the penis is buried beneath the skin and is called the *crus*. If a man has a lot of fat in his pubic area, then more of the length of the penis is buried beneath the skin. With weight loss, some of that can be reversed so that a greater portion of the penis becomes exposed; thus, it can be said to "grow." The rule of thumb doctors use is one inch of penis length gained for every 30 pounds of excess weight lost. (Sorry to all you skinny guys, but losing extra weight won't help you.)

Getting direction

The proportion of crus (penis under the skin) to exposed penis can cause variations in the direction that the penis has during an erection. Men with a shorter crus, and thus a longer penis, are more likely to have an erection that points downward, while an erect penis that has a longer crus will probably point outward, or even straight up.

Frank

When Frank came to see me, we spent half an hour talking without broaching the real reason for his visit. He admitted that he didn't go out with women, but he was blaming that on all sorts of things that didn't make sense to me. I could feel that more was bothering him than he was letting on, and I told him straight out that I thought he wasn't being truthful with me. That's when he told me that he was afraid of dating women because, if he got close enough to them to have sex, they would notice that his penis was misshapen.

Because I am not a medical doctor, I do not examine patients, but I did ask him to describe for me what his penis looked like. He said that, when he had an erection, instead of sticking straight out, as did the erect penises he'd seen in some porno films, his penis had a very large curve in it. To me, his description seemed to be within the bounds of normalcy, but I sent him to a urologist to make sure.

When I next saw him, he was a new man. The urologist had confirmed what I had thought, and knowing that he wasn't going to be made fun of gave him the confidence to start dating. The next time I heard from Frank, about a year later, he called to tell me that he was engaged.

Occasionally, a man tells me that he is concerned because his penis points in a certain direction when it is erect. As you can see from Frank's situation, this is absolutely normal. But it is true that some men have a more pronounced curve than others, and sometimes the penis also bends to the left or to the right.

Because I am not a medical doctor, my first piece of advice if you feel that your penis has an abnormal shape is to go to a urologist to make certain that this curvature doesn't indicate some problem.

In the vast majority of cases, the curve falls well within the norms of most men, and the concern is just a case of sexual ignorance. In other words, the man did not know that most penises are curved to some extent. Once in a while, a man does have a more pronounced curve than most. Even the majority of these men don't have a problem in bed, although a few may have to adjust the positions that they use. In some cases, however, a man may have *Peyronie's disease,* a condition that can make sex impossible (although, rest assured, in most cases the disease goes away on its own after a short while, as I discuss in Chapter 22).

In any case, this problem is mostly in the minds of the men who come to me with concerns about the appearance of their erect penises. Because they believe that their penises look unusual, they are afraid to date. They worry that, when the time comes to undress, their partner will react negatively.

There's one simple way to avoid worrying about how a new partner will react to the shape of your penis, and this goes for the vast majority of other doubts that people have about their sexual abilities: Wait until you have established a strong relationship before you have sex with somebody. I don't say you have to get married, but you will find the experience of making love much better if you are in love, and you integrate sex as an expression of your love rather than as a form of recreation.

So, whether your penis looks like a boomerang or is straight as an arrow, remember that the three little words "I love you" are far more important to your lover than the direction in which your penis points.

Getting on Better Terms with Your Testicles

Although a man may not be familiar with the inner workings of his penis, outwardly, he is at least on somewhat good terms with that part of his anatomy. But, when it comes to their *testicles*, too many men know almost nothing about them.

Be forewarned, however, because, by the time you've finished with this chapter, you will not only be seeing testicles differently, you'll also be feeling them in a whole new way.

Making the descent

As a baby boy is developing inside his mother's womb, his testicles are still inside his body. It is only during the last few months that the testicles poke their way outside, or descend, into the *scrotum,* a sac of skin located at the base of the penis. Occasionally, one or both of the testicles will not make the descent.

Some of these undescended testicles are of the hide-and-seek variety, meaning that, during the first year or so, they kind of come and go. As long as they make an occasional appearance, everything will be just fine, and eventually they'll get up the courage to stay where they belong.

A testicle that remains inside the body will not function properly because the temperature will be too warm. A boy who has this problem may also be embarrassed by his appearance. For these reasons, medical intervention is usually called for, which may be a type of hormonal therapy, but more likely will involve surgery.

Manufacturing hormones

In addition to testicles' vital role in the continuation of the species, men require functioning testicles for the hormones they produce, most importantly testosterone. *Testosterone* is called the "male hormone," and that name truly fits. If a boy is born without testosterone, his scrotum forms as the outer lips of a vagina and his penis as something akin to a clitoris.

Even if only one of a boy's testicles fails to form properly, a partially developed uterus and fallopian tube will develop inside him. This is because he will not have enough of another hormone, normally released by that testicle, *MIS,* which inhibits the growth of female organs.

Producing sperm

Despite the fact that the variety of contraceptive methods have allowed people to disconnect sexual intercourse from reproduction, the main purpose of having sex, from an evolutionary point of view, is still to make babies. But, although the penis is required to penetrate the woman's vagina for the best chance at success, the man needs seeds to place within her in order to accomplish this important task. These seeds, called *spermatozoa* (or more often by their nickname, sperm), are manufactured in the testicles.

Sperm are rather amazing little creatures. They are the only parts, of the body that do their work outside of it. You see, sperm don't survive well at high temperatures, particularly the temperature inside our bodies. This is why the testicles lie outside the body where they can be cooled by the soft summer breezes (at least for those of you who favor kilts or loincloths).

In order for the sperm to be successful at their task of making babies, they have to overcome many obstacles after making a long journey. You may well be familiar with their final shape — an oval head with a long tail that helps to propel it along — but sperm do not start out that way (see Figure 2-3).

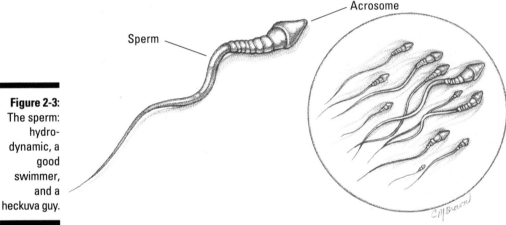

Acrosome

Sperm

Figure 2-3:
The sperm:
hydro-
dynamic, a
good
swimmer,
and a
heckuva guy.

From humble beginnings

Early in their life cycles, sperm are called germ cells. (Here's a case where I think most people would have preferred a nice, long Latin name; but, rest assured, these cells have nothing to do with what we commonly associate the word germ.)

Germ cells are produced in the *seminiferous tubules,* which are long, spaghetti-like tubes that are connected to each other, packed into a tight ball, and surrounded by a tough membrane. This package is called — drumroll, please — a *testicle.* (Between these tubes are cells that produce the male hormone testosterone.) As the germ cells travel along the tubes, slowly but surely they turn into sperm.

Their metamorphosis complete, the sperm leave the testicle and head for the *epididymis* on their way to the *vas deferens*. (If you haven't already done so, at this point I strongly suggest you look at Figure 2-4, because you might get lost without a map, and you can't stop at a gas station to ask for *these* directions.)

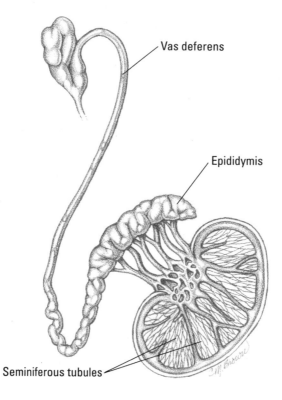

Figure 2-4:
The sperm leave the testicle and head for the epididymis and vas deferens.

Vas deferens

Epididymis

Seminiferous tubules

Meiosis: small division

Now that you've had a chance to look at the diagram and can picture in your mind's eye the journey that the spermatozoa are taking, I have to tell you about one more important transformation that they make.

All of our cells have the complete code of genetic material, called DNA (the long term is deoxyribonucleic acid, but DNA is much easier to say), unique to each individual. But, while the germ cells start out with all of this DNA, along the way they undergo a process called *meiosis* (pronounced "my-*oh*-sis"). Here are some of the important effects of meiosis:

✔ When a germ cell undergoes meiosis, it forms two new cells, each of them having only half of the DNA code: 23 bits of genetic material (called *chromosomes*) instead of the normal 46.

When a sperm teams up with a female egg, which also only has 23 chromosomes, their genetic materials intertwine, and the resulting baby ends up with a package that is a mixture of both the mother and the father.

✔ When the male germ cells divide, the sex chromosomes divide also. The male has both X and Y chromosomes; the female has only X chromosomes.

Whether the sperm that reaches the egg first has an X (female) or Y (male) chromosome determines whether the baby will be a girl or a boy.

There's one more thing about a *spermatozoon* (a single, fully developed sperm; spermatozoa is the plural) that I thought all you macho men out there would appreciate: Not only can sperm move around on their own outside the body, but they're also fully armed, liked little guided missiles. Over the head of the sperm lies the *acrosome,* which is full of enzymes that help the sperm penetrate an egg if it should be so lucky as to meet one on its journey.

When they're ready, the sperm leave the *testes* (another name for testicles) and enter the epididymis, which is a series of tiny tubes that lie on top of the testes. (For those of you into amazing statistics: if unfurled, these tubes would reach 60 feet in length.) During their journey through the epididymis, sperm learn to swim. They enter the epididymis with useless tails and leave it as little speed demons.

Vas deferens

If you go back to Figure 2-4, you see that the sperm's next stop on their voyage is the *vas deferens,* a tube that ejects the sperm into the urethra. In the urethra, the sperm are mixed with fluids from the seminal vesicles and the prostate; then they make their way out into the world through ejaculation.

The combination of these fluids and the sperm is called *semen.* The amount of semen ejaculated during sexual intercourse is generally around a teaspoonful, though it varies depending on when the man last ejaculated. The semen is whitish in color, has a distinctive smell, and is thick when it first comes out. Sperm only comprise about 5 percent of the volume, but they are the only part of the semen which can cause pregnancy.

Too few sperm (male infertility)

Just because your testicles look normal does not mean that they are fully functioning. If a couple is trying to conceive but can't seem to do it, one of the first things that doctors look for is a problem with the man's sperm. The most common problems are a low sperm count (which means that the man is not producing enough sperm) or the sperm he is producing lack sufficient *motility,* the ability to swim to the egg. The basis for the problems could be abnormal sperm production, which is more difficult to treat, or a blockage somewhere along the line, which may be corrected through surgery.

Interestingly enough, most semen analysis is done by gynecologists, specialists in the female reproductive system. A gynecologist is usually the first person that a woman consults when she has problems getting pregnant. Commonly, the gynecologist asks that the man's sperm be analyzed. Then, if the tests reveal a problem with the sperm, the man is sent to a urologist for further evaluation.

Why boys wear cups

Despite the fact that so many men adopt a tough guy, macho image, the heart of their maleness, the testicles, is highly sensitive. The testicles are so sensitive that, if you're a man reading this, you might be experiencing some pain down there just by thinking about the pain that occurs when they're struck by an object.

If a boy has never had the sensations caused by a blow to the scrotum, then he might not see the need to wear a cup over his groin area when playing rough sports. But no man who has suffered this agony would hesitate for a minute to protect himself with a cup.

At risk for testicular cancer

Even though the testicles are easily accessible, apart from trying to keep from getting kicked in that delicate spot, most men don't pay all that much attention to them. That can be unfortunate because testicular cancer is a disease that can be deadly if you don't find it in time. Although rare, testicular cancer is most often found in men from ages 15 to 35. In fact, it is the most common form of cancer in men in their twenties and thirties. Luckily, the disease is also easily curable — if you find it in time.

Because the testicles are outside the body and available for examination, you can easily feel a testicular irregularity if it is present. And the best news is that, because your testicles are so accessible, you can spare yourself the trouble of going to a doctor for the examination (as we women are forced to do with cervical cancer) by examining them yourself.

Check for lumps

Since testicular cancer usually begins as a painless lump, the sooner you find such a lump, the better your chances of having it dealt with without any serious medical consequences.

To check for lumps:

- Gently take each testicle and roll it between your thumb and forefinger to see if there is anything different about it than the way it felt the last time.
- Your testicle should feel smooth and firm with a slight softness, a lot like a grape.

✔ One guide might be to compare your two testicles to each other.

✔ If you do find something that feels different, pick up the phone right away and make an appointment to see a urologist.

✔ You should do this test once a month.

Remember that the epididymis sits on top of the testicle. Some men examining themselves for testicular cancer mistake it for a strange lump. They get a real fright before a doctor explains to them what it is. So what you need to have clear is that you are checking your testicle; that's the hard ball. The lumpy epididymis, which lies on top of the testicle, belongs there and is supposed to be lumpy.

Testicular cancer can hit any man, but men who have had one or both undescended testicles at birth (see "Making the descent" earlier in the chapter) are at higher risk. So if either or both of your testicles had not descended when you were born, make doubly sure that you perform this exam.

Sometimes a minor injury to the groin area may cause some swelling. This swelling could mask the presence of an undetected cancerous growth. This is why a monthly checkup is necessary — so you know what's normal for you from month to month, and what's not.

I know that a lot of you are squeamish about medical things (and won't go to the doctor unless you're in excruciating pain), particularly when it comes to something in your genital area. But this is important so please don't be lax about it.

If you really don't like the idea of examining yourself, and if you have a partner, maybe this is an exercise that you can assign to her. I don't know if she'll like doing it any better than you would, but you both might profit from the side effects.

Testicular pain

Men don't usually talk about private matters, especially when it comes to anything that is hanging between their legs, but it is quite common for a man to feel a twinge of pain from time to time in his scrotum. If you experience this sort of pain and it disappears after a minute or two, there is nothing to worry about. On the other hand, if you have any continuous pain, then you should go to see a urologist immediately.

The Prostate Gland

In addition to their testicles, there's one other problem area that men should have checked, and all too often don't, and that's the prostate. The prostate gland, located below the man's bladder, produces some of the fluids that are contained in the semen, giving semen its whitish color. The urethra, through which semen and urine pass, runs through the prostate, and any disease affecting the prostate can affect the urethra.

Checking the prostate

As a man ages, it is common for the prostate gland to become enlarged and cause a man to urinate more frequently. This is bothersome but not dangerous. However, the prostate also has a nasty habit of becoming cancerous, and that can be quite dangerous, though it is easily treated if discovered in time.

The way that a doctor checks the prostate for changes which could signify a cancerous growth is simply to palpate, or touch, it. So that your doctor can do that, you have to bend over and allow him to stick his fingers in your rectum. This way, your doctor can actually feel the prostate gland.

Although I don't necessarily blame any man for not wanting to rush off to the doctor to be examined in this manner, a prostate examination is no worse than the gynecological visits we women have to go through regularly, so I won't accept any excuses for not doing it. Regular prostate exams can save your life; I absolutely recommend that you not put them off.

Treating the prostate

There are various treatments for prostate conditions, some of which have side effects that affect sexual functioning. Some medications used to treat either an enlarged prostate or a cancerous one reduce sexual desire. Surgical removal of either part or all of the prostate is another measure that can be taken, which also has potential side effects.

The most common form of surgery for an enlarged prostate is called a transurethral resection of the prostate (TURP). Approximately five to 10 percent of men who are operated on experience impotence following the surgery, and 80 to 100 percent experience something called *retrograde ejaculation*. What this means is that, during ejaculation, instead of the semen flowing out of the penis, it flows backwards into the bladder. This does not affect a man's ability to have an orgasm, so some men find that retrograde ejaculation does not bother them; others report sex to be less pleasant because there is no fluid. Retrograde ejaculation would definitely cause a problem if the man was trying to impregnate a woman; in that case, artificial insemination may be necessary.

Chapter 3
It's a Female Thing

In This Chapter

▶ A tour of the female anatomy

▶ The "men" words

▶ Breasts, hanging in there

*O*n the subject of our genitals, we women are faced with a conundrum (no, that is not a new sexual term; it just means a puzzle). On the one hand, because our reproductive organs are for the most part hidden away, women in general don't have the same type of familiar relationship that a man has with his apparatus. Some women even try their best to ignore their genitals. They touch themselves as little as possible and never really look between their legs.

The problem is that these hidden organs have a way of making themselves known with a certain regularity so that, try as we might, they are impossible to totally ignore. And there are good reasons not to ignore these organs:

✔ One of the ways that a woman's apparatus can suddenly interrupt things is if she becomes pregnant. The fact that more than a million women a year in the U.S. alone have unintended pregnancies is proof that too many women still do not know all that they should about how their bodies work.

✔ Another reason for women and men to become better informed about the female anatomy is that understanding our bodies is certainly key to good sexual functioning, which is the primary purpose of this book.

✔ Understanding female anatomy is important for having a healthy outlook towards women. The idea that a woman's genitals are in some foreign, dank place — the black hole of Calcutta is one name used for it — denigrates not only a woman's genitals, but her status as a human being as well.

Although, in our society, these parts are private as they relate to an individual, there is certainly no need to keep their general nature private as well.

So whether you are a female or a male, I'm going to make sure that you are no longer faced with a mystery when you contemplate a woman's genitals. Instead, I am going to imprint a topographical map in your brain that you are never going to forget.

If you're a woman reading this, you have a definite advantage in that you can examine yourself. Many women have never taken the time to look closely at their genitals, and I recommend it highly. Because your genitals are not as convenient to view as the male apparatus, you'll need a simple tool: a hand mirror. Take off your clothes and seat yourself someplace where you can spread your legs easily. You can use available light, or, if you're in a dark spot, you can use a flashlight to illuminate the area. I suggest you do some exploring on your own, read the next few pages, and then go back and see if you can identify the various places I mention.

As far as you guys out there, if you have a partner who's willing, it certainly wouldn't do you any harm to share in this experience, although I have a few words of caution:

✔ If your partner has never examined herself before, maybe you should give her some time alone to take this little tour first, because there is no doubt that your presence will be a distraction.

✔ Second, when it's your turn to explore, do your utmost to keep the examination nonsexual, even if you do get aroused (which you probably will). If you're able to keep the moment on an educational plane, then it is a good time to ask her some questions about how she feels about her genitals, as well as what pleases her and what displeases her when you have sex.

If, after the grand tour is over, you're both so aroused that you need to have sex, then be my guest — but only if you promise to put to use what you just learned and not go back to doing the same old thing.

All Those Latin Terms

Certainly my job would be easier if the medical world didn't use so many Latin terms, which I then have to explain to you — especially since I never took Latin. But since it does, I suggest that you look at Figure 3-1 before embarking on this journey into the female anatomy. That way, you'll have a better feel for what I'm describing as we proceed, and you won't get lost on some side road.

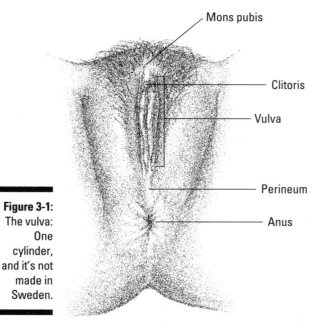

Mons pubis

Clitoris

Vulva

Perineum

Anus

Figure 3-1:
The vulva:
One
cylinder,
and it's not
made in
Sweden.

The part of the female genitals that you can see is called the *vulva,* which lies between the mons pubis and the anus. The *mons pubis* (also called mons veneris, which in Latin stands for "mound of Venus") is a layer of fatty tissue that lies above the pubic bone, basically acting as a bumper. That part of the female is easily identified because it's covered with pubic hair. The anus is . . . oh, you know what an anus is because, whichever sex you are, you have one.

Viva the vulva

The vulva has large outer lips called the *labia majora* (which is Latin for, you guessed it, large outer lips). Inside these lips are

- the *labia minora* (smaller inner lips)
- the *clitoris* (a woman's most sensitive spot)
- the *urethra* (from which urine is passed)
- and the *vestibule* (not a place to hang your hat and coat)

The vestibule is the actual entrance to the vagina, and is covered by a membrane called the *hymen.* When a woman is aroused, the *vestibular bulbs,* which lie underneath, swell with blood and become engorged, somewhat like a penis — which only makes sense, because they are made from the same spongy tissue as the penis.

Whether you're looking at Figure 3-1 or the real thing right now, it is important to remember that not all vulvas look alike. Just the way there are different models of Volvos, there are many different shaped vulvas, but they will all take you where you want to go.

In the early weeks of a baby's formation, when it is still an embryo, the male and female genitals look basically the same. That's because many of the same tissues are used to form both the male and female genitals; though, upon completion, these genitals end up taking different forms. (And a good thing, too.) For example, the tissues that form the *labia majora* in the female are the same tissues that form the *scrotum* in the male.

The labia majora are made up of two rounded mounds of tissue that form the outer boundaries of the vulva (see Figure 3-2). After puberty, hair grows on them, as well as on the mons pubis. The skin of the labia majora is usually darker than the surrounding skin of the thighs. Within the labia majora are the smaller *labia minora*. They surround the vestibule and are hairless. They join at the top to form the *prepuse,* or clitoral hood.

Inside the vestibule are the *Bartholin's glands,* whose secretions serve as one of a woman's natural lubricants during intercourse (although the major source of a woman's lubrication comes through the walls of the vagina, as I discuss later in this chapter). These secretions are also an indication that the woman has become aroused, similar to the male's erection. As a woman ages, the glands begin to shrink and secrete less fluid. For this reason, an older woman must often use a lubricant to help keep the area moist during intercourse.

Where the upper ends of the labia minora meet lies the *clitoris,* the principal organ of female sexual pleasure. Pea sized, the clitoris develops from the same tissue as does the penis. Also like the penis, the clitoris has a shaft and a head (glans) and gets engorged with blood during sexual excitement and grows, though certainly not to the extent that a penis does. The clitoris has many nerve endings and is a very erogenous organ, critical to a woman's attaining an orgasm. (See Chapter 13 for more on attaining orgasms.)

Though a lot smaller in size, the clitoris has about the same number of nerve endings as a penis, which is why many women cannot tolerate direct stimulation of the clitoris but prefer to have the area over the hood and the mons pubis stimulated instead.

The clitoris, like the penis, can accumulate *smegma* — a combination of secretions, skin cells, and bacteria — under the clitoral hood. You should be careful to clean this area thoroughly. If there is too much accumulation, you may have to ask your gynecologist to do a thorough cleaning.

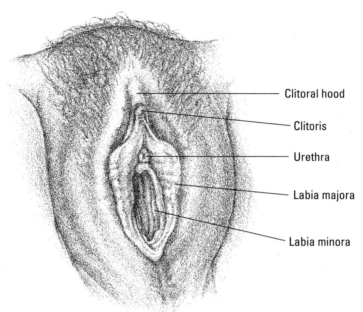

Clitoral hood

Clitoris

Urethra

Labia majora

Labia minora

Figure 3-2:
The innards
of the vulva.

Below the clitoris is the entrance to the urethra, out of which urine flows. The urethra is totally separate from the vagina, into which the penis is inserted during intercourse. Some men, and possibly even a few women, don't realize that these are two different openings, which is one of the reasons that they get squeamish about this region. But, as the penis is really too big to fit into the urethra, it should not be a source of concern. And, since urine also comes out of the penis, no man should feel that the vagina is any less clean than its male counterpart. But, if you still feel uncomfortable about this region, there's an easy solution.

If you want to be absolutely sure that both your genitals and your partner's are squeaky clean, there's nothing wrong with making wash-up of both a normal part of your sexual routine. After all, nobody ever died from being too clean.

Urinary tract infections are fairly common in women, and one reason for this is that bacteria can be pushed back inside the urethra during intercourse. Always keep this area clean, being very careful to always wipe yourself front to back and not the other way around.

The hymen: symbol of virginity

The hymen, when intact, was once considered the traditional proof of a woman's virginity. Her status as a virgin was verified by the bleeding that often occurs when the hymen is first penetrated.

In olden days, the mother of the bride would actually display the bloody sheets after the wedding night to show how pure her daughter had been before her marriage. And, if by some chance the daughter had been slightly impure, some chicken's blood would do — especially since DNA testing hadn't been invented yet.

In our modern era, however, many women break this membrane accidentally prior to their first attempt at sexual intercourse, either by inserting a tampon or while performing vigorous activities, such as bicycle riding. In the vast majority of cases, even an intact hymen has perforations so that menstrual blood can pass through, but some women are born without these and a doctor must pierce the hymen. (By the way, the fact that a woman has broken her hymen before she's had sexual intercourse doesn't change her status as a virgin. Only through actual intercourse can she change that standing.)

The vagina: the main thoroughfare

What makes women different from men is that much of our sexual apparatus is on the inside — most notably, the *vagina.* The vagina itself is a hollow, muscular tube which extends from the external opening at the vestibule all the way to the cervix, which is the entrance to the uterus.

An adult woman's vagina is about 3 to 4 inches long, but it is extremely flexible. During intercourse, the vagina stretches to accommodate the penis. When a woman gives birth, the vagina stretches even more, becoming part of the birth canal through which the baby passes on its way into the world. When there is neither a penis nor a baby in it, the vagina is collapsed like an empty balloon.

The vagina does not go straight back, but usually angles upward. (Some women have a tipped vagina, which angles downward, but this is not common.) Some women, not aware of the angle, have a difficult time inserting a tampon because they think it should go straight back, which it can't.

The walls of the vagina have three layers (see Figure 3-3). The first is the *mucosa,* or vaginal lining. The mucosa is very thick and has many folds. It responds to the woman's hormonal changes by secreting various types of fluids. Under the mucosa are a muscular layer and a layer of connective tissue (the *advunticia*) that are rich in blood.

Beneath the vagina, on the pelvic floor, are other muscles that are responsible for keeping the vagina elevated, tight, and firm. Women can do Kegel exercises, which I talk about in Chapter 13, to help tone these muscles.

Speaking of exercising, sometimes when a woman is exercising or during intercourse, air can be forced into the vagina and, when the women changes position, it goes back out, producing a sound as if she were passing gas. This is a common occurrence and should not be a cause of embarrassment.

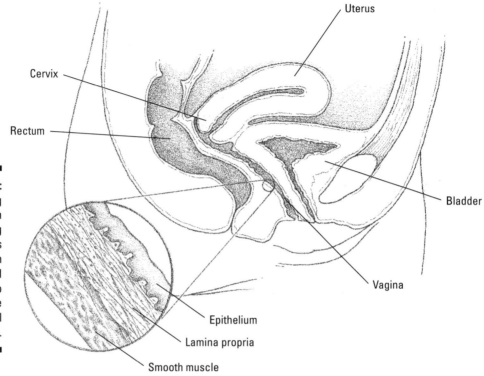

Figure 3-3:
Lubricating
fluids and an
enveloping
fullness
come from
the vaginal
walls to
enhance
sexual
pleasure.

During sexual excitement, a woman experiences several physical changes:

- The vaginal lips and clitoris swell.
- The nipples on her breasts become erect.
- The vaginal walls fill with blood in a process called *vasocongestion,* which is similar to the way blood flows into the penis during erection.

The vagina becomes lubricated by the passage of fluids through the vaginal walls. This lubrication is not manufactured by a gland, but occurs when fluid filters into the vagina from blood vessels surrounding it. The vasocongestion causes increased pressure which, in turn, causes the fluid within the blood serum to be pushed through the tissues of the vaginal wall.

This fluid has another function besides making it easier for the penis to slide in and out of the vagina. It also changes the chemical nature of the vagina, making it more alkaline and less acidic, an environment that is more hospitable to sperm.

In most mammals, the female does not provide any lubrication; instead, the male secretes the lubricant, similar to what is produced by the Cowper's gland in human males, but in much greater quantities. Researchers have noted that, when males of certain species, like horses, are aroused, a steady stream of this fluid flows out of the penis.

The vagina goes through several changes in a woman's life.

- ✔ Before puberty, the vaginal walls are thinner and the vaginal tube is smaller, which is one reason why so much damage can be done to a young girl who is sexually molested.

- ✔ During puberty, the vagina grows, and hormones cause other changes to take place. The vagina becomes elevated, and the clitoris becomes firm and erect when a woman becomes sexually aroused.

- ✔ After menopause (which I explain very soon, so be patient), a woman's hormonal levels go down, and the vaginal tissue becomes more fragile and less elastic. A woman's natural lubrication also declines at this time. Luckily, there are ways to treat all of these problems so that they don't affect good sexual functioning.

At your cervix

At the top of the vagina is the *cervix,* which is the entrance to the uterus. The cervix is actually the lower portion of the uterus, and it protrudes approximately $1/3$ of an inch into the vagina. The cervix produces a special mucus that changes according to the woman's *menstrual cycle* — the monthly process of releasing of eggs in preparation for possible pregnancy (see "The Men Words," later in this chapter).

- ✔ During the first half of the cycle, especially around the time the woman releases the egg (ovulates), her mucus is abundant, clear, and watery. It is quite receptive to sperm penetration and survival, and sperm may live in the mucus for several days.

- ✔ Once ovulation has occurred, the cervical mucus changes dramatically. It becomes thick, cloudy, and sticky, just about impenetrable to sperm trying to pass through the *os,* or opening of the cervix.

Making the cervical mucus impenetrable to sperm is one of the ways that the birth control pill prevents pregnancy. In addition, those practicing natural family planning can test the quality of the mucus as an indicator of fertility (see Chapter 7 for more information on this technique).

The uterus: It stretches, and stretches, and stretches

The *uterus* is about the size of a pear, approximately three inches long. A muscular organ, the uterus is collapsed when empty. Its inner cavity is lined by a tissue called the *endometrium,* which develops and sheds regularly as part of the menstrual cycle. As noted in Chapter 1, menstruation occurs in response to ovarian hormones.

The uterus is where the baby develops, and one look at a very pregnant woman tells you that the uterus has the ability to stretch incredibly. Luckily for us women, the uterus also goes back to its regular size after the baby has gone out into the big, wide world — or *we'd* be big and wide forever.

The ovaries and fallopian tubes

Leading into the ovaries are the fallopian tubes, each about four inches long (see Figure 3-4). The entrance to these tubes, near the ovary, is fairly large and lined with tiny "fingers," called *fimbria,* which help to guide the eggs released by the ovary down into one of the tubes.

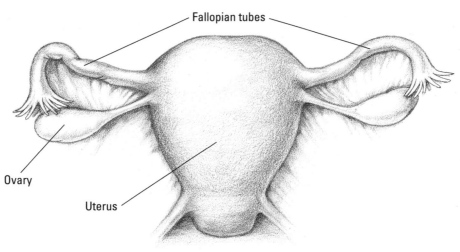

Fallopian tubes

Ovary

Uterus

Figure 3-4:
The ovaries and fallopian tubes: Where it all starts.

A woman has two ovaries, each about 1 ½ inches long. The woman's eggs — all 200,000 of them — are stored within the ovaries and then released, usually one at a time, at a signal given by the pituitary gland.

The ovaries also release the female sex hormones, estrogen and progesterone. These hormones act as the triggers for the processes that are needed to create a baby.

I describe baby-making processes in Chapter 1. If you skipped over that chapter, or maybe even if you didn't, I suggest you go back and read it now. Sex is all about making babies, and that's something you can never know too much about.

As far as the role that estrogen and progesterone play in a woman's sexual desire, the evidence seems to tilt away from their having much of a role. Women also produce the male sex hormones, *androgens,* and these may play somewhat of a role, but the evidence is not conclusive.

The "Men" Words — Menstruation and Menopause

I don't know why the two biggest female "problems" start with the prefix "men," but it wouldn't surprise me if it were caused by a Freudian slip on somebody's part somewhere along the line.

Some women would disagree with my putting the word "problem" in quotes, because they really do think of menstruation and menopause as problems. Because I'm basically an optimist, I refuse to categorize them as such.

Having your period may be inconvenient at times, and some of the aspects of menopause can be annoying, but there are also saving graces. I always believe that it's better to look at the glass as half full rather than half empty.

Menstruation — having your period

What could be good about having blood coming out of your vagina once a month, you ask?

- ✔ Number one, since menstruation is part of the process of making babies — and I love babies — it's definitely worth such a small inconvenience.

- ✔ Second, ask any woman who has problems with her menstruation, such as irregular bleeding, and you suddenly discover how nice it is to be able to know approximately when "your friend" will next be paying you a visit so that you can be prepared.

- ✔ Third, disruptions in a woman's cycle can serve as an early warning signal of possible health problems, so it's wise to be aware of your body's regular functioning.

PMS

I suppose that I can't address the topic of menstruation without also addressing Pre-Menstrual Syndrome (PMS), though I would much prefer not to. Does the onset of menstruation affect women in various physical and psychological ways? I guess that since so many women report that it does, I have to go along with this finding. But it bothers me when some women give in to PMS and use it as an excuse for all sorts of behavior, because men can then use this to justify holding women back.

Now I am not a radical feminist, by any means. I gladly let a man hold a door for me or send me flowers. But I do not endorse any policy that says that a woman can't be given significant responsibilities because of her mood swings. Both sexes have mood swings.

How many men out there have terrible tempers in part due to raging male sex hormones? Do these temper tantrums hold men back? Of course not. So neither should any so-called mood swings hold women back, and the only way to make sure that they don't is to minimize their effects.

The medical profession has associated over 150 symptoms to PMS (and you wonder why I think there's some exaggerating taking place on this subject!), which can include irritation, depression, changes in appetite, abdominal bloating, breast tenderness, poor concentration, insomnia, crying spells, and swelling of the extremities.

PMS occurs during a seven-day period after ovulation and before the menstrual period begins. Some women have only a few symptoms; many may only have these symptoms irregularly, while others get a full-blown PMS attack every month.

No scientific evidence supports any one cause of PMS, although the possible suspected causes include a hormonal deficiency, fluid balance abnormalities, and nutritional deficiencies.

If you suffer from the effects of PMS, I certainly have sympathy for you. But if you use PMS as a reason for not doing your job, you're harming all women by making it seem as if we are not worthy of holding responsibility every day of the month. We certainly need to do more research on this topic, because right now there is no proven cause or cure for PMS. Until we do learn more and can offer help to those who have PMS, I urge you and every woman to make a strong effort to cope with your symptoms without making life miserable for those around you, especially the men in your life. I believe the time has come for this country to have a woman president, and that will never happen if David Letterman and Jay Leno can have a field day poking fun at the candidate's problems with PMS.

Sex and the menses

Now let me come down from my soapbox and talk about sex and menstruation.

I am Jewish, and, for Orthodox Jews, sex is absolutely forbidden while a woman is having her period. This attitude, whether it comes from religious beliefs or just plain squeamishness at the sight of blood, is shared by many. Ironically, however, there are many women who actually feel more aroused when they are having their period. This is because the pelvic region fills with blood, similar to the flow of blood that occurs in the genitals during sexual arousal.

What if you do feel aroused during your period? There's no physical reason to avoid sex because you're menstruating. You might want to place a towel under you to protect the sheets, and if the man feels strange about having blood on his penis, he could use a condom. But if the urge hits you, there's no reason not to give in to it. Unless your religion forbids it, of course.

Studies show that orgasm can actually relieve some of the discomfort women feel while they are having their period by reducing the feeling of pelvic fullness and cramping.

One thing that you should remember is that, although, technically speaking, you should not be able to get impregnated while you're menstruating, Mother Nature sometimes plays tricks on you. You may have some vaginal bleeding that you interpret as the start of your period when it may not be, and, if you have unprotected intercourse at that time, you could wind up pregnant. If you decide to use natural family planning and rely on your menstrual cycle to plan your sexual activities, then you have to keep careful track of your period to avoid making such mistakes.

Now you would think that women would feel their sexiest at the time when they were ovulating because that's the time when they can become pregnant and hence continue the species. In fact, it's the only time that females in the rest of the animal kingdom do become aroused. Although this heightened arousal may occur in some women, no research has ever found that it's widespread, so it's a mystery as to why this trait has disappeared almost entirely in humans.

Menopause — "the change of life"

Menopause is that time in a woman's life when she stops releasing eggs and shedding the lining of her uterus through menstruation. She is no longer fertile, and there is no more risk of pregnancy. Although every woman is different, the average age that American women hit menopause is 51, so we spend the last third of our lives as menopausal women.

Now, if all that happened to women during menopause was that their monthly bout of bleeding stopped, the commercial world would already have made a celebration out of this day, complete with parties and gifts. However, the cessation of ovulation also causes a decrease in the production of the female hormones, estrogen and progesterone, and that has other effects that women sometimes find unsettling.

Easing into menopause

Menopause is not something that occurs all of a sudden. Usually the changes develop slowly and the period of change is called the *climacteric.* A woman's period may become irregular and the flow lighter or heavier. The actual length of time that it may take for the woman to cease having periods may be one to two years from the start of the climacteric.

Another classic symptom of menopause are *hot flashes,* a sudden feeling of heat that takes over the entire body. It can happen at any time of the day or night, and the number of hot flashes and their duration is different for every woman. Since the woman usually also becomes flushed, these hot flashes can be embarrassing, though there's certainly no need to feel embarrassed. Although not every woman experiences hot flashes, the normal duration for this symptom is two years. About 25 percent of women will have hot flashes for a longer time if they go untreated. (Skip ahead to the section on hormonal replacement therapy to learn more about the treatment.)

Another effect of the decrease in hormone production is changes in the vagina and bladder. The vaginal walls thin out, causing vaginal dryness. This dryness, in turn, can cause burning, irritation, and decreased lubrication, which can result in painful intercourse. Similar changes in the bladder can cause a woman to feel the urge to urinate more frequently.

Many women also experience some psychological changes, although these have not been medically proven to be tied to the effects of menopause. They may, in part, be due simply to interruptions in sleeping patterns caused by the hot flashes, or to a woman's reflections on this permanent physical change in her life, which definitely signals the end of youth.

Some harmful side effects of menopause may be *osteoporosis* — a loss of bone strength caused by lower levels of calcium being retained — and possible heart problems.

Hormonal replacement therapy

Luckily, medical science has found a way of alleviating all of the symptoms of menopause through estrogen replacement therapy. Studies show that having a woman take estrogen to replace that which she is no longer producing can alleviate many of the symptoms of menopause, as well as protect against certain kind of cancers, especially cancer of the cervix. But there have also been studies that show an added risk of breast cancer for some women using hormonal replacement therapy. Any woman beginning menopause should consult her doctor to find out what options are available to her.

Because I'm not a medical doctor, that's all I'm going to say about the physical effects of menopause. (If you're a woman approaching the proper age bracket, I recommend that you go out and buy a book solely on this subject.) The issue of menopause and sex, however, is a topic that I do cover in Chapter 16. I'll give you a preview of that discussion by saying that my philosophy is a very positive one concerning sex in the later years.

Breasts: Hanging in There

I certainly can't give you a road map to the intimate female anatomy without giving you at least a quick tour of the Alps — or, for some of you, the Appalachians. As you should realize, breast size is of no consequence, except to those men who've spent too much time at Hugh Hefner's knee. But breasts are certainly an erogenous zone, and since they do stick out, even while under wraps, they're one part of the body that gets noticed whether you're clothed or not.

Feeding babies

The main purpose of breasts is to feed babies, because after a mother gives birth she *lactates* (that is, makes milk) provided that the baby starts to suck at the nipples. This is truly a miraculous process, one that is not only good for the baby's health but also for the mother's, because it helps the uterus to contract.

Strangely, Western women in the 20th century gave up the process of feeding their babies from the breast for a period of time, but I believe that more and more women are returning to this method.

If any of you have heard that a mother who is breast-feeding can't get pregnant, think again. There is a tendency not to ovulate while breast-feeding, but it's not an absolute, as many a woman has discovered too late.

Getting sexual pleasure

There is no difference between the breasts of male and female children. But, when a girl reaches puberty, first her nipples and the *aureole,* the darker skin around the nipple, begin to enlarge. Then, as her levels of the hormone progesterone increase, the underlying tissue grows, producing a full breast.

There is a concentration of nerve endings in the nipples, and most women's nipples get erect when they become aroused. As an erogenous zone, a woman's breasts serve both the male and the female; men get excited by looking at and fondling breasts, but women also enjoy the sensations.

Many women who masturbate fondle their own breasts and nipples.

Checking for breast cancer

One woman in nine will develop breast cancer in this country. Because of this risk, it is important that every woman examine her breasts once a month. Figure 3-5 shows one technique of checking your breasts for signs of cancer.

It is important that you be consistent about the time of the month you conduct this examination because your breasts do change as you go through your menstrual cycle. The most accurate time to check is during or just after your period. By examining your breasts at the same point in your cycle, you'll be able to make a more accurate comparison.

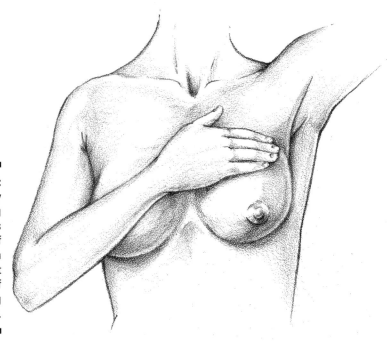

Figure 3-5:
Regularly examining your breasts for signs of cancer is an important part of staying healthy.

What you are looking for are anomalies — things that feel strange — basically a lump of some sort. If you find something, don't panic. Most such lumps are not at all dangerous, but you should consult with your physician as soon as possible. And if you have found an irregularity, be thankful that you did locate it early because, in most cases, it is easily treatable.

You should also have regular breast examinations by a health professional, who may be able to detect something that you would miss, and go for a mammogram whenever your physician tells you that it is time. The older you are, the more important these exams become, and the more regular they should be. After a woman turns 40 she should definitely go once a year (though some say it's OK to wait until you're 50), and that also applies to even younger women if they are in a high risk group. Check with your doctor to determine the best regimen for you.

Be proud of your breasts

Whatever the size of your breasts, they can provide pleasure to both you and your partner. Although small breasts may not get much recognition when you cover them with clothes, once you uncover them in front of a man, he probably won't care what your cup size is. So never feel ashamed of your breasts, but flaunt them at the appropriate moment so that they get their due.

Chapter 4
Understanding the Teen Years

*T*he other day, I received a letter from a high school senior who was going off to college. He knew that I lectured to college students, and he wanted to know what changes, if any, I'd seen among this group of young people.

My answer to him was that there certainly have been changes. Because of AIDS, colleges (and high schools too) have been putting a much greater emphasis on teaching their students about human sexuality. So the questions that I get these days are more sophisticated than those I was asked ten years ago. Most college students already know the basics, and they're looking to me for additional information. But the fact that my lectures are usually standing-room-only also shows that young people still have a lot of questions that need to be answered. That's why I continue to go to colleges all across the country, and it's also one of the reasons that I am writing this book.

If you're a teen today, you are definitely facing a different set of circumstances when it comes to sex than teens of any preceding generation. The pill, AIDS, vast numbers of single mothers, gays coming out of the closet — all are factors that just didn't exist not that long ago.

However, the challenge of being a teenager comes not just in the area of sex. Part of the job of each new generation is to climb onto the shoulders of those who have passed before them and take our civilization one step higher. It's called progress.

But to accomplish anything, you first have to learn to become independent from your parents and teachers. And so, as with every generation before you, this search for independence puts you in conflict with the adults of your time.

To give you an idea of how long this conflict has been going on, just look up some of the things that the philosopher Sophocles wrote about the young people of Greece in 5 B.C., and you'll see that he used the exact same language that adults use to describe teens today.

These conflicts that you face as a teen don't come only from the struggles with those who are older than you. They also arise directly from the changes that are taking place within yourself. The process of growing from a child into an adult is never a smooth one. The growth process comes in spurts. Not only are the adults around you confused by the changes that they see taking place in you, but these changes are just as confusing to you and to every adolescent.

Although the added inches that seem to come out of nowhere are what everybody notices, and usually to your embarrassment, it's the changes that are taking place on the inside of you that are the most significant ones. Many of these come because your hormones, which have been dormant until now, are starting to kick in, bringing with them physical and psychological growth.

Adolescence is a little like the Italian train system. You can never be sure exactly at what time the train is going to leave, nor can you be sure when it's going to arrive at the various stops along the way.

Don't Worry (Much), Be Happy (Lots)

The ages of 11 to 16 are when these changes take place in most young people, but in any particular group of young people, you'll find some experiencing changes as early as age nine or ten, and others lagging behind until maybe 16 or 17. To be the first girl to sprout breasts or the first boy to have his upper lip darkened by a light mustache is definitely embarrassing, because everybody is going to notice, you can be sure. But to be the last one in the group, even if nobody seems to notice, can cause even worse worries, because you begin to feel that you'll be flat-chested or hairless forever.

Although the best advice is to enjoy your youth and not worry about such things, I know that this is impossible. These particular changes are too sensational to ignore, particularly when they're also affecting how you think and feel.

I certainly had my share of problems, because I never passed 4 feet 7 inches. As everybody else around me kept growing taller, I stopped. It did cause me a lot of pain, but once I realized that I was not going to grow anymore, I resolved not to let my height stop me. I think you'll agree that I didn't let my size get in the way. Actually, many short people have succeeded in life because they knew that they had to work harder to get ahead and did just that.

Whatever stage you're at, I give you permission to spend five or maybe ten minutes a day taking stock of yourself and giving in to whatever feelings about yourself you may be harboring. But, after that, you have to pick yourself up and push forward. Your main duty at this time of your life is to do well in school. Luckily, how big or small you are, how developed or undeveloped you are, has no effect on your studies — unless you let it. And be sure that you don't let it. Concentrate on your work and getting good grades and, before you know it, your worries about being different from everybody else will take care of themselves.

Now, if you happen to be at either end of the spectrum, an early or late developer, I have two other suggestions:

- ✔ Look around you at the adult population.

  You can quickly see that none of us adults got stuck in childhood. So whether you are waiting for everybody to catch up to you, or if you're the one who needs to do the catching up, keeping one eye on the adults around you will help you to remember that it will all even out eventually.

- ✔ Learn as much about the process as possible.

  In this book, I only give you the short explanation of the growing-up process, probably no more than what you can find in your health textbook. But there are plenty of books meant for teenagers that explain the process in detail. In fact, I even wrote one, *Dr. Ruth Talks To Kids*. I find that if I know what is going on, even if I can't totally control it, I begin to feel more in control, and I make better choices. Really understanding what your body is going through makes it a little easier to distance yourself from the process, and that helps you to remain a little calmer about it all.

Evolving into Adulthood

At some point during the second decade of your life, your brain begins to stimulate the production of hormones that cause physical changes to take place. We don't know exactly what triggers the brain, though I believe that seeing a few too many episodes of *I Love Lucy* can slow the process down.

The human body produces many different kinds of hormones. When you're about 11 years old, your brain says, "You've had enough playing with toys; now it's time to get serious." Since your brain communicates to you by releasing chemicals, that's how it gets this message across. For those of you who can sit through the operating sequences on *ER*, here are the gory details:

- ✔ The pituitary gland releases higher levels of *follicle stimulating hormone* (FSH) and *luteinizing hormone* (LH).

✔ Together, FSH and LH activate the sex organs so that eggs (ova) develop in the female ovaries, and sperm develop in the male testes.

✔ The sex organs then produce their own hormones. Estrogen and progesterone are the two most important female hormones. Testosterone is the principal male hormone.

The physical changes

Here are the general physical changes that take place:

✔ For both sexes height and weight increase, underarm and pubic hair begins to grow, leg and arm hair becomes thicker and more apparent, perspiration increases, and levels of oil in the skin become high (which you can blame for that great bane of all teenagers, acne).

✔ In girls, breasts become larger and more pronounced, nipples stand out more clearly, and the genitals grow and get a little darker and fleshier. On the inside, the uterus and ovaries also grow. At some point during the process, *menarche* occurs. That's a woman's first menstrual period. It may take up to one and a half years from the first period, however, before her menstrual cycle becomes regular.

✔ In boys, the testicles and penis become larger. At some point, the man gains the capacity to ejaculate sperm. He also begins to have spontaneous erections (usually at the wrong time and place). Most men also experience *nocturnal emissions,* also called "wet dreams." These are spontaneous ejaculations of semen that occur during sleep.

The psychological changes

As you might expect, going from childhood, where the biggest problem was how many pogs you had in your collection, to adolescence — worrying about how many zits are on your face, when your period is going to visit you next, what to do with the bedsheets from the wet dream you had last night, or how to get the boy or girl next door to notice you — can be quite traumatic.

Now, just as not every toddler goes through the terrible twos, neither does every teenager grow sullen and moody, as is the reputation. In fact, most people enjoy these years more than any other. For, although there may be worries, there are also a lot of thrills. Firsts — be they your first car, first date, first kiss, first act of sexual intercourse, or first orgasm — are very exciting. You'll be breaking away from your parents a little bit more every day, changing schools, learning to drive, developing new friends, staying up later, squeezing pimples . . . OK, forget that last one. But each day brings new challenges, and challenges make you feel more vibrant and alive.

Now, if everything is just ducky, you don't need any help from me. But for those of you who are having problems, let me address some of the most common ones.

Friendships

Adolescence is the term we give to the teen years when a child becomes an adult. It is a time of life when having friends is most important. The biggest calamity can be staying home on a Friday or Saturday night. What does happen to some teens is that they go through a period when they don't have as many friends as they would like. Maybe your family moves, or you go away to school, or your best friend with whom you've always hung out starts dating someone seriously, leaving you out in the cold.

What you have to remember in a situation like this is that you can do something about it. The worst thing you can do is simply sit home and mope. You have to go out and make friends. If school is in session, you can

- Bring a fantastic lunch, with lots of things that you can share, like a bag of potato chips or Oreo cookies, then sit at a table where other kids are eating and offer them what you've brought.
- Join an after-school organization.
- Volunteer to help work on the next dance.
- Bring a Polaroid camera and take pictures of the other students and give them out.

If school is out, try to do things where you can spot other solitary teens and strike up a friendship.

- Go out bike riding or roller blading and try to hook up with some other kids doing the same.
- Grab your basketball, go to the nearest court, and try to get into a game.
- Visit the library, ignore the "Silence" sign, and try to strike up a conversation.
- If there's a nearby beach or pool, bring along a Frisbee or a deck of cards and try to get a game going.
- Volunteer your services some place where other teens are likely to be doing the same thing, like at a hospital, nursing home, camp, or zoo.

Don't be afraid to use the rest of your family to help you make friends. Sometimes adults can help match kids together. Instead of making a long face when your Mom suggests meeting somebody, go ahead and meet that person. You really have nothing to lose. If you've got siblings, do things with them, even if they're much younger than you. Maybe they've got friends who have older siblings too.

It may be easier to just sit home and watch MTV, but that will quickly get boring, so the sooner you begin working at making friends, the better off you'll be.

Dating

I could write a whole book on dating for teenagers, but I would like to pass on just a few tips that I think are very important.

- The first is that you should begin by going out in groups. One-on-one dates put a lot of pressure on both parties, pressure that you may not be ready for. Don't let the fact that your best friend has a steady boyfriend or girlfriend influence you. As I've said, teens develop differently, so it may just be that your friend is ready, and you're not. But it also may be that your friend is in over his or her head.

- Teens who start going steady too early often wind up in trouble. They spend too much time with each other so that they can't concentrate on their school work. They tend to isolate themselves from their other friends, which increases the intensity of their relationship, which can cause them to go too far too soon. Studies have shown that the earlier teens start dating, the earlier they are going to have sex. And if they break up, they're left feeling even more alone.

- If you meet someone who becomes really special to you, then it's only natural that you want to see a lot of each other. But to go out on dates just because some of your other friends are doing it is not a good idea.

- When you do start dating, don't pretend that suddenly your heart has taken complete control over your head. Just because you like someone doesn't mean that you have to take risks in order to see them.

  If someone is abusive, or if they overindulge in alcohol or use drugs, or if they drive dangerously, or if they ask you to go to an unsupervised party or a deserted place or anywhere that trouble might be lurking, get yourself out of there as quickly as possible.

- Always make sure that others — ideally your parents, but at least some friends — know where you are.

Sex & Marriage

It's hard to believe that the factors which affect a vital part of our lives, sex, could change so radically in a short period of time, but they definitely have. Not so long ago, young people didn't have a choice. Their parents would decide whom they were going to marry, make all the arrangements, and that was that. Sure, some people engaged in pre-marital or extra-marital sex, but not without considerable risks. An unmarried pregnant woman couldn't get an abortion, and, in most instances, she would be rejected by both her family and society. With such dire consequences hanging over their heads, most women chose to accept the status quo and not have sex until they got married.

Then, as society began to see women less as chattel and allowed them to be educated along with men, the age for getting married started to get pushed back more and more. Now it's commonplace to wait until after you've gotten your college degree or maybe your graduate degree before getting married. And that, along with other factors, began to affect people's decisions about when to have sex.

Wait for marriage?

It's commonplace today not to get married at all before having sexual intercourse. Far too many young women are becoming single mothers, a difficult and expensive life for both mother and child.

Part of the reason for the number of unintended pregnancies among teenagers is that girls are getting their menarche earlier and earlier. Where many girls weren't capable of having children at age 16 only 30 years ago, now many 12-year-olds are not only physically ready to have babies, but are actually having them.

So now we have a major dilemma. Girls can have babies at a younger age; meantime, we're asking people to wait until a later age to get married. If all young people were to listen to their elders, the period of abstinence — the time during which they're capable of having sex but are waiting until they get married — would just about double. Throw into this mixture the fact that, as a result of the birth control pill, it is quite possible to engage in sexual intercourse without getting pregnant, and you have a very anxious and confusing situation for young people.

Now, whether young people get married or not, they do pair off in great numbers as they get older. And, in fact, our society encourages them to do so all the time. Certainly just about every young person on TV has a boyfriend or girlfriend or is desperately seeking one. Even at home, aunts and uncles and grandmas are always asking even little children whether they have a boyfriend or girlfriend. Under these circumstances, is it realistic to expect our young people to put off having sex?

As is often the case, the answer is neither black nor white, but somewhere in between.

Is there a magic age?

Teens and their parents are always asking me what's the right age to begin having sex. Now, although we do have age limits for certain things — like voting, getting a driver's license, and drinking alcohol — there is no magic age for sex. In the first place, voting and driving are things that you do alone, even if others are with you while you're doing them. But sex is a shared activity. It's not just whether you are ready, it also depends on your partner.

This is not an issue that anybody else can decide for you. Sure, some adults go around saying "just say no," but they're not in your shoes.

Don't rush it

The most important thing that I can tell you is not to rush into anything. Think about your decision carefully and weigh the pros and cons.

Remember, you will never forget the first time you have sexual intercourse. So be as certain as you can be that, when you do "do it" for the first time, it will be an occasion that you'll treasure for the rest of your life — not one that you'll regret forever more.

Don't be pressured

Never, never have sex because somebody pressures you into it.

If you're with somebody who says that they'll stop seeing you unless you have sex with them, then you know what the right decision is: First, stop seeing them, and certainly never have sex with them. They're not interested in you, but in sex.

If the person you're with says that they're "dying" with the need to have sex, remember two things:

- ✔ No one has ever died from not having sex, but you could die if you have sex with a person who gives you AIDS.

- ✔ Sexual release is possible without intercourse. That person, or you, can masturbate, and if you feel like it, you can help that person achieve sexual release by using your hand.

When to have sex is a very difficult decision to make. I wish I could offer you a role model, but no one has ever lived through the particular circumstances that you face today. It truly is a different world. If you have followed your best judgment in making your decision, no one can say whether your decision, whatever it is, was absolutely right or wrong. Only time and your own life's experience will tell.

Because there are serious consequences to having sex, whatever you do, don't make the decision to have sex casually. Don't let peer pressure influence you or the person with whom you are thinking about having sex. Just look deep down inside of yourself. If you do that, I believe that you'll make the right decision *for you.*

Masturbation

In the preceding section, I mention masturbation. This is an activity that is quite common among adolescents. *Masturbation* means touching your genitals in a way that you find pleasing to the point of having an orgasm. I talk about this solo play in more detail in Chapter 19. Although many myths surround this activity, masturbation cannot do you any harm unless you overdo it to the point where it affects other areas of your life, like your schoolwork or your social life.

An issue that is often attached to masturbation is privacy, because one of the reasons that teens seek privacy is the need to masturbate. How much privacy you can get at home often depends on how much room there is. Your parents and siblings should certainly give you as much privacy as possible. But you have to be conscious of other family members' rights as well. You can't hog the bathroom or come in late at night and make a lot of noise and then expect others to respect your rights. If you want to be treated as an adult, then you have to act like one also.

Now just because many teens do masturbate, you shouldn't feel that there is something wrong with you if you don't masturbate. If you feel the need, that's fine, but it's just as fine if you don't feel like doing it. As with all aspects of your sexual life, the decision is yours — you have control.

Sexual Identity

Teenagers don't always know what their sexual identity is going to be; that is to say, they're not always sure whether they're heterosexual or homosexual. In fact, even though some pre-teens or teens engage in sexual acts with members of their own sex, that doesn't necessarily mean that they're homosexual (see Chapter 18).

The teen years are a time for learning, and it takes some teens longer to learn what type of person attracts them. Here again, a time will come when you are sure of your sexual identity, so don't make a big deal out of it if you're not sure at any one point in your adolescence.

All in the Family

As a teenager, you are beginning the process of breaking away from your family. It's absolutely necessary that you do this in order to develop into a mature individual. But breaking away from your family doesn't mean abandoning them. Yes, you want to spend more time with people your own age, particularly with your friends. But you should also spend as much time as you can with your family. You still need them, and they need you.

Sure you have a great time when you're with your friends, but there are also certain tensions. You have an image to keep up. There's a structural hierarchy; maybe one person is the leader, or several of you are vying for the top spot. And then there are the sexual tensions. Teens of the opposite sex are around, so you have to worry about whether you look good, whether you smell good, and whether you're wearing the right clothes. And there's competition, too, for the attention of those members of the opposite sex.

But, with your family, you can let your hair down. You can act silly, eat your favorite foods (even if they're not the latest fad), watch the TV show you watched as a child, and talk about topics with your family in ways that you can't with your friends. You can reminisce, look at old pictures, and try to recapture the feelings that you had as a child, which you can do with no one else but your family.

Try to get up a little earlier and have breakfast with your mom. As often as you can, share dinner with the rest of your family members. Try to do things together. Maybe you wouldn't want to be caught dead with your parents at the local mall, but spending a vacation in another city together can be a lot of fun, so don't put the idea down. Friends are great, but they may not always stick by you in times of trouble the way family will. Cut the apron strings, definitely, but don't cut yourself off entirely.

Don't Stop Here

If you're a teen, you may want to read the rest of this book. It covers some issues that you are not facing right now, but you may well run into these issues at some point in your life. It's always better to be prepared by knowing the facts.

Whatever you do, treasure your teen years. They're very special, and you won't get a second chance to enjoy them except maybe through your own children. So have fun, stay safe, and keep reading.

Part II
Getting Ready

In this part...

There are still some people out there who think that my only role is to tell people to go ahead and do whatever they please. In fact, when there was talk of Lee Iacocca running for President, he said that he would tell the people what to do and I would be his running mate and tell them how to do it. I was flattered at the time, but in truth I'm old-fashioned and a square, and I want you to create a relationship with someone before you have sex with them. So this part is all about the preliminaries to good sex: building and keeping relationships.

Chapter 5

Finding the Right Partner

· ·

· ·

*F*or many people, finding that other person for a long-term commitment is the hardest part of a relationship. Notice I said "long-term commitment." I am old-fashioned and a square. I am not in favor of one-night stands, and here are two basic reasons why I'm against them:

✔ **Good sexual functioning:** Sex is much better when it takes place within a relationship, as opposed to between strangers.

Each individual has different needs when it comes to enjoying sex to the fullest. It takes time to learn how to best please each other — time that you don't have during a one-night stand. Anyway, how pleasant is it to wake up in the morning next to someone whose name you can't remember?

✔ **Sexually transmitted diseases (STDs):** From the point of view of transmitting diseases, when you've had sex with one person, it's the same as having had sex with all of that person's past sexual partners.

Think about it. If the person you're having sex with is promiscuous — and if they're having sex with you the first time you meet them, what other word is there to describe them? — joining you in that bed, or back seat, is every other person that person has slept with, as well as the partners of their partners, and so on. That could easily amount to several hundred people!

"Wait a minute," you say, looking around, "where are all these people?" OK, I exaggerated. Those people are not really there. But they did send their representatives — their germs and viruses. And do you want those afterthoughts hanging around you? Check out Chapter 21 for the damage they can do.

There is no such thing as safe sex between two strangers. There is only the potential for safer sex. And that's only if you take all the necessary precautions.

But, no matter how many precautions you take, you can still catch a sexually transmitted disease (STD). Condoms can break. And even when they don't break, condoms offer less than adequate protection against some STDs, like herpes. And since those STDs include the deadly AIDS, only fools think that an indicator of good sex is how many times they've scored.

Luckily, many people have heard the message about the dangers involved in having many partners. Today, more and more people are looking for that long-term partner with whom they can have a long-term great relationship as well as long-term great sex.

But finding such a partner is a lot more difficult than finding someone who only meets the requirement of being good in bed. A long-term partner must have a whole list of positive qualities in order for you to be in love and develop this relationship. Learning to recognize these qualities in other people and figuring out how to attract the people who have the right qualities takes skill and patience. Many people seem unable to master the process. But, if you don't, you may end up spending strings of lonely nights by yourself or having your heart broken again and again.

Difficult, Yes; Impossible, No

Although I will never say that finding a partner is easy, for I certainly faced my own difficulties as a young woman who was an orphan and only 4 feet 7 inches tall, I will make one assertion — it is not impossible. Believe it or not, that's a very big distinction. Sitting in my office chair, I've heard too many people say that they *can't* find a partner. But that's not so.

Everyone can find a partner, even a wonderful partner. If you've been unable to find the right partner, you may just be going about it the wrong way.

The dreamers

Here's an example of a search for love that was doomed from the start:

Lonely Lisa

Lisa came to see me because she couldn't find a man. She was desperate and cried throughout half of the first session. Lisa had a nice personality and was attractive, although a little overweight. Not a big problem, but one which did require making some adjustments. But what kind of help did she come to me for? What she most wanted from me was to get her a date with a certain very famous TV star.

Not only do I not know this star, not only would I not do such a thing if I did know him, but where in heaven's name did she get the idea that this star was waiting for her to walk into his life? Taking all the factors into consideration — she didn't know him, he lived thousands of miles away, and he was one of the most sought-after bachelors in Hollywood — the odds of their ever linking up were ridiculously slim. She was setting herself up for her lonely nights by choosing such a totally unrealistic goal.

Whatever you think of Lisa, you have to understand that she is not alone. Oh, not everybody has their eyes set exclusively on one TV or movie star (although certainly millions of people fantasize about stars, and that's all right), but many of you may have a certain image of the person you want, oftentimes an unrealistic image, so you wind up just as lonely as Lisa.

Not only is it unrealistic to expect your man to look like Tom Cruise or your woman like Sharon Stone, but if you base your selection on only one aspect of a person, such as looks or job title, it insures that you miss out on meeting some very nice people who may not fit into the one cubbyhole in which you are looking.

If you are serious about finding a partner, then you have to widen your search to include anyone who might fit the bill. Naturally, I'm not suggesting that you date the first nerd you meet at the convenience store. But make sure that you base your selection process on the complete human being, not just on one attribute.

After all, looks fade, and fortunes come and go. You can't be sure of what it is you are really getting just by looking at the current packaging. On the other hand, the important qualities like warmth, *joie de vivre*, the ability to give of oneself, and an attraction for you are constants that can survive a 75-year-long marriage.

The doormats

Be careful not to become so blinded by looks, money, power, or position that you don't see when you are being used.

People who let themselves be used tend to fall into the same trap again and again, seemingly unable to learn from their mistakes.

As terrible as the heartache you must endure if this happens is the time that you waste. You meet plenty of people who could be great partners, but you don't realize it and miss making these connections. Years go by and, instead of having spent them with someone your care about and who cares about you, you spend them alone, with brief interludes of make-believe happiness dating people who turn out to be only in it for themselves.

Here's Paul's story to illustrate how easily you can fall into the trap of being used but not loved:

Heartbroken Paul

When Paul came to see me, he was absolutely heartbroken. He'd been dating this gorgeous woman for the last three months. She had recently moved to New York and was interested in becoming a model. Paul had a few connections, and he was able to open some doors for her. One evening, he took her to a party at which there were a number of people in the fashion industry. They met a top photographer, who immediately took a liking to this woman, and she dropped Paul flat and left the party with this other man.

This wasn't the first time that Paul had allowed a woman to walk all over him, and I told him that, unless he changed his ways, it wouldn't be the last time, either.

Paul needed to identify his problem in order to keep himself from repeating it over and over again. To be successful in the dating game, you must analyze your faults and the faults that others may have and come up with a mental image of your ideal partner. I'm not talking about finding perfection. Nobody is perfect — except maybe my grandson. But you do have to learn how to navigate the dating scene so that you end up forming a relationship with someone who will satisfy your needs while you satisfy theirs.

The time-wasters

Let me delve a little bit further into the subject of wasting time and offer some advice to those of you who are always waiting to win the dating lottery — some without even buying tickets.

Time-wasters fall into two basic categories:

✔ The first category are people who always have a string of excuses for not looking for a mate:

- I have to lose a few more pounds.

- I have to redecorate my apartment.

- I have to look for a new job.

- I have to get my bachelor's degree (and then my master's and then my doctorate).

- I have to wait . . . and wait . . . and wait. . . .

If you're one of these people, you can end up wasting your entire life waiting for the right moment to look for a partner.

If you're serious about finding a partner, the time to start searching is now. This may seem obvious, but look back at your past and see how much time you've wasted. And remember, it's not just the time you may have wasted, but the opportunities you've missed. Every social gathering that you skipped may have contained someone who was right for you.

✔ The other group consists of people who don't make excuses, but who won't lift a finger to help themselves. They think that the way to find a partner is to sit and wait by the phone.

That is nonsense.

If you want something in this world, you have to make an effort to get it, and the more effort you put into the search, the better will be your rewards.

In olden times, when families lived near to one another, there was a whole network of people looking to make matches for single people. Nowadays, as people move around so much, those networks have been erased. You have to make up for that loss by putting your own network together, piece by piece. It will take some effort, but it will also pay off. At the very least, you'll make some new friends. At best, you'll find someone you love and who loves you.

If you really want to find a partner, you have to go out there and look for one. Make yourself available. Go to parties. Throw parties! Tell everybody you know that you are looking. Put an ad in the personal listings. Go to a matchmaker, if that's what it takes. There's nothing to be ashamed of.

Should you use every avenue, from personal ads in newspapers to meeting people through cyberspace? Absolutely. But you do have to be more careful with these mediums. Even the absolute worst blind date, the one with bottle-thick glasses and buck teeth, comes with a reference — somebody that you know knows who they are and where they live. The people you meet impersonally can easily hide their true identities, and, if they're out to harm you, they can do so with little risk (see Chapter 20).

Now most of the people you'll meet via personal ads, cyberspace, and so forth are just like you, perfectly nice but a little lonely. But you have to take at least the most obvious precautions:

✔ Make sure that the first time you meet, it's at a well-lit public place, like a restaurant or popular bar.

✔ Don't be too quick to give out personal information. It might be best to only give a daytime office number.

✔ Take a cab home — by yourself.

Remember, it's a jungle out there, and you're not Tarzan.

The love-at-first-sight syndrome

Another group of people who can end up being miserable are those who suffer from the love-at-first-sight syndrome. The French call it *le coup de foudre* — the bolt of lightning — and think of how rarely people are hit by lightning (thank heavens!). Undoubtedly it does happen: Two people meet at a party, ride off into the sunset (or dawn), and live happily ever after. For those lucky few, it's great. But, for so many others, waiting for love at first sight only brings misery.

If you find yourself wanting nothing less than an instant attraction, you may just be avoiding the time and work it takes to build a successful relationship. When it's either love at first sight or nothing, be prepared for some problems:

- First, you might stare into the eyes of a million people and never see those sparks fly. Or the two of you might be at the bus stop, see each other, the bus comes, zips you away, and you never see each other again. Every week in New York City's *Village Voice* there are ads placed by people looking for someone they saw only fleetingly like that. Some people think it's romantic; I think it's sad. People who have these kinds of delusions often wind up old and alone.

- Another difficulty is that, while you're waiting for your Venus or Adonis to appear, you're not giving other people a chance, even though, with time, one of them might turn out to be your one true love.

  Love is an important building block in forming a relationship, but it doesn't have to be the first stone set. You can lay a foundation by developing a friendship with someone whom you later come to love. And you can love that person as deeply as you would someone you met in a love-at-first-sight situation, if you're willing to give that love the opportunity to grow at its own pace.

- An equally frustrating problem caused by the love-at-first-sight syndrome is that you may find yourself always falling in love with people who don't love you back.

  Puppy love is cute in kids, but when it's an adult going around acting like a puppy, it only turns people off. When you begin to act maturely and hold your emotions in check, not only do you wind up with egg on your face less often but you also give potential partners time to get to know you and then fall in love with you.

  If you're always crowding your potential partners by showering them with gifts and adoration that they're not ready for, you can guarantee that the only result will be to drive them away.

Believing in Yourself

Many of the problems that people have in finding a partner come from low self-esteem. If you don't believe that you are worthy of finding a partner, then it becomes very difficult to make it happen. You may end up in some of the time-wasting situations as a way to sabotage your chances of finding someone just because you don't really believe that you deserve that someone.

But you *do* deserve that certain someone. And you *can* take control of your life and make the changes necessary within yourself so you can turn those interpersonal failures into successes. You have to learn to pull your shoulders back, hold your head high, put a smile on your face, and go out there and conquer the world. You can do it!

Not everyone can do it alone, however. Some people need professional help, and, if that's the case, you should definitely go and get it (see Appendix B). And I'm not saying this only as someone who gives such help. When I wrote my autobiography, I knew I was going to have problems facing the parts of my life when I lost my family to the Nazis. I went to a psychologist I knew, and I spent several hours in his office crying into the tape recorder. It was painful, but those chapters got written.

So do I feel for any pain you may be suffering? Absolutely. But is that an excuse for not asking for help to get on with your life? Absolutely not. The Bible says seek and you shall find, and that's what you have to do.

Re-entering the Dating Scene

One of the biggest problems that people encounter who are suddenly thrust into having to date once again, either after a divorce or just the end of a long-term relationship, is that they can't seem to take their emergency brakes off.

If you've recently broken up with somebody, you've just done a lot of suffering. Even if you're the one who caused the break-up, it's never easy. And now you're supposed to go back into the dating scene as if nothing happened? It's impossible. You're carrying a lot of emotional baggage, and that's going to slow you down.

But what you don't want is to never get started in the first place. You don't want to be sitting there revving your engine but not moving an inch. You're so afraid that whatever it is that just happened to you will happen again that you can't find the courage to move on. You actually end up stopping yourself from connecting with other people.

But, when you make up your mind in advance that something bad is going to happen, you end up stopping yourself from allowing something wonderful to happen. You can't let what happened in your past, no matter how bad it was, determine what will happen in your future.

Sure you have to learn from your mistakes and be more selective the next time. But to be more selective, you have to be out there meeting people from whom to make that selection.

If you're on the rebound, here are some tips that will help you to actually bounce back:

✔ **Don't knock yourself.**

Many people blame themselves for the break-up. But, to find a partner who will treat you right this time, you have to build up your self-esteem, not tear it down. Think about the good things you can bring to a relationship, and make sure to build on those good things as you hit the dating scene.

✔ **Think best-case scenario, not worst-case.**

Always thinking negative thoughts will have an effect on how you look and how you behave. If you're going to use your imagination, use it to dream about winning the lottery instead of being hit by a truck. A positive outlook and a welcoming smile are better at attracting folks than gloom and doom.

✔ **Compare the risks with the rewards.**

What's the worst thing that can happen if you ask someone out? They'll say no. What's the worst thing that can happen if you agree to go out with someone? You'll have a miserable evening. But what's the *best* thing that can happen? You'll have a terrific time, wind up falling in love with a great person, and live happily ever after. Isn't that worth taking off that emergency brake?

Yes, it is more difficult rejoining the dating scene the second or third or fourth time around. But it's even more difficult staying home by yourself, so I suggest you take the easy way out. After giving yourself some time to mourn your last relationship, go out there and find yourself a new one.

Now that I've encouraged all of you who are on the rebound to go out and date, I have to put in one word of caution. Some people who've just broken up with a partner rush into a new relationship to prove to themselves, to the former partner, or to both that they're worthy. If you try to link up too quickly — maybe even with the first person you go out with — for the wrong reasons, then there's a very good chance that you'll end up making a mistake. If, in your haste to begin a new relationship, you choose someone who isn't a good match for you, then you'll have to break up with this new person and start over. If you're not careful, this kind of cycle could go on for years. So, although it is important to get back into the dating scene, learn from your past mistakes in order not to repeat them.

Dating When There Are Children at Home

If, after the break-up, you've been left with the kids, then you have some special problems. If your children are young, you'll be in a continual search for child care while you date. If your children are old enough to stay home by themselves, then they're also old enough to have opinions, and that, too, can make dating very difficult.

There's no magic wand that I can wave over you to make your life simpler. The only thing I can say is that I did it; so I believe that you can too.

Obviously, if you have family who live nearby that you can rely on, then you have to make the best use possible of them. Because I was an orphan, I didn't have that resource. What I did have was a lot of wonderful friends. And whenever we got together, you could count on finding my daughter fast asleep in the middle of the bed among all the coats.

Did it harm her that I dragged her around? On the contrary, I think it helped her. She got to hang around with adults, who were always on the lookout to teach her something. She got to spend more time with me instead of a baby-sitter. And her mom was a lot happier having a social life than she would have been cooped up at home with a small child — and a happy mom makes for a happy child.

Don't let your children hold you back

Whatever you do, don't become a martyr and let your children hold you back. If you do, you'll end up resenting your children, they'll sense that resentment, and you'll wind up with more ruined relationships.

Your children will have to make some sacrifices, but when they're small, they don't really realize it. My daughter, who has her own son now, always loved the attention she got from my adult friends and thought it was great fun to go to sleep in the middle of a pile of coats. She didn't miss her bed, and I would have been foolish to miss out on being with my friends out of some misplaced guilt.

I really believe in that old saying: Where there's a will, there's a way. And I want you to believe in it too.

CAUTION

Sex with your ex

Out of adultery often comes divorce. In and of itself, divorce is not a sexual issue, but you would be surprised at how many letters I get concerning sex after divorce.

Just because a divorce is much simpler to get these days doesn't make the actual separation of the two people easy. The chief reason people continue to live together after their divorce is usually financial; they can't afford two separate homes. In some of those situations, the two former partners never even speak, much less have sex. But cases also exist in which the divorced couple continues to have sex even after the courts have declared their marriage void. Some of these people tell me that, although they stopped loving their partners, they never tired of having sex with them. Others just do it out of desperation.

Another scenario that people ask my advice about is what to do when the couple no longer lives together, but one of the pair visits the other and asks to have sex with him or her. I know that some people in this situation give into such requests, but that's not my advice to them.

Unless you think that, by having sex with your ex, you might get back together — and you would like to get back together — you really shouldn't continue to have a sexual relationship after your marriage has come apart.

After you get divorced, you should be trying to build a new life for yourself. It might not be easy, I realize that, but continuing to have sex with your ex is not going to make it any easier. Maybe if you are a little desperate, it will push you to find a new partner. But if you keep yourself sexually satisfied by sleeping with your ex, you may never find the energy to start over with someone else.

Sleep overs

If you do find a new partner, and your relationship becomes sexual, you'll run into some new complications with regards to your children. If your children are young enough that they don't really suspect what goes on between a man and a woman who are sleeping together, then the easiest way to have this new person in your life sleep over is to make it into a party atmosphere. If the kids get an extra treat the first few times, it will be easier to integrate this person into the family. However, don't allow these "parties" to take place too often, or you'll be creating a situation that can get out of control.

If your children are old enough to suspect that two people sharing a bedroom are having sex, I recommend letting them know in some subtle ways that you are having sex first, before bringing the new partner to spend the night. If the kids believe that the sex part is a *fait accompli,* a done deal, too late to turn back now, then they won't resist the sleep overs as much. But if they think that they can still "protect" Mom or Dad from this new person, then they might try to cause trouble.

Chapter 6

Asking the AIDS Question

● ●

In This Chapter

▶ Broaching the subject of AIDS testing

▶ Springboarding into other issues

▶ Getting tested for AIDS

● ●

*A*t lectures, in letters, on the street, and even in ladies' rooms, people are always asking me questions. Over the last 15 years — at least for the most part — the questions have been pretty much the same. Certainly there are always some questions that come out of left field, like the phone call I received on the air about onion rings. (If you haven't heard that story yet, think of the game of horseshoes and let your imagination run wild.) But, by and large, the problems that people came to me with were universal. Then AIDS came along, and people had a new and deadly reason to question sexual practices.

Since the onset of AIDS, I now receive a whole new subset of questions having to do with that dreaded disease. Some are practical questions about condoms and the like, which I address in Chapter 21. But what has really left people confused is how to bring up the subject of AIDS testing with a partner.

Having the AIDS Discussion

In our culture, we don't talk about sex as much as we engage in sexual activities. That's not a good thing, and I have been doing my part to get couples to communicate better about their sexual likes and dislikes. But, because not everybody waits to form a strong relationship before having sex, the issue of AIDS testing can come up before the two people involved are really a couple. Suddenly, they may be faced with having to ask some very intimate and personal questions of each other before they really know each other all that well.

Now you could say that, if a couple is ready to *have* sex, then they should be ready to at least talk about it. But that's one of the issues that causes difficulties right there. Just because one party is ready to have sex doesn't mean that the other one is also. In the old days, pre-AIDS that is, it was generally the man who would fumble and grope his way around, and the woman would communicate to him with either a stop or go signal. It wasn't the greatest system — a few men got slapped, and a few women cried — but for the most part it worked. Well, it doesn't work any longer.

In the 1990s, there needs to be a new intermediate step: the AIDS discussion. If both parties are clearly interested in going to bed together, and are really looking for a simple assurance of probable good health, then this conversation may be no more than a speed bump on the way to the bedroom. But if they're not confident of the other person's desire to have sex with them, how should they handle the AIDS discussion? And the question of other STDs as well?

Let me give you some possible scenarios.

Paul and Juliette

Paul and Juliette have had five dates, and they haven't had sex yet. Their last date was with another couple. They'd gone out dancing, and, during the last few slow dances, Paul had held Juliette very close. He'd had an erection, and rather than pull away from him, Juliette had pushed her pelvis into his. To Paul, it was a clear sign that Juliette was ready to go to bed with him, but because their friends were driving, Paul had to content himself with a goodnight kiss when they dropped Juliette off at her place.

During the week, he called Juliette and asked her to dinner. He picked a place that was about six blocks from where she lived. When he arrived, he parked his car and suggested they walk. After a little bit of banter, he sucked in his breath and asked her: "Do you think it's too early in our relationship to be talking about AIDS testing?" She answered, "No, Paul I don't," and the discussion that needed to take place, did.

By posing the question that way, Paul didn't presume that they were going to have sex. He left it to Juliette to decide. If she'd wanted to wait longer, she could easily have told him so. But, because she was ready to have sex with him, the discussion was able to proceed smoothly. They were both interested in the same goal.

Fran and Tony

Fran met Tony the day after he moved into her apartment complex. She saw him again later at the grocery store, where he was stocking up on supplies, and she ended up cooking him dinner that night. He was very busy those first few weeks setting up his apartment and starting a new job, but they did get together for a drink a few times and once for a quick dinner at a local Mexican place.

Tony finally had a weekend off. This time he offered to take her to this fancy French restaurant that Fran really loved. They had a great meal and shared a bottle of champagne that went to Fran's head a little bit. When they got back to the apartment complex, instead of heading their separate ways, as they'd done previously, Tony invited Fran inside and she accepted. They had some brandy while sitting on his new sofa, and soon Fran found herself wrapped in his arms. Her clothes started coming off, and not too much later he was leading her to the bedroom, their clothes scattered over the living room floor.

As they lay down on the bed, Fran asked Tony: "You don't have any . . . uh . . . diseases, do you?"

"No way," he said, "I'm not one of those guys who'll sleep with just anybody." A little voice inside of Fran did start to whisper something, but at that point she was somewhat tipsy, very aroused, and totally naked, and so she didn't bother listening.

What that little voice inside of Fran was trying to tell her was that, although Tony was saying that he wasn't that kind of guy, here he was going to bed with someone he barely knew. Was that really the first time that this had happened to him?

Most people in Fran's position would have done exactly what she did — given in to the moment. That's why you must have the AIDS discussion long before that moment arrives. Don't wait until you're in a situation where it would not only be embarrassing to suddenly pull back, but also almost emotionally impossible to resist going ahead. That's especially true when drugs or alcohol are involved. You have to be realistic about sex and know that your ability to resist temptation is not infinite. You have to protect yourself in many ways, not just with a piece of rubber.

Speaking of rubber, what if Tony had added, "and anyway, I'm using a condom"? Would that have made it OK?

Not necessarily, because condoms can break. Relying on condoms *can* be enough of a safeguard, but only if you really know the person with whom you're about to have sex. In this case, Fran knew next to nothing about Tony, as he'd just moved to town. She certainly had no way of knowing for certain whether he was telling her the truth. He could have been lying, or he may have had diseases and not known it.

Whether or not you listen to my advice about forming a relationship first, definitely never put yourself in the type of situation that Fran did. How do you avoid that? Simple . . .

Make yourself a resolution that you will never get undressed until you're sure that it is safe to do so. If he starts to unbutton your blouse, or she grabs hold of your zipper, tell your partner to stop and explain why. Tell your partner that it's not that you don't want to become intimate, assuming that you do, but that you need to talk about safer sex first.

After having this conversation, you may both decide to renew your activities, possibly stopping at a prearranged point or maybe going all the way, depending on what was said. Whatever the final outcome turns out to be, at least you'll know that it was a calculated one and not left to chance.

Steve and Betsy

Steve and Betsy were in college. They started going out in September, and by October they were in love. They would often wind up in each other's rooms for the night, and would masturbate each other to orgasm, but Betsy wouldn't let Steve penetrate her with his penis. Steve, who wasn't a virgin, wasn't sure exactly what was going on, and then it hit him: Betsy knew that Steve had had sex with other girls and was worried about AIDS.

That night, after they had dinner together in the cafeteria, he took her for a walk to a quiet part of the campus. They sat down on a bench and Steve sprung his surprise. "I've made an appointment to be tested for AIDS tomorrow." Betsy looked at him for a few moments, not saying anything. Finally she said, "Steve, I hope you're not doing this for me. I love you, I really do, but I'm not going to have intercourse with you, or anybody, until I get married."

Steve's brilliant piece of deduction had been dead wrong. Betsy wasn't worried about AIDS. She simply intended not to have intercourse until she found the man she was going to spend the rest of her life with. Here's a case where Steve needed to have a different sort of conversation with Betsy before bringing up AIDS — one about their relationship. Betsy hadn't said anything about her commitment to wait because she'd been a little afraid that Steve might leave her over it. She was willing to offer him sexual release and was happy with the orgasms he gave her, but that was as far as she was willing to go.

Betsy should be applauded for wanting to wait. But maybe, since she was the one putting on the brakes, she should have brought the subject up earlier and saved Steve the embarrassment he felt that night on the bench.

Again, you can never assume that the other party is going to want to have intercourse with you. That's why the subject of AIDS testing can be so embarrassing to raise in the first place. But, if you use the approach that Paul did (in the first scenario), putting the question within a context that the other person can gracefully back out of, you'll find that you are less likely to stumble the way Steve did (in the preceding scenario).

Going beyond AIDS

I am concentrating on AIDS, in part because it's mostly the fear of AIDS that has driven our society to make these changes in sexual etiquette, and because it is the only really deadly STD. But just because AIDS is uppermost in everyone's minds doesn't mean that you should forget about the other STDs.

Herpes is something that was scaring people just before the AIDS crisis broke, and herpes is still rampant. If you know that you have herpes, which can break out at any moment, then you have a duty to warn your potential partner so that he or she can decide whether or not to proceed.

Some people believe that herpes is catching only when the person affected has a visible outbreak. In fact, a few days before the outbreak becomes visible, the herpes virus is present and can be transmitted to someone else. That's why, even if you have outbreaks that are very far apart, you should never assume that you can't pass the disease on to a partner.

Many of the other STDs are treatable with penicillin or some other drug (see Chapter 21), and that should be your first line of defense for you and your partners. But if you haven't gone for treatment, or if the treatment is still continuing, then you have to let your partner know.

The benefits of better communication

Although having the AIDS Talk is not necessarily something pleasant, you can derive other benefits from it besides limiting your risk of catching an STD. People have tended not to talk about sex, even the good parts. But once you've broached the subject of sex, don't give it the hot potato treatment and drop it right away. Try using it as a stepping stone so that you can broach other topics that also need to be addressed.

One topic that flows naturally from the AIDS Talk is contraception.

✔ Certainly, you should discuss the subject of condom use. Some men absolutely refuse to use them, and the woman should find this out ahead of time so that she can decide whether or not to go any further with him.

✔ If the woman intends to rely on the pill for birth control and hasn't started taking it yet, she should tell the man that he's going to have to wait, testing or not, until the gynecologist says it's OK to begin.

The next transition is one that I realize not many people will be able to make, which is to go from talking about AIDS to telling your potential new partner the best way to give you an orgasm. It's too bad that this discussion seldom takes place, because anyone who could communicate that well would rank among the absolute best of lovers. But even without going that far, you can still have some communication along those lines.

For example, if you're talking about previous partners, you could use that opening as an opportunity to make a particular point. "A few years ago I dated this guy Jack. What first attracted me to him was that he was such a gentleman. But when we started having sex, he ended up being too much of a gentleman, too squeamish to do anything but straight sex. You know what I mean?"

Even if your new partner doesn't know exactly what you mean, your partner should get the idea not to be afraid of trying some different things.

Remember, if you do bring up past partners, you don't want to do it in a way that will be threatening and that could cause any performance anxieties. On the other hand, bringing up past partners can be a good way of introducing a subject, so learn to use your past effectively, yet carefully.

And you shouldn't be afraid to prepare for that moment when the lines of communication are open. If you want to get a particular message across, try to plan some things that you might say. Even if you don't follow the script to the letter, writing some ideas down ahead of time makes it easier.

Because I don't know exactly what your desires might be, I can't give you the exact words you'll need, but I think some of the following phrases will give you some guidelines for how to work your needs into the conversation:

✔ "I'm glad you weren't afraid to bring up the subject of AIDS. I'm sure that means you won't be afraid to tell me if there's anything you'd like for me to do that gives you special pleasure."

or

✔ "I really appreciate that you brought up the topic of AIDS. I always feel so tongue-tied when the subject of sex comes up, but I really want to communicate my feelings to you."

or

> ✔ "Now that I've opened my big mouth about AIDS, I guess it won't surprise you that I like to be verbal in bed. I know it bothers some people, and if you tell me to stop, I'll do my best."

or

> ✔ "AIDS isn't the only thing I'm afraid of when it comes to sex. I really dislike it when a guy tries to get me to do certain things."

I think you get the idea. If there's some point that's very important to you, which you want to get across, use the opportunity of the AIDS Talk to at least give your partner a hint. Later, when you get more intimate, you can work up the courage to say more about it.

How to Get Tested for AIDS

Simply agreeing that you're going to be tested for AIDS isn't enough. Then you have to actually go for the test, and I want to make sure you know what that's all about. I give some more details in Chapter 21, but right here are some matters of sexual etiquette that still must be addressed.

You can get the AIDS test from your family physician, at a clinic, or at a Planned Parenthood Center. A technician draws your blood and sends it to be analyzed. Depending on the procedures used by the place you take the test, you'll get the results in two to four weeks.

Whether AIDS test results are trustworthy depends very much on how long it has been since you, or your partner, has had sex with someone else. The way laboratories detect AIDS is by checking for the presence of antibodies for the HIV virus in the blood. These antibodies take a certain amount of time to appear in your bloodstream after your first contact with the virus. How long? The Centers for Disease Control in Atlanta recommends waiting six months. HIV antibodies can be detected as early as two months from first contact, but it can take as long as six months; the longer you wait, the more certain are the results.

And then there's the matter of trust:

> ✔ First, you have to rely on whatever your partner has told you about past partners and their last sexual encounters with any of them.

> ✔ Then, for the test to mean anything, you and your potential partner can't have sex with anyone else while waiting for those results, or they'll be meaningless.

While I'm on the subject of trust, I know that there are many of you who might not insist on having a new partner undergo the AIDS test. You may decide to put your faith in the reported behavior pattern of this person — relatively few other partners, 100 percent use of condoms — and have sex with them, protecting yourself with condoms. As I said before, condoms do not offer 100 percent protection, but only you can decide what to do. I understand that to wait six months for the results of a test is a burden, but I've also had friends of mine die of AIDS, so, in my opinion, you should be as careful as you possibly can be.

I certainly suggest you read Chapter 21 carefully so that you can make the decision about how best to protect yourself with as much information guiding you as possible.

The psychological issues

If you feel nervous about talking to a partner about AIDS and the issue of testing, I have to warn you that you're going to feel even more nervous actually going for the test. You may think that you've been careful, or you've only slept with a few people, but you won't really know that you're HIV-negative until you get the results back. Faced with the reality that you may get back a result that shows you have been exposed to this deadly virus, you may have a lot of trouble going for the test. And then you face a terrible two-week waiting period until the results come back.

There are organizations that will help you with these psychological issues, and I suggest that you try and find out if there are any where you live (see Appendix B). The lab that you are considering going to might be able to suggest such an organization.

There's another reason that you might want to look into these organizations. As many precautions as you think you've taken, you may be surprised to find yourself HIV-positive. If that happens, you're going to go on an emotional roller-coaster, and you should get help to deal with it. The same organization that can help to ease your fears about going for the test will be able to help you through the crisis of getting a positive result. It's always better to be prepared, especially if you're distraught.

Confidentiality versus anonymity

Even if you're a virgin, even if you've only slept with one partner in your life, if you ever need to buy life insurance, you're going to have to get an AIDS test. Now, as you know, the problem with testing is that sometimes they give you the wrong results. Because of the stigma often attached to having AIDS, you don't want that information to get out, especially if a further test will come out negative.

All tests are supposed to be confidential; the way computers are all connected to each other, however, I don't know how much value to put in that term. There are tests that are *anonymous*. That means that the blood is given to the lab with only a number so that only you know the final result. Before you go for the AIDS test, find out if there is a way for your tests to be done anonymously. At least that will be one worry — keeping the results to yourself — that you won't have to be concerned about.

Sex without Intercourse

Some people think that the only way that they can get AIDS is through vaginal or anal intercourse. They believe that other forms of sex are perfectly safe. Mutual masturbation is safe, providing that you don't have any open cuts on your hand. If a man puts his penis between the woman's thighs or breasts, that can also be presumed as a form of safer sex, provided that he doesn't get some of his semen on his hands and then pass it on to the woman by inserting his fingers into her vagina.

Oral sex is another story. It is thought that saliva does kill HIV, and so oral sex is safer than vaginal or anal sex. But, even if oral sex is 20 times safer, it is not 100 percent safe. Let me say this again, you can get AIDS through oral sex. You can perform oral sex on a man (*fellatio*) while he's wearing a condom, and, provided that you're careful not to bite through the latex, that should be a safer form of sex. They also sell *dental dams,* small rubber sheets that are supposed to make cunnilingus (oral sex on a woman) safer. I have to tell you that I have my doubts that someone can perform oral sex on a writhing woman while keeping this dental dam in place. It's certainly safer than intercourse, but I wouldn't call it safe.

AIDS has certainly changed the way people interact sexually. I do all that I can to raise money to fight this dreadful disease, and I hope that one day our scientists discover either a cure or a vaccine, but until then you have to be very careful.

Too many young people think that their youth immunizes them from any form of danger — AIDS, driving too fast, skiing recklessly, drinking excessively — and that's just not true. Some older people believe that AIDS hasn't invaded their segment of the population yet, and that's not true either.

So, as they used to say after the shift briefings on the TV show *Hill Street Blues* — be careful out there.

Chapter 7

Using Birth Control — Reducing Your Risks

As I point out on more than one occasion throughout this book, the main evolutionary purpose of sex isn't just so that we can have those pleasurable orgasms. Sexual intercourse is the way that our species, Homo sapiens, reproduces itself. The pleasurable aspects are built in as an inducement to do our reproductive duty.

Now I haven't changed my mind on that. But, while for most of mankind's history sexual pleasure and reproduction were basically inseparable, in the latter half of the 20th century, that has all changed.

Now we can have our cake and eat it too, so to speak, because it is possible to have great sex and terrific orgasms without much risk of making a baby when we're not ready for one. And then, when we are ready to have a family, we can decide how large it is going to be and pretty much pick the timing of when each child will come into the world.

Not everyone thinks that this is a sign of progress. Many religious leaders decry the concept of recreational sex, which is sex that is intended only to provide pleasure. And, because I'm old fashioned and a square, I too will tell you repeatedly that one-night stands are not a good idea, even though it is possible to have sex with hundreds of people and never once make a baby.

But the purpose of this book isn't to debate the moral consequences of the sexual revolution. Maybe one day the publisher of this series will put out a book on morality, but until they do, you're going to have to look elsewhere for a full discussion on the subject.

DR. RUTH SAYS

The only thing that I will state, one more time, is that sex between two people who are part of a committed relationship is much better than sex between people who are basically strangers. I say this not to attach any moral stigma to other types of behavior, but simply because I truly believe that if you follow this advice, your sex life will be better.

Where I do put my foot down, however, is when people have unintended pregnancies because they do not take the proper precautions. Now I am in favor of women having the right to an abortion. But, at the same time, I would like to see a world where people would not have unintended pregnancies and so abortion would be wiped out. We do not have the perfect contraceptive, so wiping out abortion is not yet possible. But, if everybody not ready to have a baby used at least one of the methods of contraception that I describe in this chapter, we at least would be heading in the right direction.

A lot of progress has been made since I first broke new ground in 1980 by telling people on my radio show, over and over again, that they must use contraception. In those days, there were about one and a half million unintended pregnancies in the United States every year. Now, in the middle of the 1990s, that number has dropped to about a million. (You may see various statistics on this issue, but I believe this figure is correct.)

Measured statistically, that's significant progress, but a million unintended pregnancies is still much too many. That is why I am still waging the same crusade, and it's one of the main reasons why I agreed to write this book. If I can prevent even one unintended pregnancy among the readers of this book, I feel I will have done an important job. So you see, you must pay close attention to the material covered in this chapter, because what happens to you in the months and years ahead will not only affect you but will also reflect on my reputation!

The Four Basic Types of Contraception

There are four basic types of contraception:

- Sterilization
- Hormonal methods
- Barrier methods
- Natural family planning

According to the National Center for Health Statistics, in 1990 (the most recent year for which statistics are available in the U.S.) the most popular method of contraception for women between the ages of 15 and 44 was sterilization. Forty-two percent of women using contraception chose this method, compared to 28.5 percent who use the pill and 17.7 percent who use condoms. Sadly, overall contraceptive use has declined slightly among women, from 60 percent in 1988 to 59 percent in 1990.

FOOD FOR THOUGHT

A brief history of contraception

People have been trying to make the separation between sex and pregnancy for a long time. We know that, as far back as 1850 B.C., ancient Egyptians tried many different ingredients to kill sperm (act as *spermicides*), including honey, carbonate of soda, and crocodile dung. (And you complain about inserting a diaphragm or putting on a condom?)

Eventually, the Egyptian version of Planned Parenthood technicians progressed to something a bit less, shall we say, exotic. By 1550 B.C., Egyptian women were using cotton-lint tampons soaked in fermented acacia plants instead. Okay, so it's not less exotic, but it sure sounds better than crocodile dung.

In case you're curious as to how we know all of this, the Egyptians used to bury recipes for these methods of contraception along with the women's bodies so that they wouldn't become pregnant in the afterlife. (I wonder if the condom concession at Forest Lawn is still available?)

Various people at various times have come up with other items for women to insert in their vaginas to try to prevent pregnancy, including discs made of melted beeswax, oiled paper, and seaweed. The noted Casanova seemed to have found some success by placing the hollowed halves of lemons over the cervix of a woman — a precursor to the diaphragm used today, only a little more sour.

These various inserts were called *pessaries,* and, even though the sun never set on the whole British Empire at one time, in various parts of it the sun *did* set, and considerable hanky-panky went on after dark. As a result, British medical researchers cataloged more than 120 different types of vaginal barriers being used in England and in its various colonies.

We have to go back to the desert for a moment to trace the history of the first nonbarrier method of birth control for women, the *intrauterine device* (IUD). Supposedly, camel drivers used to place pebbles in the uteri of their beasts to keep the camels from getting pregnant while crossing the Sahara, and some British inventors refined that technique to create the IUD at the end of the 19th century.

And then, in 1959, the oral contraceptive pill was given its first approval by the U.S. Food and Drug Administration, an event that signified the beginning of the sexual revolution. For the first time, a woman could control her reproductive ability (and her menstrual cycle) with a single pill each day, eliminating fears of an unintended pregnancy.

We shouldn't forget the male half of the population, whose principal method of contraception is the condom. That device is said to have been named by a Doctor Condom, who was supposed to have been a court physician to Charles II of England in the 17th century. His condom was made out of sheep's intestines scented with perfume. Actually, the Italian anatomist Fallopius (identifier and namesake of the fallopian tubes) had created the first condom 100 years earlier. His main goal was not so much to protect against pregnancy as to prevent venereal disease, which the condom did very efficiently, according to his research. The condom is still used today for its ability to protect against most sexually transmitted diseases.

Remember, only one of these methods of birth control, the condom, can significantly reduce your risk of catching a sexually transmitted disease. The condom is not the most effective method of birth control (although it is certainly better than nothing), but it is a vital piece of equipment in the war against AIDS and other sexually transmitted diseases. So, if you're not with one steady partner, or if your one partner has more partners than just you, you should always have some condoms on hand — and use them!

Sterilization

Sterilization methods come in two basic types: one for women (*tubal sterilization*) and one for men (the *vasectomy*).

Both the female and male methods of sterilization have certain advantages over other kinds of birth control:

- ✔ They are one-time operations.
- ✔ They are very effective.
- ✔ They don't have side effects.
- ✔ They don't affect sexual functioning.
- ✔ You never have to worry about becoming pregnant.

The main disadvantage of sterilization is that it is permanent. If you later change your mind and want to make a baby, it is difficult — and in many cases impossible — to do so.

Many people are surprised that sterilization is the most popular method of birth control. I rarely recommend sterilization because the effects are permanent. But it is that very permanence, as well as the security of knowing that the risk of getting pregnant is extremely small, that leads so many people to choose this method — especially those who have reached an age when they think they don't want children anymore.

Tying the tubes

A common name for the female method of sterilization is *tubal ligation,* although tubal sterilization can actually be performed in a variety of ways, not all of which call for tying the tubes.

The tubes I'm talking about here are the fallopian tubes, in which the egg is fertilized by the first sperm that finds it (see Chapter 1). If these two tubes are cut and tied, the eggs and sperm should never be able to come together (see Figure 7-1). (In rare instances, the tubes grow back and a woman can become pregnant, but this only happens in 4 out of 1,000 cases.)

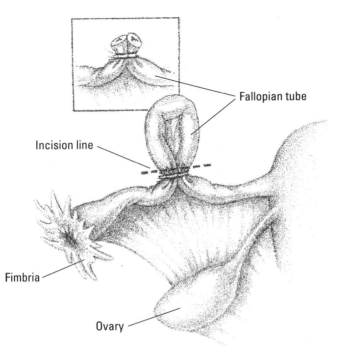

Fallopian tube

Incision line

Figure 7-1:
Tubal
ligation
gives "tying
the knot" a
whole new
meaning.

Fimbria

Ovary

As you might guess, tubal ligation requires a surgical procedure, but most women can undergo it on an outpatient basis (either in a hospital or clinic), under local anesthesia, and in under 30 minutes. The cost can be as high as $2,500, but this is a one-time charge as opposed to other methods that involve a cost for every use, like the condom or birth control pill.

Complications with the procedure are possible, including bleeding, infection, or a negative reaction to the anesthetic. In most cases, however, these complications are rare and can be dealt with easily.

Women have a number of kinds of tubal sterilization to choose from, and usually the method a woman chooses depends on other medical factors.

✔ One of the two most common types of tubal ligation is called a *laparoscopy.*

- First, the abdomen is inflated with an injection of harmless gas, which allows the surgeon to see the organs more clearly.

- The surgeon then inserts a rodlike instrument, called a *laparoscope,* through a small incision. The laparoscope has a "camera" and light to help locate the tubes.

- Finally, either with the same instrument or another, the operation to cut and tie the tubes is performed. Complications are rare.

✔ A *mini-laparotomy* is the other popular method. It is similar to the laparoscopy, but it does not require a viewing instrument. It is done within 48 hours of giving birth, when the abdomen is still enlarged and viewing is easier for the surgeon.

✔ More rarely performed is a *full laparotomy.* This is a major surgery, requiring a much larger incision, full anesthesia, and hospitalization for five to seven days, followed by several weeks of further recovery.

✔ *Vaginal procedures* are another option, but they are rarely performed because of the higher risk of infection.

✔ Last is the *hysterectomy,* which is the surgical removal of the uterus. This, too, is major surgery, and it is rarely used merely as a method of sterilization. Instead, a hysterectomy may be performed to correct another medical problem, with sterilization occurring as a side effect. With a hysterectomy, the tubes may not actually be involved, but without a uterus, pregnancy is impossible.

With any of the tubal methods of sterilization, the woman's organs function normally so that she still ovulates, has her full set of female hormones, and has her monthly period. The eggs, which continue to be released monthly, simply dissolve the way any unused cells do. (Remember, the egg is microscopic in size, so it really can't do any damage floating inside of you for a while.)

After sterilization, sexual functioning also remains the same, or is sometimes improved because the woman no longer has to concern herself about becoming pregnant. But remember, if you undergo one of these procedures, you have to assume that you will never want to have children again. I am one of those who doesn't like to say never, but with so many women opting for sterilization, I guess I'm in the minority.

Vasectomy

The male version of sterilization, the *vasectomy,* is also a surgical procedure that is performed on an outpatient basis. In a vasectomy, the tubes that carry the sperm (the vas deferens) are cut and tied (see Figure 7-2). Only very rarely do the tubes grow back together, so that only 2 out of 1,000 men who are sterilized cause a pregnancy in the first year.

One difference between the male and female sterilization is that some sperm remain in the man's system after the operation, so you must use another method of contraception for at least the first 15 ejaculations. You can be certain that all of the sperm have been passed out by getting a simple lab test done on the semen. Ask your doctor for more details.

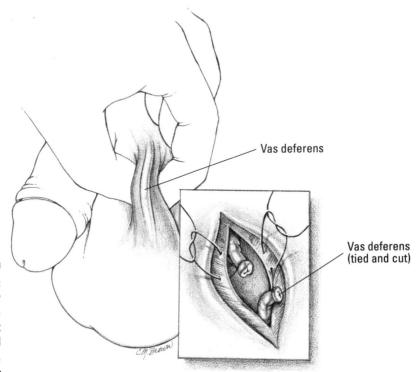

Vas deferens

Vas deferens
(tied and cut)

Figure 7-2:
A vasectomy
is the male
equivalent
of the tubal
ligation.

Some men worry that undergoing a vasectomy will in some way reduce their
sexual prowess, but you don't need to worry about this. A man feels no difference in sexual performance after a vasectomy because he still is able to have
erections and ejaculate.

The only change after a vasectomy is that, after the system has been cleaned
out, the semen no longer contains any sperm. Because sperm make up only
5 percent of the volume of the ejaculate, a man who undergoes this procedure
will not be able to tell any difference, nor will his hormones be affected in any
way. The testes continue to manufacture sperm, but instead of being ejaculated, the sperm are absorbed by the body.

Vasectomies are much less expensive than tubal sterilizations, ranging in price
from $250 to $500. Trying to reverse the procedure, however, is much more
expensive than having the procedure done in the first place. Reversing the
procedure requires microsurgery, and very often such surgery is not effective.
This is why having a vasectomy is considered to be permanent.

Attempts have been made to create a reversible vasectomy by installing a valve instead of cutting the vas deferens, but these have not been effective. The sperm, those little devils, have managed to find ways of getting through.

Research continues to be done about vasectomies and their effects. Be sure to ask your doctor for all the latest information before you agree to the procedure.

Hormonal methods

The ancient Greeks had this weird idea that our temperaments and bodily functions were controlled by what they called *the four humors:* blood, mucus, yellow bile, and black bile. Because my television producer and good friend is Greek, I know how some Greeks tend to believe that they discovered everything, but in this case it happens to be true, although they got the details slightly wrong.

The human body secretes close to 50 different hormones in the endocrine system. These *hormones* are chemical substances that go directly into the bloodstream to our various organs and control how they work. The hormones that affect the sex and reproductive systems are absolutely vital to their functioning, and, conversely, by controlling these hormones, we can now affect the functioning of our reproduction with great accuracy. The contraceptive pill works exactly like that, inhibiting pregnancy through the use of hormones.

The pill

The pill is a very effective method of birth control — almost as effective as sterilization, in fact — assuming full compliance (that is, assuming that the woman takes the pill regularly and without fail). Because the pill made having sex almost risk free, it is credited for starting the sexual revolution in the 1960s, when the use of oral contraceptives became widespread.

The pill has undergone many transformations since those early days. Although the active ingredients in the pill are basically the same hormones that a woman's body creates to regulate her menstrual cycle, estrogen and progestin, the high doses used when the pill first came out caused many side effects. Today's lower dosages mean that these side effects, especially the negative ones, are greatly reduced.

These days, pills come in two types:

- *Combination pills,* which contain both estrogen and progestin, keep the ovaries from releasing eggs.
- The so-called *mini-pills* contain only progestin.

The pill can prevent ovulation, but its main method of preventing conception is to thicken the cervical mucus so that the sperm cannot penetrate it.

If you use the pill, it is important for you to remember that you must take it every day, and preferably at the same time of the day — say, every morning — for the hormones to work best. (When using the combination pill, the woman goes off the hormones for seven days to allow for withdrawal bleeding, which simulates normal menstrual flow; however, in most cases she continues to take pills during this time in order to enforce the habit, but these are placebos, without hormones.)

The failure rate of the pill is tied closely to compliance, so if you are on the pill and don't want to become pregnant, make sure that you follow to the letter the directions that your doctor gives you.

Besides preventing pregnancy, the pill has several advantages, including

- ✔ More regular periods
- ✔ Less menstrual flow
- ✔ Less menstrual cramping
- ✔ Less iron deficiency anemia
- ✔ Fewer ectopic pregnancies
- ✔ Less pelvic inflammatory disease
- ✔ Less acne
- ✔ Less premenstrual tension
- ✔ Less rheumatoid arthritis
- ✔ Protection against endometrial and ovarian cancer, two of the most common types of cancer in women

When you start taking the pill, you may experience a little bleeding between periods, but it is usually a temporary phenomenon.

Some women are afraid that the pill may cause cancer of the breast or uterus because the hormones used have been linked to these cancers in animal studies. Whether or not there was once such a risk, at the doses presently prescribed, no scientific evidence indicates that this is so. In fact, the pill has been shown to reduce the risk of cancer of the ovary or endometrium.

Just about every woman of child-bearing age can take the pill, except those women who are over 35 and who smoke. That's because the pill can cause some risks to the cardiovascular system, and older women and women who smoke are more susceptible to these problems. Some other physical conditions, such as diabetes or a history of blood clots, can make the pill unsuitable for a woman, which is why the pill must be prescribed by a physician.

The initial visit usually costs between $35 and $125, though it can be less if you visit a clinic. The pills themselves cost between $15 and $25 per month, though again the cost may be lower at a clinic, or through Planned Parenthood.

Do not try to save yourself the cost of a doctor's visit by using someone else's prescription — that's a prescription for trouble.

And I must repeat the warning concerning STDs. The pill offers absolutely no protection against AIDS or any other sexually transmitted disease, and you must use the pill in conjunction with a condom if there is any risk that you may catch a disease from your partner.

If you are using other drugs — including antibiotics — while you're on the pill, check with your doctor to make sure that these medications won't interfere with your method of birth control. In many cases, your doctor will advise you to use an additional form of protection at this time.

Norplant

The main problem with the pill is compliance. Some women forget to take their daily pill and wind up pregnant. Norplant was created as an alternative to the pill for women who worry about this problem.

Norplant uses a slightly different hormone, called *levonorgestrel,* which keeps the ovaries from releasing eggs and thickens the cervical mucus. The drug is contained in six soft capsules, about the size of a matchstick, which are inserted under the skin of the upper arm and continually release the hormone.

After the Norplant capsules have been inserted, which must be done by a physician trained in the process, they protect a woman against pregnancy for five years. But use of Norplant is reversible, so any time a woman wants to end her use of Norplant, she can have the capsules removed. Again, they must be removed by a physician trained in the process.

Norplant costs about $500 to $750 to be implanted; removal costs from $100 to $200. Some family-planning clinics may provide financing.

The side effects of Norplant, both positive and negative, are about the same as for the pill, although some women are candidates for Norplant who cannot take the pill. The most common side effect of Norplant is irregular bleeding. Although this irregularity usually diminishes after about nine months, a small number of women may find that it continues up to five years. Some women have also run into problems when having the Norplant capsules removed, encountering complications during what is usually an easy procedure.

Because of the problems with Norplant removal, a new implant system, called *Implanon*, is now being tested. Instead of five inserts, Implanon uses only one, which is good for only three years compared to Norplant's five. Implanon has another benefit over Norplant in addition to using fewer rods. The Norplant rods, tiny as they may be, are often visible and can be felt by a partner. This may lead a man to assume that a woman may be ready to have sex with him because she has protected herself from pregnancy, when, in fact, she does not want to have sex with him. The Implanon rod, on the other hand, is less noticeable than the five Norplant rods. I'll be waiting along with the rest of you to see how the testing goes.

Depo-Provera

Another alternative to the pill is *Depo-Provera.* Like the preceding methods, Depo-Provera involves a hormone, but instead of taking a daily pill or having rods inserted into your arm, you get a shot every 12 weeks.

Certainly, a woman who doesn't like injections won't choose this product. And, although its side effects are the same as the pill's, if they are not to your liking, you can't simply stop taking it, like the pills, or have the rods removed, like Norplant. Instead, you must wait until the full 12 weeks have passed for the effects of the shot to go away. That also holds true if you want to get pregnant, though most people aren't in such a rush to have a baby that they can't wait such a short time. Despite these deficiencies, Depa-Provera is gaining in popularity.

The costs of the injection range from $30 to $75. But, again, they may be less at a clinic.

The intrauterine device (IUD)

The IUD is the modern outgrowth of the pebbles that camel herders would put inside their animals to prevent pregnancy. Perhaps pebbles would also work on women, but I don't suggest you try it — they haven't been approved by the FDA. The IUD, which is approved, is a small plastic device containing either a hormone or copper that is inserted into a women's uterus. IUDs work either by preventing the fertilization of the egg or by preventing implantation of a fertilized egg in the uterine wall.

The IUD has faced a lot of controversy, so much so that many women think it is no longer an option. One brand of IUD, the Dalkon Shield, did have problems and has been removed from the market. Some other manufacturers then pulled their brands out of the American market in fear of potential lawsuits. However, the World Health Organization and the American Medical Association rate the IUD as one of the safest and most effective temporary methods of birth control for women.

Because of this controversy and because IUDs are of two basic types — ones that contain hormones and the ones that contain copper — you should definitely speak with a doctor or clinician before making up your mind.

Inserted into the uterus through the cervix during menstruation, the IUD can be left in place for up to eight years (some must be replaced every year, some after four years). Exactly how this device prevents pregnancy depends on the type of IUD that you're using.

A critical component of the IUD is the string that hangs down from the end and protrudes through the cervix into the vagina. The IUD is very good at protecting against pregnancy — if it is in place. Occasionally, the IUD can slip out, and you may not realize that it's gone. If that happens, you are no longer protected against pregnancy. That's why you should regularly check to feel if the string is in place.

The advantage of the IUD is that — apart from checking for the string — you don't have to worry about it. And the IUD does not change either the hormone levels or copper levels in a woman's body.

You may have some cramping when the IUD is first inserted, and some women have heavier bleeding for the first few months; a few women may develop a pelvic infection. Even rarer are problems with the IUD being pushed up into the uterus and causing other types of complications. But, all in all, compared to other forms of birth control, and especially to using no birth control at all, the IUD is safer than most methods. (But remember that, if you are not in a monogamous relationship, you still need to protect yourself from STDs.)

The cost of an exam and insertion ranges from $150 to $300.

On the horizon

If I ever find Aladdin's magic lamp and the genie grants me three wishes, I definitely know what at least one of those wishes will be, and that is the perfect method of birth control. Each of the birth control methods that are available currently have drawbacks of one sort or another.

But since I don't believe in genies — or even dream of Jeannies — I would like to see a lot more money invested into this area of research. However, some money is being spent, and some new developments have come of it.

The vaginal ring

A new method of hormonal control of pregnancy is on the horizon (see "The barrier methods" up next). The *vaginal ring* is inserted like the diaphragm. It stays in place for three weeks of the month, and is removed for one week during menstruation. The ring does not act as a barrier, like the diaphragm; instead, it releases the same types of hormones that are found in the pill. Each ring contains enough hormones for three cycles, so you must get a new one every three months.

Although the ring could cause some of the same side effects as the pill, these effects should be milder. This is because the vaginal ring is placed right next to the cervix, so the woman receives an even lower dosage of hormones than she would if she were taking the low-dose contraceptive pill. Yet she still receives all the same benefits of the hormones in the pill (see the earlier section on the pill).

The vaginal ring is still being studied. If this form of contraceptive interests you, check with your doctor every now and then to see if the ring has been approved.

The male pill

A male version of the contraceptive pill is currently under study. Like the female pill, this male contraceptive involves adding hormones — in this case, a synthetic version of the male hormone, testosterone — which will cause production of sperm to shut down for about a week. But, because taking this hormone orally could cause liver damage, the male version of the female pill will never be a pill; it will have to be an injection. This contraceptive is still undergoing tests and probably won't be ready until long after the year 2000.

The barrier methods

The aim of the barrier methods is to block the sperm from getting at the egg. Applying military tactics to this job, the logical place to begin is at the narrowest opening: the cervix. Casanova first tried a barrier method using hollowed-out halves of lemons at the cervix, but these days latex has pretty much taken over from the citrus family.

The diaphragm and cervical cap

The diaphragm is a shallow, dome-shaped cup. It has a flexible rim to allow for insertion, because it needs to be folded in order to be placed into the vagina (see Figure 7-3). The diaphragm is made to block the whole rear part of the vagina, including the cervix, protecting that entranceway from invasion by any attacking sperm.

Because sperm don't give up all that easily, the diaphragm is designed to work in conjunction with a spermicidal cream or jelly. The diaphragm must be left in place for at least eight hours after sexual intercourse to give the spermicide sufficient time to kill all the sperm. It can be left in the vagina for up to 24 hours.

The cervical cap works the same way as the diaphragm, the difference being one of shape: The cap is smaller and fits more tightly over the cervix. The cap is usually recommended for women whose pelvic muscles are not strong enough to hold a diaphragm in place. Because of the tighter fit, however, some women complain about difficulties in removing the cervical cap.

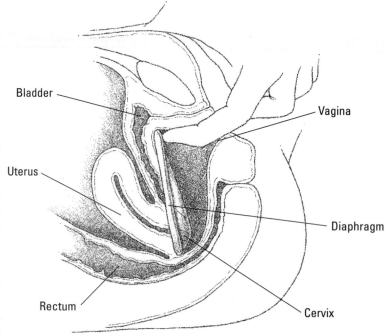

Figure 7-3: One of the main reasons diaphragms are sometimes ineffective is that they are not inserted correctly.

Bladder

Vagina

Uterus

Diaphragm

Rectum

Cervix

Although neither the diaphragm nor cervical cap has any side effects, they are not the easiest methods of birth control to use.

- ✔ The diaphragm or the cap can be cumbersome to insert because you not only have to put cream or jelly on it and then place it in the vagina, you have to insert it carefully enough so that you are sure that it is seated properly.

- ✔ Even though you can insert the diaphragm or cap up to six hours before intercourse — so that you can plan ahead of time and not have to interrupt a hot date to put in your diaphragm — if another episode of sexual intercourse is going to take place after the first, additional spermicide must be added.

You cannot use either the diaphragm or cervical cap during the time of menstruation.

The diaphragm does not come close to offering as much protection against pregnancy as some of the other methods I cover. In fact, with normal use, 18 out of 100 women who use the diaphragm become pregnant during the first year. Even among the women who learn to use the diaphragm perfectly, 6 out of 100 become pregnant. On the other hand, if you're not happy messing with your hormones, or if your system won't let you, then the diaphragm is a good alternative.

Romancing the diaphragm

If you didn't plan on having sex and so didn't put your diaphragm in place ahead of time, that doesn't mean that the act of putting in the diaphragm has to break up that romantic moment. Instead, try integrating the insertion of your diaphragm into foreplay.

If you're turning your nose up at this suggestion, that's probably because you're a bit squeamish about placing your diaphragm into your vagina when by yourself, not to mention with an audience, albeit of one.

But what you have to remember is that men are visual creatures. The more up close and personal they get with what are normally your private parts, the more excited they become. So, although the thought of putting in your diaphragm in front of your man may turn you off, I guarantee that it will be a turn-on for a number of men.

If you don't believe me, try it out. And if it turns out to make you more excited as well, you might find the extra lubrication useful in the insertion process.

The spermicides used with the diaphragm do offer some protection against AIDS and other sexually transmitted diseases, but not enough to really count on. If you're at all worried about being at risk, make sure that you also use a condom.

Doctor's fit required

Because both the diaphragm and cervical cap must be fitted, you must visit a physician in order to get this type of birth control. That visit may cost anywhere from $50 to $125, while the devices themselves cost between $13 and $25.

Both the diaphragm and the cap should last for several years, but you should hold them up to the light regularly to check them for wear, primarily holes. And, if you undergo a physical change, such as a pregnancy or significant weight loss or gain, you should go for another fitting before using the device again.

Progress report

Scientists have been tinkering with the diaphragm and have come up with a new, improved version, assuming the tests hold up, called Lea's Shield. The shield offers several advantages over the diaphragm:

- ✔ It is made of silicone rather than latex (some people are allergic to latex).
- ✔ It has a one-way air vent that allows for a snugger fit.
- ✔ It has a built-in loop to make it easier to remove.
- ✔ Because the shield is a one-size-fits-all device, unlike the diaphragm and cervical cap, Lea's Shield may one day be sold over the counter.

The condom

When the pill first came out, that's all anybody could talk about, and the lowly condom was relegated to the back of the shelf. But then along came AIDS, and the condom's ability to protect its user from transmitting diseases pushed it again to the forefront.

I doubt that anyone over the age of 12 doesn't know exactly what a condom is, but, to be thorough, I'll now launch into a description of this rising media star.

The condom is a sheath that fits over the penis, blocking the sperm from being released into the vagina. Most condoms are made of latex, although some are made out of animal tissue (usually lambskin), and a new one just coming out is made of polyurethane, which is supposed to better transmit sensations between partners.

Lambskin condoms have microscopic holes that, while small enough to stop the sperm in midbackstroke, are big enough to allow viruses safe passage into the vagina. These condoms do not offer adequate protection against HIV.

Condoms are widely available at drugstores, some supermarkets and convenience stores, and in dispensers in many public restrooms. When you purchase a condom, it comes rolled up in a package. You place the condom on the erect penis and roll it down along the shaft, leaving a small pocket at the top to collect the semen (for you graphically inclined readers, see Figure 7-4). Be sure to smooth out any air bubbles.

The days of the boring condom are over. Now you can buy them in various colors, different sizes, and with unique packaging. You can also purchase dry or lubricated condoms (even flavored ones!). Some of those that are lubricated include a spermicide for added protection.

Speaking of sizes, condoms for most men are like socks in that they are pretty much a one-size-fits-all piece of equipment. But for men built a lot larger or smaller than average, it is important to look for a condom with a different fit. Men with smaller penises may have a problem with some condoms slipping off during intercourse. They should purchase condoms with a "snugger fit." Among the brands that make this type are Lifestyle and Exotica. Men who are more amply endowed risk splitting a regular condom, but there is a brand aimed at this market called Maxxum. If you have problems finding these condoms in your area, I suggest calling Condomania at 1-800-9-CONDOM and ordering some by mail.

If you are using a dry condom and decide to add a lubricant, make sure that the lubricant is a water-based one, like KY Jelly. Oil-based lubricants, like Vaseline or other products made from mineral or vegetable oils, including Reddi Whip, can break down the latex and make the condom porous. This breakdown can happen very quickly, so do not use any of these products with a condom.

Figure 7-4:
Although how to use a condom may seem obvious, many people wind up paying a high price for not knowing as much as they thought they did.

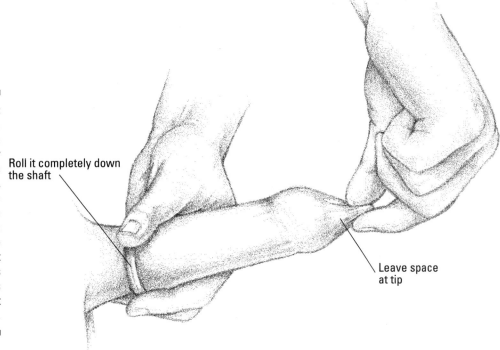

Roll it completely down the shaft

Leave space at tip

Removal is tricky

The trickiest part of using a condom can be removing it. Always be very careful to make sure that there is no leakage because, if the sperm are allowed to escape from their little rubber prison, they could make their way up into the vagina and pull off the escapade that you are trying to prevent.

✔ Either the man or woman should hold onto the base of the condom to keep it on the shaft of the penis while the man pulls his penis from the vagina.

✔ To minimize the risk of leakage, you should remove the condom before the man loses his erection entirely.

Condoms aren't perfect

Although the condom is relatively risk free to the man (unless he happens to be allergic to latex), it is not the best of methods as far as offering protection from pregnancy. Of 100 women whose partners use condoms, approximately 12 will become pregnant during a year of typical use. That's because condoms can break during use or because spillage of semen takes place during the removal process.

Obviously, the more careful you are using a condom, the more protection it can offer. But the biggest reason for condom failure is failure to use it in the first place. In other words, a couple may say that their method of birth control is the condom, but then they use condoms only occasionally.

If you are going to rely on condoms to protect against pregnancy or STDs, you have to use them all the time.

Condoms and the pleasure principle

Although many women applaud the condom because it forces men to take responsibility for something that has long been left to women, men often complain that wearing a condom during sex diminishes their sensations.

Now, for some men who have problems with premature ejaculation, reducing their sensations can be a good thing. But I understand that, for the rest of you men reading this book, it's a drawback.

If I could snap my fingers and make AIDS and all the other STDs out there disappear, I would be doing my best imitation of a Flamenco dancer all day long, I assure you. But the sad truth is that we do not have either a cure or a vaccine against AIDS, so you really have no choice but to use a condom when having sex that has any risk of passing along a disease. I know it adds to the man's frustration to use condoms when the woman is also using a method of birth control, but at least in those situations, if you stay in the relationship long enough, there's a chance that one day you'll be able to throw those condoms away.

Condoms don't last forever

Speaking of throwing away condoms reminds me of something. Some men carry condoms in their wallets on the off chance that they'll get lucky. That's OK as long as you think of that condom the way you think of the oil in your car, which should be changed every 3,000 miles.

I don't want to put a time limit on how long a condom can stay in a wallet before it should be declared damaged goods. That depends on a lot of factors, including how hot it is outside and how big a tush you have. But I will say that a year is way too long, even if you're a skinny guy living in Alaska.

By the way, this advice doesn't only apply to wallets. There are a number of places a man may keep a "safety," including the glove compartment or trunk of his or his parents' car, his lunch box, his tool kit, or his kilt. Whatever that place is, if it is subject to extremes of cold or heat, assume that, after a while, the condom will no longer be reliably "safe."

The female condom

Because too many men have been giving women flak for forcing them to wear condoms, a female condom has been developed that allows women to protect themselves against sexually transmitted diseases. The female condom is a loose-fitting pouch with a closed end that you insert deep inside your vagina. Like a diaphragm, the female condom can be inserted ahead of time or right before intercourse. The open end is left outside the vagina, and the male inserts his penis into it when entering the vagina for intercourse.

Although condoms for men can cost as little as 25 cents, the female condom costs closer to a dollar. Because it offers women the freedom of self-reliance when it comes to protecting themselves against AIDS, I believe this is a small price.

Foams, creams, and gels

Available over the counter are many contraceptive foams, creams, and gels. They do not require a prescription, and apart from possible temporary allergic reactions to the chemicals of which they are made — which may affect the woman, the man, or both — they have relatively few side effects. They also are relatively ineffective when used by themselves.

Of 100 women who use a contraceptive foam, cream, jelly, or suppository, 21 will become pregnant during the first year of typical use, although if perfectly used, the number drops to 3.

The spermicides in these products do offer some protection against HIV and other STDs, but I don't recommend that you rely solely on these products to remain disease free.

Most of these products come with applicators to place them inside the vagina. You use each product a little differently, but in general you should put it in place at least ten minutes before intercourse (though this can be integrated into part of foreplay). Additional spermicide should be added each time you intend to repeat sexual intercourse.

These products are easy to buy and easy to use, but they're much more effective when used in conjunction with either a diaphragm, cervical cap, or condom.

Natural family planning

Certainly the best way to avoid becoming pregnant is never to have sexual intercourse. This is called *abstinence*.

Another way is to be abstinent during the time of month when the woman is fertile and can become pregnant (see Chapter 1 for a discussion of these times). This reliance on the time of the month that a woman is fertile is called *natural family planning* (or periodic abstinence, or fertility awareness method, or the calendar or rhythm method).

Natural family planning is based on the regular patterns of fertility that most women have. Right away, you can see the number-one drawback these methods share. Many women are not all that regular, and even those who are regular sometimes have irregular months. When that happens, an unintended pregnancy can result.

Determining the time of fertility

To use any of these methods, you must first try to predict when you will next ovulate. Unless you already know that you're "regular," meaning that your period always comes at the same time in your cycle, your first step is to determine what pattern you follow. If your pattern tends to be very irregular, natural family planning carries more risk of pregnancy for you.

Calendar method

Your fertile period is not just the day that you ovulate. The egg is thought to live for one to three days, but sperm can live inside the vagina from two to seven days. This means that, if you have had sexual intercourse before the time that you ovulate, any of those sperm might still be hanging around the fallopian tubes when the egg comes along, ready to ambush the egg and impregnate the woman.

To be safe from pregnancy, you should think of a nine-day period as being risky — five days before you ovulate, the day of ovulation, and three days after that. During that fertile period, you should either abstain from sexual intercourse or use a barrier method.

The other 19 days that comprise the cycle are considered to be "safe," and — theoretically — you can have sexual intercourse during those days without using any other method of birth control and not become pregnant. But nothing is ever certain when those sneaky eggs and sperm are involved, so be aware of the risks.

By now this should be a reflex, but I will give you this warning once again. Even if you are presumably safe from becoming pregnant, that doesn't mean that you are safe from getting a sexually transmitted disease. Unless you are certain that your partner is 100 percent safe, you should make sure that a condom is in place before attempting intercourse.

Basal body temperature

You can use other indications of when you are fertile in conjunction with the calendar method. One is *the basal body temperature method.*

A woman's temperature rises slightly (between .4 and .8 degrees) when she ovulates. If you take your temperature every morning before you get out of bed using a special high-resolution thermometer, and discover a rise one day, and if you are sure that you don't have an infection of some sort to account for the rise, then you can presume that you have ovulated and should refrain from unprotected sex.

Of course, any sperm that were deposited ahead of time would be able to impregnate you, so this method can only serve as a proof that the calendar method is working.

If you are trying to get pregnant, however, the basal body temperature is a good predictor of when you should be having intercourse to make a baby.

Cervical mucus

Another way of checking whether or not you are ovulating is to examine your cervical mucus, which thins out when you are ovulating to allow the sperm to pass through. By continually checking the cervical mucus, you can notice when it begins to thin out, indicating that you have ovulated. It's tough to interpret your mucus without training, so I recommend that you take a class — which is offered by some hospitals — on how to identify the changes in your mucus if you plan to try this technique.

As with the basal body temperature method, although this is a reliable method of telling when a woman has ovulated and so provides useful information if you are trying to become pregnant, by itself it does not let you know when you are about to ovulate. Therefore, any sperm already deposited in your vagina could impregnate you.

One more way that you can tell if you have ovulated is by recognizing the actual sensations of ovulation, called *mittelschmerz*. Usually, only one of the two ovaries will release an egg. Some women can sense when this happens by a slight pain in their lower abdomen, on either the right or left side. Not every woman has these sensations, so it is not commonly discussed.

Using the sympto-thermal method

When these three methods — the calendar method, the basal body temperature method, and the cervical mucus method — are combined, it is called the sympto-thermal method. This method can serve as a relatively accurate guide for deciding when to abstain from sex or use a barrier method.

Under normal usage, of 100 women using the periodic abstinence method — meaning they refrain from having intercourse during what they believe is their fertile period — 20 will become pregnant. However, if perfect use can be obtained, the number drops to three.

But perfect use is rare, because outside factors can play havoc with natural family planning.

- ✔ If a woman lacks sleep, this can cause her temperature to vary.

- ✔ If she has a vaginal infection, which she may not be aware of, the consistency of her cervical mucus can change.

- ✔ And then there are her ovaries, either one of which may decide to evict an egg for nonpayment of rent at any old time.

For more about natural family planning, see Appendix B.

Facts about Birth Control Myths

OK, so your head is filled with all the facts about birth control. What worries me now is that you may still have some other "facts" floating around up there, which are really myths, and which can get you into big trouble.

To make sure that you can truly distinguish between fact and myth, I'm going to spell out the myths to you and then dispel them just as quickly.

Douching does not prevent pregnancy

The first myth concerns douching, which is useless both for hygiene and birth control purposes.

The concept of washing out the sperm before they can make their way up into the uterus dates back to at least the time of ancient Egypt (so you see that this falsehood can truly be said to be of mythical proportions). The ingredients used in these douches have changed over the years. When I was young, vinegar was supposed to do the trick; more recently I've heard that Coca-Cola is a douche of choice.

The fact is that, by the time you finish with intercourse and douche, many sperm have already begun their trip towards the egg and are beyond your ability to flush them out.

Although the advertisers on Madison Avenue may not try to convince you to try douching as a contraceptive, they do try to sell the concept of douching as a way of maintaining personal hygiene. Some experts think that these products should be avoided because they kill helpful bacteria, and they certainly don't do any good. If you have nothing better to do with your money, I suggest you give it to the charity of your choice rather than buy these commercial douches.

One time is all it takes

Like the wives' tale about douching, another myth that has gotten a lot of women in trouble is that a woman cannot get pregnant from her first attempt at sexual intercourse.

If her hymen is intact, a virgin may bleed, and she may also suffer a little discomfort. But these factors are irrelevant to the joining of sperm and egg, so first-timers have to take the same precautions as everyone else.

You can get pregnant without orgasms

Some people believe that if the woman doesn't have an orgasm then she can't become pregnant.

Although it is true that the vaginal contractions of orgasm cause the cervix to dip into the pool of sperm-laden semen at the bottom of her vagina and can help foster pregnancy, it is also too true that some of the sperm are going to make their way up the cervix whether the woman has multiple orgasms or none at all.

My advice is to go ahead and have those orgasms . . . after you've taken care of birth control.

Stand-ups don't stop sperm

Some people think that sperm cannot defy gravity, so that, if the couple has sex standing up, she won't get pregnant.

Wrong again, folks. Those sperm are strong swimmers and can go upstream as well as down.

Pregnancy and periods can mix

Some people trust that if a woman is menstruating, then she can't become pregnant.

Although menstruation does limit the odds of becoming pregnant, it is not a 100-percent, sure-fire way to prevent pregnancy. Some women have irregular bleeding, which is not true menstruation. Misinterpreting this bleeding can throw off your strategy for preventing pregnancy.

Pulling out is no protection

And then there's that most dangerous of myths, which has caused more pregnancies than any other: the epic tale of the withdrawal method.

Through the ages, men have sworn to probably millions of women that they have great control over their ejaculations and that, as soon as they feel their orgasm coming, they will remove the penis from the vagina so she won't get pregnant.

This theory has a lot of holes in it:

- ✔ In the first place, a lot of men who think they have matters under control, don't. They wind up ejaculating before they can pull out.

- ✔ Some men, in the heat of excitement, forget their promise and don't pull out.

- ✔ Even if the man does pull out before he ejaculates, it's already too late. The pre-ejaculatory fluid produced by the Cowper's gland is filled with sperm, and those sperm are already making their way up into the uterus long before their brethren are being expelled onto milady's stomach or thighs.

So, although *coitus interruptus* — the fancy Latin name for this not-so-fancy method of birth control — may be better than nothing, it's not much better. And, of course, it offers little protection against the spread of sexually transmitted diseases.

If Your Method Fails

If a man and a woman are trying to have a baby together, then finding out that the woman is pregnant can be one of the happiest moments of their lives. On the other hand, finding out about an unintended pregnancy can be one of the loneliest and scariest moments of an unmarried woman's life. It can also be difficult for her partner. And it can be upsetting even for married couples, if they didn't plan on a pregnacy

I certainly can't tell any woman what she should do under those circumstances, but I can let you know what your options are.

Keeping the baby

One option is to carry the baby to term and keep it. More and more single women are certainly doing this. Some of these young mothers feel that having a baby is a rite of passage to adulthood, many actually following in their mother's footsteps.

I strongly disagree with this attitude, because a baby brought up in a household without a father is usually missing both the male half of the child's upbringing and often the financial support too (although, whether you are married to the father of your baby or not, he has a legal obligation to help you take care of that baby, financially speaking, and you should insist on those rights). These women, often from disadvantaged homes, would be better off preparing themselves for adulthood by finishing their education than trying to rush into it by having a child.

Now there are also older women who have the financial means to bring up a child by themselves, and, since they can't find an acceptable husband, they decide to become single parents so as not to miss out on the joys of motherhood. Thanks to Dan Quayle, the TV character of Murphy Brown became the epitome of this type of woman.

To some degree, I agreed with the then-vice president's criticism, because the "Murphy Browns" of the world are really the exception rather than the rule. As a successful newswoman, she definitely had the financial wherewithal to raise a child on her own. But that is not the case with most single mothers, and I believe there is a danger in glamorizing single motherhood on TV, because doing so may lure some women into following in Murphy's footsteps even though they do not have anything approaching her finances.

But one thing is for certain, with so many single women having babies, the stigma that was once attached to the status of unwed mother has all but vanished. People may still raise their eyebrows, but they certainly won't stone you.

If keeping the baby is an option you choose, I wish you the best of luck. I went through it with my first child, and I certainly enjoyed motherhood no end. But, though I know you will have many moments of joy through the years, you will also face many difficulties.

Of course, you can also marry the father of your child. But I urge you to do this only if the two of you love each other and want to raise a family together. Many loving couples have been made by the unintended conception of a baby, and it can work. But it's not the best way to start a marriage.

Putting the baby up for adoption

Another option is to have the baby and give it up for adoption. There are many couples who can't have children who would make wonderful parents for your child. The social worker at any major hospital should be able to guide you into finding a qualified adoption agency.

But giving up a baby for adoption isn't as easy as it may seem. As the baby grows inside of you, you will not be able to keep yourself from growing attached to it, and once you actually see it, the task of giving it up will be heart-wrenching. The emotions that giving a baby up for adoption entail are one of the big reasons why I say over and over again how important it is to do everything you can to avoid an unintended pregnancy.

Another thing to consider is that, before a baby can be given up for adoption, the father has to agree also. If the father isn't available, that could cause later complications if he then decides that he wants to raise the baby.

Although in some cases adoptions have been reversed, be very certain that you want to give up the child before you actually do so. Every child deserves a secure set of parents.

Ending the pregnancy early

Some women may choose abortion. An *abortion* is the termination of a pregnancy by the loss or destruction of the fetus before it has reached *viability* — the ability to sustain itself outside the womb.

Some abortions are spontaneous, meaning the woman's body rejects the baby for some reason. This is called a *miscarriage*. Although we don't always know what causes a miscarriage, very often it is discovered afterwards that there was something seriously wrong with the fetus.

Abortions can also be artificially induced, usually by a physician. Ninety percent of all abortions performed in this country are done in the first 12 weeks of pregnancy, when the embryo or fetus is barely visible or quite small. The usual method of an early abortion is *vacuum aspiration*. The cervix is numbed and the embryo or fetus is removed with vacuum suction through a narrow tube that is inserted through the cervix. Normally, the procedure takes about five minutes, is done on an outpatient basis, and has few complications.

If you wait longer than 12 weeks, everything gets a lot more complicated because the fetus has grown in size so that it can no longer simply be aspirated. The types of procedures range from dilation and curettage (D&C), which involves a scraping of the uterine lining, to dilation and evacuation, which involves a scraping and aspiration, to the saline abortion, in which a saline solution is injected into the uterine cavity. All these procedures are more difficult to perform than simple vacuum aspiration and involve added risks to the woman.

Emergency contraception

Women can be given a large dose of estrogen and progesterone, something like the early pill, inducing what would normally be termed a miscarriage. This dosage of hormones has been nicknamed *the morning-after pill,* but in reality it can be administered up to 72 hours after sexual intercourse.

A pill that has the same effect as the morning-after pill, but using a lot less of the drugs, now exists. It's called RU 486 and was developed in France. RU 486 can be used whether the woman is certain that she is pregnant or not, which is especially useful in cases of contraceptive failure (a condom breaking, for example) or rape.

RU 486 works by blocking the effects of progesterone, which is key to establishing pregnancy. Two days after taking the RU 486 pill, the woman is given a dose of prostaglandin; after that, most women experience bleeding and the passage of tissue within four hours. RU 486 can be effective at preventing pregnancy up to ten days after a woman has missed her period.

As of this writing, RU 486 is not yet approved in this country, but it is available in Europe.

A woman's right

Abortion is a very controversial topic because many people, either for religious or moral reasons, believe that the embryo or fetus is no different than a baby and should not be destroyed. The Supreme Court has ruled, in a landmark decision, *Roe v. Wade*, that a woman's right to privacy overrides the state's ability to control what she does to her own body, effectively legalizing abortions. But, although that decision took care of the legal issues, it did not change the minds of those who are against abortion, and so the controversy continues to rage.

Abortions really upset me, but what used to happen before abortions were legalized is even more odious to me. At that time, safe abortions, either done in other countries where they are legal or done by real doctors in the United States surreptitiously, were available only to the rich, which forced poor women or women of only modest means to seek out unsafe, illegal abortions that often left them seriously injured or dead.

Abortion, legal or not, should never be used as a form of birth control. The methods of birth control that exist may not be perfect, but they are quite effective and much better alternatives to abortion. But, no matter how conscientious a women is, contraceptive failures do occur, as do rapes. Because of those circumstances beyond the control of women, I believe that we must retain the right to have an abortion when needed.

Making your decision

It was a lot easier for me to outline these choices than it would be for you to select one of them if you are faced with an unintended pregnancy. This is even more true if you are alone, without the assistance and guidance of the father of the child.

My advice is not to try and make the decision of what to do alone. Seek out guidance or counseling from someone, preferably someone who has helped others who've faced the same problems; family members may love you, but their own emotions may supersede your needs.

Planned Parenthood, where I used to work, is a nationwide agency that specializes in this field. Their counselors are usually well trained and very good at helping women go through the decision-making process.

Other agencies and clinics also advertise that they are capable of guiding you, but some of these places may not be impartial. Some may have a greater interest in getting you to say yes to something that they make money from or strongly believe in rather than in offering you objective advice.

I often recommend that people consult with their religious leaders on many issues, but, on the issue of abortion, some religious leaders may not be able to be objective regarding your own particular circumstances or needs. Get as much spiritual guidance as you can. Seek out the guidance of whomever you feel can help you. But remember, the final decision rests with you.

Chapter 8

Courtship, Marriage, and Commitment

. . . .

. . . .

Courtship, marriage, and commitment — there are three old-fashioned words for you to contemplate. You know that, if you were to study the United States from only what you read in the media and what you saw on television, you might conclude that these family values were gone forever. While I have to admit that they're, how shall I put it, on the run, they're not totally dead yet and certainly not forgotten, at least not by this grandmother.

One day we may reach a point in our society where children are "manufactured," that is to say, either cloned from DNA or put together in a petri dish from donated eggs and sperm. In my opinion that would be terrible, but it may happen. At that point, the raison d'être — the essential reason — for marriage will have changed so much that maybe the concept will die out. But for now, in this scientifically backward era when most people can't even program their VCRs, marriage is still a viable social institution because it provides the best environment in which to raise children.

Yes, I know that there are plenty of single mothers and fathers who are doing a good job of raising their children, but let's face it, the toll that this is taking on both the parents and the children makes it far from an ideal lifestyle. Since women have jumped into the workforce in such great numbers, I'm not sure that even two parents are enough anymore, and so I certainly do not believe that any of you should consciously try to become single parents.

Now if you don't believe in marriage, then I suppose that you could skip this chapter. But before you skip ahead, let me say one thing to you. Right now you may be saying to yourself, and anyone else who will listen, that you never want to marry. You may always have been single, or you may have once (or twice or three times) been married and decided to swear off from this rite. That's fine. I respect your opinion as long as you respect mine. But opinions do change, and so, when it comes to marriage, never say never. Leave your options open in case you do one day fall deeply in love with someone, so much so that you'll want to swear to each other that you'll spend the rest of your lives together.

Courtship

In the old days, there was no such thing as dating. If you so much as wanted to talk to a girl, you had to first ask her father for her hand in marriage. The concept of spending an evening together, and maybe of even having sex together without first taking your vows of holy matrimony, was just not permitted (not that it wasn't tried).

Nowadays, most couples start out dating and then, if they happen to fall in love and it lasts a while, they decide to take the plunge. Sometimes they live together, more often than not they have sex together. When, during this process, does courtship begin? Or does it exist altogether anymore?

It certainly does exist. Here's a case I know of:

Anthony and Rose

Anthony was about ten years older than Rose when they met. He'd been looking for someone who would make a good mother for his children, and as far as he was concerned, Rose was it. Anthony didn't have any doubts, and he was intent on marrying the girl he had his sights on.

Anthony didn't just take Rose on a date. He took her to the fanciest restaurants. And Anthony didn't send flowers only on Valentine's Day. Rose would receive these enormous bouquets almost every day at her office.

Rose liked Anthony, but when he started showering her with all of this attention, she wasn't quite prepared. She hadn't been thinking of getting married just yet, but it was obvious from the way Anthony was treating her that a wedding was on his mind.

Rose had had boyfriends before, but nobody had ever treated her like Anthony did. She was very flattered by all the attention he was showing her, but she also realized that if he asked her to marry him and she said no, he would probably move on. He had fully committed himself to his quest, and he wasn't the type to accept no for an answer and then just hang around.

It wasn't until the moment that Anthony actually popped the question that Rose made up her mind. She knew that Anthony was a one-in-a-million find, and she decided that she'd have a hard time doing better — besides, she found that she loved him — so she said yes. And as far as I know, they've been living happily ever after.

I have to make a confession here. Anthony wasn't American; he had been raised in Italy, so his ideas of how a male should react were different than those of the average American. (That also holds true on the highway, which Anthony seems to think is actually the autostrada.) American men tend to be cooler about these things. They won't necessarily commit themselves the way Anthony did, and that's too bad. Men who won't commit themselves think that, by holding back, they're keeping some of their freedom, but that's not true.

Giving in totally to your emotions, by diving right in without holding anything back, actually makes you feel a lot freer.

- ✔ You don't have to put on a show for your friends, pretending that you don't care all that much.
- ✔ You don't have to tell jokes about your date behind her back, which you later regret when you're actually holding her.
- ✔ You don't have to feel badly because you're going dancing with your girl instead of watching the game with the guys.

It's not that she's wrangled you into marrying her. You're the one who made the choice, who made the commitment to marry this woman, and you're happy to live by it. Being able to say to somebody, "I love you" — that's real freedom. Only giving a piece of yourself, instead of your whole self, means that you're tied down to a sham, and that's what ends up being a shackle around your ankle.

Remember, you can't be tied down to a marriage with somebody if you're the one who tied the knot.

Can women do the courting?

I tell women all the time that they have to learn to take the initiative. They may even have to convince a man to fall in love with them. But, at some point, he's going to have to take over the courtship process, or the woman is going to feel cheated.

I know, some of you are saying that that is a sexist statement. Do I have hard evidence that a relationship is not going to work out if the woman takes the role that has traditionally belonged to the man? No. But in my gut I feel that way. I sense that the whole relationship will end up being topsy-turvy, and at some point the woman will meet a man who makes her feel special, and she's going to leave the guy she courted.

The interpersonal relationships between men and women are changing every day. So many more women are becoming bosses, having male secretaries, asking men out for a date, that I cannot predict what the future will hold. There may come a time when women and men share the courtship process equally. But I don't believe that that time has come yet, and, unless you are one of those people who always has to be on the cutting edge, I suggest that you follow at least some of the tried-and-true traditions. After all, you are planning for a lifelong marriage, so you want to minimize the mistakes.

Proving your love to a woman

Remembering that you want to give your whole self, don't be afraid to go overboard. Now that doesn't mean that you have to max your credit card in order to win a woman over.

I believe that what women want more than anything else is your attention. Here are some things I recommend that you can do to prove your love to her:

- **Use the telephone:** Don't just call her when you want to go out, but also call her to find out how she is. If she lives alone, you can even call her in the middle of the night just to tell her that you love her. She won't mind, and, when she falls back asleep, she'll dream about you.

- **Send flowers:** Some men wrack their brains trying to think of an appropriate present, and then give her something that's totally unromantic, like an electric broom. Most women enjoy receiving flowers, so use that to your advantage. Flowers aren't that expensive, you can order them by picking up a phone, and they'll be delivered right to her door so that you don't even have to schlep them. What could be a better gift?

- **Take charge:** Most people enjoy it when someone else takes charge once in a while. You might think that it's the polite thing to ask your date which restaurant she wants to go to, but, if you're paying, that puts her in an awkward position. She might like Chez Chuck's, but she also might know what the tab will turn out to be. So, if you are the one asking her out, you decide where to go.

- **Tell her how you feel:** Women crave intimacy, and that doesn't mean "I'll show you mine if you show me yours." A lot of men confuse sex with intimacy, but making love isn't enough for most women. She wants to know what you're feeling, so tell her. If you want to look at the outside of her, that's fine, but in exchange you have to let her see the inside of you.

- **Build up a bank of shared experiences:** You can just go to a concert together, or you can go to a concert held under the stars at a park as you lie on a blanket and share the wine, cheese, and grapes that you brought.

You can just drive up and down Main Street, or you can take a drive to the countryside to see the spectacular fall foliage. You can shovel out your car together, or you can go night skiing by torchlight. How she sees you will depend somewhat on the circumstances; so, to put yourself in the best possible light, treat her to a few special moments.

✔ **Look your best:** Some men pay a lot of attention to the way they look, while others don't. If you're of the latter type, it's time to change your tune. She wants to be proud of the man she's going out with, so try to look your best when you're with her.

Although these tips are mainly for men, it takes two to make a relationship work. You ladies can read these suggestions and, if you get any ideas, go for it.

Commitment

Some people get married who do not plan on a lifetime commitment. In the movie *Jurassic Park,* Ian Malcolm, the character played by Jeff Goldblum, says, "I'm always looking for the next ex-Mrs. Malcolm." If you approach marriage with that attitude, there's a good chance that you will get your wish. No one is perfect. No two people share identical tastes in every way. There is going to be conflict in every marriage. It would be unnatural if there weren't; after all, you're not clones.

Your tolerance for that conflict is going to depend very much on how committed you are to the marriage in the first place. If you approach marriage with that proverbial ten-foot pole stuck out in front of you, then any marriage you enter into is destined to fail.

Love isn't enough

Think of a marriage as a house of cards. If the cards are merely placed together, the least little wind will bring them tumbling down. But if you glue the cards together, then they're likely to withstand all but the strongest gale. *Commitment is the glue that holds a marriage together.*

Aha, you thought it was love, right? You thought that, as long as you love each other, you can make it through any storm. You'd be surprised at how many people there are who love each other and can never stay married. It's not the love that's missing in their life together, it's the commitment.

Maybe she's more committed to her job. Maybe he's unwilling to commit because he wants to have sex with other women. Maybe they're both unwilling to commit in case they meet somebody who might be better for them. It doesn't mean that they don't love each other.

Children and commitment

Having children is supposed to be a sign of commitment, but you can't count on that, at least not anymore. With the example of so many single parents, especially single mothers, raising children on their own, couples just don't look at children as reason enough to stay together any longer. I don't think that it's right to have children if you don't at least think of yourselves as committed, but, sadly, too many people disagree with me. I say "sadly" not because they disagree with me, but because of what it does to the children.

Children are much better off growing up with two parents living under the same roof. Some people dispute that, but they'll never convince me. Now that doesn't mean that I never advise a man or a woman to split from their spouse when there are children involved, because I do. If two people are really incompatible, if they're fighting all the time, and maybe even taking it out on the children, then divorce is the best recourse. But it's not a win-win situation. The situation may be better for everyone concerned after the divorce, but the end result still can't be compared to a whole, functional family.

It's one thing to grow up never having had a father or a mother around. But, if a child has had two parents, and suddenly they split up, it's bound to affect the child. One way it affects them is that they blame themselves. They shouldn't feel guilty, because it is rarely the kids who cause the split, but, no matter how much you tell them that they are not the reason for the breakup, they won't believe it. Even if they accept the fact that they didn't do anything to cause the divorce, they'll still think that there was something they could have done to stop it.

Putting your marriage first

So if love isn't enough, and kids aren't enough, what is this thing called commitment? Its components are going to be different for each and every person involved in a marriage, but the basic philosophy is the same. Commitment is a willingness to put the marriage ahead of the individual whenever necessary.

Every marriage undergoes trials of one sort or another. One partner may become sick. Money problems may crop up. Parents can put pressure both on their offspring and his or her spouse. Just the everyday stress of having kids and jobs creates conflicts. And some unlucky souls will face all of the above.

Some pressures are actually easier to handle as a couple than individually. If a natural disaster strikes, like a flood or earthquake, it's obviously better to be two people struggling to go on with your lives rather than one. Even if you've lost all the treasures you've accumulated over the years, at least you still have someone with whom to share the memories of the past.

Other situations can be especially hard on a marriage. If you have a boss who expects you to work late every night, not only do you have to struggle with your own anger, but then you have to go home and get nasty looks from your spouse, who is sick of being alone every night. When one person is caught in the middle and can't bear the pressure, then one side will have to go. In this particular case, it could be the job, or it could be the marriage.

Factors that tear at a marriage

Finding this "marriage glue" is especially hard in the present era, which is why the divorce rate stands at 50 percent. What are some of the factors in our society today that tear at marriages?

- **The two-career family model:** Any type of wound needs time to heal, be it a physical one or a psychological one. That's why it is important for two married people to spend time together. But when both work, and there's also the job of taking care of their home, which often falls most heavily on the woman, even little problems can develop into crushing mountains of anger.

- **Our mobile society:** If you've always lived in one town, you've got a whole support system of family and neighbors and friends. When you move, you can build new networks, but they're never as strong as family ties, and they take time, so that, if you move every few years, then it's almost impossible to find people you can really rely on. Not having people you can turn to for help can make it very difficult to cope, especially if you have children.

- **The media:** Now, in the past, you may have worried about keeping up with the Joneses, but since the Jones family lived right next door, their house was probably similar to yours, and basically you lived the same lifestyle. But today, instead of living next door, "the Joneses" are on your television screen, or in your newspapers and magazines, or on your computer network. You are deluged with new gadgets to buy, new places to go, new sports to take up. Sitting on a rocking chair on your front porch making small talk is not one of the options being pushed, because no one can make a profit off of that. But that's exactly what a marriage needs most. Far too many options are available, and spending quality time with your spouse is made to seem like one of the least worthy.

- **The divorce model:** Divorce used to be frowned upon by society at large, and so a couple's expectations were different. Divorce wasn't just one of several options, but was looked on as a last resort. Peer pressure was a strong force keeping a couple from getting a divorce, and that pressure came from family, neighbors, and people on the job. Now there's been a total reversal. These days, your friends may actually encourage you to get a divorce. Nobody at work cares whether you're divorced or not, and maybe your boss even prefers it, because now you can work later. Your family may still not like the idea, but they probably live a thousand miles away, so their vote doesn't mean all that much.

✔ **The sexual revolution:** There have always been people who have had affairs, but with the consequence for adultery in Biblical times being stoning, it was something that people tried to keep under wraps. Today we are told that everyone is cheating and that you're a fool if you stick with the same person. Yes, times have changed, but not so drastically as all that. But all this talk about sex does make it harder to accept a so-so sex life with one mate for a lifetime.

All of these things are responsible for the rising number of divorces. But, if you make yourself aware of these things and do all you can to counter their effects, divorce doesn't have to be the final chapter of your marriage.

Strengthening Your Marriage

Now we have to look into what you can do to keep your marriage, be it an existing one or one that is still in your hope chest, from breaking up on the rocks of the 21st century.

Communicate

Nothing is more essential in a marriage than talking with one another. Telling each other your problems is a way of keeping them from growing to the point where they can no longer be solved. But, you have to be willing to obey certain rules:

✔ You have to listen to the other person.

✔ You have to communicate in such a way that you don't cause a fight, which means no put-downs, no threats, no needling.

✔ You have to pick the time and place where communications are going to work best. Don't start talking about a problem when you're running out the door, late for work. All that will accomplish is to start a screaming match.

Here are some other hints for keeping the discussion flowing freely and keeping your marriage healthy and happy:

- ✔ **Keep problems outside the bedroom:** Don't bring up problems about sex while you're having sex; always bring up sexual problems outside the bedroom. Emotions are at a fever pitch when you're making love, and if you add the wrong catalyst you'll get an explosion.

- ✔ **Don't argue about kids in front of them:** Never argue about something having to do with the children in front of them. Doing so will give your children the wrong message and, if they choose sides, distort the final outcome. You should always present a united front when you do talk to your children, even if the disagreement hasn't been settled. If you give children mixed messages, you'll wind up with mixed results.

- ✔ **Think before you speak:** Think before you say something — if it's going to hurt the other person's feelings, maybe it is better left unsaid.

- ✔ **Don't be greedy with compliments:** Everybody likes to hear good news, so pass it on. This is especially important if the other person has invested a lot of time and energy into a project, be it cooking a meal or washing the car.

- ✔ **Make a date to talk:** If you're not finding enough time to communicate without planning for it, then make a date to talk. Certainly, if something pressing is on your mind, then you have to find time to talk it out. But even if you don't have a particular problem to discuss, remember that, in order to keep those lines of communication open, you have to use them on a regular basis.

Try to pick a time for conversation when the clock isn't ticking. In other words, if your husband gets up early, don't plan on talking to him when you get into bed because he'll be concerned that it's cutting into his sleep. On the other hand, if you really need to say something, and he has to take a shower, jump right in there with him. You are married, after all.

- ✔ **Bring up pleasant memories:** Going over the good times you shared together can be a soothing balm and help with the healing process of problems you are currently experiencing. Don't hide that wedding album in the back of a closet; instead, keep it out where it can serve as a re-minder of one of the happiest days of your life.

Do things together

It helps if you and your spouse have things to talk about. If you share a hobby, there will always be a topic of conversation that you'll be mutually interested in. It can be as simple as reading the same book to something more compli-cated, like sharing in the running of a small business.

✔ **Go for walks:** There's no better time to discuss something than when you're going for a stroll.

- You have privacy because there's only the two of you.

- There are few distractions — and if you have a cellular phone, don't take it (unless a real emergency is pending).

- By walking, you'll be expending energy — energy that might otherwise be used in fighting. You'll find that, if you discuss issues while being active instead of passive, you'll be much less likely to squabble over the little things.

✔ **Go out on dates:** I know that, with children, it can be hard to find the time and the money to go on dates, but it really is important to have some large periods of time that you can devote to each other. If there aren't any grandparents around, try to find another couple with whom you can exchange baby-sitting duties. If you can't afford a fancy restaurant, go to McDonald's, order your Big Mac to go, and park somewhere quiet for an hour or so.

✔ **Get a lock for your bedroom door:** I'm always surprised to find couples who don't have this little necessity. Your kids need to know that there are times when Mommy and Daddy want to be alone, whether it's just to talk or for other, more private reasons. A hook-and-eye type lock costs only about a dollar, and it can be the best investment you'll ever make.

✔ **Turn down the volume:** Some people seem to always need background noise, be it the TV or radio or a CD playing. Even if it's not loud enough to stop conversation, this noise is a distraction to conversation. Because time for communication is short as it is, both of you have to give each other your full attention if you want to really impart information. And, when you get in your car together, don't automatically switch on the radio. Drive time can be great conversation time, unless it gets drowned out by some DJ.

✔ **Organize and prioritize:** With busy schedules, it's hard not to get scattered. You keep saying "We'll talk soon," and even though you share the same living space, soon becomes later, becomes never. Yes, there are things that you have to do, but are they all more important than talking to each other? Make a list of what you have to do (dress the kids, walk the dog) and put conversation with your spouse as close to the top as you can.

✔ **Let the machine pick it up or take it off the hook:** Now I love telephones, and I'm on them for hours each day, but just because the telephone has a loud ring doesn't mean that it always gets first crack at our attention. Sometimes you just have to decide that you won't let the phone interrupt. If the two of you have finally found time to sit down and have a conversation, it makes no sense to interrupt those precious moments to talk to somebody else. There's nobody more important to you than your spouse, right?

Keep together when you're apart

In the days when the only way to communicate over long distances was with pen and ink, people actually wrote to each other. Now that the typewriter is already passé, and we have computers and e-mail and whatever so that it should be easier to write, people do it less and less.

✔ If you've got half an hour, and your spouse isn't around, write him or her a letter. Explain how you feel so that you'll get a jump start when you do get the chance to talk. How your letter gets there, the post office or e-mail, is up to you.

✔ You can also jot down brief notes on Post-it notes and leave them someplace where your spouse is sure to see them. Just make sure that those short notes aren't always passing on a chore, or your spouse will dread seeing them rather than view them as something to look forward to.

It's a good idea to write yourself notes about what you need to communicate to your partner. How many times have you said to your spouse, "There's something I had to tell you, but I've forgotten it"? If you'd written it down, you wouldn't have that problem. So next time, do just that.

It's very easy to let communication between you and your spouse drift away into nothingness. Communication is something that you have to work at, and both of you have to put it near the top of your list of priorities in order to be successful at it.

Sex and Marriage

Surveys of people with happy marriages have all shown that sex is an important ingredient. It's not the most important ingredient, and most people find that their sex lives do decrease as the years go by, but you cannot let your sex life degenerate into nothingness. Sex is an important way of communicating your love, and, like the other ways of communicating, it takes some effort on your part to make certain that there is enough of it to keep your marriage together.

Obviously, if either partner is sexually frustrated, it is not going to be good for a marriage. Even if the word orgasm is not stated in your marriage vows, being able to derive sexual satisfaction with your spouse is certainly implied. But the sexual union between husband and wife brings more than just the easing of sexual tensions to a marriage. It also brings intimacy, which is another important component to the glue that holds the two of you together.

I regularly receive letters from women who will not let their husbands see them naked because they are ashamed of the way they look. Some of these women have satisfying sex lives, so it's not that they're not having sex, but they do keep this particular barrier up. This always causes me concern, in part because of the low self-esteem that these women have for themselves, but also because it shows a lack of intimacy.

A marriage needs intimacy because it shows the world, and the couple themselves, that there really is a special bond between them. That doesn't mean you can't set any boundaries, but the fewer there are, the more intimate you will be. And I'm not only talking about physical intimacy. Being naked together is certainly a good feeling, but you also have to let your partner see into your psyche. If you hide your hopes, your dreams, your desires from your spouse, then you become strangers in some very basic areas, which is not good for a marriage.

You can also carry intimacy too far and think nothing of, say, burping loudly in front of your spouse as if he or she weren't there. That's not intimacy, that's being gross. No matter how intimate you are, you should never lose respect for your partner. Now, if your intimacy stretches into the bathroom, then there's certainly nothing wrong with exercising any bodily function in front of each other, but that doesn't give you license to turn the rest of the house into a toilet.

The ultimate intimacy

The ultimate intimacy has nothing to do with sex and is usually done with your clothes on. It's not complicated or difficult, and it can be done over and over, yet it is very, very rare.

The ultimate intimacy is to totally give yourself to your partner.

All of us hold things back from the rest of the world, including our spouses. Some of these things aren't important to anyone else and should be held back. If you've got an itch behind your left ear, there is no reason to announce it to the world before you scratch it. That's trivial.

But what if there's an itch in your psyche? What if you were a six-foot-tall, beefy truck driver who always wanted to write poetry but were afraid people would laugh at you? Would you reveal that side of yourself to your wife? And if not, why not? Would you be afraid of seeming weak to her? Do you think you've got to keep up a certain image in order for her to love you?

Every time you hide behind a screen of some sort, you are decreasing the intimacy you have with your spouse and building walls between you instead of bridges.

You may think that, if you let somebody peer inside to your very core, it will weaken you. That might be true if you let just anyone in, but this is your husband or wife we're talking about. And if they love you as much as you love them, rather than weaken you, sharing this kind of intimacy will strengthen the both of you as well as your marriage.

Don't play games with each other

What ruins the intimacy between a husband and wife is when they play games with each other, which means when they keep score.

- ✔ He did that, so I won't do this.
- ✔ She didn't let me do this, so I won't let her do that.
- ✔ Last year we didn't go to the dance, so I won't go to his family picnic.

Every time you look up at that scoreboard, you are destroying a piece of your marriage. You are not supposed to be on different teams, you're supposed to be on the same team.

Now, even teammates squabble. There's no such thing as a perfect marriage; things will go wrong, and you'll have your ups and downs. But, if your goal is to be perfectly intimate, to be as close to each other as possible, then you'll work those problems out and continue to make progress. But, if you stop thinking that way, if you start believing that your relationship is a competition, then very soon it will become one, and it will cease to be a marriage.

There is no better feeling in the world than to be one with the person you love. During sex, the intensity of that oneness can be terrific, but that feeling is also a source of strength and comfort 24 hours a day. Work towards having the kind of marriage where you really do feel that you're in this life together. Put in the effort it requires. Break a sweat once in a while. You won't regret it, I promise you.

The 5th Wave   By Rich Tennant

"It's an agreement Arthur and I made-he agrees to stay home from the gym 2 nights a week, and I guarantee that he'll still burn over 300 calories each night."

Chapter 9

Romantic Getaways and Honeymoons

• •

In This Chapter

▶ Making your vacation sexy

▶ Honeymooning

▶ Getting romantic when you're not alone

▶ Vacationing on a budget

• •

The old saying there's no place like home doesn't always apply to sex. In fact, many people have had their most exciting sexual experiences while far, far from home, be it on their honeymoon or just a relaxing vacation. Relaxation is certainly a key word, because the more relaxed you are the better sex you'll have.

Another important ingredient is time. I've stressed over and over that the more time you put into lovemaking the more you'll get out of it. I realize that in the 1990s many people find it hard to put aside time to have sex at all, much less spend quality time lying languidly about naked in bed for hours, but hopefully that won't be true on your vacation. When you take your trip, you'll have read this chapter and will know exactly how to put the zing into your next voyage away from home, be it across the ocean or at a nearby motel. But, to make a vacation sexy, you have to plan ahead . . . and not just to make sure that you have a seat on the plane.

Vacation Foreplay

As I tell you in Chapter 11, the longer foreplay lasts, the stronger is its effect. Now, as far as I am concerned, foreplay can start immediately after you've had an orgasm, through afterplay, and I extend this philosophy to vacations as well.

The minute you begin to plan for a vacation — and that can be the second the plane touches down coming home from the last one — you should use the anticipation to better your sex life, not only on your next vacation, but all during the time leading up to it.

Fantasize

How do you begin your vacation foreplay? Fantasize.

Fantasy is a very important part of this process. By daydreaming about your up-coming vacation, you can begin to relieve the stress of all the work days before you actually take off for parts unknown.

- ✔ Take a break during the day and picture having sex during this vacation. By doing this, you begin the process of foreplay.

- ✔ While you and your partner are actually having sex, fantasize that you're on that vacation together. Pretend that you're on that white-sand beach, or in that cozy tent, or even in your own backyard hammock.

Fantasy can almost always heighten the sensations of lovemaking, particularly when the setting is one that has strong appeal.

So you see, through fantasy, you can make a future vacation into a great sexual stimulator for months prior to packing your bags. And then, by the time that you do arrive at that getaway, you'll be primed to have the best possible sex ever.

Make plans together

Sexual energy doesn't transfer itself between two people only when they're actually having sex. A very important part of being a couple is communication, and what better way to communicate than to plan for an up-coming vacation? Spending time with your partner going over pamphlets and brochures, looking at maps, and discussing the pros and cons of each location is a great way to interact. Your budget may be fixed, but all of the other choices are wide open, so make the most of choosing between beach or mountains; hotel or campsite; great food or wonderful vistas.

Now both of you may well have to compromise, but with the whole wide world laid out in front of you, if the two of you can't find a place that you both would enjoy spending a relaxing week or two, then I have serious doubts as to whether you belong together in the first place.

Prepare for your trip

You have many ways besides just making the nuts-and-bolts plans to stretch out the anticipation of a vacation:

- ✔ If you're going to a foreign country where you don't speak the language, you can take language lessons together. If you can't afford that, then buy a set of tapes and listen to them while you're together in the car. (Make sure that you learn the phrases that make for good lovemaking in each country you'll visit.)

- ✔ To familiarize yourself with the foods of the country you're going to visit, have some meals at restaurants that serve the native fare. Or have a romantic evening at home trying some new recipes or take-out food from these restaurants.

- ✔ If your vacation is going to involve sports, then you can train together. Even a bicycle ride to build stamina can be part of vacation foreplay.

- ✔ If you're going to need some clothes for the vacation, go together to a clothing store and help each other pick out what you'll need. When you try on different garments, picture what you'll look like when you're actually there. Make sure that you include something sensual and eye-catching.

- ✔ If there's a movie that has your vacation spot as its location, go rent it. Try pretending that you're the characters in that film. How could you make it sexier?

- ✔ You can also rent travel films. If you've been to that place before, you can take out your own travel pictures and videos. (I hope you've taken some romantic views.)

- ✔ If you want to get fancy, you can even decorate your bedroom with some touches of the place that you're going. A potted palm and some mosquito netting might not only liven up your fantasy life but make your bedroom look a whole lot spiffier as well.

Look for whatever ways you can to build the anticipation and use the energy from those feelings to enhance your sex life while you're still at home. Believe me, the most important part of the body when it comes to sex is not your genitals but your brain. Learn to use your brain creatively, and you'll improve your sex life, not just for the time you're on vacation, but all year long.

What Makes a Vacation Sexy?

To some people, a sexy vacation means only one thing — lying under the sun on a beach on some tropical island. Certainly the atmosphere of a tropical paradise is sexy, especially if the only thing you're wearing all day is a bathing suit, or even less. But to my way of thinking, sexy means stimulating, and that stimulation has to work, not just on your skin, but also on your brain. That's why there are plenty of sexy destinations where the closest grain of sand is hundreds of miles away.

Stimulation of every sort

Many people agree that one of the sexiest places in the entire world is Paris, which even in summer can be cold and gray. But, though you may not get even a hint of a tan in the City of Lights, Paris can stimulate every one of your senses in ways no place else can.

Sharing the finest of foods, gazing at some of the world's greatest art treasures, hearing the beautiful sounds of French being spoken, window shopping among the most fashionable boutiques, and just strolling under the unique Paris skies can't help but make your senses perk up, definitely including your libido — which many people find works overtime whenever they are visiting this French jewel. You may not spend as much time on your back while you're in Paris as you would on a Caribbean isle, but let me assure you, the time you do spend locked in embrace will be memorable.

Atmosphere

While Paris combines so many sensory stimuli, almost any other place in the world you choose will have its share, too. It's only a matter of looking for these stimuli and being aware of how they affect your mood.

- ✔ New York City, with its hustle and bustle, offers an atmosphere where making love can become part of some giant construction project, with the traffic noise a unique background that makes you feel like you're roaring down the track on the subway.

- ✔ Rome, with the ruins of its ancient empire scattered about the city, allows you to pretend you're the emperor and empress of your own sexual empire.

- ✔ Vacationing in wintry climes makes the warmth you'll find huddling under the covers especially cozy and inviting.

Any place can make for a sexy vacation, as long as you import your own sensuality to it.

Vacations for Hobbyists

If the two of you have a hobby and combine your travels with your hobby, that can make a vacation especially fun. I know two people who collect gemstones, and they have a great time going out into the desert to spend a week looking for new stones.

"Digging for rocks in the desert? How can that be sexy?"

If that question pops into your mind, then you still don't get it. Look, no vacation is going to be constant sex. Even honeymooners need to come up for air once in a while.

The idea isn't to pick a vacation locale which offers the best sites for sex, but to pick a place that offers you other types of stimulating activities that keep your mind alert. That way, when you do have sex, all of your senses will be in high gear rather than in neutral. That's what's going to give you great sex instead of so-so sex.

If you enjoy digging for rocks, if finding a specific stone excites you, then at the end of the day you'll be in the perfect mood for sex. On the other hand, if such a vacation doesn't turn you on, well, there's a whole world to explore so cross the deserts off your list and see what sites do appeal to you and to your partner.

Differing expectations

If you both share the same hobby, then a vacation that is centered around that hobby will be great. But if you have different hobbies, then you have to be cautious. If you like to play golf and your wife doesn't, then I can guarantee you that picking a resort with a golf course so that you can spend six hours a day on the links while your wife sits in the room will have her fuming, and your sex life is going to be below par.

Now, if you like to golf, and your wife loves to scuba dive, and the resort has both, then there's nothing wrong with splitting up during the day in order to get back together at night, provided you agree on this beforehand.

What might make such a situation even better is if there are two couples; half of each pair share the same zeal for one activity, and the other half for another (those halves don't need to be of the same sex). That way, each person has companionship both during the day and the night.

Differing skills

I love to ski, and so does my husband, but when we go skiing, we never go on the slopes together. The reason is that we don't ski at the same level, and it would be no fun for him if I were to hold him back. My advice for any couple who are not of equal skill at a sport, and who go to a place where that sport is the main activity, is to split up during the day. Concentrate on the sport, learn to get better at it, enjoy it to its fullest — and then spend the night together.

One of the main reasons that sex can be better on a vacation than at home is that you're both relaxed. If you've spent the day on the ski slope arguing because you go too fast and she goes too slow, then those added hours of companionship aren't going to help you much when you hit the sack that night. This advice applies to skiers, tennis players, golfers, or any other sport where differences in ability can ruin the fun of one or both partners.

Honeymooners

Should honeymooners act any differently than other couples? That depends on their relationship. If you have been living together for two years, if you have already gone on several vacations together, and if this is really just one more, then I wouldn't place any added pressure on this particular vacation to be more sensuous than any other. Obviously, you'll have more time for sex than at home, and the glow from the wedding will rub off so that romance should be thick in the air, but you also don't want to set yourself up for disappointment. If you've already had sex 500 times, you can't realistically expect the earth to move on the 501st.

Some couples who live together take a "vacation" from each other, in the sexual sense, for a month or so prior to the wedding in order to try to make the honeymoon a little extra special. That could work, and there's certainly no harm in being celibate for a short period in order to add some spice to the wedding night. But again, a month without sex is not the same as never having had sex before. This short spell of celibacy may intensify the feelings you have when you do have sex again for the first time, but don't allow your expectations to get overblown, or you may end up regretting the time you spent keeping your distance.

Having sex for the first time on your honeymoon

Now what about you "real" honeymooners, the ones who wait until you're married to have sex? I wish each and every one of you a fabulous honeymoon with mucho orgasms, but I must also throw in a word of caution.

Many couples, especially if they are both inexperienced, take a while to develop sexually. There's a very good chance that the woman's orgasm may prove elusive or that the man will be so excited that he won't last long enough to penetrate his new wife (see Chapter 10).

There will be plenty to get excited about during your honeymoon, as just the sights of each other's bodies will be new, and certainly lying together naked, if that's something you've never done before, will feel exquisite. But sexual performance may need time to develop, and you shouldn't panic if things don't go right the first time. After a while, you'll learn how each other's body responds, and you'll become better lovers, especially if you pay attention to what I tell you in this book.

Where to honeymoon

As far as the setting of a honeymoon goes, I do believe that the traditional island is a good idea, though not necessarily because it will improve your sex life. The idea behind a honeymoon is to get to know each other sexually, of course, but also in every other way. You want to become closer, and so the fewer distractions, the easier it is to concentrate on each other.

Of course, you don't need a tropical paradise to focus all your attention on each other. All you really need are the basics, which are a room with a bed and a lock on the door. But, if you can afford to go away, then being on your own little island will make the experience that much better.

Too much of a good thing

I have one more caution to give honeymooners, and that is not to overdo it. I know that, supposedly, you can't have too much of a good thing, but in reality that's not true.

Certainly, if you take in too much sun and fry your skin to a crisp, you're not going to be in the mood for sex. Or, if you play several hours of tennis after spending several months behind your desk at the office, then the muscle cramps you'll have the next day will definitely cramp your style when it comes to making love. And, if you have a few too many of those tropical rum punches and spend the night worshipping the porcelain god, then that will also put a crimp in your sex life.

And just the way you can abuse the sun, exercise, liquor, or food, you can also abuse sex. There's even a name for one of the diseases a woman can get from too much sex with a new partner. It's called *Honeymoon Cystitis*, and it's basically a vaginal infection. So, while I encourage every honeymoon couple to enjoy sex to the fullest, if it seems that certain parts are feeling slightly worn out, then listen to Mother Nature and give it a rest. You'll have the rest of your lives to have sex, so a few orgasms more or less on your honeymoon won't make that much of a difference.

Getting married on your honeymoon

A growing trend these days is to get married on your honeymoon. Now, if one of my kids were to take off on a vacation and come back to announce that they'd gotten married, I'd have a fit, let me tell you. But there are definitely circumstances where it's appropriate, especially when it's not a first marriage for either partner.

Sometimes the family, or at least the immediate family, can take part in such weddings. A wedding at Disney World, for example, would certainly be an appropriate family setting. And, with people living so far from their families these days, if both sides of the family are going to have to travel anyway, why not bring them to a place that offers them other opportunities to have fun in addition to the wedding?

People who do get married on their honeymoon cite several reasons for choosing this alternative. One is expense. With weddings costing so much, by taking off on your own, you can literally save tens of thousands of dollars. Another major reason is to avoid the time and stress that a big wedding brings. People spend months planning their wedding and — between picking a date that both the church and catering hall have available, selecting your bridal party, sorting through the guest list, and all the other details that are required — having a wedding is no cinch. And, when both people work at full-time jobs, they just may not have the time to plan a full wedding.

On the other hand, bringing back a video of your wedding for two is not necessarily going to satisfy your mother, who had been anticipating that last dance with you since you were little, or your father who had always dreamed of walking you down the aisle.

I believe in tradition, but I recognize that, these days, some of our traditions are no longer practical. And so, while I think it's a pity to exclude your family from your wedding, you have to live in the real world.

Second honeymoons

Second honeymoons are a great idea because you've not only decided to renew your wedding vows, but you're also putting aside a period of time to be with each other. If you have kids and jobs and in-laws and all the other things that married life brings, then those private moments spent on a cruise ship, or even in a motel room, are truly something to treasure.

On a recent Valentine's Day, I was on the Princess Cruises' Love Boat along with 1,600 people who renewed their marriage vows. A minister officiated at the wedding ceremony, and then I got up and gave a little talk. I gave the couples specific instructions on what to do right after the festivities were over — and, by the way that the deck cleared and everybody disappeared downstairs to their cabins, and, by the way the boat rocked afterwards, I think every couple followed my advice exactly!

Many of the couples on the boat were over 50, and, for many of these couples, their sex lives had probably started to wane. Some of this decrease in sexual activity came from circumstances — their busy lives, the lack of privacy from having kids that stay up later than they do, and so on — and some from the physical changes that come with age (for more about that, see Chapter 16).

Now that doesn't mean that sparks can't be made to fly — and they were certainly flying on that Love Boat — but you also shouldn't expect rockets to go off. Hopefully, you know each other's bodies well enough so that you can both derive a lot of pleasure from sex. But don't think that, because the word *honeymoon* is attached to this vacation, the sexual feelings will be quite as powerful as they were during the first one.

Vacations with Kids

It's great to anticipate how sexy your next vacation is going to be, but if you take the kids along, there's a possibility that you'll end up having even less sex than you do at home. The reason for that is that many families end up sharing a room, and nothing puts a bigger damper on sex than having your kids sleeping in the bed next to you.

Obviously, exactly to what extent kids affect your sex life depends on the ages of your children. If they're young enough that they go to bed early and wouldn't wake up if a freight train went through the room, then your sex life may not be overly disrupted. And, while babies do get up in the night, they also nap during the day — and, since you're on vacation, there's no reason not to have your sexual escapades in the afternoon, if that's when baby gives you some time off.

Older children are another story. If they go to bed at the same time you do, and they're sharing your room or tent or camper, then you can say good-bye to having sex. If that's likely to happen, then my advice is to try to plan ahead so that you do give yourself a few nights alone. I know that every couple has to live within their budget, but, because a vacation can be ruined if you're sexually frustrated, put aside some funds to insure that you can get some privacy.

Here are some tips that you may find helpful, depending on the age of your children:

- ✔ The simplest, though most expensive, solution is to rent a separate room for the two of you, maybe even down the hall instead of adjoining, for one or two nights a week.

- ✔ If your kids need a baby-sitter, call ahead and pick places that have that service and, one or two nights, rent another room just for yourselves for the evening.

- ✔ Pick a place to stay that has a supervised play area for children, and then go back up to the room while they're at the pool or beach for some of what a song of note calls "afternoon delight."

- ✔ On a rainy afternoon, drop the kids at a nearby movie theater and head quickly back to the hotel.

- ✔ You may find that renting a house is not only less expensive than staying in hotels, especially since you don't have to eat every meal in a restaurant, but that you'll also have the luxury of having your own bedroom.

- ✔ The cheapest solution is to bring along a watch that has an alarm and set it for two in the morning, when, hopefully, the little darlings will be sound enough asleep that you can have at least a minimum of privacy.

Vacations with a Parent

When a parent has lost a spouse, you may want to take him or her along with you so that he or she is not left alone for the weeks that you're away, or just to give him or her the opportunity of getting away from home. Sleeping accommodations with a parent that you take on vacation can easily be made separate, so that finding the time for sex won't necessarily be a problem. (Actually, taking Grandma or Grandpa along may solve some of the problems you might have in finding time for sex if you have kids, because a grandparent can act as a babysitter and take the children for a walk for an hour or two, giving you some peace.) But romance needs more than just sex, it also requires intimacy, and having another adult along can make that hard to come by.

Though our society looks at senior citizens as being sexless, they're certainly not. Even if they don't have a partner, they definitely remember what it was like to have one. They should understand that you need some time alone, and they probably are already concerned about being a burden, so your parent won't mind letting you go off on your own with your spouse to take a walk or go for a swim or whatever, so that you can be by yourselves now and then.

Vacation Variations

Variety is certainly a way of adding spice to your sex life, and vacations offer ample opportunity for spicy sexual variation.

Vacations at nudist camps

At the end of this chapter, one of the places about which I offer some information is a *naturist,* or nudist, resort. Now, nudist camps are not places where you go especially to have sex. In fact, most are fairly strict about such things. Although you're free to run around naked, which you may find sexy, sex itself is reserved as an indoor activity — unless there are some spots off the beaten path where you can indulge yourself fully in your love for the sun and your partner at the same time.

If you're looking for a place to shed your inhibitions as well as your clothes, you've got plenty of places from which to choose.

✔ The American Association For Nude Recreation has more than 46,000 members.

✔ Nudist clubs are all over the world, with about 200 in the U.S.

✔ You can even take a nudist cruise.

Vacations at sea

Personally, I really enjoy going on a cruise ship, but you know why? They always have a masseur or masseuse on board, and I make sure that I get at least one massage every day. Now, if your partner is good at it, you can offer each other private massages, though you don't need to be on a boat to do that.

Cruise ships pamper you, and since they usually stop at different ports of call, you get a chance to sightsee in an area while keeping all of your belongings in one place. Other benefits of cruise ships are

✔ You get great food (though don't be tempted to eat too much or you'll be too stuffed for sex).

✔ Cruises offer plenty of activities, both on board and in the various ports, and you can meet lots of nice people, a few of whom you may swear you will get together with again some day, but probably never will.

✔ If you want to stay in your cabin the whole time and never see anyone or anything, there's room service 24 hours a day. Just make sure that you ask for a room with a double bed!

Having sex out of doors

Many people enjoy having sex outdoors. That's absolutely a great idea if both partners are into it, but don't let yourselves get too carried away. Here are some tips for making your romp in the sun (or moonlight) an enjoyable one:

✔ Make sure that the place you pick really is private.

✔ Put a blanket underneath you. You don't need to catch poison ivy to have a good time.

✔ If you're under the sun, make sure that you put suntan lotion on the parts of you that haven't yet been exposed to the sun. This is especially important if you're on a boat where the sun's rays get amplified by the water.

✔ You may want to consider some sort of bug repellent so that you don't let your big moment under the sun get interrupted by something as tiny as a mosquito.

Places to Visit

This is a sex book, not a travel book, and as I said early on in this chapter, planning your vacation is half the fun, so I want you to do your homework. But I did decide to give you a few places to consider, just as a jumping off point. Hopefully, some of my insights into why these places are great for a romantic holiday will help you to decide when considering other places. I don't know about you, but I always find the hardest part isn't in finding *a* great place, but choosing from among so many.

The Caribbean

If you live in the East or Midwest, the Caribbean is a great tropical playground. Because the chain of islands is cut off from the full force of the Atlantic, the waters on the Caribbean side of these islands are placid and warm. The climate is also ideal — hot temperatures are especially conducive to romance — and most of the islands have long, private beaches where you can really get to know each other. There are hundreds of resorts in the Caribbean; the following is just a small sampling.

Young Island, St. Vincent

Young Island is a resort that is on its own little island, just off the larger Caribbean nation of St. Vincent. There are only 20 or so cabanas scattered about the island. The ones at the top are the most secluded, and hence the most popular with honeymooners, but being a few yards from the beach isn't bad either.

The resort offers sailing, snorkeling, its own sailboat, tennis, spectacular vistas from sunset point, and plenty of nighttime activities, as well as things to do and see on the main island of St. Vincent. A vacation on Young Island is definitely of the type for two people who are looking forward to spending as much time as possible gazing into each other's eyes. And why not, you're in love, aren't you?

Club Orient, St. Martin

On an island that is half French and half Dutch, you'd expect to find care-free living, and you won't find any place more care-free than Club Orient. Here, you don't even have to decide what to wear, since the whole resort is clothing-optional. You don't even have to unpack!

Club Orient has 84 red pine chalets and studios imported from Finland. Since the aim is to relax, although there's tennis, volleyball, snorkeling, and sailing, you won't find any telephones, radios, or televisions in the rooms. Only *you* provide the indoor entertainment, and that shouldn't be difficult after running around in your birthday suit all day.

Maho Bay Campgrounds, St. Johns

Maho Bay isn't just for those interested in saving money by roughing it a bit, it's also for those who want to help conserve the Caribbean's natural beauty, because this unique resort was constructed for the *ecotourist,* the person who wants to view his environment without destroying it.

This resort was built on land leased from a national park by a New Yorker who wanted to keep it as pristine as possible and decided that tents were the only way to go. He designed special tent-cottages, which make good use of natural light and the cooling trade winds. Guests walk on wooden decks so as not to damage the natural flora, and just about everything is built out of recycled materials.

Maho Bay is one of the Caribbean's most popular resorts, almost always fully booked, and two new developments have now been added further up the mountain. Harmony and Estate Concordia offer a few more touches of civilization, but are as in tune with the environment as possible, from the solar-generated electricity that turns the fans to the compost pile for biodegradable waste.

Since sex is certainly one of Mother Nature's best gifts, how could it not flourish in such an environmentally conscious atmosphere?

Mexico

Somehow water and romance seem to go together, so how about a resort that has 250 pools! Westin's Las Brisas resort in Acapulco not only features the beautiful waters of Santa Lucia Bay, but the rooms are tucked into the hillside with patios overlooking either a private or semi-private pool. The decor is a romantic pink and white, and you can even drive around in your own pink and white Jeep.

With all that water, the main outdoor activities are swimming, sailing, snorkeling, water-skiing, scuba diving, and fishing. Landlubbers get to play golf and tennis. And, if you bring the kids along, there's even child care.

Hawaii

The Hawaiian Islands have long been a traditional honeymoon locale, but they're well suited for lovers of all types. If you want to get away from it all, I suggest visiting the island of Maui. The Lahaina/Kaanapali Beach area offers all the action of Waikiki, but only minutes away are lush tropical sights.

The Westin Maui has 12 acres of its own tropical gardens, plus five pools, a 150-foot water slide, and a $2 million art collection, in case the natural beauty isn't enough for you.

If you're willing to get up early for one of your mornings, I suggest going to the top of Mt. Haleakala to see the sunrise. Ask at your hotel about a tour in which they take you up in a van and then give you a bicycle to get back down the side of the volcano. You won't need any muscles to pedal, but you better hang on tight to those brakes, because this ride will challenge your favorite roller coaster for chills and thrills.

Club Med

Club Med isn't just one place but a whole planet full, because you can find them in Europe, Africa, Asia, the Americas, and the South Pacific. The basic concept at these 100 or so resorts is that you pay one price, and they take care of everything, so you don't have a worry in the world. Many have really great facilities for children, even teaching them circus tricks. You can leave your children in the morning and not have to worry about them all day; with so many other children to play with, they won't even miss you. If you can't figure out what to do with all that free time, then I've been wasting my time.

Among the most romantic Club Med villages is the one in Bora Bora, where you'll share a cabin for two with views of a blue lagoon. Another popular Club Med option for honeymooners (and over 7,000 people spent their honeymoons with the Club last year) is the Club Med sailing cruise ships. They go island hopping all over the world, so you can vary the scenery of your time spent away from home.

Europe

A European vacation or honeymoon is not going to be relaxing, but it is certainly going to be invigorating, and many couch potatoes out there need to get their engines started more than they need a new place to rest their butts.

The Swiss Alps

If you're not into culture, which you'll find in any of the great European cities, then how about majesty? My favorite European destination is the Swiss Alps, where we go for long hikes in summer or for skiing in winter. The vistas are magnificent, and, as far as I'm concerned, a day's worth of exercise is the best stimulant there is.

English-speaking countries

For those of you who are leery of going to a foreign country because of the language barrier, why not visit England or Ireland? London is one of the great cities of the world, and you can go to the theater every night, which will provide wonderful intellectual stimulation — and, as you know, the brain is the main organ as far as sex is concerned.

Although I recommend the countryside only in summer — as it can get very cold at other times of the year, and central heating is scarce, a stay in a lovely English or Irish village is very relaxing and provides an ideal place to get in touch with each other.

Amsterdam

Amsterdam is another European city that I recommend visiting. Every other street has a canal running down its middle, so you go from the hustle and bustle to peace and quiet. And if you might like visiting a red light district to get your sexual engines started, Amsterdam's is one of the largest. I advise against using the services of any of these prostitutes because of the risk of disease, but just fantasizing about what goes on when they close their curtains could make for an enjoyable evening.

Florence

Although I can't tell you about every possible European highlight, since there are so many, I just want to add one more, and that's Florence. Florence is a jewel of a city, with incredible works of art at its many museums. If you can, try staying just outside of the city in a country inn so that you can share in some of the warmth of the Italian people as well as their ancient culture.

Israel

Now I recognize that, apart from some ardent Jews, Israel is not the first place most people would pick as a romantic getaway. But since Israel has a special place in my heart, I had to include it on my list, and since I lost my virginity there, I see no reason why other honeymooners should not do the same!

Israel has great beaches, wonderful natural places to explore, like the Dead Sea, and historical artifacts that you can find nowhere else on Earth. All the events that you may have read about in the Bible took place in this region, and so, when you settle down in bed together at night, you can imagine yourselves back in ancient times obeying God's command to be fruitful and multiply. What could be sexier than that?

Africa

I once went on an African safari in Kenya and Tanzania, thanks to Robin Leach and his TV show, *Lifestyles of the Rich and Famous,* and it was quite a thrill. The trip I went on was of a premier class; although we were living in tents, it was as close to living in a hotel in the bush as you could get. I realize that not everyone can afford such luxurious accommodations, but if it's something you've always dreamed of, then why not save up for it?

Life is too short to forgo our dreams, and if making love to the sounds of wild animals in the distance turns you on, then by all means you should get to do it at least once in your life.

The Good Old Continental U.S.A.

What's great about traveling within the limits of the United States is that you can find just about any type of scenery that you could possibly want. There are vast beaches, soaring mountains, bustling cities, vast empty plains, a Grand Canyon, a Big Sur, and a Little Big Horn.

The one negative to traveling in your own country is that the temptation is there to do things that you also enjoy at home: eating a Big Mac, doing the crossword puzzle, watching the ball game, having a Bud, having sex the same old way.

My advice is that, when you're on vacation, try to do things that are different. If you've never had Thai food, then that's the time to try it. If white water rafting sounds invigorating, then go for it. Wear that bikini or see-through teddy for him. Pull over and pick those wildflowers for her (unless they're legally protected). Make a point of using different positions or making love at different times of the day or night.

By breaking out of your routines, you will not only be taking advantage of your vacation time, but you may even pick up some new habits that you'll enjoy sharing all year long.

The Poconos

The resorts in the Pocono mountains have tried to paint themselves as the ideal place for a romantic getaway or honeymoon, and since they've gone out of their way to add some sexy touches to their rooms — like indoor swimming pools and glass tubs shaped like champagne glasses — then why not go out of your way to use them?

One piece of advice that I would like to offer is to do your homework when picking which Pocono resort to visit. Some are better than others, so try to get a personal recommendation either from friends who have been there or from a travel agent that you trust. And remember, the pools and glass tubs are only in the most costly rooms.

The gambling capitals: Las Vegas and Atlantic City

I am as far from a high roller as you can get. As soon as I lose $10 in the slot machines, I'm out of there. But for many people, gambling is an exciting pastime.

I could give you many words of caution on this subject, but I'll only stick to my area of expertise. If you both win, the sex will be great, but if you both lose, the sex will probably be lousy. So remember when you're betting that it's not only money that's riding on that table.

On the other hand, the gambling strips at these cities never shut down, so they offer you the opportunity to live life according to your schedule, not someone else's. That can be very attractive, and very sensuous. Just don't get so caught up in the 24-hour activities that you don't leave any time for sex.

Desert Shadow Inn of Palm Springs

I didn't think it fair to only list a nudist resort that is off-shore, so I'm adding one of many land-locked nudist resorts, the Desert Shadow Inn, which combines luxury, a beautiful setting, and nature.

Again, nudists don't think of walking around without clothes as being sexy, but a lot of other people do, and a stay at a place like this might do more for you than going somewhere else where you have to keep your clothes on when you leave your hotel room.

The Beverly Hills Hotel and Bungalows

I fly all over the country all year round, and I would need a whole book to tell you of all the places I've been, and what's sexy about them, but I couldn't very well have a chapter on travel without mentioning my favorite hotel in the country: The Beverly Hills Hotel and Bungalows.

This hotel had been closed for several years for remodeling, and boy was I disappointed. But now it's back, better than ever, and there are several reasons why I believe that it makes for a true romantic getaway.

It's all done in pink, and, because it's grounds are vast, even though you're in Los Angeles (actually Beverly Hills), you might just as well be in some tropical paradise. Yet, at the same time, you're in the heart of show business. You will see movie moguls at the Polo Lounge, and people will get phone calls by the pool (even if it's only a friend who was told to call them there just to have their name announced over the loudspeaker). There are starlets; there are men with fat cigars; and there's an aura around the place that makes you feel as if Marilyn Monroe or Clark Gable might really walk by. It has that old-time Hollywood glamour, and to me that's very sexy. Of course, it's also *very* expensive. But it's worth saving up for.

Sexy but Cheap Vacations

I think vacations are very important — everyone needs some time to relax — but a vacation doesn't have to cost a fortune to be relaxing or sexy. (In fact, some people can't relax on a vacation if they constantly feel that the meter is running.) So here are some tips on having a vacation that won't cost a lot but can still offer possibilities for great sex.

Camping

The key for making camping fun and sexy is to know what you're doing. Sleeping in a tent that leaks or picking a spot that swarms of mosquitoes call home can ruin a vacation. If you've never gone camping before, my advice is to try it out with some other experienced hands first. Then, when you've learned the ropes, the two of you can go out on your own.

To make camping sexy, you have to include Mother Nature. I don't mean that you have to make love under the stars, because your naked bodies will make tempting targets for every flying insect for miles. No, what I'm talking about is learning to appreciate your surroundings. Staring out at a mountain lake is so peaceful, so relaxing, that if you're with someone you love, you just can't help wanting to put your arms around them. Or, if you go for a walk, try to look for the little things of beauty and point them out to each other. Communing with nature is good for the soul, and also for the libido.

The local motel

There are several reasons to visit a motel. One is the presence of young children at home whose constant interruptions can really spoil a couple's love life. But you don't have to have kids at home to make going to a motel special. One of the reasons people travel is for a change of scenery. All of us tend to feel freer when we're away from our home base. So, whether this motel is an hour's drive away or down the street, going there can make a difference to your love life.

Sexing up the home front

As the old saying goes, if you can't bring Mohammed to the mountain, bring the mountain to Mohammed. Some people stay home because they can't afford to go away, others prefer to spend their vacations at home so that they can accomplish certain tasks that, otherwise, they'd never get around to, including major projects like putting up paneling or painting.

But even if you've been working all day, don't waste your nights. It is still a vacation. You're not going to your regular job, so try to do a few other things differently.

- Dress up for dinner at home or dine naked.
- Put some scented candles in the bedroom (it might help kill the smell of the paint, too).
- Take a bath together.
- Buy a new feather duster and play with it in bed.
- Get some washable crayons and doodle all over each other.
- Cover each other with whipped cream and have dessert.

You get the picture. Don't fill your vacation with drudgery, but put aside some time to have fun as well.

The 5th Wave **By Rich Tennant**

"I KNOW WHAT A ROMANTIC GETAWAY IS. IT'S WHEN MY PARENTS TELL ME TO GET AWAY FROM THE HOUSE FOR A FEW HOURS."

Part III
Doing It

The 5th Wave   By Rich Tennant

"IF WE ARE GOING TO DO THIS, CAN I ASK THAT WE _NOT_ DO IT IN THE ROOM YOU KEEP YOUR PIRANHA FISH COLLECTION?"

In this part...

*I*f you want to be a rock'n' roll star, first you have to learn to play the guitar. If you want to be a computer wiz, first you have to learn to point and click. And if you want to become a great lover, you have to develop certain skills that you'll find in these chapters. By the way, you mustn't stop reading until the end, because what goes on after you "do it" is just as important as all the rest of "doing it."

Chapter 10
The First Time

*O*ne of the great things about sex is that, after you do it, after you experience that great feeling that only sex can bring, you get to do it over and over again, literally thousands of times during a lifetime. Talk about a gift that keeps on giving . . . and it doesn't even need batteries!

To the extent that, when you have sex, you are probably going to wind up with an orgasm or two, there are similarities among all sexual episodes. But you'll also find that each time is very different. At times when passions are running high, your orgasm will feel like an explosion. Other times, sex has a more gentle quality but is still very satisfying. However, the one time that is like no other — because it can only happen once — is your first time.

Virginity Is Not a Renewable Resource

Many people have the wrong attitude about the first time. They look at it as a barrier to reaching adulthood, one which they must cross as soon as possible. Or else they feel that it is a sign of weakness, as if everybody walking down the street knows that they're a virgin and is laughing behind their backs. Whatever your own feelings about being a virgin, society then reinforces that image through peer pressure and the storylines of movies and television shows in which the hero is a macho guy who always gets the girl — and always gets her into bed.

Even your own family can pressure you. Great aunts are forever asking young-sters why they don't have boyfriends or girlfriends yet. There are mothers who take their teenage daughters to the gynecologist to be fitted for a diaphragm or get a prescription for the pill even though the daughters don't have boyfriends and aren't ready for what, to them, is a very embarrassing step. And then there are even some fathers who, when their sons reach a certain age, march them off to visit a prostitute and prove their manhood.

What's the rush?

I say, what's the rush?

Yes, the sooner you start having sex, the more sex you'll have had over the course of a lifetime. But if you're not ready for sex, or if you have sex with the wrong people, you'll end up a lousy lover, and you'll never have great sex. And then there are those who start off so quickly that they burn out and give up on sex altogether.

There are no guarantees that having your first sexual encounter at an early age means that you won't regret it later on. That's why I believe that you shouldn't jump into bed with someone just to get it over with, though I know that many people still do exactly that.

A few men lose their virginity to prostitutes; many men go only one level up: a local girl who is known to "put out." This is usually some girl who desperately craves attention, especially that of men. Maybe she is overweight and thinks she can't find someone who'll have sex with her because he loves her, or maybe she was sexually molested as a child and has a very low sense of self-esteem, but the one thing that every guy in the neighborhood knows about her is that she never says no. It may be an older brother, or some of the other guys who have used her services, but they bring the young man to this girl.

Many young people of both sexes, in America at least, lose their virginity in the backseat of a car. They barely are able to get their clothes off, they're worried that someone will see them, they're in cramped quarters that make every move uncomfortable, and their goal is to get it over with as quickly as possible.

Treasured memories

To me, all of these scenarios are sad. Unless you were drunk out of your mind (another sad scene), you will never forget when, where, and with whom you lost your virginity. That memory can be a cold one — with someone you barely knew — or it can be a warm, loving memory — with a man or woman you really cared for, and who cared for you. It doesn't matter that you may no longer be together; what really matters is that, at the time, all of the vibrations were good ones.

Although I don't necessarily expect you to wait until you are married to have sex for the first time, I do caution you not to throw the moment away, but to treasure it and respect it. Make it special and you'll enjoy replaying the moment over and over again in your head. Make it sordid and, whenever it crops up, you'll want to push it out of your mind. Isn't it obvious which is the better set of memories?

First Time's No Charm

Let me admit something here, something that I say in other parts of this book as well, and that is your first time may not be the greatest from purely a sexual point of view. Most women do not have an orgasm their first time. And, for very many men, their first time is over so quickly that they aren't even sure that it really happened at all. Then why, you might ask, if people don't have such great sex their first time around, am I putting so much emphasis on making it special?

Making it special

Sex is not just having an orgasm. Sex is a form of communicating with your partner, sharing a gamut of sensations from the touch of your skin together to kissing, caressing, and then, finally, orgasm. When two people are really in love, they don't just want an orgasm, they want to melt into each other and become one. You certainly wouldn't want to become one with a promiscuous person or a prostitute.

You may not be able to have great sex the first time, but that doesn't mean that the entire experience can't be a great one. There are several reasons to make the first time special:

- Your first sexual experience can affect your view of sex for the rest of your life. You can have a wonderful, pleasurable, and loving experience (even if it's not one for the highlight films) if the person with whom you share that first time is somebody important to you, and if you are both doing it out of love for one another and not just to relieve your sexual frustrations.

- Another reason not to share your first time with a stranger or casual acquaintance is that, whether or not you have great sex, at the very least you don't want it to be an embarrassing moment, which it certainly could be.

Most people fumble around a bit their first time. Some women experience a bit of pain when their hymen is penetrated. Some men have difficulties figuring out exactly how to put their penis into the woman's vagina. Isn't it better to know that the person you are with cares about you and will try to protect your feelings? If the most vivid memory you have of your first time is of being highly embarrassed, of someone maybe even laughing at you, what kind of a souvenir is that?

✔ Of course, there are also those sexually transmitted diseases, like AIDS. Promiscuous people, which includes prostitutes and the "easy lay," are much more likely to be infected with some disease.

You're not the last virgin in America

"But Dr. Ruth," I hear you cry plaintively, "I'm the only one of my friends left who is still a virgin. I can't go on like this. I have to get laid!"

If that is really your only problem, then I suggest a little white lie.

The next time your friends kid you about being a virgin, tell them that you're not one anymore. You don't have to say more than that, except maybe to give them a wink. Since a good number of them are probably exaggerating their sexual prowess also, I don't think that they'll question you too much.

I am tempted to write that it is amazing how times have changed, so that something that was once a virtue to be honored — that is, virginity — is now a badge of dishonor. I say "tempted" because, although it may appear that virginity is passé, in fact it's not. Certainly most men today would still prefer that the woman they marry be a virgin — at least they say they do. And, in this day and age of rampant diseases, I believe that most women would jump at the chance to get their hands on a virgin for a husband.

So you see, virginity is still treasured, it just seems as if it isn't.

Now the truth is that the majority of people do not wait until they get married to have sex. The main reasons so many people are having sex before they get married these days are the widespread availability of contraceptives to prevent unintended pregnancies, and the fact that people are waiting until they are much older than they used to to get married.

But having sex before you get married is quite a different thing than having sex with just anybody. You may not end up marrying the boyfriend or girlfriend you have in your college years. But, if you spend two or three years constantly in one another's company, if you say that you love each other and show it in a hundred ways, then you certainly have a relationship in which sex can blossom. Such a union is much closer to marriage than a one-night stand. Thousands of miles closer.

The dangers of Demon Rum

I've got one more point to make before I get off my soapbox on this issue and get to the nuts and bolts — so to speak — of your first time, and that has to do with liquor (and, I suppose, other drugs as well). A lot of people have lost their virginity unwittingly because they were too high to know what was happening to them.

The binge drinking that goes on at our college campuses has definitely gotten out of hand. I don't object to drinking per se, but the bingeing that takes place arises mostly from peer pressure, and I do object whenever anybody does anything for the wrong reasons.

So, if you want to get falling-down drunk from time to time, if that gives you pleasure, be my guest. But I ask you not to do it in situations where you might wind up getting hurt. Obviously, driving when you drink is out of the question. But also, particularly if you are a woman, don't imbibe great quantities of alcohol if you know you're going to wind up someplace private with a lot of drunken people of the opposite sex.

In other words, if you're a woman at a fraternity party and you have drunk more than you can handle, you've got problems. I have heard from too many young women that they've lost their virginity at such affairs, and it makes me sad. So don't do it.

Giving the Green Light

The first step in losing your virginity is to let the other person know that you are ready. Even for two people who have been married for 20 years, giving the go-ahead signal can sometimes be a problem. (She's trying on some new clothes in front of him, getting dressed and undressed; he gets turned on, but she's not even close to being in the mood because the red dress she thought would go perfectly with her new bag is the wrong shade and clashes. . . .)

If you've been telling a boyfriend or girlfriend "no" over and over again for quite some time, you can't expect him or her to guess when you're finally ready. And, in any case, it's going to take a little preparation on both your parts, so it isn't something you want to spring on your partner at the last minute.

Using protection

In Chapter 6, I discuss in great detail AIDS testing and how to bring up that subject, so I won't get into it here. But testing for AIDS is something that you need to do ahead of time, as is choosing a method of contraception. Because you're going to be nervous the first time, no matter what, there's no point in adding to your sense of unease by having doubts as to whether you're protected against an unintended pregnancy.

Don't fall for the myth that you can't get pregnant your first time, because you most certainly can. (I debunk this and other myths about getting pregnant in Chapter 1.)

✔ If you're on the pill, don't forget that it does not protect you against sexually transmitted diseases. You may want to use a condom as well, so you have to plan for that possibility by making your purchase ahead of time. (You don't want to use the one your boyfriend's been carrying around in his wallet for the last six months, even if he did write your name on it in Magic Marker after you found it in there!)

✔ If you've decided on another method, like the diaphragm, you have to go to your gynecologist or to a clinic to have it fitted.

Because condoms are widely available, men don't have such a problem with getting protection, unless they're too embarrassed to buy them. I sometimes wonder whether men object to using condoms mostly because of the way the condoms feel or because it's their responsibility to buy them. However, I know that, as a reader of this book, you won't have that problem because you realize how important it is to be protected.

Setting the stage

Exactly how you tell your partner that you're ready to have sex depends on several factors:

✔ Is your partner a virgin, somewhat experienced, very experienced? A very experienced partner can provide more support, but you may actually be less nervous with an inexperienced person, because he or she will be less likely to notice if you make any "mistakes."

✔ How far have the two of you already gone? If you're already into heavy petting — or even oral sex — you'll be much less inhibited.

✔ Is there a place where you already go to kiss and hug and maybe pet? Having privacy is particularly important your first time, because you don't need to be made any more nervous than you'll already be.

Giving notice

Assuming that you've already taken care of the AIDS testing matter and the use of contraceptives, should you tell your partner ahead of time that tonight's the night, or should you wait until you're actually snuggling up? I know that many people, when they are nervous about something, don't like to think about it ahead of time but prefer to just take the plunge — no pun intended. There are times when I agree with that philosophy, but not when it comes to sex.

If your first sexual experience has some negative sides to it, it will affect the next time you try. Although you certainly cannot guarantee perfection, you do want to be mentally prepared, and your partner should be as well. If you and your partner are half naked and caressing each other — something that you've done before — and suddenly you give the green light to go all the way, your partner's already turned on and his or her first reaction is going to be, "Hooray, let's go for it."

That's only normal. You, on the other hand, may want to go slowly, gently. That's why it's better to tell your partner ahead of time, before you get to that place where you're going to have sex. Let him or her know that you are ready, say that you're nervous, and ask to take things slowly. If your partner approaches the situation with the mind-set to tread lightly, then you're both likely to do so, and you'll be more likely to enjoy it.

The First Time for Women

Although I certainly hope that all goes well for any of you women having intercourse for the first time, there are two possible stumbling blocks that you should be aware of: breaking the hymen and the possibility of vaginismus.

Breaking the hymen

The *hymen* is a piece of tissue that covers the entrance to the vagina (see Chapter 3). Not every virgin has an intact hymen. Many women break their hymens either when playing sports, particularly bicycling or horseback riding, or by using tampons. If your hymen is already broken, then having sex for the first time probably won't cause you any pain or bleeding. If it's not broken, then you may feel some pain, and you will bleed a little. The pain, however, is very brief and most probably, in the heat of the moment, you will quickly forget it.

If you're concerned about bleeding the first time you have sex, just make sure that you put a towel underneath you.

If you're too tight

Vaginismus is an involuntary tightening of the vaginal muscles that usually occurs if the woman is nervous. Because you will probably be nervous the first time, vaginismus could happen to you. I'm not saying it will happen, so don't get too worked up over the possibility or you may actually cause yourself to tighten up. Just be aware that it does sometimes happen and don't think that it is a permanent condition.

Some women write to me and complain that they are just built too small to have sex. Many of these women are just experiencing vaginismus and don't realize it. The vagina is made to expand — after all, a baby can come out of there — so there's certainly room for a penis.

How can you tell if your partner's difficulty with penetrating your vagina is caused by vaginismus or just lousy aim? First of all, you can probably feel that your vaginal muscles are tighter than normal. But a simple check with your own finger will also give you an answer. Even if you've never tried to put your fingers in your vagina before, just know that it should be very easy to slip them in there; if it's not, then you are experiencing vaginismus.

What should you do if you experience vaginismus?

- ✔ Engage in plenty of foreplay with your partner (read the next chapter to find out more about foreplay). If you're excited, then vaginismus is less likely to be a problem. So, if your partner didn't give you enough foreplay, go back and start again.

  Being excited will also mean that you are lubricating. If you can't get your juices flowing but still want to go ahead with trying to have intercourse, you can use a lubricant.

  Be aware that Vaseline and other oil-based products can cause the latex in a condom to deteriorate very quickly. If your partner is using a condom, and you are not producing enough lubrication or don't have a water-based lubricant like KY Jelly on hand, you have to stop short of intercourse.

✔ Relax. The one thing you should not do is try too hard. Just because you can't have sexual intercourse one day doesn't mean that you won't be able to do it the next. Very few women have vaginismus so severe that they require treatment. Just give it a little time, and I'm sure you'll be fine.

✔ I have heard from women who have a sort of permanent vaginismus, so that the entrance to their vagina is always tight. They have reported that by using a series of larger and larger expanding *speculums* (the instrument used by your gynecologist to examine your vagina), they have been able to expand their muscles to permit intercourse, which was very painful to them before. This rarely happens, but it's good to know that, if you run into this problem, there is hope.

✔ Another tip I can pass on to make your first time easier is to put a pillow under your behind. Changing the angle of entry may make it easier for the man to penetrate your vagina, making the whole process easier for you as well.

What to expect

As far as the pleasure you will derive from this first time, you should keep one thing in mind: The majority of women cannot reach an orgasm through intercourse alone. Some women eventually do learn how; others never do. Whichever group you turn out to be in, do not expect to have an orgasm through intercourse your very first time. Now that doesn't mean that you can't have an orgasm at all. Your partner can give you an orgasm using his fingers or tongue or big toe, but he probably won't be able to do it just with his penis inside your vagina.

The First Time for Men

A man may face many hidden traps during his first time having sex; for the vast majority of men, even if they do have problems, they will overcome them eventually.

Controlling your erection

Being nervous can wreak havoc with your ability to have an erection — and who wouldn't be nervous at a time like this? Some men can't get an erection before things get started. Others have an erection, but, when they have difficulties trying to slip their penis into the woman, they quickly develop a case of the nerves, and there goes Mr. Happy. Even if your erection doesn't disappear altogether, if your penis gets a little soft, then you will definitely have problems putting it where you so want it to go.

If any of these problems happens, hopefully you have taken my advice and your partner is someone who cares for you. You can take a minute to two to calm your nerves and then have her help you to get a new erection by rubbing or sucking on your penis. Then you can try again.

Your partner can also help by parting the lips of her vagina with her fingers to make it easier for you to enter. If she's not excited and lubricating, you can use a lubricant. Remember, don't use a lubricant that's oil-based if you're using a condom; if you have one handy, use a condom that's already lubricated.

Premature ejaculation

The problem that is more likely to cause trouble your first time is *premature ejaculation.* Now I'm not talking about the standard form of premature ejaculation in which a man ejaculates faster than he wants to once he is inside the woman. In that scenario, once you're inside, you've at least reached your initial goal: the loss of your virginity. But some men get so excited by the thought of what they are about to do that they have their orgasm before they penetrate, which is immediately followed by a loss of their erection and the impossibility of intercourse.

Is this embarrassing? You bet. Is it the end of the world? Definitely not.

Even if you are going to have problems with premature ejaculation (which you can learn how to treat in Chapter 22), a man can usually keep his erection at least through the process of penetration, so you will probably be successful the next time you try. If you are really such a jackrabbit that, after a half dozen times, you haven't managed to keep yourself from ejaculating before you penetrate your partner, then you should definitely try the exercises that I recommend in Chapter 22; if they don't work, then go to see a sex therapist. (I give you tips for choosing a sex therapist in Appendix A.)

Working through the problem

For the most part, the problems men encounter — either not having an erection or not being able to control their ability to ejaculate — are mental problems rather than physical ones. Physical causes of impotence are difficult to treat, but the mental problems can usually be corrected, so don't give up hope.

The most important thing for both men and women to remember is that the first time is only the first step on the road to sexual fulfillment. As long as you make sure that you are sexually literate (which means that you read this book very carefully and pay attention to the advice you find on these pages), I have no doubt that you can become a great lover in no time at all.

The First Time All Over Again

As much sexual experience as you might have, there's always a certain tension when you have sex with a new partner for the first time. Some people get practically addicted to that tension, which is the reason that they keep jumping from bed to bed. But for many people, that tension causes the same types of problems that can be encountered during the very first time, and even some new ones.

The one advantage a virgin has is a clean slate. There's no extra baggage caused by bad experiences. And a virgin hasn't developed a set of habits without which orgasm is not attainable. For the inexperienced person, everything is possible.

The longer your previous relationship lasted, the harder it will be to have sex with a new person for the first time. You'll not only be nervous about your own performance, but there will be an almost irresistible urge to compare this new person with your former partner.

Try as hard as you can not to give into the urge to compare partners. No two people are alike, so sex with each new person is going to be different. Since the old person is now out of your life, what good can it do you to compare? If this new person is a lousy lover, but you like them enough for other reasons to stay together, then make a point of teaching them how to become a better lover. You can't teach a new sex partner how to make love to you the identical way your old lover did — and you'd be better off not dredging up those old memories anyway. Instead, you have to help each new partner become the best lover he or she can possibly be.

Another stumbling block to having sex with a new partner can be the negative baggage that you might be bringing with you. If you're coming out of a rotten relationship, especially one in which you were abused in some way, then you're going to be gun-shy; that's only natural. You have to let the new person know that you're extra sensitive so that they can be careful of what they say or do. It can take longer to heal an emotional wound than a physical one, but the right person can help speed up the healing process immensely.

If you're coming out of a very long-term relationship, one that has perhaps lasted a decade or two, then another factor that will make it more difficult to adapt to this new person in your life is that you and your body are now a good deal older. Unless you're Jane Fonda, your body is no longer what it was, and you're going to be a bit self-conscious about that. My advice to you is to try to get over that hump as quickly as possible.

Your new partner wouldn't be going to bed with you if he or she didn't find you attractive. So resist the temptation of trying to hide your body. Adopt the philosophy of the nudists, which is that you can actually feel freer naked than with clothes on because you no longer have to worry about hiding your body. Don't slip quickly under the covers, but flaunt your body. If the other person gets turned off, then you're just facilitating the inevitable, but I almost guarantee you that that won't happen.

Hopefully, during your past relationships, you at least learned how your body responds, and that's a very important piece of information. Don't be shy about telling this new person what pleases you. This knowledge may be all that you've been able to bring out of your past relationship, and it would be a shame to let it go to waste.

Chapter 11
Foreplay: Mood Magic

- -

In This Chapter
▶ Speaking terms of endearment
▶ Taking your time
▶ Creating an atmosphere
▶ Mapping the body — where cartography meets sex

- -

*F*oreplay is probably one of the most misunderstood words in the sexual vocabulary. There are still some men out there who, when they hear the word *foreplay*, think of golf instead of sex. But slowly and surely, the male population is learning that foreplay is as important to good sex as using a nine iron is to good golf.

In its simplest form, foreplay means the touching and caressing that goes on between two people just prior to intercourse. Foreplay helps both partners experience the physical manifestations of arousal necessary for sexual satisfaction.

Foreplay for Life

According to my philosophy, not only must foreplay be extended as long as possible when the two of you get into bed, but foreplay should begin as early as the *afterplay* — the caressing that goes on after sexual intercourse — of the previous sexual encounter.

In other words, I believe that afterplay can be considered part of the foreplay for the next lovemaking session, whether your next lovemaking takes place the same night or a week later.

If you're interested in becoming the best lover you can be, foreplay should be something you take into consideration with each interaction that the two of you have.

Right now, some of you are probably saying, "Hold it, Dr. Ruth, you mean to say when I ask my wife to pass the salt at dinner it's part of foreplay?"

My response is — absolutely. Which is why you shouldn't simply say "Pass the salt," but you should add an endearment, like "Honey" or "Love" or even just her name. You see, the better you treat her, and the better she treats you, the better will be your sex life.

If you're still having trouble buying this idea, consider the opposite tack:

- ✔ How sexy is it when someone calls you a jerk?
- ✔ If someone is rude to you, does it get your testosterone flowing or your adrenaline?

Of course such behavior is not sexy, especially if it takes place regularly. But, in the same way that rude behavior kindles the flames of anger, kind behavior kindles the sparks of love.

If you are kind and loving even during the most mundane moments, you are setting yourself up for terrific sex when the time for lovemaking does come around.

Linking the Emotional to the Physical

To be clearer about the difference between what's considered standard foreplay and my Dr. Ruth version, I'd like to separate, for a moment, the physical effects from the emotional effects of foreplay, especially regarding the role they play in the arousal levels of women.

People usually think of foreplay as a simple cause-and-effect mechanism, setting the stage for intercourse to take place from the physical point of view:

- ✔ In order for sexual intercourse to take place, the man's penis must be erect.
- ✔ It helps sexual intercourse if the woman's vagina is lubricating.

Exciting both partners so that these physical manifestations of sexual arousal take place is the minimal role of foreplay.

Because a young man can get an erection simply by thinking about the lovemaking that is going to take place, his version of foreplay could be just walking into the bedroom. That will change as he gets older, but, since most young men don't know that and in the heat of passion don't much care either, many of them grow impatient and try to make foreplay last as short a time as possible.

You may have heard that women don't reach their sexual peak until they're in their thirties. There is no physical reason for this, and in many women there is absolutely no truth to this either. Some women do find that sex gets better as they get older, however, and I believe that one of the reasons has nothing to do with women but instead has to do with their men.

For some men, it is only when they are out of their twenties that they begin to appreciate the effects of foreplay, and so it is only then that their women begin to get enough foreplay to fully appreciate sex themselves. And once women begin enjoying sex more, they begin wanting to have sex more often.

The Sexual Response Cycle

The reason that there are sex therapists in the world, such as myself, is due in great part to Dr. William Masters and Dr. Virginia Johnson, who studied the sexual response cycle in the late 1950s and early 1960s.

How did they study the sexual response cycle? They observed more than 10,000 sexual acts in their laboratories. Since I think even the most serious voyeur would have had enough after about the first 1,000, you can appreciate that they were really very dedicated scientists.

And scientists they were, because when I say *observe,* I don't just mean watch. The people who took part in these studies were wired up so that Masters and Johnson could tell exactly what was going on, including how much lubrication the woman was making and the quantity of ejaculate the man released.

As a result of these studies, Masters and Johnson came up with four distinct phases for human sexual response. Later, Dr. Helen Singer Kaplan, under whom I trained, created her own model, which included elements of theirs as well as one of her own.

Examining an individual's *sexual response cycle* is integral to the diagnosis that sex therapists make of anyone who comes to them with a sexual problem. It is also very important for you to understand the various categories of the sexual response cycle in order to become the best possible lover, so read the following definitions very carefully.

✔ **Sexual Desire Phase:** The Sexual Desire Phase, sometimes called the *libido,* precedes actual physical or psychological stimulation. This is the part of the model that is Dr. Kaplan's alone. Dr. Kaplan believes that these inner sexual feelings are triggered by certain chemicals in the body, to the greatest degree by *testosterone,* the male sex hormone, which is also present in females. It is upon these feelings that sexual excitement builds.

Dr. Kaplan examined and labeled this phase because of her work in sexual therapy, where she noted that some people's desire for sex was so low that they rarely or never reached the other phases of the cycle. It was only by studying what was going on in this earlier stage that she could discover what was causing their difficulties.

✔ **Excitement Phase:** The Excitement Phase arises when the genitals experience *vasocongestion*, which is a swelling caused by an increase in blood filling the tissues.

In men, this excitement leads to an erection. In women, this excitement leads to a swelling of the clitoris and vaginal lips, increased vaginal lubrication, increased breast size, and erection of the nipples. Other physical signs of this phase include increased heartbeat, breathing rate, and blood pressure. Arm and leg muscles may begin to tense; in some people, there is a "sex flush" on the upper abdomen that may spread to the chest area.

This phase is usually generated by one or a combination of physical, visual, or psychological stimuli, which can be caused either by oneself or a partner.

✔ **Plateau Phase:** In the Plateau Phase, certain aspects of the Excitement Phase reach a slightly higher level, with tensions building.

According to Masters and Johnson, men exhibit two physical signs during this period:

- First, a few droplets of fluid are released at the head of the penis to act as a lubricant for the sperm. (These droplets also contain sperm, which is what makes the withdrawal method so risky. Chapter 7 gives more information on the pitfalls of the so-called pull-out method of birth control.)

- Also, the man's testes enlarge and are pulled closer to the body.

Dr. Kaplan incorporates all of these reactions of the Plateau Phase as an extension of the Excitement Phase because the individual does not sense any difference between the excitement and plateau stages, making these subtle differences of no value to her in treating a sexual dysfunction.

✔ **Orgasm Phase:** During the Orgasm Phase, in both men and women, your body goes through a whole series of muscular contractions and spasms, including facial contortions, an increased respiratory rate and heart beat, and a further increase in blood pressure. Your genitals also experience strong contractions.

The man undergoes the further contraction of ejaculation, which occurs in two stages: the moment of inevitability, characterized by sensations that mark the so-called point of no return (which I talk more about in Chapter 22), followed immediately by ejaculation.

✔ **Resolution Phase:** In this last phase (which only Masters and Johnson include), the body slowly returns to normal — the physical conditions that existed before the excitement stage began. This Resolution Phase is much longer for women than for men, making it the basis for afterplay.

In addition, men have the *refractory period*, which is the time needed after orgasm before the man can respond to more sexual stimulation and have another erection and orgasm. In young men, this period can be as short as a few minutes; the length of the refractory period grows as a man ages.

 The man reaches the Excitement Phase much more quickly than the woman, and the woman has a much longer Resolution Phase. It's to help compensate for this difference that I suggest extending the concept of foreplay as much as possible.

Flowers as Foreplay

Have you men ever thought of offering flowers as an act of foreplay?

You certainly consider flowers as part of courtship, as well as a sign of love. But such gifts are also part of foreplay. When a woman receives a bouquet of flowers from her loved one, there's every chance that she will feel sexually excited by this. She may even start lubricating a little.

 Because women do take longer to get fully aroused, the earlier you send her these flowers, the more time she will have to reap a positive effect from them. My advice is not to bring flowers home with you, but rather to send them ahead of time. With any luck, by the time you walk through the door, the woman you love will already be well on her way to the Excitement Phase of sexual arousal.

 Although I am all in favor of variety and spontaneity — so that it is quite all right to use that excitation that she is feeling and occasionally jump right into bed before going out on that date — the longer you can extend foreplay, the better the end result will usually be.

Thinking ahead

Foreplay isn't just an art to be practiced on your partner, it can also be a method of visualization for yourself so that, when the time comes to make love, you're absolutely ready. For this kind of foreplay to work best, you should have a particular time planned for the lovemaking session.

If you're not living with your partner, and you have a date on Saturday night, then you can take a quick break during the day to visualize some of what will be going on as the evening progresses. If you do have a live-in partner, then from time to time make plans in advance to have sex so that you can luxuriate in brief fantasies during the course of the day in order to prepare.

Dinner for two

One way to prolong foreplay is to have a romantic dinner. Now, a romantic dinner doesn't have to be an expensive dinner. Sure, a beautiful restaurant with attentive waiters and wonderful food helps set the mood, but so does Chinese take-out eaten on the floor, so long as the two of you devote your attention to each other.

Paying total attention to one another is very important. I've heard of many fights that have occurred among couples as a result of a meal out at a restaurant. Maybe she got so picky about the food that it made him upset, or he started ogling a beautiful woman, making his partner angry. And too much food or drink can certainly put both parties down for the count, as far as a later sexual episode is concerned.

A romantic meal is not romantic only because of the setting or the food but because of the intimacy of spending an hour or so together *focused only on one another.* That means that the communication between the two people — which includes talking, touching, and staring into each other's eyes — is the key ingredient.

That's why you can have a very romantic evening at home, because your home can have fewer distractions. On the other hand, if your little dear ones are at home feeding their spinach puree to the dog, or if only one partner always assumes the duties of cooking and cleaning for such an evening, then that is not going to be so romantic, and you're better off going to a restaurant, even if it's an inexpensive one.

Using your lips

In my book, *The Art of Arousal*, I chose a painting by the Italian Renaissance painter Correggio to be the artwork for the cover. The picture depicts the god, Jupiter, transformed into a cloud, kissing Io. To me, that image illustrates one of the great ways to kiss: so lightly, so softly, with the lips barely touching, so that it seems as if you are kissing a cloud. But there are so many ways to kiss — passionately or lightly, with mouths open or closed, with tongues probing or not — that kissing is truly a gift of the gods.

Most of us think of lovers kissing as automatic, and for most people it is. But not for everyone. I regularly get letters — mostly from women — who complain that their husbands don't kiss them enough. Some of these men do kiss, but only perfunctorily. Others don't kiss at all.

My first piece of advice for people who feel that their lovers aren't kissing them enough is to check their breath. That's not to say that bad breath is usually at fault, but because it's a simple thing to cure, it should be the first line of attack. (Since you can't check your breath yourself, you'll have to ask your partner to do it, or, if that's too embarrassing, maybe your dentist or a good friend can help.)

If it's your partner, not you, who has the problem with frequent bad breath, I suggest you come right out and say so — though not necessarily in the middle of an embrace. Make sure that you have some mouthwash in the medicine chest and then let them know, gently, that they tend to have a problem with bad breath. Show your partner how much you prefer the minty flavor of mouthwash by rewarding him or her with a big kiss.

Another problem with kissing is *French,* or deep-tongue, *kissing.* Some people adore this form of play, while others hate it. Because so many people are orally oriented — witness how much eating and gum-chewing we do — to those people who really want to engage in deep kissing, it's a problem if their mates don't. Since I don't believe in forcing anybody to do anything, the best advice I can give to people who like their kisses to be deep and long is to find out before you get married if there's going to be a problem. Sometimes these problems crop up later in life, but at least you will have tried to head them off at the pass.

Here again, some people who avoid French kissing do so for a reason; they have problems breathing through their noses. If you really love this art form, and your partner can't satisfy you because of a breathing problem, have your partner go see a doctor, as help may be available.

Kissing isn't limited to mouths. You can kiss each other all over your bodies, and both the kisser and kissee should be thoroughly enjoying the experience. If you don't want to have oral sex because you are squeamish about the messy results, you can still cover your lover's genitals with light kisses, because that is rarely sufficient stimulation to induce orgasm. A few gentle kisses now and then on your partner's genitals will at least let your partner know that, even though you don't want to give them an orgasm that way, it's not because you are repulsed by this part of their anatomy, but just that you prefer to have sex in other ways.

The art of massage

In an earlier section of this chapter, "Dinner for two," I recommend that you and your partner touch each other as one type of communication you can use at a restaurant. But, in a public place, this can only go so far — holding hands, maybe playing footsie.

I know that some people use the cover of a tablecloth to go further, but that's not something that I recommend. You might get so lost in the moment that you forget that other people are around, and when they notice what you're up to — and they will, as people-watching is part of what going to a restaurant is all about — you're both going to be embarrassed.

But once you're back at your home, you can do all the touching that you want. Now what often happens is that the touching that people do as they remove their clothes leads right to sex. But if you're in the mood for stretching things out — and this is not something that has to happen every time — then giving each other a massage is a sensual and relaxing way to begin.

Make the moment as sensuous as you can.

- ✔ Dim the lights or use candles.

- ✔ Use some massage oils.

- ✔ Whatever you do, don't rush the massage; try to really feel each other as much as possible.

- ✔ Alternate between strong rubs and gentle caresses. Let the sensitive nerve-endings in your fingertips help you get to know your partner in a new way.

Another sensuous way of prolonging foreplay is to play in some water. Climbing into a hot tub or Jacuzzi together is a great way to unwind, especially at night with only the soft lights glowing from underneath the water.

Hot tubs are a great place to have foreplay, but they can be a dangerous place to have sex. The soothing effects from the elevated water temperature can cause physical problems, especially if your blood pressure and heart beat are on the rise from sexual excitement. It's not that I'm saying never to have sex in your hot tub, as the temptation is certainly going to be irresistible at times, but this chapter is about foreplay, and that's what I recommend that the tub be used for.

If you don't have a hot tub, you can substitute a bathtub or shower. Washing is a way of gently exploring each other's bodies while rendering a service at the same time.

Some people will not engage in sex with their partners because they are not sure how clean their genitals are. Well, if a woman is washing a man's penis, for example, she can be absolutely sure that it is clean. You may well laugh at this piece of advice, but it is something that I have recommended to many couples where squeamishness or body odors were a problem, and it usually works.

Body mapping

Although you certainly touch your partner's body all over during massage, the goal then is to create sensations, not discover which parts of your partner's body are the most sensitive. With *body mapping,* on the other hand, you aim to discover all of the most sensitive parts of one another's bodies: the breasts, the wrists, the thighs. . . .

The art of body mapping is not only something you do to another person; it is also something that you can do to yourself. Sometimes it is not just where you are touched that creates the best sensations, but how you are touched. Since only you can feel which ways of touching — gentle, rough, continuous, feathery — bring you the most pleasure, you may have to experiment on yourself as well as on your partner.

Body mapping is one of those gifts that keep on giving because, after you and your partner have explored your bodies and discovered the most sensuous places and what feels best on them, you'll be able to use those techniques again and again throughout your love life. So body mapping is far from just a way to extend foreplay; it is an exercise that each couple should engage in at least once in order to build a data-bank of information for future lovemaking.

You have now entered . . . the erogenous zone

Erogenous zones are the parts of your body that, due to the concentration of nerve endings, are more sensitive to stimulation than the other parts.

Now some erogenous zones are pretty universal. Most women enjoy having a man pay attention to their breasts — and most men don't mind obliging them in this. But, guys, don't forget what you learned in body mapping. If she likes a soft touch rather than a rough one, or vice versa, then that's what you should do.

Remember that, in foreplay, you're trying to arouse each other, so you have to do what is going to help *your partner* become the most aroused. That's not to say that, if you really enjoy kissing her nipples but that's not number one on her list, you can't do some nipple kissing. You can, and you should. But if she really likes to have her nipples softly feathered with the tip of your finger, then you should also do some of that as well.

Erogenous zones can be anywhere on your body, but here are some of the more popular ones:

- The buttocks
- The perineum (that little line between the anus and the genitals)
- Behind the knees
- The nape of the neck
- And, of course, the genitals

Following the map

It doesn't do you any good to have a map if you don't use it, so once you've discovered which parts of the body your lover likes to have caressed, kissed, licked, sucked, nibbled, tickled, massaged, kneaded, stroked, nuzzled, probed, cupped, pinched, rubbed, oiled, and in case I left anything out, everything else, go ahead and do exactly that.

Switching Gears: Engaging the Genitals

No matter how long you extend the more languorous, romantic aspects of foreplay, eventually you reach the point of engaging in traditional foreplay involving the genitals. Remember that the ultimate goal of foreplay is to get both partners ready to have an orgasm. Also keep in mind that a young man does not need very much preparation, but a woman almost always does. The reasons are both physical and psychological.

Looking under the hood — foreplay for her

The physical reason that women usually need more time to have an orgasm is that the main source of a woman's orgasm is her clitoris.

Most women need direct physical contact on their clitorises to have an orgasm. For the average woman, sexual intercourse alone does not give the clitoris sufficient stimulation for her to have an orgasm. This is because the penis does not come into direct contact with the clitoris during sex. One way to solve this problem is for the man to stimulate the woman's clitoris before sexual intercourse, and that is a primary function of foreplay.

Some women can get sufficiently aroused during foreplay that they can then have an orgasm during intercourse without further direct stimulation to the clitoris. Others need that direct stimulation and so might have their orgasms either before or after intercourse, or will use a position for intercourse that enables direct clitoral stimulation. I get to positions in Chapter 12. For now, just concentrate on foreplay's role in giving a woman an orgasm.

Stimulating the clitoris

In dealing with the clitoris, there is a small Catch-22.

The clitoris is very sensitive, which is why it can produce an orgasm when stimulated. But, because it is so sensitive, stimulating the clitoris can also be painful. The solution to this problem is good communication between the man and the woman — and a soft touch.

Every woman's clitoris is different, and only she knows what kind of stimulation she likes.

If you're a woman, it's very important that you tell your partner what works best for you. You don't have to do this in words. If you are uncomfortable talking about it, you can guide his hand with yours. Let him know how hard he should rub, whether he should touch the clitoris itself or just the area around the clitoris, what rhythms to use — fast or slow — and when to change those rhythms, if need be.

After a while, if the man is paying attention, he'll get the hang of it and be able to give you an orgasm without any further instruction.

Using more than just fingers

You may have heard me say that a man can use his finger or his tongue or his big toe to stimulate the clitoris. That's true, though I think that the big toe method hasn't broken into the main stream quite yet. From what people report to me, fingers are the number-one choice, the tongue is number two, and in third place is something that doesn't grow on people: *vibrators.*

Many people think of vibrators as good only for self-pleasuring, but if a woman needs really strong stimulation, or if the man is of an advanced age or incapacitated in some way so that this aspect of foreplay is too tiresome or impossible, then there's nothing wrong in the man using a vibrator to perform this task. (You should take some precautions when using a vibrator, and I go into those in Chapter 19.) But, in most cases, a mechanical device is not needed, and fingers serve quite nicely.

One cautionary note is that fingers are tipped by nails, which can be quite sharp. Most men don't have long nails, so that usually isn't a problem, but if you notice any sharp edges, file them off beforehand.

A nice addition to the finger is lubrication in order to minimize the friction on the clitoris. In most cases, the woman's own lubrication will do fine, and the man can dip his finger into the woman's vagina occasionally to make sure that the area around the clitoris stays moist. Saliva can also be used as a lubricant. There are plenty of products sold for this purpose, as well, if the woman's own natural lubricants have dried up due to age or if she has a problem lubricating.

All lubricants are not the same. There's a variety that you can purchase in any drug store, like KY Jelly, which, although absolutely functional, doesn't have a lot of pizzazz. But, if you make your purchase at either an adult store or through a catalog, you can choose from a large selection that come in various flavors and colors.

No matter how excited a woman gets and how much lubrication she makes, it is often not an inexhaustible supply. Sometimes she can run out of lubrication and then foreplay, or later intercourse, can become painful. Both partners should be aware of how moist the area is and make whatever adjustments are necessary.

The man shouldn't limit his attention to just the clitoris. The whole vulva is quite sensitive (see Chapter 3), and the woman may also like having one or more fingers placed inside of her vagina. For this, you might want to try a two-hand approach.

If a man lets his fingers do the walking and explores all around a woman's genitals, he may run into the anus, just down the road from the vagina. Now, although the anus is also a sensitive area, unless it's just been cleaned, a lot of germs are likely to be lurking about. These germs do not belong inside the vagina, where they can multiply and cause infections. So the man should take every precaution to keep his fingers away from the source of germs if he is then going to put them into the woman's vagina.

The tongue: Master of foreplay

The tongue seems to have been perfectly constructed for the art of foreplay, and not just for kissing.

- Tongues provide their own lubrication in the form of saliva.
- Tongues are softer than fingertips and have no sharp instruments attached to them like nails.
- Tongues can also be manipulated in many different types of strokes, from the long lap to the short dart.

It's no wonder that a man who has perfected the art of *cunnilingus,* oral sex upon a woman, is considered to be a great lover by many women.

Not all women enjoy oral sex. For a variety of reasons, some women do not like to have cunnilingus performed on them.

- Some women may prefer to have their lover's face next to theirs.

> ✔ Some women may object because of religious beliefs.
>
> ✔ Some women may feel guilty, thinking that they may have to return the favor, which is something that they are not willing to do.

Whatever the woman's reason, this is a wish to be respected. If the woman you are with does not want to engage in oral sex, just put it aside, at least for the time being.

Checking the dipstick — foreplay for him

As a man gets older, he is less easily able to get an erection.

In adolescent males, erections occur at any time, sometimes even at quite embarrassing times, like when the teacher calls them up to the blackboard. (I'm not saying that blackboards, per se, are arousing, but if a guy has been sitting a long time and suddenly gets up, blood flow will increase, and some of that blood is likely to go to his penis, particularly if he was just thinking about the cute girl sitting in front of him.)

As a man gets older, he is still able to have *psychogenic erections* (erections that pop up by themselves), but eventually he loses even that ability and will not be able to have an erection without physical stimulation (I discuss this change in Chapter 22). That stimulation, whether a necessity or not, has to be considered part of foreplay.

In many cases, your partner can easily figure out which caresses work best to get a rise out of you. Some men, however, especially those who have masturbated a lot, have developed a specific pattern to getting their erections which only they can produce, so it's possible that a man will have to start the process of foreplay on himself. Once he is erect, the woman can take over.

Fellatio

Oral sex on a man, called *fellatio,* can be performed to various degrees.

One thing that the woman should know is that the most sensitive area of the penis is usually on the underside, just below the head, so there is no need to "deep throat" a man to give him intense pleasure.

A woman can simply lick the penis, without actually putting the whole organ in her mouth, and still provide the man with a lot of pleasure. When women tell me that they have a problem with fellatio, I often tell them to think of the penis as an ice cream cone and pretend that they are licking it.

When a woman performs oral sex as a part of foreplay, she needn't be concerned about the man ejaculating, although she may well encounter some

Cowper's fluid (pre-ejaculatory secretions). If she wants to make sure that she doesn't go too far in pleasing him, she should stop every once in a while and ask him what stage of arousal he is in. If he indicates that orgasm is close, and if oral foreplay is all she wants to do, she should stop.

Actually, the preceding tip goes for any part of foreplay, especially if the man has any problems with premature ejaculation. As in Chapter 22, it is relatively simple for a man to learn to sense the *premonitory sensation,* the point of no return. All men should learn to recognize the premonitory sensation so that they don't ejaculate before they want to, either in foreplay or during intercourse.

Good communications, whether verbal or just via actions, are an integral part to all aspects of sex, and no one should hesitate to tell the other to stop doing something — either because it's uncomfortable or because it feels too good.

Other zones

The penis isn't the only part of the man that can be used to arouse him. Here are a few, but not all, of the parts of a man's body which can also be integrated into foreplay:

- ✔ The testicles definitely are an erogenous zone (though one that should be handled rather gently, because the wrong move could put a quick end to all the work you've put into foreplay).
- ✔ Many men enjoy having their nipples either stroked or sucked.
- ✔ Also on this list of erogenous zones is the anus. Again, be careful not to spread germs from the anus to other parts of the genitals.

When to End Foreplay

How can you tell when you've had enough foreplay? You can't. Again, that's why communication is so vital to good sex. Assuming the main point of extended foreplay is to get the woman ready to have an orgasm, she has to let her partner know when she's ready. Ready for what? That's a very good question.

If the woman is capable of getting sufficiently aroused to have an orgasm during intercourse, then the answer is that she should tell her partner, either verbally or by touching him in some way, that he should now put his penis into her vagina. But, if she's not capable of having an orgasm this way, she may want him to continue to stimulate her clitoris up until the point where she does have an orgasm.

There's no right or wrong answer here. The couple should concentrate on what works best so that, in the end, both partners are satisfied. Every couple is different and so it's up to each couple to write their own ending. As long as both partners are working towards the same goal, then the good guys (and that means both of you) will always win.

Chapter 12
Variations on a Theme

* *

* *

*F*oreplay, I think we can agree, is an erotic activity which has, as its goal, the arousal of both partners. In this chapter, I advance from foreplay to "doing it" — another politely ambiguous term. But what is "it"?

Is "it" only sexual intercourse? Now, my edition of Webster's dictionary defines sexual intercourse as "genital contact, usually between humans, especially the insertion of the penis into the vagina followed by ejaculation."

But that definition leaves out a lot of what happens between two people when they are "doing it." What happened to oral sex, anal sex, mutual masturbation? Aren't people having sex when they're doing those things? And since women can't ejaculate, and so many women cannot have an orgasm from intercourse alone, aren't they entitled to some pleasure from "it?"

Semantics was never my strong point, so let me just give you a brief description of what this chapter is about: any activity between two consenting adults, who are not virgins, which produces orgasms (I tell you all about orgasms in the next chapter).

Why am I excluding virgins? If two teenagers have oral sex, but not intercourse, are they still virgins? Since there's no chance of a pregnancy occurring, I suppose you have to say that yes they are. But if two people who have had intercourse decide on a particular evening to pick from the sexual menu only oral sex, and could in mid-course decide to change their minds and have intercourse, then I think there is a distinction. It's not a strong one, but we have to draw the line somewhere.

So whether we call it "doing it," "going all the way," "having sex," or "playing hide the salami," basically we will be discussing different ways two people can help each other to experience one or more orgasms.

Getting There Is Half the Fun

Although orgasm is certainly one of the goals of intercourse for both partners, how you reach that goal is where the fun comes in.

Now this is not the *Kama Sutra,* so I am not going to give you every possible position, especially because I don't suppose that many of you are acrobats. (My lawyer suggested I put several paragraphs at this point stating that I am not responsible for any injuries that may occur as a result of lovemaking using any of these positions. In this case, I'll take his advice up to a point and say that you should always use caution, particularly if you know that you have a particular weakness like a bad back. On the other hand, one of the reasons I always tell couples to lock the door when they are having sex is to keep children and lawyers out of the bedroom.)

What I do give you in this chapter are the basics, along with the advantages of each position. Don't look for any preaching here, because I don't believe that the use of one position is any more moral or normal than another. Certainly, some positions are more popular than others, but there are good reasons for that.

There's a risk in reading this chapter — you may get sexually aroused. Don't be alarmed if reading this chapter turns you on. In fact, maybe you should become alarmed if you don't feel certain sensations "down there."

The Good Old Missionary Position

The missionary position is no more than the male-superior position; that is, the man on top, woman on the bottom, and peanut butter in between. (Scratch that last part. You'd end up sticking to each other and have to call 911.)

Because humans have probably been using the male-superior position since the time of the cave man, you may wonder why it is called the missionary position. According to Polish anthropologist, Bronislaw Malinowski, this position was nicknamed that by the indigenous people of the South Pacific. It seems that South Pacific folks didn't limit themselves to only one position, and when the missionaries arrived they were shocked by this "sinful" behavior. Along with teaching the natives about Christianity, the missionaries also advocated the use of the male-superior position, and that's how it got its name.

If you've ever seen other animals mating, you know that this position is pretty much unique to humans. This is partially because, for many other species, the male-superior position would be impossible (think of turtles, for example) or at best awkward (giraffes).

Now one reason we humans might have made the missionary position so popular is that it differentiates us from animals, but it also has several physical drawbacks. (See the section, "Recognizing drawbacks," for details.) But I don't think that only practical considerations popularized this position, or that men want to show that they are not animals, or even the idea that men want to be the aggressors and get on top. (Certainly when a big male lion grabs his mate's neck in his jaws as he mounts her from behind, he's not being wimpy.)

Face-to-face wins out

I believe most researchers agree that, because we humans communicate so much with each other, either through speech or touch or looks, a position that puts us face to face during sex is the one that most people will choose. Of course, I suppose we shouldn't negate as a factor for this position's popularity that it conveniently allows both partners to remain under the covers during the chilly months.

The missionary position is not entirely static, as there are variations. Although the woman has to spread her legs to allow the man entry, she doesn't just have to lie flat on her back. Most women bend their knees somewhat, but they can actually put their knees in a whole range of positions, including wrapped around the man's back.

In the missionary position, the man doesn't have quite the same range of motion that the woman has, but he can try to ride higher — that is, in a more upright position — which may allow his pubic bone to rub against the clitoris, giving it more stimulation.

Recognizing drawbacks

As popular as the missionary position may be, it does have some drawbacks.

- ✔ The most obvious drawback of the missionary position is that the penis thrusting in and out of the vagina does not provide sufficient stimulation to the clitoris for many women to reach orgasm.

  Nor can the man reach the clitoris with his fingers because he is resting on his arms; therefore, the clitoral stimulation necessary for a woman's orgasm is not often present.

- ✔ The woman's range of motion is quite limited in the missionary position, other than to thrust upwards in time with her partner.

- ✔ If the act of intercourse goes on too long, or if the man is tired or weak for some other reason, the missionary position can be uncomfortable.

- ✔ Research has shown that, if a man is tensing his muscles, as he must do to hold himself up, it affects his ability to control ejaculation, so the missionary position can aggravate problems of premature ejaculation.

Some men ask me why women don't just stimulate themselves, since they can usually reach their own clitoris in the missionary position. Although I can't give them an exact answer, I believe that the reason lies in the same psychological factors that keep many women from masturbating. To some degree, this comes from a society which tells women that it's not nice to touch down there (though, of course, society has said the same thing to young men, and it doesn't keep more than a small fraction from doing it).

Women do seem to prefer to be stimulated rather than to stimulate themselves, however, and that's really all we need to know. So, whether you like it or not, and I think most men like it, the power of the female orgasm during sex is in men's hands . . . or tongues, or big toes.

Orgasmic variation

A variation of the missionary position is to have the woman lie back on the edge of the bed or table or boat deck (see, I never want you to become predictable) while the man keeps his feet on the ground, assuming this platform is the right height to allow penetration comfortably for both. Because his weight is no longer on his arms, the man can now use his hands to touch the woman's clitoris and stimulate her to orgasm.

This variation is one of several positions that allow the man to reach a woman's clitoris. These positions are why I say that it is possible for a woman to have an orgasm during intercourse. Often the key is to use a position other than the missionary position.

These other positions also can make a simultaneous orgasm more feasible, though it is still a tricky operation. Because the woman usually takes longer, the man has to be able to keep his level of arousal sufficiently high to remain erect but not so high as to have an orgasm, while keeping in close contact with his lover to try to gauge when she is going to be ready to have her orgasm and, at that point, try to get into higher gear. The problem comes from that little devil of a psychological factor, *spectatoring* — becoming too involved in the process to relax and enjoy it.

The Female-Superior Position

Now that we are approaching equality of the sexes, there's no reason for only men to take the superior position. Actually, none of these positions is new, although they do go in and out of fashion. We do know that more women are going on top of their men than did a decade or two ago.

It's kind of surprising that the female-superior position isn't more popular, actually, because the female-superior position offers several major advantages:

- ✔ The most important advantage of the female-superior position is that the man can caress the woman's clitoris with his fingers.

- ✔ The man can both see and fondle the woman's breasts — a double turn-on for men, who are more visually oriented when it comes to sex.

- ✔ Men also report being able to "last" longer in the female-superior position.

- ✔ From the woman's point of view, she can control the depth of penetration and speed of thrust (which sound more like the controls on a Boeing 747 than sexual descriptions). Because every woman develops her own unique pattern that suits her best, this kind of control can be very helpful to bring her to a fulfilling orgasm.

The female-superior position can be more tiring to the woman, especially if it takes her a while to have her orgasm. If she suddenly starts wondering why things are taking so long because she's losing strength, then the spectatoring reflex may set in (see previous section), making it even more difficult for her to have an orgasm. But, although some women find being on top a bit too athletic for their enjoyment, it's a position worth attempting at least once in a while.

In case you're assuming that the woman always has to be facing the man's head when she goes on top, that is not the case. She can also turn around so that her buttocks are facing his face. In fact, in the same love-making session she can turn both ways (or spin like a top, if she's so inclined).

For the female-superior position to work best, the man needs to have a very strong erection. If this position doesn't work for you at night, try it in the morning, when a man's erections are usually the hardest ones of the day.

Taking Her from Behind

The taking-her-from-behind position is not anal sex but vaginal sex, where the man enters the woman from behind, the way most animals do. Penetration can be a little more tricky to achieve this way, but most couples can figure out a way to make this position work for them.

Doggy style, as this position is called, allows the man to reach around and stimulate the woman's clitoris and also gives him an exciting rear view that many men like. This position can be a little hard on the woman's knees, but that is basically its only drawback. One reason this position is not more popular is probably that the woman's view isn't very scenic, unless there's a nice Cezanne landscape in front of her, or a mirror.

In any rear-entry position, the man can thrust deeper into the woman, and so the possibility exists of his hitting an ovary or other organ. This can be as painful to her as hitting a testicle is to him, so caution is advised.

Some people enjoy having their anuses penetrated by a finger as they're about to reach orgasm. This is certainly a possibility for the man to do to the woman in any of the rear-entry positions. Once the finger has gone into the anus, be very careful not to then put that finger into the vagina so as not to give the woman a vaginal infection.

The standing canine

Depending on the height of the two partners, rear entry can sometimes be accomplished while both partners have their feet on the ground, with the woman bending over, probably holding onto a chair or some other sturdy object.

This is one of those semi-acrobatic positions that are good for adding variety and keeping boredom out of the bedroom, but not always satisfactory to either partner because the couple has to concentrate on their sexual arousal while also trying to keep their balance.

One hint I can offer for making this position work for you, at least in a trial run, is to pay attention to your respective heights and make alterations if necessary. Because I am only 4-feet 7-inches tall, I can't reach the microphone or be seen over the podium when giving a lecture (you didn't think I was going to talk about how I manage these sexual positions, did you?), so I ask for a box to be placed behind the podium.

If there is a big height disparity between the partners, the woman or man can stand on an object, like a phone book, so that the man can place his penis inside of her without either one having to do a deep knee bend, a position which is hard to hold while trying to enjoy sex.

Splitting the difference

Another position, called the *cuissade,* is half-missionary and half-rear-entry (and maybe half-baked, too, but I don't want any of you to accuse me of having left out your favorite position).

- ✔ The woman lies on her back but turns half way and puts her leg up into the air (she gets extra points from the judges if she keeps her toes pointed North).
- ✔ The man straddles the leg on the bed and enters her, while holding himself up with his arms.

This position will definitely cause some heavy breathing, but whether or not any orgasms result will depend mostly on your physical stamina.

Spooning

Another variation of the doggy style, and a much more relaxing one, is the spoon position. Here, the man still enters the woman's vagina from the back but, instead of the woman being on her knees, she's lying down on her side. Many couples are familiar with this position because it's only a short thrust away from a position in which they sometimes sleep.

East Side, West Side, Side by Side

In the side-by-side position, also called the *scissors position,* the woman lies on her back and the man lies next to her; he swivels his hips, interlaces his legs with hers, and enters her vagina from the side. If you're not very good at tying knots, then you may have some initial difficulties getting into this position, but it is a very good one, so don't give up. (If you really have difficulties, contact your nearest sailor.)

Here, again, the man can easily stimulate the woman's clitoris while thrusting inside of her, as well as touch her breasts (and she can touch his). Each partner can see the other's face and, if the temperature is low (or modesty is high), everyone can stay snugly under the covers. It makes you wonder why you'd even bother with the missionary position (unless you have some missionaries visiting you from the South Pacific).

Lap Dancing

Lap dancing is a position that's recently become popular (at least that's what I hear) in certain strip clubs. The way it's practiced in the clubs, however, the man keeps his clothes on, making certain aspects of the act more difficult.

The basic idea, when not done in public, is for the man to sit down and the woman to then sit on top of him so that his penis slips into her vagina. If the woman is sitting so that she is facing him, she doesn't have the control over thrusting that she does in the female-superior position, and, with a woman sitting on top of him, the man can't do very much thrusting either. But, if you sit on his penis with your back to him, then you can keep your feet on the floor and go up and down as you would in the female-superior position.

The Oceanic Position

What positions did the natives in the South Pacific favor before those missionaries got there? One, which has been nicknamed *the Oceanic Position,* would be just about impossible for most Westerners of today. It seems that, because the natives didn't have chairs, they spent a lot time squatting, which they then adapted to sex. The woman lies down and spreads her legs and the man then squats over her and inserts his penis into her. Supposedly, this gave the man the ability to prolong intercourse for long periods. But, unless they happen to be catchers on a baseball team, I doubt that most men could last very long at all in this position.

Standing Up

Unless your bodies match up perfectly well in terms of height and shape, the standing-up position winds up being a difficult one to achieve. If the man is strong enough, he can pick the woman up so that they can fit, but the exertion is likely to lessen his enjoyment, to say the least.

Personally, I think that the standing-up position appears a lot more frequently in porno movies than in people's bedrooms. But, since I'm not invited into most bedrooms, maybe more sexual athletes are out there than I realize.

The standing-up position is sometimes depicted with both partners in the shower. It appears to be very romantic, but, as you may know, more accidents occur in the bath and shower than anywhere else, including our nation's highways. Throw some acrobatic sex into this mixture and the likelihood of injuring yourself approaches that of speeding along at 100 mph on a side street.

I am all for experimentation and making sex fun, but sex isn't an athletic event. Nor are any Olympic medals given out for degrees of sexual difficulty. Orgasms by themselves are a great reward, and, if you can have them without risking life and limb, then I see no reason to go the extreme route. On the other hand, while I like to ski down a mountain, other people like to hot-dog it, so if you can experiment safely, and it gives you an extra kick, be my guest.

Oral Sex: Using Your Mouth

Cunnilingus and fellatio as a form of foreplay are covered in Chapter 11, but obviously either or both partners can continue to excite the other's sex organ with their mouths and tongues until their partner has an orgasm. Of course, there is the issue of the ejaculate, which does bother some women.

You can engage in fellatio without necessarily having the man ejaculate into your mouth.

- ✔ It's best if the man helps out by letting you know when he is close to having his orgasm. That way, you can put your mouth out of range while continuing to help him climax with your hands and fingers.

- ✔ After a while, you may be able to sense certain signs, such as a strengthening of the erection, which indicate an approaching orgasm, and duck out of the way without forcing the man to spoil his concentration.

- ✔ You can keep a towel or tissue close by so that, if the man does ejaculate into your mouth, you can easily spit it out without swallowing it. On the other hand, if you do swallow it, not much harm can come of it. Some women actually even like the taste.

One area I haven't touched upon yet are the positions that you can use for oral sex. Certainly there is no right way or wrong way; whatever suits you is best. But one way does have a name of its own — "69", which refers to mutual oral sex. The name comes from the shape of the two bodies as they lie against each other, upside down to one another. Although it really doesn't matter which partner is on top, the man usually is the one to assume this role because he is likely to have to strain his neck more if he is on the bottom. (Sometimes a pillow under his neck can help.) It may be most comfortable for both partners if both lie on their sides.

What the man has to remember is that oral sex doesn't have to be strictly oral. Because most women like the sensation of having something in their vaginas when they are sexually aroused, the man can insert one or two fingers while performing oral sex to imitate the thrusting of a penis. This feeling of having her clitoris stimulated at the same time as she feels her vagina stretched is what makes some women like oral sex so much.

Anal Sex: Handle with Care

The anus does have a lot of nerve endings, so anal sex can be pleasurable to both the man and the woman, though of course the woman is not going to have an orgasm from anal sex alone.

Anal sex has certain guidelines that you must follow if you're going to perform anal sex safely.

- ✔ The first guideline has to do with cleanliness. The basic purpose of the anus is to keep fecal matter, which is full of germs, inside the colon until it is time to be released. Obviously, merely wiping the area with some tissue isn't going to remove all of the germs, so you must wash the area thoroughly.

- ✔ There are many folds on the inside of the anus, so even an enema won't necessarily remove all germs; therefore, you must definitely use a condom during anal sex.

- ✔ Because the anus was not designed to be penetrated from the outside, you need to use a lubricant to help keep the anal tissue from ripping.

- ✔ Of course, you must never insert the penis into the vagina following anal sex without first removing the condom.

If the male half of a heterosexual couple would like to try out the sensations of anal intercourse, the woman could either use her fingers or try a small dildo (there are some made especially for this purpose) or a small vibrator (see Chapter 19).

Outercourse: Heavy Petting Revisited

In the old days, outercourse used to be called *heavy petting* — a phrase which is pretty much going out of style, as are the reasons behind it. In past generations, the concept of premarital sexual intercourse was not one that many couples would engage in, but since their sexual tensions weren't any lower than those of today, they would mutually release each other from these tensions by masturbating each other.

Some of today's young people may not have the same moral or religious reasons for refraining from sexual intercourse, but because of the fear of AIDS, many are reverting to the method used by their parents and just giving it a new name.

Who's on third?

In deciding how far a couple would go, young people used to use baseball terminology. If he got his arm around her at the movies, he was at first base; if he touched her breast, he had reached second; and so on. Home base was intercourse, which left third base for everything in between.

Today's name for third base is *outercourse,* which can range from each partner remaining dressed and rubbing up against the other, to some fumbling around through clothes to touch each other's genitals, to full nudity and a combination of rubbing and touching.

Remember, some STDs like herpes and genital warts can be passed from one partner to another without penetration. If you're engaging in full body contact in the nude, you should be aware that you're at risk of contracting or spreading a venereal disease. (Chapter 21 deals with STDs and how to reduce your risk of getting them.)

Avoiding date rape

Another reason that performing outercourse in the nude can be somewhat dangerous is that sometimes matters can get out of hand, and outercourse becomes intercourse. Sometimes, this is mutually consented upon, and sometimes it is not. When it's not, it's often called *date rape,* a situation that I have some reservations about.

I am certainly against rape of any sort, and if two people are having outercourse with their clothes on and the man forces himself on the woman, then I believe that is rape. But if a woman allows herself to get into bed with a naked man without any of her clothes on, then, to my way of thinking, she shares some of the responsibility if something happens that she doesn't want to have happen. I'm not excusing the man; I'm just saying that the woman has allowed things to go too far if she is really sure that she does not want to have intercourse.

Certainly, if the couple has been going out for a long time and have a relationship, the woman should be able to have more confidence in such a situation. But if it is really only a date, even if it is the third or fourth or fifth date, she is playing with fire with such behavior. Sorry to say, some women are being burned.

Safe Sex: Playing Alone Together

I generally do not use the term safe sex, because safety from sexually transmitted diseases in most sexual scenarios is not 100 percent. Condoms do break, some viruses can penetrate condoms, and oral sex is not 100-percent safe either.

The one form of sex that is absolutely safe is self-masturbation.

Now you can masturbate alone or with a partner who is also self-masturbating. As long as neither of you touches the other, so that no bodily fluids are exchanged in any way, this sex is absolutely safe sex. You cannot give yourself a sexually transmitted disease, nor can you give a sexually transmitted disease to someone with whom you don't have direct contact.

At one time, self-masturbation with a partner would probably have been considered kinky. I still don't believe that it is practiced by many couples, but I'm sure that some do. It's certainly not as satisfying as the other methods, even if you do hold each other before and afterwards. But self-masturbation does serve a purpose, and it is worth considering if you are both very concerned about STDs and want something more than self-masturbation while alone.

Sex during Pregnancy

Since reproduction is the evolutionary reason that sex exists in the first place, it does happen now and again that a woman will find herself pregnant as a result of having had sex. If this is an unintended pregnancy, then it's a good thing that you're reading this book, so that it doesn't have to happen again. But just because you're pregnant, your sex life doesn't have to take a nine-month hiatus.

Orgasms are okay, with changes

Some women feel even more aroused while pregnant than when they're not pregnant, because the added blood flow in the area mimics the vasocongestion that occurs during sexual excitation. But, although sex can continue unabated during pregnancy, you will need to make some changes and take some precautions.

A question that many pregnant women have is whether or not it is dangerous to the fetus if the woman has an orgasm. The answer is no.

Although an orgasm will trigger contractions in both pregnant and nonpregnant women, including contractions in the uterus, these contractions are not the same type of contractions associated with labor. Nor will they trigger labor contractions. So pregnant women can have all the orgasms they want up until the moment of giving birth. Some obstetricians even suggest to an overdue woman that she have sex because it will relax her and possibly facilitate the birth.

Change positions

Although you can safely have orgasms during pregnancy, you will have to make changes in the ways that you get those orgasms. As your belly gets bigger, certain positions become less comfortable and possibly even dangerous. Some blood vessels can be cut off if you lie on your back too long, especially if there is a man on top of you, so the missionary position is one that you should drop once you reach your fourth month of pregnancy.

But that shouldn't prevent any couple from enjoying sex, because the other positions already described work quite well. These include any of the positions in which the woman is either on top or lying on her side.

Some women feel self-conscious about their bellies, and thus refrain from using the female-superior position because their bellies show so prominently. Although it's easy for me to say that you shouldn't be ashamed of something that you and your partner created, if you are self-conscious and ashamed, maybe you can overcome that negative view. Certainly the father should do all he can to reassure you that he's not turned off; in truth, many men do enjoy the added voluptuousness that a pregnant woman displays. So speak up guys and let her know that she's attractive to you.

But, if the woman is really bothered by the fact that she has a lot of stretch marks, for example, and many women do feel that way, then she certainly shouldn't be forced to show them off while having sex. If she would like to continue using the female-superior position, one solution would be to wear a light nightgown.

Condom usage

Some physicians recommend the use of condoms for vaginal sex during pregnancy because of hormone-like substances in semen that can trigger uterine contractions and because of a possible risk of infection. Your doctor will let you know if your situation requires condom use.

Sex without intercourse

Some couples worry about sexual intercourse during pregnancy, fearing that the thrusting of the penis could damage the baby. In most cases, sexual intercourse cannot do any damage, but there are certain conditions that would prevent a couple from having intercourse. Only about three out of 100 women will have such a problem, and your obstetrician will be able to warn you if you are one of them after seeing the results of your *sonogram,* a picture made by sound waves which is now a routine part of pregnancy care. Obviously, if after intercourse you notice any spotting or pain, then do not have intercourse again until you've consulted with your doctor. If there is reason to avoid intercourse, that should not stop you from enjoying sex and from seeking satisfaction, but only cause you to limit the ways in which you do this.

If the man uses his finger to masturbate his partner, or if she masturbates herself, more care must be taken than when doing this during normal times. Because her vaginal area has more blood flowing to it than normal, it will be more sensitive and so more prone to scratches and irritations caused by fingernails or calluses. If a woman does find that she is subject to these types of irritations, be sure to use plenty of lubricant the next time you have sex.

Fathers may not know best

Some couples think that anal intercourse is safer for the baby than vaginal sex, but that is not true. In fact, during anal sex the rectum is pushed up against the vagina, increasing the chances of germs entering the vagina and causing an infection. Therefore, it would be better for a couple to stick to vaginal sex than to switch to anal sex.

This switch to anal sex is often initiated by Dad, since he may feel that his penis may do some sort of damage to the baby. This is part of a general concern which a father can have and which sometimes puts a damper on sex. He begins to treat the pregnant woman as a mother instead of a wife and suddenly stops wanting to have sex. This is not only unnecessary, it could be counter-productive because it may make the new mother feel unwanted or unloved. So, although both partners have to be more careful and more sensitive during this time, the one thing they do not have to become is asexual.

What about the baby? Will it bother him or her if the couple has sex? It may wake the baby and cause him to move around, and that's a good sign, because it shows that the baby's alert. The baby may react in some other physical ways, such as increased heartbeat, but the parents' having sex will in no way harm the baby. So there's no need to have any concern on his or her behalf.

Be prepared for physical changes

Both husband and wife should be aware of another physical change that will take place in a pregnant woman: and that is, what will happen to her breasts and nipples. As the pregnancy progresses, the breasts become enlarged, as do the nipples, with the *aureole,* the circle around the nipple itself, growing rounder and darker. The nipple may well protrude more and become darker in color. Just as with the enlargement of her belly, the couple should not feel awkward about these changes. But, as with the belly, the couple may need to change their sexual routine involving her breasts.

When stimulated, the nipples of a pregnant woman release a hormone which can cause uterine contractions. Although there is no scientific proof that this hormone can trigger actual labor, most doctors advise that breast stimulation be kept to a minimum.

There's one more change that the couple should be aware of and that is the smell of the woman's vagina. During pregnancy, the vagina produces additional "good" bacteria called *lactobacillus.* These bacteria help to protect the baby, and, while doing their work, they make the vagina more acidic, thus changing its odor. This is certainly not a problem, and shouldn't cause the man any concern when performing oral sex.

Speaking of oral sex, some people believe that if a pregnant woman performs oral sex on a man and swallows his semen, it can cause her to have contractions. This is an old wives' tale and should be ignored.

If oral sex is part of the couple's repertoire, including swallowing the semen, there is no reason for the woman to stop doing this just because she is pregnant. In fact, because there are couples for whom vaginal sex is contramanded, oral sex is a great substitute.

Oral sex is a good way for the man to give a pregnant woman an orgasm, but he must never blow into the vagina. The forced air could make its way into her blood vessels, which are dilated during pregnancy.

Post-partum sex

Even after a birth with absolutely no complications for the woman, the couple cannot have sexual intercourse for several weeks.

Then, even after the doctor has given the OK, the woman may not yet be ready. Part of the reason may be physical, having a new baby who gets up several times during the night is rather tiring, and the sudden decrease of hormones caused by giving birth can result in a case of "the blues." There may also be psychological factors having to do with becoming a mother, especially if it's for the first time.

This can be a frustrating time for the father, but he has to learn patience. It is important to keep the lines of communication open so that the new mother can let him know how she is feeling and when she may be ready to try to resume having sex. Certainly he should feel free to masturbate in order to relieve his sexual tensions.

While there is no set time that the two partners should aim for as far as renewing their sex lives, you should not let your relationship slip too deeply into becoming an asexual one. If you need to make special arrangements, like hiring a baby-sitter and going to a motel, in order to get reacquainted, then you should do so.

Some couples actually split up because they never resume their sex life after having a baby, so make sure that this never happens to you.

Chapter 13

The Big O

*U*nfortunately, some people adopt a take-it-or-leave-it attitude towards orgasms. But, without orgasms, probably none of us would be here. After all, it's because men and women seek this intense instant of pleasure that people have managed to hang onto this planet by reproducing themselves over the millennia. So we have a lot to be thankful for when it comes to orgasms, and we shouldn't take them for granted.

What Is an Orgasm, Anyway?

It's important to understand what an orgasm is because some women come to me wondering whether they've ever experienced one. For those of you who have experienced intense orgasms, this might seem a ridiculous question. But many women have never shared in this experience at all, and there are also some who've had what is called a *missed orgasm,* in which the body goes through all of the physical manifestations of an orgasm, but the woman doesn't really feel it (I go into missed orgasms in Chapter 23). So whether they've just missed a passing orgasm or never even come close, there are millions of women, and a few men, who don't know what an orgasm is.

An *orgasm* is an intense feeling of physical pleasure that we human beings experience as the culmination of sexual stimulation. When you experience an orgasm, your breathing becomes fast and heavy, your pulse races, the deep muscles in the genital area contract, and your toes may even curl up. In men, orgasm is almost always accompanied by *ejaculation,* the forceful ejection of semen from the penis, necessary for procreation. Women also feel orgasms, although their orgasms are not needed for procreation.

As with every other bodily process, what's going on inside your body during an orgasm is a lot more technical than what you're feeling.

- In a man, first the prostate, seminal vesicles, and upper portion of the vas deferens, called the *ampulla,* contract, which forces out the secretions that form the *ejaculate;* then the muscles that surround the penis do their part to actually eject the ejaculate in what is called the Expulsion Phase. The first two or three of these contractions are quite strong, and they're followed by some diminishing spurts.

- For women, the uterus and the first third of the vagina, controlled by the underlying muscles, called the *puboccocygeus* (PC) muscle, incur the most contractions during orgasm.

But, as I am fond of saying, your main sex organ is located not "down there" but "up here" — in your brain. So the real importance of all that heavy breathing, those strong contractions, and ejaculating spurts is the pleasure that you register from the overall feeling, and *that* I can't describe for you; you'll just have to experience it for yourself.

Kegelling is not a new dance

The same muscles that contract in a woman during orgasm can sometimes be weakened from the stretching that occurs during childbirth.

You can strengthen these muscles again by doing the *Kegel exercises,* named after the doctor who developed them. Dr. Kegel's primary purpose was to help women regain control of urination after childbirth, but these muscles have also been found to increase the pleasurable sensation during intercourse when strengthened.

Here's how you do these exercises:

1. **First locate the muscles surrounding your vagina.**

   The best way of doing this is to feel which muscles you use when you try to stop the flow of urine. These are the PC muscles.

2. **Practice squeezing these muscles.**

   It may help to insert your finger into your vagina and then squeeze down upon it.

3. **Gradually build up the number of repetitions and the length of each squeeze.**

   Just as with any exercise, increasing your effort will strengthen your PC muscles.

You can do these exercises at any time, even while talking on the phone to your boss. After about six weeks of doing the Kegel exercises, you should begin to feel a difference when you have sex.

Men, you also have a set of PC muscles, and by doing the same exercises I describe in this section, you too can develop your muscles. Doing this can give you some added control over your ejaculations.

The rocky relationship between women and orgasms

As with the male orgasm, the female orgasm is strongly linked to her own genitals, although many women also report a more diffused sensation that takes place all over their bodies. Female orgasms tend to come in more varieties than male orgasms. Because of that, women's orgasms have been an issue of contention ever since the days of Sigmund Freud in the early 1900s.

This section summarizes a little of the history of this controversy for you, but if you really want to keep up to date, you probably should consult your daily paper. It seems that there's a new discovery on this subject every week — or at least a new discovery is claimed.

Freud's "contribution"

The Austrian psychiatrist, Sigmund Freud, believed that there were two kinds of orgasms: the *immature orgasm,* which a woman reached through clitoral stimulation only, and the *mature* or *vaginal orgasm,* which he believed was more intense. His theory had the effect of making women seek orgasm through intercourse alone — which, for most women, is impossible.

Ernest Hemingway, although not a sex researcher, added to the problem by writing about a sexual episode in his novel, *For Whom The Bell Tolls,* in which "the earth moved" for a woman during sex. Suddenly, not only were women not supposed to rely on their clitoral feelings, but they had to have special effects at the same time. And you men think you have it tough!

In the 1960s, Masters and Johnson, the experts who observed more than 10,000 episodes of intercourse (see Chapter 11 if you're curious) did a lot of research and decided that all female orgasms came — so to speak — as a result of clitoral stimulation, either direct or indirect. So the pressure was off, and women could enjoy their orgasms any way they wanted to. But that didn't last long.

The G-spot: myth or fact?

Forty years ago, a gynecologist named Ernest Grafenberg claimed to have found a spot in the vagina that seemingly could give women orgasms without clitoral stimulation. In 1982, three researchers wrote a book about this spot, calling it the Grafenberg Spot, or G-spot, and ever since its publication, I am constantly being asked questions by women desperately looking for their own G-spots.

One reason these women are so concerned is that a G-spot orgasm is supposed to be much stronger than a mere clitoral orgasm; it may even include a supposed female ejaculation. To some degree, the G-spot orgasm relates back to Freud's "mature" orgasm, because the G-spot is said to be located within the vagina, and so a woman can have a G-spot orgasm during sexual intercourse.

It seems odd to me that such a wonderful thing as the G-spot wasn't better known before recently. I've spoken to many gynecologists, and none has been able to provide me with any hard evidence of its existence. More research has been done, but I haven't seen anything to convince me that this G-spot definitely exists.

Now I'm not against the G-spot. After all, if there is some special place within the vagina that gives women fabulous orgasms, who am I to complain? My problem with the G-spot is that there has never been any scientifically validated proof that it exists. Yet thousands, and for all I know, millions of women are now looking for their G-spots.

Actually, because of where the G-spot is said to be located, a woman would have a very hard time finding it by herself. Instead, she has to send her partner on a Lewis and Clark expedition up her vagina. When they don't find this pot of gold, some women blame their men for being inadequate explorers. Then the two of them end up having a fight over it, and their entire sex life goes down the tubes.

I'm not a big believer in lotteries, but every once in a while, when the jackpot gets really big, I go out and spend a couple of bucks on a ticket. The odds are long, but so what, how much have I wasted? That's my philosophy about the G-spot. If a couple wants to look for the woman's G-spot, it's no big deal, as long as they don't invest too much in this search. If they find a place in her vagina that gives her a lot of pleasure, great. If they don't, they should just forget about it.

Climaxing during Intercourse

The G-spot isn't the only elusive object of desire in the world of sex. Another is for the woman to have her orgasm during sexual intercourse, as opposed to before or after intercourse. Again, the statistics show that most women have difficulties attaining this goal.

Because the missionary, or male-superior, position is the one least likely to generate this phenomenon, in Chapter 12 I suggest some other positions that couples can try if they want the woman to reach orgasm during sexual intercourse.

The simultaneous orgasm

The other Holy Grail of sex is the simultaneous orgasm, when both partners have their orgasms at about the same time. I can understand the desire for simultaneous orgasms, because sex is something that you do together, like sharing a meal. If the waiter screws up and brings one person's dish first, it's always an embarrassing moment. The person who hasn't been served says, "Go ahead and eat," and the other person is left with a choice of either eating while filled with guilt, or waiting and having a cold meal.

But, although it would be great to share the orgasmic moment, it's just not always possible. And striving for that achievement can lead to a lessening of the enjoyment of sex. If the man is always having to ask, "Are you ready, are you close?" it disturbs the woman's concentration and can put her orgasm further away. Eventually, the man begins to lose interest. So, because of their search for terrific sex, a couple may wind up with lousy sex.

Having sex with someone is not like being a trapeze artist, where the timing has to be just right or else one of you falls to the ground. If you can have simultaneous orgasms, even once in a while, great, but don't make a big deal out of it if you can't. You're more likely to ruin your sex lives than to perfect them.

Multiple orgasms

Are two orgasms better than one? How about three, four, five, or six?

The obvious answer isn't necessarily the right one here. I believe that it depends somewhat on what you think an orgasm is. If your definition of an orgasm is a very strong, intense feeling that leaves you satisfied afterwards, then there's really no need for another one. Returning to the food comparison, if you've had a full meal, even if someone put down your favorite dish in front of you, would it appeal to you? Probably not.

On the other hand, there was a craze a few years back of restaurants that offered *grazing menus* where, instead of one big dish, they'd bring you lots of little dishes with different foods. That's a little what multiple orgasms are like: Each orgasm is nice, but it doesn't leave you satisfied, and you wind up needing another, and maybe another, until you finally do get that feeling of satisfaction. Is it better to do it that way than to have one big orgasm? Only the individual can answer that question.

You may have noticed that the last few paragraphs were gender neutral. While it's true that people who are multiorgasmic are mostly women, some people have touted the male multiple orgasm. They teach a method of delaying orgasm, including doing the exercises to strengthen the PC muscles, that is basically an extension of the method used to teach men how not to be premature ejaculators (see Chapter 22). The man practices the method until he gets so good at it that he not only can delay his orgasms indefinitely, but can actually have an orgasm without ejaculating. I've never met anybody who could do this, so I don't really know how effective this method is, or even how pleasurable, but supposedly it can be done.

An alternative method of having an orgasm, practiced by some religious men in India, is considered a sexual dysfunction in the Western world. It is called *retrograde ejaculation.* In retrograde ejaculation, instead of the semen going out of the penis, it goes into the bladder and is later excreted with the urine. Ironically, those Indian men teach themselves this technique because they believe they are saving their sperm, which supposedly gives them extra strength. Actually, all they are doing is delaying its loss.

Although all orgasms are pleasurable, they are not all identical. As the years pass, they often become less intense, especially in men. I have more to say about this in Chapter 16.

Don't try — let it come

When it comes to sex, we humans cannot be too aware of what we are doing or our sexual powers go haywire. Anytime we become overly conscious of the sexual process, we begin to lose our ability to perform. This is particularly true for men who have difficulties having an erection. If they enter a sexual situation expecting to fail, it's almost guaranteed that they will. The same can be true for a woman who has any difficulties attaining an orgasm. If she is trying too hard to climax, it will only make it more difficult for her to do so.

This effect is called *spectatoring,* and in this respect, sex resembles many sports where, if you try too hard to hit the ball or to get the basket into the net, it just won't work. The idea is to let your body take control while your mind relaxes. Under normal conditions, this method works fine, and both partners can have orgasms. But as soon as they are forced to become aware of the timing of their orgasms so that they reach them together, the couple becomes too conscious of the process and actually loses control they might otherwise have, which is what makes simultaneous orgasms so elusive.

If you're lucky, an experience like the simultaneous orgasm will happen by itself once in a while and provide some extra enjoyment. But if you try too hard, the odds are against it happening at all.

Chapter 14

Afterplay: Embracing the Moment

- -

In This Chapter

▶ Cuddling creates closeness

▶ Afterplay helps women wind down

▶ Telling your partner about your needs

▶ Afterplay leads to more foreplay leads to more sex

- -

*A*fterplay is so simple to do that there's really no excuse for not doing it. The only reason that most people don't do it, I believe, is that they can't be bothered to learn. Anyone, even a genius, may know absolutely nothing about a particular subject, and that's OK. But if someone refuses to try to learn about something, then, in my book, that person's a real dunce. And, as far as afterplay is concerned, too many people, both men and women (but especially men), don't want to even hear about it.

Uncover Those Ears

All too often, after a man has his orgasm, he doesn't care what happens to his partner, physiologically speaking, when she's had hers. These men cover their ears when they hear the word *afterplay*. It's similar to the reaction that they have when their wives mention taking down the storm windows in spring; they head for the attic to hide.

If you want to become a terrific lover, especially in showing your partner that you really love her, then knowledge of afterplay is vital. So I want you to pay close attention.

The simplest of techniques

In terms of technique, there's not really all that much to afterplay. We're not talking rocket science here. In fact, we're not even talking paper airplane making.

All afterplay requires is that the man take a little bit of time to hold and caress his partner, both physically and verbally, after she has had her orgasm. Does that sound complicated? Or strenuous? Should it tax the intelligence or the stamina of either the strongest or weakest of men? Of course not.

Nevertheless, afterplay remains the most neglected part of good sexual functioning. The important issue with afterplay is not that people have problems figuring out how to engage in afterplay; it's that they're not even making the attempt.

 Although the male half of the couple is usually the main obstacle to engaging in afterplay, women need to read this chapter just as much as men do. Many of us women don't know enough about afterplay either. And if you don't ask for afterplay, you will certainly never receive it.

Stay in bed

 To fully appreciate the need for afterplay, look at sexuality researchers Masters and Johnson and their study of 10,000 episodes of sexual intercourse. As I mention in Chapter 11, Masters and Johnson didn't just watch their subjects; they had them wired up to all types of machines that measured their various physical responses during an episode of sex. They measured each person's heart rate; they measured their blood pressure; they measured how much sweat people gave off. And one of the things they noticed was that women take a longer time than men to come down from the high that they get during sex.

After a man has an orgasm, it's not only his penis that shrinks like a balloon with a hole in it; all other physical manifestations, such as heartbeat and excitation, also come down rapidly. But, just as a woman usually needs a longer time than a man to get sexually excited, she also needs more time to descend from that luscious plateau of sexual excitement.

So, if the man ends the sexual experience by rolling over and going to sleep, the woman is left to come down on her own, which is a lot less satisfying to her than doing it in the arms of a conscious partner. And it isn't just by choosing the arms of Morpheus, the god of sleep, that men sidestep the issue of afterplay. Some men get up to have a snack or watch television. Some head right for the showers, which may be a habit picked up from sports, but which leaves the woman not only feeling unfulfilled, but wondering if she somehow made the man feel unclean by having sex with him.

Some men not only leave the bed, but leave the house or apartment altogether. True, they may not live there, but that doesn't mean that, as soon as the sex act is finished, they have to rush to put on their clothes and bolt for the door. (Unless, that is, the man is having an affair with a married woman and he hears the husband's car turning into the driveway.)

Both partners must recognize that a woman needs to bathe in the afterglow of her orgasm for a little while in order for the sex act to be complete for her. How long is a little while? For some women it can be as short as a minute or two. Others need a little longer than that. I'm certainly not suggesting that the man has to spend as much time in afterplay as in foreplay or sex. He just needs to recognize that afterplay is a woman's legitimate need, and he should lovingly address that need.

Staying Awake

Now, I know what a lot of you men are saying out there right about now: "But Dr. Ruth, it's not that I'm insensitive, it's just that I can't help falling asleep."

And you know what my answer is to that? Nonsense.

Of course you can stop yourself from falling asleep after sex if you put a little effort into it. Sex does use up a certain amount of energy, but if you've just come off the court after a tough game of basketball, do you rush home and go to sleep? No, more likely you go with the guys to a local tavern and unwind over a couple of beers. And that's all that afterplay is, unwinding after a sexual episode.

"But Dr. Ruth," you say, "after that game, I'm not lying in a warm, comfortable bed, and I didn't just have an orgasm, which leaves me totally relaxed, not just physically tired."

OK, that's true, and I'm not telling you that you can't go to sleep. Sex does often take place in bed, and it's also more often than not at night, close to the time when you would normally go to sleep. I'll grant you that. But I'm not asking you to pull an all-nighter. Just take a few moments to hold your partner and show her how much she means to you.

Pleading special circumstances

If your lover wants to stay up talking for another hour or two, that's not afterplay, that's a gabfest, and you have a right to put an end to it. And I'll even agree that there are times when the circumstances are such that falling right asleep is fine, too. If you have an early morning meeting the next day, or you've got to get up early to go run the marathon, then it's perfectly OK to say to your partner: "Excuse me, honey, but I really have to go to sleep now." If you normally "give good afterplay," then she'll no doubt give you a pass. It's the men who fall asleep every time with whom I have a bone to pick.

I once received a letter from a man who told me that he owned his own business, which caused him a lot of stress; because of that, he had a hard time falling asleep at night during the week. The one exception was after he had sex with his wife. Then he'd fall right to sleep; instead of getting two or three hours of sleep that night, he'd get the eight hours he needed. Because I wouldn't want to be accused of causing a man to have sleepless nights, I gave him an official Dr. Ruth dispensation from afterplay during weeknights, but only if he promised to make an extra special effort to cuddle and caress his wife after having sex on weekends.

There are no hard and fast rules concerning afterplay except that you be considerate enough to recognize this need in a woman and to make as strong an effort as you can to meet this need as often as possible. Again, I'm not asking you to dig a ditch or break up boulders, but only to hold your lover tenderly for a few moments after she has her orgasm.

Communicating the need

Now, if you are a woman whose man is from the roll-over-and-start-snoring-as-soon-as-it's-over school of sex, then you have to speak up. But never speak up about this during lovemaking. All it will probably do is lead to a fight that will ruin whatever pleasure you did get, and his as well.

Always try to communicate sexual matters during a quiet time, when you're likely to have enough time to talk without being interrupted and when you have the privacy you need to speak openly about sexual functioning. A stroll around the neighborhood after a good dinner would do nicely. Explain to your partner that you really would appreciate it if he wouldn't go right to sleep after having sex. Tell him why, let him know how good it will make you feel, and how good you want to make him feel, and also tell him that he doesn't have to engage in afterplay every time you have sex.

Afterplay Creates Foreplay

Men who take time for afterplay will be rewarded not only with more satisfied, and hence happier, wives or lovers, but also with better sex lives. You see, I look at afterplay as really the beginning of foreplay for the next sexual episode. Throughout this book I tell you that the more you stretch out foreplay, the better sex will be the next time. So if you can start foreplay with afterplay right after you have sex, you won't be wasting a single second. Just imagine what that's going to do for your sex life!

Chapter 15
Keeping the Fires Burning

· ·

In This Chapter

▶ Learning to communicate with your partner

▶ Creating a sense of romance

▶ Trying new things

· ·

Tom Ewel and Marilyn Monroe starred in a wonderful film called *The Seven Year Itch*. The premise was that after a certain period of time, presumably seven years, a man would begin to get tired of his wife and go outside of his marriage to find some excitement. That movie was made in 1955, and was considered risqué at the time, but an awful lot has happened to relationships since then.

First the divorce rate started to rise dramatically, and people weren't waiting seven years anymore. It didn't take very much to cause a couple to break up, and even children, who were often the glue that held a couple together, weren't holding things together like they used to. I would see many couples who were having problems, and, with all the temptations that seemed to abound, I wasn't always successful at patching things between them.

And then came a new era, the era of AIDS. Suddenly all that green grass on the other side of the fence was looking kind of brownish. Couples who are having problems and that might well have caused them to split up ten years ago are now more willing to try to work things out, and not just for the sake of the kids. People today are scared of starting a new relationship, and so they're willing to put in the effort to at least try to save the one they're in.

Now, of course, if a couple comes to see me in my office that means their relationship is already somewhat rocky. Your job, if you're married, is to steer clear of any shoals, and some suggestions of how best to do that is the subject of this chapter.

Communicate, Communicate, Communicate

What's the number-one rule for staying out of marital trouble? Keep the lines of communication open and flowing with information. If you're dissatisfied with the state of your relationship, let your partner know about it — *but* do it in a nice way and at an appropriate time.

If you've ever wondered what goes on in a sex therapist's office, let me tell you: Most of what happens is that people sit down and tell me all of the problems that they wouldn't or couldn't say to their spouses (see Appendix A). My job is to listen. For me to be most effective, it is better if I get to hear both sides of the story. After that, I have to try to get them to talk to one another, sometimes with me as a referee, at least for the first few times. I may pass along some advice, but, if my type of therapy is going to work, the most important exchanges have to be the ones that take place between the partners.

My job isn't necessarily to always patch things up. Sometimes it's my duty to help the couple untie the knot and separate. If two people no longer love each other, there really is no point in trying to help them stay together. Even if I were successful in the short run, in the long run the same problems would crop up again and again. Either they'd waste the rest of their lives being miserable, or eventually they would break up anyway.

But enough about people being miserable, because I want you to be happy, joyous, ecstatic! If you're not any of those things, then let's begin, right now, to change your life around so that you will be all those and more.

The first step is to take the first step

When people write me a letter or call my office to make an appointment, I always congratulate them because they've already taken the first step towards a better relationship and a better life. Why? Because they've acknowledged that there is a problem. You would be surprised to know how many people are miserable and won't admit it, even to themselves. They keep doing the same things over and over again and don't let themselves see that something is drastically wrong with their lives.

Ellen and Bob

Ellen and Bob were one of those couples about whom everybody said their lives were perfect. And from the outside, their lives did seem perfect. From Bob's point of view, also, everything was just about perfect. But from Ellen's point of view, things were far from perfect.

When Bob had sexual relations with Ellen, he knew just how to bring her to orgasm, and so sexual satisfaction was not a problem for either of them. But Bob lived his life by the book, and sex was for Friday night and at no other time. When Bob came home on Fridays, he often brought Ellen a little gift, and he would give her a hug after dinner. This was his version of foreplay, and there was nothing wrong with it, per se. The problem was that, on the other six nights of the week, he barely had time for his wife. He'd watch Monday Night Football, go bowling on Tuesday, act as scout leader on Wednesday, and so on. He was having a good time, but Ellen felt abandoned. She needed more attention and romance from Bob the rest of the week. She said it often enough, but he never really took it seriously, and so, basically, Ellen was miserable.

Ellen's call to my office was the first step in fixing her problem. She came to see me and told me what had been happening, and then I asked to see Bob. He was shocked that Ellen had visited me, but after he and I talked, he was more than willing to pay more attention to his wife. He did love her, after all. He had just gotten wrapped up in certain habits in which she wasn't included. A few simple changes, such as both of them taking up tennis, really turned their marriage around.

It's easy to take your partner for granted. Life, today, can get filled with all types of activities, many work related, some community or charity related, and some simply leisure activities. I once chastised Johnny Carson on the air for keeping people up watching him instead of attending to their partners, and, although he may be off the air now, all of the other late night talk-show hosts are equally to blame. Putting television ahead of your spouse is dumb. And I'm not just talking about sex here. If you don't spend some quality time communicating with your spouse, your sex life is going to suffer in the long run also.

Men: Talk to your wives

I didn't choose the case of Ellen and Bob, where the man was not communicating sufficiently for his wife's needs, by chance. Although there are certainly couples in which it is the wife who is too busy to spend time with her husband, in general, it's the other way around. Women need to have more romance in their relationships than do men. Some recent research indicates that the brains of men and women are different, so maybe that has something to do with it, but it could just as well be a cultural bias as a physical cause. The fact remains that many men either ignore or are oblivious to the needs of their wives or partners when it comes to romance or closeness or whatever you want to call it.

I am not advocating that every man suddenly turn into Prince Charming. In the first place, no man is going to be able to totally turn his personality inside out, and he really doesn't need to. But there is a threshold in communications, a point below which a woman will feel that something is missing. Now if your wife fixes you good meals to satisfy your hunger, you shouldn't feel that it's demeaning to give her a fix on a regular basis of your attention, especially because you will get something out of this as well.

There isn't a man out there who doesn't have some desires or feelings or thoughts on his mind that he would like to communicate to someone. Your partner is the perfect person to do that with, and once you start talking about life, you'll find that there's so much more to talk about.

The art of conversation

As you know, I'm European, and we Europeans place much more emphasis on good conversation than do Americans. I suppose part of the reason for this comes from the vast distances that exist in America, so that often the nearest neighbors live miles away, and there's just nobody with whom to talk. But whatever the underlying reason, the art of conversation is not that well practiced in America. And the more hours we spend looking at television and computer screens, the less skillful at conversation we become.

Having a conversation should actually be fun, as long as ideas are exchanged. I don't consider saying every thought that pops into your head to be the same thing as having a conversation. Certainly many people are afflicted with what is commonly referred to as "motor mouth," and that does turn everybody off who wants to start a conversation with them.

It takes two or more people to have a conversation. If you expect people to listen to what you have to say, then you have to return the favor and listen to them. And when you respond, try to make sure that it's to the point, so the other person knows that, while he or she was speaking, you were listening and not just planning what you were going to say next.

When you're listening to somebody, try to catch the undercurrents of what they're saying, as well as the actual words. This is part of the skill set that any therapist must possess, because very often clients don't open up right away; instead, they turn around and around the subject they really want to discuss. It's up to the therapist to see what the real issue is.

But you don't need years of training to spot a hidden agenda. If you pay close attention to what the other person is saying, you too can discover what they really want to say but don't know how to.

The easiest way of understanding what other people are trying to say is to put yourself in their place. Remember who they are, what kind of person they are, what they do, and use that information while you're listening. For example, if your wife never pays attention to sports, and she suddenly is talking to you about baseball or football, it is unlikely that she has developed an interest in that sport overnight. She's probably trying to use a sports analogy to tell you something else, so listen carefully and try to understand the message that she is passing on.

If your spouse is talkative and he or she suddenly stops talking, doesn't that usually get your attention? Often it means that he or she is angry with you and, therefore, has decided to cut off communications. When you fail to communicate, you are also using silence as a way of saying something: that you don't care enough about the other person to bother communicating with that person. Think about that the next time you're in a room with your spouse and no words are passing through your lips.

Your brain never shuts off

Some people say to me, "I don't know what to say." Now, when it comes to starting a conversation with a stranger, when you're trying to make a good first impression, I can understand that you might become tongue-tied. There's a good chance that the conversation you start up will be rejected, and that's enough to make anybody hesitate.

But, if you start talking to your spouse, you're not talking to a stranger, so you don't have to be afraid. As far as what you can say, just listen to yourself for a few moments. You see, your brain never shuts off. You are in constant communication with yourself. All you have to do is share some of that communication with your spouse. If you had a great lunch, say so. If you read an interesting article in the paper, bring it up. If you're wondering what tomorrow's weather is going to be, ask about it. It's not that hard if you give it a chance.

Set the Stage for Romance

Candy, flowers, cards, gifts of any sort or variety — all serve the same purpose: to show that you care. Although it is wonderful and sometimes important to give gifts — such as on a birthday, anniversary, or other important occasion, so as not to send a negative message (like, "I don't love you enough to care") — what the soul really craves is not material things but personal attention.

So if you either can't afford, or don't wish to give your spouse gifts with monetary value, give something that doesn't cost you any money. Like a massage. Or a night off from cooking. Or even just a walk around the block. Show your spouse that you really do care by giving of yourself.

Be alone together

Another important ingredient for creating a romantic atmosphere is being alone — just the two of you.

You can set the most beautiful table, with candles and flowers and a $100-bottle of champagne, but if the kids are sitting at their usual places or your mother-in-law is sitting between you, let's face it, the decor won't mean a thing. It would be more romantic if the two of you went to a greasy spoon diner alone.

I know that it's not always easy to make time for each other. With so many men and women in the work force, time is in short supply. But having some time alone together is very important to a relationship, so you have to give it a high priority. If you've got kids, get a baby-sitter. If you don't have kids, leave that file at the office for a change.

Make plans

Many people insist on spontaneity. They don't like to make plans, saying that it takes away from the moment. Well, I say hogwash and double hogwash.

- ✔ The first hogwash is for the misconception that a planned romantic evening offers any less than an unplanned one. If the problem is that these romantic evenings are few and far apart, then it is certainly going to add more romance to your life if you have a planned romantic evening than if you don't have a romantic evening at all.

- ✔ The second hogwash has to do with the structure of foreplay, which I discuss in Chapter 11. Foreplay does not begin when the man touches the woman's left breast. I realize that's a misconception that many men have — that foreplay is all physical — but it isn't true. Yes, there's a physical component to foreplay, and part of foreplay is to stimulate the woman so that she will have an orgasm. But foreplay can start long before the couple is within hands' grasp.

Remember, foreplay can start as early as the afterplay of a sexual episode. So it certainly can be part of a planned romantic evening. Here are some examples:

- ✔ That first good morning kiss . . . if it's accompanied by a wink

- ✔ A compliment dropped as your partner is stepping out of a morning shower

- ✔ A phone call during the day in which you mention the night's planned activities

- ✔ Flowers sent to her office in the afternoon, or a bottle of wine brought home

If you begin to build the sense of excitement right from the moment you both open your eyes, you'll both be more than ready for sex by the time you actually begin to undress for lovemaking.

Remember that the longer you stretch out foreplay, the stronger will be its effects on both of you. What's wonderful about stretching out foreplay is that it doesn't have to take up a lot of time. A kiss, a wink, a compliment, a phone call, these things don't require much extra time out of your day, but they can pay off with a big dividend at the end.

Don't confuse romance with sex

A very big mistake that many men make is to confuse romance with sex. Yes the two are linked, but they don't have to be tied together like Siamese twins. You can also act romantic without there being a requirement for sex. Let me restate that, you *should* act romantic even when you're not going to have sex with your partner.

If a man only acts romantic because he wants to have sex, then those things that he's doing won't be romantic anymore. I've confused you men, right? I've just told you to stretch out foreplay with romantic moments during the course of the day, and now it seems like I'm telling you not to. Could I actually mean two contradictory statements? Yes.

Let me explain. Stretching foreplay out is certainly romantic. But if you only act romantic when you want sex, then these same deeds lose their romance. I think a case history is called for here:

Nancy and Barry

Barry thought of himself as a very romantic guy . . . at least whenever he was in the mood for sex. He knew that Nancy loved flowers, so any time that he was thinking about making love to Nancy, he would bring flowers home.

The problem was that, just because Barry was in the mood for lovemaking, didn't mean Nancy was. But as soon as she saw Barry walk in the door holding a bouquet of flowers, Nancy knew what he wanted. Pretty soon, instead of looking at flowers as beautiful gifts of nature, she began to think of them like the treats she would feed their dog when she wanted him to do a trick.

One day, Nancy had a really terrible time at the office. Everything seemed to go wrong, and she was feeling very irritable when she walked into the apartment. No sooner had she removed her coat, but there was Barry, holding a bouquet of flowers with a big smile on his face. It was more than Nancy could take, and she grabbed the flowers, threw them into the garbage, and marched into the bedroom, leaving Barry open-mouthed.

What Barry didn't realize was that, because he only brought home flowers when he wanted sex, those flowers were putting pressure on Nancy — pressure that, on that particular day, put her over the top. Barry had to learn to bring Nancy flowers on nights when sex wasn't on his agenda. And, if he wanted to start foreplay early, he needed to vary his ways of doing so, so that he wouldn't seem to be pressuring Nancy into having sex just by bringing home something a little special.

Use Variety to Spice Up Your Sex Life

Variety adds to romance in many ways. If you always go to the same restaurant when you go out to dinner, that can get boring, and boredom doesn't help keep those romantic fires burning. By trying a new place, you get to sample new foods and a new atmosphere. The experience will give you new things to talk about, even if it turns out that the new restaurant isn't as good as your regular haunt.

The need for variety is also true in the bedroom. If you always make love exactly the same way, it can become boring. Some women actually come to dread the way a man will always touch her in the exact same way. It doesn't make her feel special or wanted, it makes her feel like an old shoe.

Make some new moves

Now a lot of men are out there right now saying, "But I like my old shoes best." That may be true, but if Cindy Crawford were coming over to your house, would you put on your old shoes? I don't think so. And if Cindy Crawford was going to go to bed with you, would you put on your old moves? Of course not. You'd try every trick in the book to make her feel great, and that's what you should be doing for your partner. She may not be Cindy Crawford (or whomever you fantasize about taking to that deserted island), but you can treat her as though she is, and you'll both wind up profiting from the experience.

I'm not saying you have to go to Fantasy Island every time you make love. There are certainly times when you both have just enough energy to want to have sex, but you don't have the added energy that it would take to be creative. Even if you make love the same way nine out of ten times, at least that tenth time, try something a little different. If you stay in the same rut, it will only get more and more entrenched, and then you'll never be able to get out of it.

Dressing it up

Here's an example of something that really did happen to me that I think will help elucidate creativity in lovemaking. I was doing my radio show when I received a phone call from a man who said that he'd been living with his girlfriend for several years, and they always had great sex. (He also made sure to tell me that they used contraceptives.) He said he was getting married in a few weeks, and he needed an idea to make the wedding night special.

I thought about it for an instant and then told him that, after his new wife came out of the bathroom, he should go in and take off all of his clothes, except for a top hat. I thought that was pretty clever, but he one-upped me. He asked me where he should wear the top hat!

Variety can mean making love someplace you've never done it, like the kitchen floor or on the dining-room table (just make sure that the legs are darn sturdy). You can add variety by making love at a different time of the day, like early in the morning or in the middle of the afternoon. You can make love with most of your clothes on — or with only one of you naked and the other one fully clothed. Let your imagination fly and see where it takes you.

The one thing I must caution you about, however, is never to pressure your partner into doing something that he or she doesn't want to do. It's fine to be creative, but you have to create something you'll both enjoy.

Don't be a lazy lover

You know that you only get negative results from being lazy at school or at work, so why do you think that you can be lazy when it comes to sex? A lazy lover is a lousy lover. The more energy you put into your lovemaking, the better a lover you'll be.

Now, by energy, I don't necessarily mean more *physical* energy, although that's worth trying if the two of you tend to be passive. The energy I'm talking about is spirit. The more of yourself you put into your lovemaking, the more you'll get out of it. It is easy for a woman to remain passive and, although that's OK from time to time, if you always remain passive, you're letting yourself fall into a dangerous trap. When one partner is always the one who initiates sex, and the other partner doesn't actively participate, the sex won't be as good for either partner, and problems are likely to occur after a time.

Take charge of your sex life, and you can achieve tremendous results.

Create an Adventure

In addition to using variety, it's also important to be a little daring. Take a risk on a new position (see Chapter 12 for a selection). What's the worst that can happen? Now when I say don't be afraid to take risks, I'm not suggesting you do anything really dangerous, especially concerning unsafe sex. But, within reason, the sex act has many variations that don't involve any real harm beyond the risk that one or both of you won't be able to sustain the position or have an orgasm. So you miss one orgasm, that's no big deal. On the other hand, if you decide that you like a new position, it can bring you many, many orgasms over the course of a lifetime.

Visit a sex shop

Many people wouldn't be caught dead in a sex shop, and my question to them is: Why not? When you're hungry, you go to the supermarket. When you need clothes, you go to a department store. So, if you need a little more variety in your sex life, what's wrong with going to a sex shop?

The number one excuse is: What if the neighbors see me? If the neighbors are in the sex shop, then they probably couldn't care less. If someone does say something, say that you're buying a present for a bachelor or bachelorette party. But the simplest solution is to go to a sex shop that's not near where you live. After all, I'm not telling you to go to a sex shop once a week. Once in a lifetime might be enough, but you should at least go that one time, even if you don't buy anything.

What might you find in one of these stores? There are many different varieties of sex stores. Some feature mostly X-rated movies. Others have a large selection of so-called *marital aids,* like vibrators and dildos. Some have sexy lingerie, while others have lots of leather products. Sex stores often cater to a particular audience, so that one store may have a lot of whips and chains, and another won't have any.

 Whatever you do, don't go into a sex store with a serious attitude, or you'll wind up being disappointed. Sex is supposed to be fun, and the gadgets and gizmos featured in these stores are supposed to add to the fun of lovemaking. If you're not comfortable using any of these products, then simply browse.

Use a mail-order catalog

If you don't dare go into a sex store, or if there's not one near you, the next best thing is to get a catalog. That way, you can do your browsing without fear of the neighbors peeking in. All adult catalog companies send their catalogs in plain wrappers, and the same goes when they ship their merchandise, so even your mail carrier won't suspect a thing.

There are different catalogs for different tastes. Some catalogs, like *Adam & Eve,* are erotic in and of themselves — with lots of pictures taken from the X-rated videos they sell, featuring men and women in all sorts of poses, along with pictures of half-naked men and women wearing some of the exotic outfits. These catalogs sell many different types of dildos and vibrators and oils and games, and the copy leans towards words like "hot," "steamy," and "banned."

I'll warn you right now, many women (and maybe a few men) would be offended by these erotic catalogs. Because these catalogs feature photos of so many half-naked women with great bodies, many women feel intimidated by them. To these women, such catalogs are more of a turn off than a turn on.

On the other hand, most men find these catalogs exciting in and of themselves, so looking at them will probably get their batteries started up. So if you can at least tolerate thumbing through the pages (and the guys aren't half bad looking in any case), then one of these catalogs could spice up your love life, even if you don't order anything from them.

Then there are catalogs that take a more, shall I say, intellectual approach. Catalogs mailed out by places like The Townsend Institute, for example, feature how-to videos which, while they are certainly also X-rated, are instructional in nature rather than just fictional stories featuring lots of sex. Catalogs like this also show books and creams and vibrators, but in a much more subdued context and without any nudity.

For the purchase of vibrators and other sex toys, I've long recommended the catalog of *Eve's Garden,* which is very classily done, and the people at *Good Vibrations* put out a nice, calm catalog too. Their operators can also answer any questions you have about their products. See Appendix B for how to contact these companies and others.

Watch X-rated videos

The VCR has certainly changed things in the X-rated video market. Where once such movies were hard to come by, now they are easily available. You can watch them by the dozen in the privacy of your own home. I get a lot of questions concerning these videos, so I know that they raise several issues that many couples do face.

Because men are more turned on by visual stimuli, these videos are aimed primarily at the male market. That's good for a man looking to find some erotic material to masturbate to, but it's not always good for couples. Many women find such movies abhorrent. Some dislike them because they depict sex so explicitly. Other women don't mind the sex but feel threatened by the gorgeous bodies of the women featured in these films. And then there are the women who dislike the sex, the women, the men . . . basically every aspect of these X-rated videos.

Certainly nobody should be forced to watch anything that they don't like, but you shouldn't take these movies all that seriously either. After all, there are blockbuster films that feature violence and bodies flying all over the place, and, to my mind, that is much worse than showing people having sex.

Some X-rated films supposedly have more of a plot and are more sensitive to a female audience. I don't believe that the difference will be enough to convince a woman who hates this variety of film to watch all the way through, but these films do offer a compromise. However, since the filmmakers know that the market for X-rated films is still mostly male, the sex quotient has to be made sufficiently strong to appeal to that half of the audience.

People often ask me for my recommendations, and, although I'd like to oblige, that would necessitate me becoming an X-rated movie reviewer. I don't mind watching these films, but their overall quality is such that I couldn't stand to see dozens of them, much less hundreds.

There is one film, however, that I do recommend regularly (though I have to admit it's not that easy to obtain). It's a film called *A Ripple In Time,* and it features an older woman, in her 50s I believe, rather than the typical nubile, young blonde. This is a film that I recommend for older adults to watch who want to spice up their sex life. You can order this film by calling 1-800-843-0305.

Take Charge of Your Sex Life

The success of your sex life is not something that you should leave to chance. Work on it, on a regular basis, and you can definitely reap rewards that are worth the effort you put in.

The other side of that coin is that, if you ignore your sex life, if you allow it to slowly peter out, so to speak, it will be much more difficult to get those fires burning again. So take my advice and start right now.

Part IV
Changing Patterns

The 5th Wave   By Rich Tennant

"JUST TO SPICE THINGS UP, I THOUGHT I'D WEAR THE FRENCH TICKLER INSIDE OUT THIS TIME TO ADD TO <u>MY</u> EXCITEMENT."

In this part...

You know the old saying, variety is the spice of life. So, in this part, I'm going to give you lots and lots of variety.

Now some of this variety won't be right for you, and that's OK. The only way for variety to exist is if we don't all want the same exact thing. But don't be closed-minded. What you don't find to your liking today may become your favorite part of sex some time in the future.

Chapter 16
Sex in the Golden Years

*P*eople have a funny way of trying to paint something that is basically negative so it appears really positive. For example, you've heard people say that stepping in you-know-what or having it rain on your wedding day brings good luck. Although I'm an optimist, I recognize that these sayings are just ways of making people feel good when something not-so-good happens to them.

Some people might say that the phrase "sex in the golden years" fits into the category of simply putting a positive spin on a mostly negative issue. Others might even say it is an oxymoron, because as soon as people get their first Social Security check, sex goes out the window.

Now, I'm not going to lie to you and deny that there are negative aspects to growing older as far as sex is concerned. After all, since so many other physical attributes begin to grow dimmer, why should a person's sexual apparatus remain perfectly fit? And, in fact, it doesn't. But, when it comes to sex, not all of the aging factors are negative. And let me make one thing absolutely clear: People can continue having sex right up into their 90s.

Female Changes

Menopause is a fact of life for every woman, although each of us goes through it at a different age and with different levels of symptoms (see Chapter 3). The end result, however, is the same for all. Every woman who reaches menopause experiences the following changes:

✔ She stops having her menstrual cycle.

✔ She becomes incapable of being impregnated.

✔ She drastically lowers her production of the sex hormones, estrogen and progesterone.

These changes have several physical effects on sexual functioning. Vaginal lubrication lessens or stops altogether, and the vagina itself becomes drier and less flexible. Intercourse is often painful. Sounds pretty bad, right? Painful intercourse could certainly put a complete halt to your sex life. But there's a simple and very effective solution: use a lubricant.

By replacing the natural lubricants that diminish as you age with artificial ones, you can maintain your usual sexual functioning. An older woman's clitoris is still sensitive, she can still have orgasms, and she can have comfortable intercourse.

I am not a medical doctor, so I won't go into any detail, but, just as a lubricant can solve the problem of vaginal dryness, some of the other side effects of menopause can be treated with hormonal replacement therapy. This treatment is not necessarily right for every woman, but I recommend that every woman consult a gynecologist about this issue, and maybe even find one who specializes in this area.

So the negative side of menopause can be pretty easily taken care of. Now look at the positive aspects:

✔ A post-menopausal woman no longer has periods (although some forms of estrogen replacement therapy will restore the period of a post-menopausal woman). Now sex during one's period is certainly not dangerous, but most couples tend to refrain from "doing it" during those few days, especially if the woman has cramps or headaches. With menstruation gone forever, you no longer have good days and bad days, so that every day of the month is good for sex.

✔ With the end of menstruation comes the impossibility of becoming pregnant. For many women, whether they use one or more methods of contraception, the risk of an unintended pregnancy does put somewhat of a damper on their enjoyment of sex. They may not realize it when they are young enough to bear children, but once the risk disappears, they suddenly blossom sexually. I've known many, many women who found sex to be a lot more enjoyable after menopause just because they were freed of this particular worry.

Male Changes

The changes that men undergo vary more from person to person than do the changes women go through, though testosterone levels generally begin to decline in men starting in their 40s. Every woman goes through menopause but, although every man does go through certain changes, the results are not always the same. Some men merely have a decrease in their sexual prowess, which I'll get into in a moment, while others become impotent. Obviously, the latter result is a serious problem, but even impotence does not have to spell the end of a sexual relationship.

You know you're getting older when...

Let me begin with the early symptoms of a male's aging in regards to sex. A younger man can have an erection merely by thinking about something that turns him on. That is called a *psychogenic erection* (see Chapter 2). He sees an erotic photograph or thinks of the last time he and his wife made love and, voilá, his penis becomes hard and erect.

As a man grows older, psychogenic erections become a little less hard. Eventually, a time may come when he is no longer able to have an erection merely by thinking about something sexy. Now this does not happen overnight. He still has psychogenic erections for a time, but they become fewer and fewer and need more and more stimulation to take effect. Then, at some point, they stop altogether.

Does this spell the end of his sex life? Absolutely not! Unless, of course, he doesn't realize what has occurred.

Howard and Sarah

Howard and Sarah had been married for 25 years. Howard was usually the one to initiate sex, but Sarah had always been a willing partner. Sarah loved Howard very much and was sure that he had never cheated on her.

As they both approached 50, they began to have sex less frequently, but when they did engage in it, it was still very satisfying to Sarah. As the frequency declined, Sarah began to feel sexually frustrated, and so she decided to try to get things going.

She had a few sheer nightgowns in the bottom of her drawer. In the past, whenever she would put one of these on before going to bed, she could be sure that Howard would get excited by this, and they would end up making love. She tried this approach a couple of times, and nothing happened. One time she even reached over to touch his penis, and it was totally limp.

Sarah didn't know what was happening. She exercised regularly, but she had put on a little weight, so she thought that maybe Howard didn't find her attractive anymore. Then she became suspicious. Maybe Howard was "giving at the office" and had nothing left to give her. She became more and more irritated with Howard, and six months went by without them having sex. At that point, Sarah came to see me.

Had Howard been cheating on Sarah? Absolutely not. What he told me when I interviewed him was that his penis had abandoned him. He would look at his wife in her sexy negligee and want to have an erection, but nothing would happen. He was so ashamed by this that he wouldn't admit it to his wife. Because neither of them would talk about it, and because neither of them suspected the real cause, what should have been a simple matter developed into a major storm.

Curing Howard

What Howard needed was very simple: physical stimulation. He needed to have his penis touched in order to get an erection. He had discovered this himself because he, too, had grown sexually frustrated because he wasn't having sex with his wife and had begun to masturbate. But, because he hadn't wanted to touch himself in front of her to get an erection, he hadn't used this knowledge to get their sex life going.

Howard and Sarah did have a period of awkwardness to get over because they had to develop a new set of signals. In the past, they hadn't usually verbalized their desire for sex. Howard would initiate some sort of sexual contact. If Sarah was interested in having sex, she'd confirm his desire for sex by reaching over and touching his already erect penis, and they'd be off to the races. Other times Sarah would get things going by putting on one of her sheer nightgowns. But Sarah had never had to "give" Howard an erection because he'd always arrived in bed, shall we say, prepared. Howard felt strange asking Sarah to fondle his penis in order to get an erection, and Sarah didn't feel comfortable reaching over to touch his penis, not knowing whether he wanted to have an erection or not.

Now the lack of an erection didn't mean that Howard didn't want to make love. He just had to learn to tell Sarah, verbally, that he was interested. Once she knew for sure that he was interested, and if she was interested back, she would use her hands to give him an erection.

Fellatio and the older couple

As a man gets older, he may require greater amounts of stimulation in order to get an erection. Some men find that oral sex works better than the use of hands. If the wife has always been willing to perform fellatio, then the couple has no problems. If she has never performed fellatio, however, then problems can occur. Not only may she have always felt disgusted by the idea, but, if she feels that she is being forced into performing oral sex, she will be even more resentful about having to start.

I get many letters from widows who face this problem. A woman's sex life with her husband may have dwindled slowly, and both had become used to it. But then, after her husband passes away, she meets a man who isn't only interested in companionship, but who wants to have sex with her. The problem is that he cannot have an erection all that easily and requests oral sex. The woman is in a quandary. At her age, men may be hard to find, so she doesn't want to lose his companionship over the sexual issue. And, because she knows that there are so many other widows around who would be happy to do whatever a man who was interested in them wanted done, she feels she doesn't have a lot of leverage in this area. So she writes to me and asks what she should do.

This is a tough question for me to answer. On the one hand, I do not believe that anyone should do anything under pressure. But if the alternative is to lose the man and be lonely, that's no good either. I usually suggest a compromise, which is to have the woman try oral sex. Maybe she won't find fellatio so horrible once she gets used to it. Maybe she'll even learn to like it. Don't be surprised by that, because I do get women who report exactly that turn of events to me. Or maybe she'll hate fellatio and have to give up on this man. If fellatio is really the only way that he is going to have an erection, then you really can't blame him for insisting on it.

An end to premature ejaculation: an aging plus

I'm not finished dealing with the negative effects of aging and men, but I didn't want to continue a list of negative items without mentioning a silver lining.

Many men who suffer from premature ejaculation when they're younger find that, as they age, that particular problem often goes away. As their capacity for sex diminishes, men gain lasting power, which, for women who really enjoy intercourse, can be the start of a whole new phase of their sex lives.

Impotency

Just the way that a man's inability to have a psychogenic erection comes on slowly, so does the onset of impotency. An impotent man first finds that his erections are becoming softer and don't last as long. At some point (and remember: not all men become impotent), he cannot have an erection at all.

In many cases, impotency is a side effect of another disease or the drugs used to treat another problem (see Chapter 17). Diabetes can cause impotency. So can some of the medicines used to treat heart problems. Many men are too ashamed to ask their doctor about problems with impotency. Sometimes they just figure that sex for them is over when that does not have to be the case.

Always check with your physician about impotency, especially if you are taking any kind of medication. Different medications have different side effects. Sometimes, if you complain to your doctor about problems with impotency, he can put you on a different type of drug, and the impotency will go away.

But, if a man is just not able to have an erection any longer, that does not mean that he can never perform sexual intercourse again. A variety of implant devices are available to allow a man to have erections whenever he wants them. For more information on this topic, see Chapter 22.

The Psychological Bonuses

Now that I may have depressed some of you male readers, let me return to those silver linings. These are not just of benefit to you men, but to both partners, which makes the silver linings even brighter, don't you agree?

When two people first get married, their libido is so high that they make time for sex, even if time is short. It also helps if no children are in the house, so that sex can occur almost any time and not just after the kids have gone to bed.

As the years go by, and particularly as children arrive on the scene, finding time for sex can become more difficult. And, in these days where both men and women are in the work force, not only is the time often in short supply, but also the energy.

In the so-called *golden years,* time suddenly grows in much larger supply. The kids are (hopefully) out of the house, and, even if both partners aren't fully retired, in all likelihood they're not working full time, so that they can make love at various hours of the day, and in various places, not just at night in the bedroom with the door locked.

Making love in the morning isn't only advisable because it adds variety and offers daylight. The male sex hormone, testosterone, is at its highest level in the morning, so that, if a man has problems with impotency, they are least likely to show up in the morning. Also, after a good night's rest, energy levels may be higher. If you need to have a cup of coffee, maybe even that morning bowl of bran flakes, that's OK. Since you won't be in a rush, you can partake of a leisurely breakfast and then go back to bed.

Just as during any other period in your relationship, the more effort you put into better lovemaking during your golden years, the more you'll get out of it.

Chapter 17

Sex If You Have a Disability or an Illness

- -

In This Chapter

▶ Sexual relationships for paralysis victims

▶ Sex after a heart attack

▶ Sex and diabetes medications

▶ Sex for the mentally impaired

▶ Sex in institutions

- -

*T*he very first person I ever treated after I became a sex therapist was in a wheelchair. One of my dear friends, Dr. Asa Ruskin, who has since passed away, was head of rehabilitative medicine at a New York hospital, and he sent this young man to me. Even though I was new on the job, I was able to help him, and that has always left a particular soft spot in my heart for people with disabilities.

Later on, I taught a course in human sexuality open only to the disabled at Brooklyn College. This turned out to be another wonderful experience. The students were great, and they taught me a great deal about their lifestyle and their courage. As a result, I vowed that I would never do another class like it again. My reasoning was that the lessons that these students had to offer were so important and so inspiring that I wanted to see these students integrated into regular classes on human sexuality, rather than sectioned off by themselves.

As you can guess, I believe very strongly that people with disabilities should be able to exercise all of their sexual capacities to the full limit of their abilities. Sadly, they are not always permitted to do so, although that's as much the fault of the society they live in as of their disabilities. Medical conditions can also affect your ability to enjoy sex. I discuss the major ones in this chapter. Problems caused by testicular or prostate disease are discussed in Chapter 2. Problems caused by mastectomy and hysterectomy are discussed in Chapter 23.

We Are All Sexual Beings

In our society, sexuality is usually not something to be flaunted. Although we may admire a brightly plumed bird, despite the fact that those wildly colored feathers have no other purpose than to attract a mate, because of our Puritan ethic, many of us look down upon a human being who flaunts his or her sexuality.

Now I definitely respect everyone's right to consider sex as something that should only be done in private, but I disagree with those who go too far and think that anything having to do with sex is dirty and ugly. Considering that every single one of us has sexual urges, and that none of us would be here if it weren't for sex, people who think this way are sadly mistaken in their attitudes.

Sadly, we often take an ostrich-with-its-head-in-the-sand attitude towards people with disabilities. Some people in our society prefer not to see those who aren't reasonably fit. They'd prefer that people with disabilities stay in an institution or at least have the "decency" to remain at home. Too many among us tend to look at the disabled as somehow subhuman and want as little to do with them as possible. We forget that, inside those bodies that may be crippled or blind or just old and infirm, are fellow human beings — and any of us can join them in disability at any time.

Now, when you put the two attitudes together — our attitudes about sex and our attitudes about the handicapped — then you really wind up with a concept that few people are willing to accept openly and that all too many find themselves uncomfortable with: a sexually active, handicapped person.

This reaction is ridiculous, of course. But, because these attitudes are handed down to us both by our families and by our peers, no one is totally to blame, and everyone shares in the fault. What is important to understand, for those of us who are not disabled, is that those feelings of discomfort that have been handed down to us are not natural, and that we can change them if we are willing to try.

So, although much of the advice in this chapter is aimed at people who have disabilities, I wish that any of you reading these words who are blessed with all of your physical and mental faculties would appreciate that, not only is it OK for people with disabilities to have sexual feelings and to engage in sex, but it would be unnatural if they didn't.

Sex and Disabilities

Saying that terrific sex is possible and desirable for people with disabilities isn't the same thing as saying that it is easy to come by.

Perhaps the most difficult part of sexuality for many people with disabilities is finding a partner. And some people who were once physically fit and had a partner, lose that partner after they become disabled. No one can say whether losing a partner is worse than not having one in the first place; both are very, very difficult circumstances — particularly when the person involved faces physical difficulties as well. But if the disabled person's partner does leave, adding an emotional loss to the physical one, this combination can be unbearably painful.

Finding a partner

The most important characteristics for a person with disabilities to have in finding a partner are to be open-minded and persistent. You have to learn to have faith in the fact that there are people in the world whose criteria for deciding whom they want to have as a partner is the inner person, not a person's physical attributes or how much money he or she has. These individuals are willing to look beyond physical problems because they fall in love with others based on who they are as human beings.

For that to happen, for such a person to discover the inner you, you who are disabled must allow your inner being to shine through. Now this isn't easy. Often people with disabilities tend either to hide themselves in shame or to cover their weaknesses with anger. Although these two common responses are quite understandable, you must let as many people as possible see the real you, the happy you, the sensitive you, the sexy you. Then, hopefully, you'll find someone to be your partner.

Some people who become the partner of a person with disabilities are themselves disabled; they may even have the same disability. But, if you are going to act unpleasant, if you are going to make it especially difficult for someone to love you, then it doesn't matter whether the person you meet has a disability or not. People may be sympathetic to others with disabilities, but that doesn't mean that they're going to want to spend time with a self-absorbed grouch.

Most disabled people have to struggle every day just to get by, so I know that you possess plenty of strength and courage. But I also know that, when it's an effort just to get down the street, it's easy to give up on something long-term like finding a partner. But you can't let yourself give up. You have to persevere, because finding someone to share your life with is a goal worth every ounce of determination you put into realizing it.

One benefit to showing your bright side is that, even if you never find a partner with whom to form a loving and sexual relationship, you will certainly make new friends. People are attracted to a sunny disposition, they can't help themselves. If you smile, if you give people compliments, if you tell a funny joke, if you give them a big hello, they will respond positively. On the other hand, if you have a sour face, if you mumble, if you complain, then you will turn people off.

Many of you may be saying, "But I have a disability; I have enough troubles. Why do I have to reach out? Why do I have to be the first one to smile?"

Well, you know what? I give the exact same advice to a physically able person who is looking for a partner. Your disposition does play a role in attracting others, and just because you have a good excuse for feeling rotten doesn't change the fact that negative feelings repel people. That's just the way it is; if you want to attract people, then you just have to act attractive.

Partnering the person with disabilities

You can't compare pain, so I could never make a comparison between the hurt felt by those who become disabled, in whatever way, and the suffering of their partner, but I must acknowledge the partners' pain. Without warning, a marriage that included a long list of activities that both partners enjoyed, like skiing or tennis or making love on the dining room table, becomes one full of obstacles instead. Yes, the physically fit partners still have their health, but as long as they remain with their partners, their hopes, dreams, aspirations, and fantasies can be just as damaged as those of their disabled lovers.

Sadly, but often understandably, many of these partners leave the marriage. They refuse to accept the limitations that living with a disabled person puts on their lives. Sure, it would be great if everyone could be heroic, but not everybody can, and we shouldn't condemn these people, because we don't know what we would do if we were in their shoes.

Keeping the relationship alive

Some couples, when the one partner's health first fails, swear that they will stay together and work things out, just the way they did on their wedding day. But that is not always possible. Sometimes it's the fault of the healthy partner, who just can't find the strength any longer to take care of a disabled partner and still manage his or her own life. And sometimes it's the fault of the disabled person, who places too many demands with too little consideration for the partner.

However difficult it is to have a disability, you, the disabled person, must be willing to give your partner a hand. Yes, you may have lost certain faculties, but you have to be willing to exercise the ones you still have to your fullest.

Because this is a book about sex, let me address that particular subject. If a man has an accident and, as a result, loses his ability to have erections, that doesn't mean that his wife has to spend the rest of her life sexually frustrated. If he can still move his fingers, if he can still use his tongue, if he can hold a vibrator, he owes it to his wife to fulfill her needs. If the man abandons his wife sexually, while at the same time asking her for all sorts of other help, not to mention sympathy, then she just might not be able to bear all those burdens. The same holds true for a disabled woman who withholds sexual favors.

If a healthy spouse locked into a marriage with a disabled person who refused to engage in any sex came to me, I wouldn't necessarily advise that person to stay within such a marriage. I might feel badly saying it, but I just might have to say that that person has to think of themselves also.

You should also remember that the glue that keeps a loving partnership together is a lot more than just sex. You have to tell your partner how much you love him; you have to thank her for putting in the extra effort that your disability may cause; in short, you have to shore up your entire relationship if you are going to have a successful marriage.

An inspiring man

One of the advantages of being Dr. Ruth is that I get to meet all sorts of people. On one of my television programs, I interviewed a man who was quadriplegic, and he was willing to talk on national television about the great a sex life he had with his wife. He did the best that he could with what God left to him, and he had a very successful marriage.

He is definitely inspirational, and thankfully he is not alone. Many people with physical disabilities have great sex. Anyone who saw *Coming Home*, a 1978 movie about a soldier who returns from Vietnam in a wheelchair, was given a demonstration of how sexual and sexy the relationship of a disabled man and a healthy woman can be. So a disability does not have to put an end to a couple's sex life, although it will almost definitely mean that they will have to put more effort into seeing that the fires do keep burning brightly.

If you and your partner are facing a disability, I cannot recommend too strongly that you see a sex therapist or marriage counselor — in particular, one who has experience working in such areas (see Appendix A). Both of you may have worries and fears that play a role in your sexual functioning, maybe even a bigger role than the actual disability. You both need to talk these problems out, and rarely can a couple accomplish this without professional help. The same is true of other types of strains, in addition to the sexual ones, that can tear at your relationship. It's not easy undergoing such trials, and there's no shame in seeking help to overcome them.

Sex after a Heart Attack

When most people hear the term *disabled* or *physically challenged,* they immediately think of someone who has an affliction that is easily seen, such as a person who is in a wheelchair, who uses a cane, or who signs instead of speaks. But not every ailment is visible, and one of the most common problems which affects sexual functioning is a heart attack.

Overcoming fear

You may well have heard rumors of famous men who died because of a heart attack while in the throes of passion. I can't attest to the truth of any of these. But I *can* tell you that, for the average person who suffers a heart attack or undergoes heart surgery or even has angina, problems with sex almost always result. It's not that these people don't want to have sex; it's that they're afraid. They worry that, as a result of engaging in intercourse or having an orgasm, they will trigger another heart attack — this time, a fatal one.

This is not a foundless fear. Certainly, for a time after you've had a heart attack, your doctor will not allow you to have sex. But just because you're given the green light, doesn't mean that you will feel ready. It doesn't take much to make a man lose his ability to have an erection, so you can imagine that the fear of provoking a heart attack would certainly be sufficient to cause impotence. For women, the usual problem is *anorgasmia,* the inability to have an orgasm, which is equally understandable.

The best treatment for fear of sex after a heart attack is reassurance by your physician or cardiologist. I believe that this should take place in the hospital while you are still recuperating. Sexual performance is almost always a concern of someone who has had heart problems; it helps speed recovery if your fears can be alleviated as quickly as possible. If you need further tests to determine what you can and cannot do, then, by all means, you should get them. No doctor should consider the loss of sex as no big deal, because it *is* a big deal — not only for the patient, but also for the patient's partner.

By the way, it's not only the patient who may suffer from impotence or anorgasmia, it can also be the partner, who is just as afraid of causing a crisis with his or her partner's heart. The partner may need just as much reassurance as the patient.

One way to overcome the fears associated with sex is to make masturbation the first step and slowly work your way up to intercourse. Masturbation is also something that you can perform on your partner so that he or she doesn't have to be sexually frustrated during your recovery.

It may not all be in your head

Fear isn't the only factor that could be causing impotence. Heart problems are usually accompanied by vascular problems, and — because a man's erection is caused by blood flowing into the penis — sometimes the impotence a man experiences after a heart attack has physical rather than mental causes.

Angina, shortness of breath, and palpitations are problems associated with heart conditions, and, although they may not be deadly, they can certainly put a crimp in your sex life. Very often these symptoms show up after you've had an orgasm, during the period that your heartbeat is on its way down. Now, if every time you have an orgasm you get an angina attack, which is a sharp pain in the chest area, then that's not going to improve your desire for sex, is it? Here, again, you should consult with your physician or cardiologist. Don't be ashamed to ask specific questions. Your doctor may have suggestions that will help you have a relatively normal sex life, and you have every right to find out.

What can you do?

Here are some specific tips that might help you if you have heart trouble.

- ✔ If you have a heart condition, don't engage in sexual activity when you're angry or under a lot of stress. At these times, the heart is already beating faster, and sex would only tax its abilities even more.

- ✔ See if one of the new drugs like calcium channel blockers or beta blockers can be prescribed for you. These drugs can make sex easier on your heart.

- ✔ Some heart patients decide for themselves to take their medication, like propranolol (Inderal) or nitroglycerin, before having sex, thinking that they can prevent heart troubles. Do not attempt such techniques without first checking with your physician. (Propranolol is used on a schedule, so taking it out of schedule could be risky.)

The medications that are prescribed for heart conditions, such as beta-blockers, antihypertensives, and diuretics, can cause sexual functioning problems of their own. Sometimes your doctor can prescribe alternative medicines that will still be effective without getting in the way of your sexual functioning, so ask questions of your cardiologist.

I have spoken to many cardiologists on this issue, and the lack of communication is shared by both the medical profession and the patients. Some cardiologists gloss over the sexual aspects, but many times it's the patients who are too shy to discuss with their cardiologist that they're having sexual problems. This is especially true of older people, who form the biggest proportion of heart patients. They may believe that, at their age, sex isn't important. But sex is important, and it can play an important role in your recovery. So don't ignore sexual problems; speak out.

Drugs that can affect your sex life

Many drugs have side effects, and many of those side effects pertain to your sex life. The following is a list of drugs that can affect various sexual functions. Take note, these drugs will not affect everyone the same way, but if you are taking one or more of these drugs and you do notice that it is affecting your sexual functioning, speak to your doctor about it. There may a different drug available, or perhaps a different dosage, that will restore your sexual functioning.

Drugs that can affect sexual desire (names in parentheses are brand names):

antidepressants, hypnotics, antipsychotic and antianxiety drugs such as: antihistamines, barbiturates, chlordiazepoxide (Librium), chlorpromazine (Thorazine), cimetidine (Tagamet), clonidine (Catapres), diazepam (Valium), disulfiram (Anabuse), estrogens (used in men to treat prostate cancer), methyldopa (Aldomet), propranolol (Inderal), reserpine (Serpasil), tricyclic antidepressants (TADs), and birth control pills

Drugs that can affect ejaculation:

anticholinergics, barbiturates, chlorpromazine (Thorazine), clonidine (Catapres), estrogens, guanethidine (Ismelin), methyldopa (Aldomet), monoamine oxidase inhibitors, phenoxybenzamine (Dibenzyline), reserpine (Serpasil), thiazide diuretics, thioridazine (Mellaril), and tricyclic antidepressants

Drugs that can affect erections:

anticholinergics, antihistamines, barbiturates, chlordiazepoxide (Librium), chlorpromazine (Thorazine), cimetidine (Tagamet), clonidine (Catapres), diazepam (Valium), digitalis, disulfiram (Antabuse); estrogens, ethionamide (Trecator-SC), guanethidine (Imelin), hydroxyprogesterone (for prostate cancer), lithium (Lithonate), methantheline (Banthine), methyldopa (Aldomet), monoamine oxidase inhibitors (MAOs), reserpine (Serpasil), thioridazine (Mellaril), and tricyclic antidepressants

Drugs that can affect orgasm in women:

anticholinergics, clonidine (Catapres), methyldopa (Aldomet), monoamine oxidase inhibitors, and tricyclic antidepressants

I believe that it would also be a good idea to consult with a sex therapist who is trained in working with people with heart ailments. Sex therapists aren't shy about speaking to you about your sexual functioning, and, if necessary, they can act as an intermediary and speak to your doctor in order to find out exactly what sexual activities you can perform safely. See Appendix A for more about choosing a sex therapist.

Sex and the Diabetic

You may be aware that one of the side effects of diabetes in men can be impotence. The fact that so many people do know about this possibility means that many men who are diabetic suffer needlessly with impotence. In these cases, the impotence is caused not by the disease, but by the anxiety they feel.

If you're a diabetic having problems with your erections, either a softening of the erections or no erections at all, I suggest that you do visit a sex therapist for several reasons:

✔ The therapist may be able to help restore some or all of your lost functioning, if the cause is not physical.

✔ Even without a firm erection, sexual enjoyment and ejaculation can still be satisfying. A therapist can help you explore these possibilities.

✔ You should visit this sex counselor with your spouse, because she may need reassurance that the problems are being caused by the disease and not because you now find her unattractive or have taken an outside lover.

✔ You should also consult with your doctor because there are products on the market that may be able to restore your ability to have an erection. One of these, a drug called alprostadil, being marketed as Caverject, has just been given approval for sale by the FDA. It is self-administered into the base of your penis and can induce an erection within 5 to 20 minutes.

Diabetic women have also been found to have diminished sexual functioning. The intensity of the orgasmic response is sometimes lessened, and she may develop a greater need for increased manual or oral stimulation of the clitoris in order to have an orgasm. Again, a sex therapist can help you deal with these symptoms.

Sex and the Mentally Impaired

Many people feel that, because mentally impaired or intellectually disabled people have only the intelligence of a child, they should be treated like children with regard to all of their abilities. They believe that the mentally impaired should be "protected" from sex the way we protect children. As a result of such policies, especially if the person lives in a group setting, family or staff make an effort to eliminate any form of sexual interest or expression from these people's lives. They are given no privacy and not even allowed to masturbate.

In many cases, this attitude comes in conflict with reality because, although a person's mental level may be stuck in childhood, physically, he or she goes on to become an adult. The men have erections, nocturnal emissions, and a fully developed libido (sex drive) with all of the sexual desires that brings. The woman's sex drive also can develop fully, and physically she will have to adapt to having her menstrual periods. So, although, for some mentally impaired individuals, sex education can be limited to teaching them not to undress or touch their genitals in public, many others would benefit from learning about safer sex practices and how to handle a relationship.

Because the degree of mental proficiency is different for each of these individuals, exactly how much they should be taught, and how much freedom regarding sex they should be given, depends on the individual. Some mentally disabled people marry and have children; for others, such activities would not be appropriate.

The one thing that anyone — parent, relative, or caretaker — dealing with a mentally disabled person who reaches adolescence cannot do is ignore sex. As the mentally disabled person grows up physically, his or her hormones will kick in, causing a variety of changes, such as the growth of pubic and underarm hair. Just as with average teenagers, someone must teach mentally disabled teenagers that these changes are normal. Girls must learn to use a pad or tampon. Boys must be told about wet dreams. Both sexes have to understand about the sexual feelings that they are starting to have. Both have to learn about masturbation and that they should do it in private.

Another point to consider is companionship. Everyone needs companionship, and so it is only natural that people pair off. Sometimes that companionship develops into a romance, and then a sexual relationship. Some institutions allow this to take place, making sure that contraception is used, while others do not. But even keeping men separated from women cannot insure that sexual contact won't arise.

The best approach is to offer all mentally impaired persons sex education so that they can learn to deal with this aspect of their lives. They will benefit from it, and so will those who take care of them. We cannot deny people who have mental impairments the right to fulfill the same needs that the rest of us have, and so we have an obligation to help them learn as much as they are able to absorb.

Sex and the Institutionalized

Just as people who take care of the mentally disabled must accept the sexuality of those under their care, so must those who tend to any person who is chronically institutionalized, including those with chronic disabilities and the elderly who are in nursing homes for the elderly. For the vast majority of these people, whatever disabilities they do have, sexual dysfunction is not what placed them in the institution.

Institutionalized individuals deserve to have both their sexuality and their privacy respected. If they need to have the door closed in order to masturbate, they should not be disturbed. Many times, people confined to a nursing home form relationships. In these cases, I believe that *dating rooms* should be set aside, with a clear "Do Not Disturb" sign visible, so that they can enjoy their companionship in whatever way they see fit. Remember, even if a couple does not have intercourse, the pleasure of touching each other, hugging, or kissing is intensified if the couple is permitted to be alone.

In some cases, the couple cannot have sex without assistance, and I advocate that, just the way the staff would help them to bathe or to void, staff should be trained to help disabled individuals enjoy the benefits of sex. Sex is not only for the young and beautiful, but for everybody, and this assistance should be provided in a nonjudgmental way.

What may be most important to creating an environment where healthy sexual relationships can flourish in these settings is to make certain that the staff is given the necessary counseling to be able to handle such issues just as competently as they give other types of care. Because of the values of our society, helping people to have sex does not always come naturally, but I believe that, given the proper guidance, we can make our institutions a little warmer than they are now by including as much loving as possible.

Uncompromising Compromised Sex

In all probability, sex for a person with disabilities or a medical condition is going to involve some compromises. Not every position will be possible; maybe even some very basic sex acts, like intercourse, are impossible. But that doesn't mean that the two people having sex can't derive a lot of pleasure from their activities. The important thing is not to look at your sex lives as limited, but to try and make the most of the sexual performance that you can have. Discuss your situation with your doctor to find the full range of what is possible for you.

Remember, sex isn't just orgasms. The pleasure that comes from making love (and here I think that it is very important to use that term) comes also from touching each other, kissing each other, caressing each other.

The human body and the human spirit are amazing things. Very often, the body of a disabled person compensates for one loss through the development of other senses. A blind person may find that his or her sense of hearing has improved considerably. A deaf person may develop a keener sense of smell. And so disabled people may well find that the parts of the sex act that are available to them become more exquisitely pleasurable than they might be to others.

That's why you should never give up. Try to enjoy sex to whatever extent you can, and make sure that your partner enjoys it, too. You may find that, in the end, you are gaining as much enjoyment as any nondisabled person does and, by fully appreciating the sensations that you do have, maybe even more so. And your partner will find life more fulfilling as well.

The 5th Wave
By Rich Tennant

"MOM AND DAD GET LIKE THIS EVERYTIME THEY WATCH BACK-TO-BACK EPISODES OF 'THE LOVE BOAT'".

Chapter 18

Same Sex Relationships

· ·

In This Chapter

▶ The roots of homosexuality

▶ Indicators (and nonindicators) of homosexuality

▶ Coming out

▶ Gay sex

· ·

Much of this book deals with heterosexual relationships; that is, relationships between men and women. *Homosexuality* is when men or women are sexually attracted only to others of the same sex as themselves (*hetero,* of course, meaning different, and *homo* meaning the same). Which one you are — heterosexual or homosexual, that is, straight or gay — is called your *sexual orientation.*

I am often asked why it is that some people prefer to have sexual relations with members of their own sex instead of with the opposite sex.

From the letters I get, I know that many people believe that homosexuals actually choose the homosexual lifestyle over heterosexuality. They think that a gay person makes a conscious choice at some point in his or her life to be gay, for one reason or another, and so they also believe that gay people could just as easily change their minds and switch to heterosexuality. Of course, the implication is that they should change back to the more "normal" sexual orientation.

The truth is that we don't know the *etiology* of homosexuality — the reasons why some people are gay while most others are not. In spite of the research done on the subject, no conclusive results have been found.

Here are some of the many theories proposed over the years:

✔ Aristotle believed that men who like to be sodomized have an extra nerve running down their spinal cord that ends in the rectum.

✔ Before Aristotle, Persian physicians concluded that the way a boy masturbated, holding the penis either tightly or loosely, would cause him to be either homosexual or heterosexual.

✔ Sigmund Freud thought that homosexuality developed when a boy
identified with his mother rather than with his father.

For many years, homosexuality was defined as a mental illness, and treatment
was aimed at restoring "normal" sexuality. It wasn't until 1973 that the American Psychiatric Association recognized that homosexuality was not a mental
illness.

Here is what modern science has to say about homosexuality:

✔ Research with twins has demonstrated that there is a genetic component
to homosexuality, but genetics is not thought to account for all cases.

✔ Anatomical studies of the brain have shown some apparent structural
differences between homosexuals and heterosexuals, but to date this
research, while continuing, is still speculative.

Although we have been studying the issue for thousands of years, we still can
come to no conclusion about what determines sexual orientation. All we do
know is that homosexuality among men and women has existed for as long as
history has been recorded, that homosexual lifestyles are no more likely to
disappear than heterosexual ones, and, as far as I am concerned, that homosexuals should be treated with the same respect as every other human being.

The Right to Be Gay

Is it important to know why some people live a different lifestyle? In a perfectly
open society that attached no consequences to one's sexual orientation,
knowing what caused different sexual orientations might not be important. But,
because some people in our society publicly advocate that homosexual men
and lesbians be prevented from — or even punished for — living their lifestyles,
I do think it certainly has relevance.

You see, if gay people do have a choice in their lifestyles, then some could
perhaps legitimately argue that society should try and control how they live.
(There are some lesbians who say that they do choose lesbianism for political
reasons, but that is beyond the scope of this book.) Society singles out a
number of different modes of behavior to restrict. Some think that, because we
ban things like prostitution and sex with minors, so too, potentially (and I'm not
saying I advocate this, because I don't), could we ban homosexuality in our
society. Sodomy was certainly illegal all across the country for many years and
is still outlawed in some states (see Chapter 24).

But what if sexual orientation is beyond our choice? What if we are born with our sexual orientation and cannot change it? Can you really fault homosexuals then? Should society pass laws forbidding gays from having sex if that is the only way that sex is pleasing to them?

Now, as a Jew, I know that the Bible specifically bans homosexual acts, and therefore many believers in the Bible consider homosexuals to be sinners. The problem with relying on the Bible is that it says so much that it is open to interpretation, and — of necessity — some of that interpretation may be more human than divine. Some religious denominations, like the Episcopalians, voice support for homosexual priests despite these Biblical injunctions. And many Christians support our armed forces despite the facts that one of the Ten Commandments says "Thou Shalt Not Kill" and Jesus instructed his followers to turn the other cheek. The only thing we can know for certain is that we are all here on this Earth together.

Separation of church and state

In America, we believe in separation between church and state. Believers in the Bible are certainly free to stop themselves from committing certain sexual acts, but, under the U.S. Constitution, their beliefs do not confer on them the right to force others to believe or behave as they do.

Sexual practices between gay men and women, when done safely, do no one any harm. Although gay sexuality may not fit the mold used by most people, I believe that we shouldn't criticize gays for behavior over which they may really have no control, and which doesn't harm anyone anyway. Nobody is forcing anyone to be gay, and neither should anyone force someone not to be gay.

As fellow humans, we in the majority heterosexual population must learn to be more open-minded and not condemn those gay men and women who live among us. Rather, we should treat them as we would any other of our brothers and sisters on this planet.

No carte blanche

What two consenting adults, whatever their sexual orientation, do in the privacy of their home is their own business. Now this doesn't mean that I give blanket absolution to every form of homosexual behavior. For example, I believe that some of the activities that take place in public areas, like at gay bars and bathhouses, go too far — especially, in this era of AIDS.

Homosexuals are as capable of responsible sex as are heterosexuals. And they're just as capable of irresponsible sex as well. Considering that heterosexuals have a 50 percent divorce rate and often have multiple sexual partners over time, it's unreasonable to expect that homosexuals should be any different — picking one partner and staying with him or her for a lifetime.

But that a serious effort must be made to form a relationship before having sex applies to both lifestyles equally. And that safer sex practices be employed all the time applies to all sexually active people — gay and straight.

Determining Your Orientation — without a Compass

I am sure that many heterosexuals are reading this chapter out of curiosity, and that's great. Now some straight readers may get turned on by reading about gay sex, and that may confuse them. They may suddenly start to wonder whether or not they themselves are gay. So, before getting to the sexual part of this discussion, I'd like to familiarize you with the very beginning of the process: uncovering your sexual orientation.

What turns you on

Getting excited by reading about gay sex, or even having fantasies about engaging in sexual relations with a member of your own sex, does not mean that you are gay.

A gay person definitely knows whether he or she is gay, and that identification does not come because of an occasional gay fantasy.

In addition to gay fantasies, a common occurrence among young teen males is to do some sexual experimenting with another male. This might take the form of masturbating together, or actually masturbating each other. This type of behavior doesn't usually go any further than that; it stops on its own. Again, sexual experimentation among teenagers is pretty common and does not indicate any homosexual tendencies.

What does indicate that a young person is actually a homosexual?

The best indicator of homosexuality is if you can *only* get sexually excited by thinking about having sex with someone of your own sex, even though the only sexual activity you may be having at the time may be with members of the opposite sex.

Living in the closet

Saying that someone is "in the closet" has a range of meanings. Basically, it refers to someone who does not admit openly that he or she is gay. Some people who get married, have children, and spend an entire lifetime living with and regularly having sex with a member of the opposite sex, are really not heterosexual at all. In order to get excited, these people have to fantasize about having sex with a member of their own sex.

There are different ways that people who appear to be openly heterosexual may actually lead clandestine gay sex lives:

✔ Some people visit gay bars when the opportunity presents itself, go to areas where gay prostitutes are known to hang out, or merely masturbate while looking at gay magazines.

✔ Some people lead a gay lifestyle only when in the presence of other gays, but put on a front of being heterosexual in other settings, such as at work or school.

✔ Some people may never actually engage in any form of gay sex, but, nevertheless, deep down inside, are gay.

Many of these people, especially in today's more liberal atmosphere, do end up "coming out of the closet" at some point in their lives. But others box themselves in so tightly that they just don't feel that they could survive the revelation, and so they hide their gayness for their entire lives.

Coming Out

Prior to 1969, few gays would consider publicly revealing their sexual orientation (also called *coming out),* but a riot in New York — caused by a police raid of a gay bar called The Stonewall — politicized many gays and started what was called the Gay Liberation Movement. This movement insists that the homosexual lifestyle be treated the same as the heterosexual one, and that gay people have rights equal to those of everyone else. Many laws have been passed since then that give gays much more freedom than they once had to practice their lifestyles. But many members of our society still frown on gays — oftentimes, including the people who are closest to gays: their families.

Coming out to family and friends

The adolescent years are never easy for anyone, but they are certainly a lot more difficult for gay young people. Not only do gay teens have to confront their own emerging sexuality, which is different from that of most of their peers, but they must then face the rebuke that their sexuality often brings from their immediate families. Revealing one's homosexuality is never easy — for young or old — but it can be particularly difficult for teens, who are dependent on their families and have not yet established their own private lives with their own place to live and a job to provide financial support. In fact, the rates of suicide for young homosexuals are much higher than for heterosexuals of the same age, in great part because many are unable to cope if faced by rejection from their families.

There is no single pattern for how families react when a son or a daughter comes out of the closet. Some parents may have suspected for a while and learned to accept it, so there is a general sense of relief that the subject is out in the open. Other parents react very negatively, upset that many of their expectations for their child — the traditional heterosexual marriage followed by a number of grandchildren — have suddenly disappeared. They may also react negatively, in part, because they feel that their child's homosexuality reflects badly on them — and the way they raised that child — in the eyes of the rest of the family as well as friends and neighbors. In some families, the reaction is split, with one parent accepting the son or daughter's announcement and the other going so far as to cut off all contact.

Parenthood is never easy, but, because the expectations of most parents are turned topsy-turvy by the announcement that their child is gay, it's normal that there might be some mixed emotions in the beginning. Getting past those feelings and rebuilding your family's unity is the key, and I don't believe that you can help do that without some preparation. If you are forewarned about how your family may react, and have been told ways to handle these reactions, you are much more likely to end up being accepted by your family.

Up until recently, the decision of whether or not to tell your family that you were gay was one which was entirely up to you. Sadly, that has not been the case for many homosexual men who contracted AIDS. Testing HIV-positive has been the reason pushing too many men in the last decade to tell their families about their sexual orientation. I want all of you — gay and straight — to think of that sad scene the next time you consider practicing unsafe sex.

The most important advice I can give to those of you who are gay and who have not revealed your sexual identity to your family is to immediately find a counselor who has worked with other gay people facing this problem to give you guidance (see Appendix B). The counselor's experience in this area can be invaluable to you in obtaining the best possible results from your circumstances.

Coming out to the world

Most gay people come out to a potential sex partner first. That can be a very scary experience in itself. What if that person turns out to be straight? Rejection is always traumatic, but especially if the other person is actually repulsed by the offer, as a straight person approached sexually by someone of their own sex often is.

Eventually, most gay people do meet other people who share their lifestyle, and the support that they get from others helps them to then declare their sexual orientation to their families and friends. One new way that is helping many teens is via computer bulletin boards (see Chapter 20). Using this method of communication, they can learn about the gay lifestyle without having to reveal their own identity until they are ready to do so.

Coming out in your profession or on the job can be much more risky. Openness about one's sexual orientation doesn't always translate well in the business world. Because of this, many gay people who do not hide their status at home are very careful about whom they tell at the office. Some companies will not hire a homosexual simply because of the strain that an HIV-positive person might put on their health benefits program. In other cases, some employers are becoming less tolerant of their homosexual employees, either because of their own fear of AIDS or because of a concern that their other employees may react negatively.

This on-the-job discrimination against homosexuals can backfire in the battle against AIDS because it can lead the gay person, for appearance's sake, to avoid forming a relationship, thus forcing him into the dangerous world of anonymous sex, where the risk of getting and spreading AIDS is so much higher.

Not so long ago, more and more gay people were letting their secret out. But, since the advent of AIDS, many gay men have decided to keep their sexual orientation private once again.

Because a gay person can never know exactly what the outcome of his or her coming out will be, it is always a heavy burden. If everything goes right, gay men and women may feel as though a tremendous weight has been lifted from their shoulders because they no longer have to lead dual lives. On the other hand, if they end up losing contact with certain family members and friends, many find it a heavy price to pay for admitting their true identity.

Coming out when you're married, with children

The gay man or woman who marries someone of the opposite sex, and also has children, faces a double burden if they decide to later reveal sexual identities. In addition to his or her own suffering, his or her partner and children undoubtedly suffer tremendously.

Although the gay person certainly feels a sense of loss at leaving the spouse and children, the likelihood is that the gay person will eventually blossom within the gay community. However, for the partner who is being left behind the grieving process can sometimes be worse than that caused by a death. That person now has not only lost a spouse but also has had their own sexual worth badly damaged. The partner whom they loved, and whom they thought found them sexually attractive, may actually never have felt that way. This realization comes as a crushing blow, and, although the newly identified gay person will be welcomed by the gay community, his or her former spouse often finds no comparative support. Because this phenomenon has spread in the last decade, support groups are now forming in various places to help such abandoned spouses. But, still, many of these people end up facing their loss alone.

These negative consequences are not because the gay people made a bad decision at the time they came out. Rather, I believe that these gay people made a bad decision when they got married in the first place. By allowing society to pressure them into leading a lifestyle they were not suited to, they end up causing many other people a lot of pain and suffering later on — in addition to the suffering they endured themselves while leading a life not truly their own.

Outing

Some people within the gay community believe that all gay people should reveal their homosexuality. These people sometimes act on this belief and reveal the secretly gay person's sexual orientation in a process called *outing*.

As you might expect, I am totally against outing. I have seen the pain and suffering that gay people go through when they freely decide to reveal their true selves, and nobody has the right to force someone else to undergo that process.

Finding support

Not so many years ago, children who were born left-handed were forced to learn to write with their right hands. Society has since learned to accept lefties, and in some endeavors, such as sports, many lefties actually have an advantage.

I hope that one day everyone will feel the same way about gay people that we feel about lefties. The pressures that our society puts on gays to keep their sexuality hidden causes untold damage. And the guilt for this lies not on gay people, but on all of us for trying to force them into adopting a false sexual identity.

Gary

I had a young man come to see me who was very distressed. He'd known he was gay since he was about 14. He was a "Navy brat," and desperately wanted to please his father and also join the Navy, but he knew he couldn't do that as a homosexual, so he hid his sexual orientation. Because he needed sexual release, he would go into gay bars for impersonal sex, but he would never allow himself to become close to any gay man, because he knew it would be much harder to hide a relationship than to hide mere sexual intercourse.

Gary did not join the Navy, but he still was very fearful of his parents discovering his homosexuality. The reason that Gary came to see me was that, for the first time, he had developed a crush on another man — a coworker. They'd had sex, but Gary didn't know how to handle the situation. He asked me to help him forget this man, but, of course, what he needed was instruction on how to tell his family who he really was so that he could fully develop as a human being.

Although everyone focuses on the AIDS crisis among homosexuals — and it certainly has had a horrible effect on this population — at the same time, gays have been building networks to help each other live more satisfying lives. They've organized politically, with groups such as The National Gay and Lesbian Task Force, so that in major cities where there are large gay communities they have gained many, if not most, of the same civil rights of heterosexuals. There are gay resorts where they can gather without feeling different. And I just saw a new book, *The Gay Lesbian and Bisexual Students' Guide* (NYU Press), which lists all of the colleges in America and rates them as far as the hospitality they provide to gays.

All these changes have made life a lot more pleasant for homosexuals since the Stonewall incident, but far too many people still remain ignorant and discriminate against others because of their sexual orientation.

Homosexual Sex between Men

There are a wide array of male-to-male sexual practices — many of them identical to heterosexual practices — and, in a gay relationship, the feelings of love and caring can be as strong as in any heterosexual relationship.

Because of the traumatic effect that AIDS has had on the gay community, I am listing gay sexual practices in order of their safety, as that is of major concern to both gays and straights. It is particularly important that young homosexual males hear the message about safer sex because, while the older population that has seen so many of its members suffer and die has adopted safer sex practices, reports indicate that young gay men are once again flirting with danger in their habits.

✔ At the safest end of the spectrum is *voyeurism*; that is, watching others who are having sex. This might be compared to straight men going to topless clubs; although, because of the atmosphere of the gay bar and bath scene, voyeurism is more likely to be accompanied by masturbation among homosexuals.

✔ Group masturbation is another common practice in certain homosexual communities. This may either be solo masturbation done in the presence of others, or mutual masturbation, which is sometimes done in *cycle jerks* where one man masturbates the next, who masturbates the next, and so on. Because of the dangers of AIDS, most major cities have developed *J/O Clubs* (the J/O stands for "jerk off" or "jack off"), which are places where gay men may masturbate together. These clubs usually have strict rules against other, dangerous forms of sex.

✔ Kissing is something that appeals to some gay men, though not all. There are some gay men for whom kissing is the primary or only form of physical contact they have with other men.

✔ *Frontage* is the term applied to the practice of two men rubbing their bodies against each other, usually until climax. This is a considered a safe form of sexual activity.

✔ *Fellatio,* oral-penile sex, is considered to be the most common form of sex between men.

Because the risks of transmitting an STD are greater if one person ejaculates into the mouth of the other, ejaculating in the mouth is often avoided. Because of the leak of Cowper's fluid, however, such oral sex still has some danger to it unless the person on whom fellatio is being performed wears a condom. Kissing other bodily parts includes little risk, except for anal kissing, or *rimming,* from which many STDs can be passed on.

✔ The most risky form of gay male sex is *penile-anal sex*. This is when one man inserts his penis into the anus of his partner and thrusts until he achieves orgasm. The person whose anus is being penetrated, the *bottom,* may also find pleasure from having his prostate and rectum stimulated in this manner. The transmission of STDs is at its highest during anal sex because the ejaculate can contain the viruses. Because the rectal lining is often torn or abraded during this sexual practice, the viruses then gain easy access to the blood stream.

> The use of condoms is a must for safer penile-anal sex; although, because of the amount of physical activity, condoms are more likely to break during anal sex than during vaginal sex. So, even with a condom, anal sex remains a risky activity.

The relationships between homosexual men have undergone several transformations since the Gay Liberation Movement began. Many gay men, especially in bigger cities with large gay populations, at first became ultra-promiscuous. They had sex with literally hundreds of other men, even if they also formed a relationship with one other man.

With the arrival of the AIDS epidemic, however, many homosexuals chose to have sex only with one partner; however, for many, it was too late. They had already contracted the disease. Sadly, some younger homosexuals are returning to unsafe sexual practices. We can only hope that they use safer sex before it is too late.

Lesbian Sex

Much of what is considered to be lesbian sex resembles what heterosexuals consider to be foreplay (see Chapter 11), because intercourse between two women is not possible. These activities include touching, kissing, licking, and sucking over the entire body.

- Because, in a lesbian couple, both partners have breasts — which, in women, are especially strong erogenous zones — these are usually a central part of sexual activity, including the rubbing of both sets of breasts up against each other as well as much nipple play.

- Body-to-body rubbing is another important method of sexual activity. When two women lie face to face, one on top of the other, pressing their genitals together and grinding them one against the other, this is called *tribadism*. In the 19th century, lesbians were sometimes referred to as *tribades* because of this practice. One reason that lesbians use this technique is that it allows the hands and mouth to be free to stimulate other parts of the body.

- Since the clitoris is the most sensitive part of a woman and, through its stimulation, she achieves orgasm, it is naturally central to lesbian sexual activity. Most lesbians enjoy touching and rubbing the clitoris, as well as the entire genital area, using fingers and sometimes vibrators.

- Oral sex is also popular. The use of the "69" position, during which both partners can perform cunnilingus on each other at the same time (see Chapter 12 for the heterosexual version of the 69), is common to some lesbians. Others avoid it, however, because they find that simultaneous sex is too distracting. Those women prefer to take turns.

✔ Vaginal penetration by a partner's finger or tongue is common, as is the insertion of foreign objects. Some lesbians use dildos. But, because many dildos are shaped like a penis, some controversy exists in the lesbian community as to their use. Many lesbians reject dildos because they are male-defined, and there is a strong political factor in the lesbian lifestyle. (Dildos are covered in Chapter 19.) See Figure 18-1 for some dildos that aren't shaped like penises.

✔ Other lesbian sexual practices include stimulation of the anus, including *rimming* (moving the tongue around the edge of the anus) and penetration of the anus with a finger or dildo.

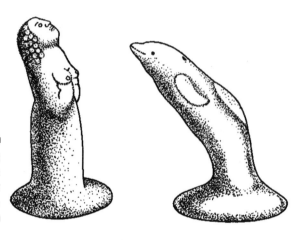
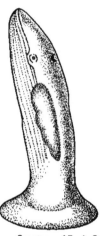

Figure 18-1:
Dildos come
in many
shapes.

Courtesy of Eve's Garden

Although orgasm is certainly a goal of lesbian sex, the lesbian community believes that all sex play is valid and that the goal should be pleasure, whether that leads to orgasm or not. However, some studies have reported that the frequency of orgasm for lesbians who have partners is higher than that of heterosexual women. Researchers have speculated that lesbians tend to arouse each other more slowly and communicate more during the sex act, telling each other more explicitly what is sexually pleasing.

The relationships of lesbian women have tended to be more couple-oriented than the relationships of homosexual men, both from an emotional and a physical point of view. Lesbians seem more interested in intimacy, and less demanding sexually.

Chapter 19
Solo Play and Fantasy

· ·

In This Chapter

▶ How masturbation got such a bad rap

▶ When to say when

▶ Who masturbates?

▶ How it's done

▶ Masturbation and make-believe

· ·

*T*o start off, I've got good news and better news. The good news is that I'm going to give you permission to do something that some other people may have told you not to do. The better news is that hair won't grow on your palms if you do it.

The Mythology of Masturbation

For any of you who haven't heard the myth about hairy palms, let me explain. Masturbation has long been frowned upon, and in ancient times there were viable reasons for this, besides the fact that Vaseline hadn't been invented yet.

    ✔ If people, particularly men, were masturbating, then they wouldn't be propagating as much. And, in the early days of mankind, when infant mortality was high and life expectancy low, making babies was important for survival of the species.

    ✔ Masturbation was frowned upon by the elders of the tribes because they believed that each man was born with only a certain amount of sperm, and if he wasted that sperm masturbating, he'd have none left to impregnate a woman. (I wonder what their attitude would have been if they'd known that a man can make 50,000 sperm a minute. Let the good times roll?)

The story of Onan

The early Jews certainly were against the *spilling of seed* (an old-fashioned term for masturbating). You can read about their concern in the story of Onan in Genesis in the Bible, out of which came the word *onanism* as a synonym for masturbation. Actually, Biblical scholars now believe that, rather than masturbating, Onan practiced *coitus interruptus* (withdrawing before ejaculation) so that he wouldn't impregnate his brother's widow, as customs and religious law dictate he do. How the scholars came to that conclusion is beyond me, but in any case, if Onan had known what everyone who's reading this book knows about the sperm in pre-ejaculatory fluid, he would have stuck to the original version and masturbated instead.

Over the years, this ban on masturbation was never completely lifted, and in certain time periods, during the Victorian Era in England for example, the crusade against masturbation grew to a fever pitch; the list of ills that masturbation was said to cause included insanity, epilepsy, headaches, nosebleeds, asthma, heart murmurs, rashes, and odors.

Worse than the supposed symptoms were the weapons that parents used to try to curb their children's masturbatory activities, which included restraints of all kinds and such medical procedures as circumcision, *castration* (removal of the testes), and *cliterectomy* (removal of the clitoris) — a terrible practice which is still widely used throughout Africa and performed on millions of women, not only to curb masturbation, but all sexual pleasure.

But, whether the ban on masturbation was based on cultural or religious beliefs, the elders knew (from their own experience, no doubt) that young boys and girls don't always listen to their elders (surprise, surprise). So they invented some myths about masturbation that would have the persuasive powers that laws wouldn't.

Many of the myths against what was labeled "self-abuse" were based on the notion that the consequences of masturbating included a physical sign that would reveal to the world that the individual was a masturbator. This threat of public exposure was supposed to coerce potential "self-abusers" to keep their hands away from their genitals. Among these scare tactics was the myth of the hairy palm, but, because the possibility of having to comb your palm every morning wasn't always scary enough, the elders also threw in things like going blind or insane.

Neither the bans nor the myths have stopped in this century. Many religions forbid masturbation, and the ad agency for an acne treatment got into the picture and suggested that masturbation causes pimples. ("Oh no, a zit, now everyone at school will know why I close the door in my room!") All of these myths are, of course, nonsense.

Too Much of a Good Thing?

Not a whit of scientific evidence shows that an orgasm obtained through masturbation is any different from one obtained during sexual intercourse, or that it could cause you any harm. But that doesn't mean that masturbation doesn't have any negative consequences. Masturbation can be abused, as can anything — including the things we need to survive, such as the food we eat (look at how many overweight people there are in the world today) and the air we breathe (as in hyperventilation).

Some people are guilty of overdoing a good thing when it comes to masturbation and get hooked on gratifying themselves, sometimes masturbating many times a day. They do it to such an extreme that they don't leave themselves the time or energy for much of anything else, including finding a partner.

OK, so how much masturbation is too much? That's a question I'm often asked, but I can't answer it directly. You see, this question really has to be turned around in order to get the right answer. In other words, if you are living a satisfying life, if you've got friends, are doing well at work or in school, are in a loving partnership with someone, and you're both satisfied with your sex life together, then it doesn't really matter how often you masturbate. On the other hand, if you are lonely and out of sorts, and you rely on masturbation to make yourself feel better instead of going about the business of making your life work the way you want it to, then you may be masturbating too much, no matter how rarely it is that you actually masturbate.

Masturbation is a good form of sexual release, but sometimes you need that sexual tension to get you going, to give you the incentive to find a partner, seek out new friends, look for a new job, or whatever. So, if you need to get your life in order and do masturbate a lot, I suggest you cut down. You don't have to stop altogether, but, if you can reduce the number of times you do it, you may find that you can begin to add some other positive aspects to your life.

What you're looking for is a happy medium. If you're single and are actively seeking a partner, then there's nothing wrong with masturbating in order to keep yourself from feeling sexually frustrated. Just don't do it so much that you wind up being more attached to your genitals than to the world outside.

If your partner is satisfied with your sex life, and you would like more orgasms than the two of you are having together, then it's OK to masturbate when the mood strikes you. But do make an effort to see if your partner would be willing to engage in sex with you more often. Don't be lazy and rely on masturbation to satisfy all your sexual needs, because a sexless marriage is not fulfilling and will likely not last very long.

Masturbation for Life

Today we know that masturbation is a healthy part of growing up. It can start in infancy and continue right through adulthood.

Masturbation in infancy

Going back to the very beginning, did you know that some male babies are born with an erection, and some girl babies are born lubricating? I wouldn't be surprised to learn that some babies massage their genitals while still in the womb.

Many children touch themselves "down there" because it feels good, although they cannot derive the full pleasure of masturbation because they can't yet have an orgasm. Most parents stop their children when they catch them playing with themselves, and that's OK, but how the parents do this can be very important to their children's sexual development.

You see, there's nothing wrong with teaching children the lesson that our society frowns on enjoying any form of sexual pleasure in public. But, hopefully, you can pass along this information without giving children the idea that masturbation (or sex) is bad per se. If you yell at your children or slap their hands, they're going to get the wrong message: that sexual pleasure, in and of itself, is bad. As a result, when these children become adults, they may not allow themselves to fully enjoy sex.

You can teach children not to pick their noses in front of others without giving them a complex, so you should be able to do the same thing about touching their "private parts." Probably the reason that many parents have difficulties in this particular area is that they were made to feel ashamed when they were little, and they still haven't overcome those feelings themselves. So parents end up passing on these feelings of shame to their children. But, if you can make yourself aware of what you're doing, then, hopefully, you can tone down the way you admonish your child in order not to give him or her the same sense of shame that you might have.

What parents must explain to their children is that it's OK to touch one's own genitals, but only in private. How many parents actually give the first half of the masturbation speech, the part that says it's OK? Probably very few. And how many parents actually give their children the privacy to masturbate; in other words, knocking before they walk into their child's room and walking away if asked to do so, without asking all sorts of questions? Also probably very few. And so, in the vast majority of cases, masturbation starts out as something forbidden that a person must do on the sly, and these early experiences shape much of our society's attitudes about sex in general.

Teenage masturbation

Although infants are very aware of their sexual organs, as children grow up, they go through what psychiatrist Sigmund Freud termed the *latency stage,* when they pretty much put sex out of their minds. That's the period when boys think that all girls are yucky, and girls think that all boys are even worse.

At some point — and that point is different for every child (it can start as early as the preteens or not begin until the late teens) — the sex hormones kick in and puberty begins. The child starts to develop what are called the *secondary sex characteristics,* which include things like growing pubic hair and developing breasts. At that point, an interest in sex also starts up, and that's when masturbation is likely to begin.

Surveys have shown again and again that boys masturbate more than girls. By the time most men reach adulthood, more than 90 percent have masturbated to orgasm at least once. For women, the percentage is closer to 60 percent. Some of this difference may be explained by the fact that many women who masturbate report that they do not begin until they are in their 20s or 30s, while men report that they usually begin in their early teens. However, even when adults are asked the question, more males report masturbating than females.

I believe that there are several reasons for this:

- ✔ A boy's genitals are just handier to reach. A boy becomes used to touching himself when he urinates, and so less of a taboo surrounds those parts.

- ✔ Males also become aroused a lot more quickly than females, so they can more easily grasp the opportunity to masturbate.

- ✔ Society is a lot more strict and repressive with females than with males, making it less likely for females to masturbate.

As more and more women become sexually literate, they are giving themselves the freedom to explore their own sexuality, so I believe that those percentages will become a lot closer as time passes.

Masturbation in adulthood

There's this huge misconception that, when a person reaches adulthood, masturbation stops. That is certainly not the case for single adults, and it isn't the case for married adults either.

Many married people masturbate. Although some do it for "negative" reasons (that is to say, they do it because they are not satisfied with their sex lives with their spouses), many more do it simply out of enjoyment. Some people find that they derive greater sexual pleasure from masturbation than from sexual intercourse. Others have a higher sex drive than their partners and require sex more often. Still others integrate masturbation into sex play with their spouses.

These cases illustrate two sides of masturbation:

John and Mary

When John and Mary first got married, they had sex just about every day. After five years and two children, the frequency dropped precipitously to about once a month. Although Mary wasn't looking for sex every day, once a month was too little for her. But, though she tried to lure John into having sex more often, it usually didn't work.

One night Mary woke to find John out of bed. She got up to look for him and was surprised to find him in the study, where he had a porno tape playing and his hand on his penis. Since he hadn't heard her, she tiptoed back into bed and didn't say anything to him, but that's when she sought my help.

When I finally spoke with John, he admitted that he would masturbate once or twice a week in front of the TV set late at night. The reason he gave me was that he got really turned on by porno films, but Mary wouldn't watch them with him. He started watching them on the sneak, and it developed into a habit that he couldn't seem to break, even though he felt guilty about not having sex with Mary as often as she would like.

I helped them to develop a compromise. Mary agreed to watch a porno film with John once a month, but she got to veto certain subject matters. John agreed to have sex with Mary at least once a week, which was all she really wanted, and then, if he still had the desire to masturbate, he could.

I suppose there have always been wives who've lost out to masturbation, but the temptations that are available these days — pornographic films for playing on a home tape machine, magazines on every newsstand, sex phone lines, cybersex, and everything else — seem to have increased the frequency that people report such problems to me, either privately or in letters. The best solution is a compromise, such as the one Mary and John worked out. Rarely do two people have exactly the same sex drives, so there's no reason for John not to masturbate, as long as he isn't taking anything away from Mary's enjoyment of sex.

Jim and Jackie

This was a second marriage for both Jim and Jackie. Jim's first wife had died of cancer, and Jackie was divorced. With his first wife, Jim had a fairly sedate marriage. He and his wife had sex about once a week, and both had been satisfied with that. In Jackie, he found just the opposite of his first wife. Jackie seemed to want sex every night, and at first Jim had been thrilled. But, although Jim had forced himself to keep up with Jackie during their courtship, six months after the wedding day he was beginning to wear out. He worked long hours and couldn't continue to have sex with Jackie every night, and he started to beg off more and more.

Jackie still felt those strong urges to relieve her sexual tensions, but because she never knew in advance whether or not Jim would agree to have sex with her, she became more and more frustrated.

Although I am normally all for spontaneity, in this case, I decided that what was needed was a structure to Jackie and Jim's sex life. Jim agreed that he would have sex with Jackie twice a week, and they would pick which days would work best ahead of time. This way, Jim could reserve his energies on those days for sex with Jackie, while Jackie was free to satisfy herself through masturbation on the other days.

Communication is often the key to solving marital problems like these, and if it takes a therapist of some sort to break the ice, then by all means go ahead and visit one (see Appendix A for help on choosing a sex therapist).

How to Masturbate

Although I'm sure that most of you already know how to masturbate, I don't want it said that I left such a basic part of good sexual functioning out, so here are some instructions.

Before I get into specifics, let me say loud and clear that the best tip that I can give you is to do what feels best to you. There's no right way or wrong way. You can use your left hand or your right hand or both hands. Whatever turns you on, as the saying goes . . . and it couldn't apply more than in the case of masturbation.

Male techniques

A common word for masturbation is *a hand job,* and the hand is certainly the most popular instrument used by men for masturbation. What are the alternatives, you ask?

Some boys masturbate by rubbing up against the bedsheets. Some men masturbate by putting their penises inside of a specially made, life-size rubber doll. Sex shops also sell devices that simulate a vagina. Many, though not all, of these devices are made to look like a vagina, and the man can add lubrication to make the rubber *feel* more like one too. I don't know how popular these alternatives are, although my guess is that the vast majority of men rely on their own appendages.

Some men put a lubricant, such as Vaseline, either in their hand or on the shaft of their penis. Some men prefer to masturbate lying down, others standing up, and others don't care what position they're in. Most men enjoy looking at erotica of some sort while they masturbate, so the only kind of atmosphere they require is enough light to see the foldout properly.

Younger men sometimes practice group masturbation, nicknamed a *circle jerk* because the guys involved usually sit in a circle. Although this may appear to have homosexual overtones, it really doesn't for most of the males (see Chapter 18).

Mutual masturbation between two young men is not all that uncommon either; again, it does not mean that either of the participants is gay. Research shows that about 25 percent of heterosexual males engage in such activities in their early teens, while 90 percent of homosexual teens do.

Female techniques

Although males all tend to masturbate pretty much the same way, females don't. The key, of course, is clitoral stimulation, but the ways, women achieve clitoral stimulation vary. Certainly many use their hands, the way men do, but many women who feel the need to masturbate are reluctant to touch themselves. And many women require more stimulation than their hands can provide.

Out of those needs has developed a multimillion-dollar industry in the manufacture and sale of vibrators. Vibrators come in many different types, each with its own pluses and minuses. I wrote some material that accompanies one particular device that oscillates instead of vibrates, called the Eroscillator. The following descriptions will give you a good idea of the choices that are available. (If you want more information, I suggest you call one of the companies listed in Appendix B, and they will gladly send you a catalog.)

I'm all in favor of vibrators if a woman needs the extra sensations on her clitoris in order to become orgasmic, and I often recommend them to women. The problem that vibrators have is that the sensations they offer can become addictive. In other words, no man, sans vibrator in hand, can achieve the same level of sensation that a vibrator can. If a woman becomes used to having her orgasms via a vibrator, and she then has sex with a man, she may well end up disappointed.

In my opinion, a vibrator is great for learning how to have an orgasm if you can't do it with just your hands. A vibrator is also very good for giving yourself a special treat now and again. But if you plan on having sex with a man some-time in the future, then don't make a habit out of using only a vibrator to have your orgasms. Vary the techniques you use so that, when sex becomes a shared experience with a man, you'll be in peak form.

Plug-in vibrators

Plug-in vibrators are the most powerful ones available; some women find them too powerful. Many plug-in vibrators are marketed as body massagers. Un-doubtedly, some people use them only as body massagers, but certainly a great portion of their sales are to women who use them to stimulate the area around the clitoris. Among the brands of plug-in vibrators are the Hitachi Magic Wand (see Figure 19-1), Magic Touch, and the Sunbeam Stick Massager. You can also purchase attachments which can help to pinpoint the vibrations on a particular spot: the clitoris.

Figure 19-1:
The Magic
Wand has
been called
the
"Cadillac"
of vibrators.

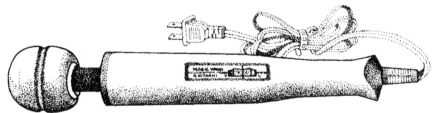

Courtesy of Eve's Garden

The Eroscillator is a plug-in type, but instead of vibrating, it oscillates, up to 3600 times a minute, which provides different and intense sensations that women who've tried it say they prefer. This device has several heads and, because it comes with a step-down transformer, is safe to use around water.

Other plug-ins include the double-headed massagers and the coil-operated vibrators. The double-headed machines multiply the possibilities (such as stimulating the clitoris and anus at the same time), and a man can even place his penis between the two vibrators. The coil-operated vibrators are smaller than the wand-type, a lot quieter, and also more easily carried in a purse. The Prelude 3 was one of the first of this type (see Figure 19-2).

Figure 19-2:
The Prelude 3 has attachments for extra pleasure.

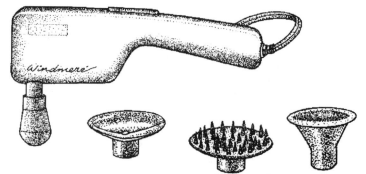

Courtesy of Eve's Garden

Because the coil-operated vibrators were really developed more for sexual play than for massage, there is a long list of various attachments that you can use. These attachments offer different types of stimulation, and I usually suggest to a woman that she try out several different varieties to discover which ones give her the most pleasure.

Battery-operated vibrators

Battery-operated vibrators are less expensive than the plug-in type, they're more easily carried, and they offer more gentle vibrations — which can be a plus or a minus, depending on your particular needs.

Many battery-operated vibrators come in the shape of a penis and are called *phallic-shaped.* Because it's clitoral stimulation that most women need, a penis-shaped vibrator is not a necessity for every woman, although many women certainly enjoy the vibrations inside their vaginas as well. You can also find battery-operated vibrators that are long and smooth but not actually penis-shaped, some of which come in small sizes so that they are both portable and concealable in a purse or luggage.

Some vibrators don't look at all like what they are. The Hitachi Mini Massager is small, square rather than phallic-shaped, and has a cover to hide the head — very discreet in appearance. Also, some are devices meant to be entirely inserted into the vagina nicknamed *vibrating eggs.*

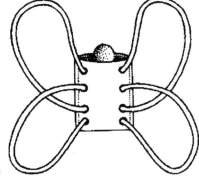

Courtesy of Eve's Garden

Figure 19-3:
The butterfly
is your little
secret.

Butterflies are vibrators that come attached to bikini-like straps so that they can be worn, like a bikini bottom, for hands-free vibrating (see Figure 19-3). You can also buy a butterfly pouch, which can hold one of the smaller battery-operated vibrators.

Although I see nothing wrong with walking around in public with a vibrator secretly working its magic on your clitoris (and certainly knowing that nobody knows that you're being stimulated would add to the erotic effect), I must caution anyone who wants to use one of these not to do so while driving a car. Remember, we're all after safer sex.

Other equipment

Most vibrators are made for clitoral stimulation, but what if you want or need to feel something inside of your vagina while the vibrator is doing its job on the outside? That's where a *dildo* comes in. A dildo is a phallic (penis-shaped) object that you insert into your vagina to simulate the feelings that you would get from a real penis. Dildos have been around a lot longer than vibrators. In olden days, dildos were carved out of wood, ivory, or jade. Nowadays, silicone rubber seems to be the material of choice.

Many dildos are made to look exactly like an erect penis, and they come in all sizes. But because lesbians form a large group of dildo users, and many prefer a dildo that doesn't look like a penis, you can purchase dildos that come in all different shapes, from some that are simply smooth to others that look like a woman or a fish or a whale (see Chapter 18). There are double dildos so that two women can simulate intercourse on each other and harnesses so that a woman can strap on a dildo to use on a partner, but I'm getting away from masturbation here, which is the theme of this chapter.

I do what???

If you're still not sure of how to masturbate successfully, then you might be interested in a tape produced by Betty Dodson, Ph.D., who has made a career out of the practice. She gives classes to women on the art of self-pleasuring, but if you can't attend one of her classes, the next best thing is to buy a copy of her video, *Selfloving: Video Portrait of a Women's Sexuality Seminar.*

Betty filmed one of her workshops in which ten women, ages 28 to 60, sit around, nude, and practice what Betty preaches. Nothing is left to the imagination, so be prepared to see it all, knowing that afterwards you won't have any questions left about how to use a vibrator and what the results can be. You can purchase the video through Eve's Garden (see Appendix B).

Water works

Another medium that seems to satisfy many women is flowing water. Many women masturbate by running the water in a bathtub, lying down in the tub, and placing their buttocks up against the end of the tub so that the running water lands right on their clitorises. The temperature, strength of the flow, and so on can be adjusted to suit the individual. Women report that this technique gives them a very satisfying orgasm without the need for direct contact using their hands or a piece of equipment.

Hand-held shower heads, particularly the ones with massaging jets, are also very good. And, if you have access to a Jacuzzi, you can use the water jets in those to good effect. With any of these methods, you'll not only have a great orgasm, but you'll also be exceptionally clean.

Speaking of clean, if you're ever in Europe where you have access to a bidet, here's a tip: Although these porcelain accessories that sit next to the toilet were developed for hygiene purposes, lots of women have found them to have other, more exciting uses.

Fantasy

Men are definitely stimulated by visual images, which is why 99 percent of the magazines which show naked people are aimed at men. Although women certainly appreciate a good-looking guy, seeing a close-up of his genitals will not generally serve as a turnon. What most women prefer as erotic stimulation is fantasy.

Now men fantasize also, and many men fantasize while masturbating, but the method of choice for men is still visual. Women, on the other hand, usually spend more time masturbating in order to reach their orgasm, so that they can leisurely construct a nice, long fantasy that will get them in the right mood for an orgasm.

Other people's fantasies

If fantasies interest you, and you want specific ones, I suggest you buy one of Nancy Friday's books. She has assembled several collections of women and men's fantasies *(My Secret Garden, Women On Top,* and so on) that most definitely make for interesting and highly arousing reading. But, as you know, although I wouldn't be upset if you became aroused while reading this book, that's not my main purpose, so I'll leave the recounting of other people's fantasies to Nancy Friday and stick to giving you advice — and I do have advice to give you concerning fantasies.

Anything goes

First of all, there's no such thing as a wrong fantasy. In fantasy, you don't have to worry about safer sex, what the neighbors would say, or anything else. If you want to make love to Alexander the Great and his whole army, be my guest. If you want to fantasize about Hannibal and his elephants, go ahead. Literally, whatever turns you on is A-OK.

"But Dr. Ruth," people always ask me, "if I fantasize about someone of the same sex, doesn't that mean that I'm gay?" The answer to that is no. But it doesn't mean that you're not gay either. Now, if you can only have an orgasm while fantasizing about someone of the same sex, even when you are with a partner of the opposite sex, that's a different story. But if you occasionally fantasize about someone of the same sex, it doesn't mean that you're gay. For more about sexual orientation, see Chapter 18.

Sharing your fantasies

Another question I often get asked is: "Should I share my fantasies with my spouse or lover?" The significant word here is *caution*. Some partners don't mind hearing their lovers' fantasies; some even get aroused by them, but some get very jealous. If you feel the need to talk about your fantasies with your partner, do it very carefully. Here are some tips:

> ✔ **Make the first one very tame.** Maybe your favorite fantasy is being a Dallas Cowboys cheerleader caught naked in the locker room with the whole team. That's fine, but tell him that it's being found naked in your office after hours by him. If he reacts positively, then you can work your way up to telling him your real fantasies down the road.
>
> ✔ **Use common sense.** If your husband is built like Woody Allen and you tell him you're always fantasizing about Arnold Schwarzenegger, how do you think that's going to make him feel?
>
> ✔ **Remember the Golden Rule.** If you tell your partner about your fantasies, be prepared to hear his or her fantasies back. If you think that you might get jealous, then don't open that Pandora's box in the first place.

A fantasy is a fantasy is a fantasy . . .

I've run into people who were intent on making their fantasy become a reality, and most of the time that does not work. Obviously, if your fantasy is rather simple, like being covered in whipped cream and having it licked off by your partner, then it may be possible to have your dream come true. (And yes, the pun was intended.) On the other hand, many fantasies could either get you into trouble (the kind that have to do with making love in public places, for example), or make you very disappointed (your Woody Allen might wreck his back carrying you over the threshold).

My last piece of advice regarding fantasies holds true for nonsexual fantasies as well as the sexual ones, and that's to remember that they are fantasies. Some people trick themselves into believing that their fantasies are real. If your fantasy lover, for example, is a movie or TV star, that's great. Plenty of people have fantasies about their favorite stars. But if you're single and you go so far as to turn down dates because they're not with that famous movie star, then you're in big trouble. In your fantasies, you can make love to anyone; in real life, you have to find a partner who wants you. Fantasies are wonderful tools; just be careful how you use them.

Chapter 20
Cybersex and Other Variations

When teenagers first get their hands on a new dictionary, what are the first words they look up? And when high schoolers are handed out their biology textbooks on the first day of school, do they hunt right away for the picture of a frog? Of course not. That's why it wouldn't surprise me if some of you have turned to this chapter before reading any of the others.

Now I'm not going to scold you for doing that, because I never blame anyone for wanting to learn about any aspect of human sexuality. So, if you believe that this chapter is where your knowledge is weakest, then that's great.

I can't deny that I was the same way. When I was a little girl, I made a precarious climb to unlock a cabinet on the top shelf where my parents kept what was called in those days a marriage manual, which basically taught people about human sexuality. (My parents could have used that book before they were married because, ironically, the only reason that this little contraception-pusher is in the world is because they failed to use any.) By making an artificial mountain out of some chairs, I was not only taking the risk of getting caught, but I could easily have tumbled down and broken my neck. So I recognize that we are all curious about sexual matters, and the higher that cabinet is — that is to say, the more forbidden it seems — the stronger our interest and that's fine. *But*...

Even though reading about kinky acts, looking at pornographic pictures, using those thoughts as part of fantasy, and sometimes even sharing those thoughts with a partner can be helpful to good sexual functioning, actually engaging in what most of us consider deviant sexual behavior is another story. From my experience as a sex therapist, the end results just don't turn out positively. Although sex can be a wonderful part of the glue that holds a couple together, pushed to its extremes, sex can just as easily be the storm that tears them apart. Even if both partners willingly enter into the world of "extreme" sex, the odds are that they won't exit it together.

Sex creates very powerful feelings that need to be kept under control. In that respect, sex is very like the human appetites for such items as liquor, drugs, or gambling. For some people, all they need is one taste of it, and they plunge down the abyss called addiction. So, while I'm all for people having a glass or two of wine with dinner, you have to be aware that you may be one of those people who cannot have even one sip of alcohol without setting off a chain reaction that you can't control. I'm even more in favor of people enjoying sex than alcohol, but you have to understand that sex, too, can be abused.

The biggest dangers of going into the outer fringes of sexual behavior used to be that you might find your relationship left in ruins, or maybe a string of them destroyed. Nowadays, the dangers have been multiplied a hundredfold as the risks of catching an incurable, deadly disease lie just around the corner of most of these forms of sex.

My advice is to tread very carefully. Peek through that knothole in the fence if you want, but don't try to climb over it. That fence is there for a reason, and you should heed the warnings to keep out.

Cybersex: Sex and the Computer

I suppose that, since they've computerized everything else, sex isn't going to escape this revolution. And I have to admit that even I, a grandmother who doesn't know how to turn one of those computer contraptions on, have moved onto the information superhighway ("going online") with a CD-ROM version of my *Encyclopedia of Sex*.

When it comes to passing on information about sex, I say great. When it comes to other forms of what's been dubbed cybersex, I say maybe. You're an adult. You can decide for yourself. Just make sure that children are protected from inappropriate material (see Chapter 25).

The French minitels

Although the word *Internet* is on everybody's mind right now, the French were using computers to communicate many years before that revolution hit these shores. The French phone company launched a system of *minitels,* which are basically small computers that are used only to communicate. Quickly, young French people discovered that this was a good way of making new friends, and being French, naturally many of these new friendships turned into romances.

Chatting via computer is one step further removed from sex than speaking on the phone. With computers, not only are your looks removed, but even your voice. Some people also think that your soul is removed from the process, but that's another story.

Computer sex forums

The big advantage that computer sex forums offer is that they are organized according to subject matter. That means that you can quickly find other people who share your tastes and communicate with them, passing on ideas, places to go, and things to do. The Internet being absolutely without guidelines, when I say that you can chat about any topic, I mean *any* topic. Some of the names of these forums should give you a clue as to what's out there: "Pumps, Leather, S&M," "Water Sports," "Piercing," "Dressing for Pleasure," "Dominance and Submission Only," "Loop and Lash B&D," "Zoo Animal Lovers," "Ten Things Every Lesbian Should Know About Love and Sex," "Penis Names," and "Below the Ankles — Feet." Had enough?

Although some people merely "listen" in to what others are saying in these forums, most people actively participate. Some are looking to find people who could be their friends and, if it turns into something more romantic or sexual, that's fine. Such people are no different than anyone who attends a singles dance or goes to a singles bar. Sometimes, these people end up meeting the person they've been communicating with, and sometimes it remains only a cyberfriendship.

Other people go online looking only for *cybersex,* which may frequently result in masturbation. When that is the main aim of the particular forum, it is called a J/O (for jerk off) session. The people who inhabit these forums regularly call themselves cybersluts — and who am I to disagree?

Anonymity online

Before you go exploring cyberspace, I have some words concerning personal information: It's up to you how much personal information you want to share.

After meeting someone in one of these forums, you might decide to exchange phone numbers and talk, and then maybe even meet. If you're looking for a partner, it is certainly better to get to know someone in person rather than only via your computer.

The difference between a blind date with someone who comes recommended by a friend or member of your family and one in which you've only met in cyberspace is that the cyberdate could be putting on a completely false front and, while seeming quite nice, actually be psychotic. They may sound absolutely sane on the computer, but they could easily be hiding a darker side. I'm not telling you to be completely paranoid, because the vast majority of the people you'll meet will be absolutely normal, but, because some danger is lurking out there, a little paranoia is appropriate.

Don't be too quick to give out any personal information. If you do meet someone, have the meeting in a very public place where you can easily get away and not be followed.

The top online services

All of the online services offer access to pictures and "chat" facilities. On some systems, the adult material, especially the more unusual, kinky, adult material, is fairly well hidden. When you're looking for such material, often the best thing to do is to ask around in adult-oriented chat areas of the system you use.

America Online (AOL)

With more than 3 million users, a lot of people can find each other on America Online.

AOL's chat rooms, in an area called the People Connection, include Gay & Lesbian, Romance Connection, Over 40, The Meeting Place, Thirty Something, Male 4 Male, Female 4 Male, Bondage, Le Chateau (BDSM). In each room, written conversations are taking place live all the time. You can simply read and watch, or participate. There are also private rooms, where individuals can go off and talk on their own. You can remain anonymous by using a "screen name" as your handle.

AOL also has Internet access for World Wide Web, newsgroups, and e-mail, which are covered later in this chapter.

CompuServe

CompuServe has chat facilities similar to AOL's. Because CompuServe was one of the original online services, the chat areas are called "CB," and you can "tune into" a channel. Run the CB Simulator under the Services menu, search among the channels, and you'll find adult sexual discussions.

Channel 10 (in the Access CB .Adult I band) seems to be a popular place to hang out: It's not for the faint of heart.

Specialized chat areas, called HSX Forum Conference Rooms, are available for conversations that many would consider too personal — at least, for the general chat areas.

CompuServe has Internet access as well.

Prodigy

Prodigy has an Adults Only section, but mind your manners: They watch for explicit language. You can create alternative identities (but anyone can figure out who you are) — so be careful. To get to the major action, click on "jump" on any menu page, type in **Lifestyles Board,** click on "choose a topic," and go to Alternative Lifestyles. Another section, for sexual issues, is in the Health bulletin board.

Prodigy also has excellent access to the Internet.

Adult BBSs

If you're handy with a *modem,* you can access some of the most popular adult bulletin board systems (BBSs) that are focused on sex and adult-oriented materials. Check the back of computer magazines (such as *Boardwatch Magazine,* which lists the Top 100 BBSs yearly), your local newspaper, bulletin board books (*BBSs For Dummies* comes to mind. . .) to get you started. Virtually every topic that you can imagine is covered — Personals, "XXX," and many have chat facilities — you name it, and someone is hosting a BBS about it.

The Internet

You can't turn on the TV without hearing about it. Whether the hype comes close to the reality is an argument we can't have now, but you can find almost anything by looking around a little (and I'll tell you where to start!)

In each of the following areas, you can find a FAQ (Frequently Asked Questions) section to help you before you dive in too seriously. (IDG Books Worldwide's *Internet For Dummies* has good information about the Internet as a whole.)

E-mail ecstasy

Thirty million people have access to e-mail — and love letters have never been the same! Just be careful whom you send to!

E-mail (meaning electronic mail) works among all of the major online systems, the Internet, many individuals with Internet accounts, and corporations and educational institutions. E-mail is by far the most popular use of the Internet.

Many e-mail systems also allow you to send pictures along with text. Each e-mail system works a little bit differently, but all the systems talk to each other and you can send a message to anyone on any system. For example, on AOL, go to the Members keyword and click on Member Directory to search for your long-lost friend. With 3 million people, you have a reasonable chance of finding your cyber-sophisticated correspondent.

With 30 million people on the Internet, the systems that are being developed to allow similar look-ups will be quite popular.

Wicked World Wide Web

In existence for less than two years, the World Wide Web is an easy, graphical way to access the Internet. It now has more than 100,000 sites and more than 5 million documents. You can search for sex in many forms and persuasions, and get valuable information about Safe Sex as well.

The easiest way to find things on the Web is by using one of the popular search tools. (Their Internet addresses are in parentheses.) For example, using the Netscape browser, click on NetSearch and it will bring up InfoSeek (www.infoseek.com), a search engine that allows you to look through Web Pages and more by whatever word you type in. It's no surprise that the word "sex" is the most popularly searched word on the system!

You can also use Yahoo (www.yahoo.com) to find preselected topics from art to zoology. To find the sexuality section, click on Society & Culture, and then scroll down to the Sexuality Links. There were hundreds of "links" at last count.

Other popular search engines include Lycos (http://lycos.cs.cmu.edu) and WebCrawler (http://webcrawler.com), which also let you search to your heart's desire.

Naughty newsgroups

Think of the Internet's UseNet newsgroups as the largest bulletin board system in the world, with more than 250 newsgroups devoted to sexual issues. You can get pictures, sounds, movies, and text stories. There are discussions of fetishes, erotica, gay and lesbian issues, and sex toys, to name a few. The primary newsgroups can be found in two areas, under *alt.binaries.pictures*, and *alt.sex*. There are also active discussions under the *alt.personals* area, and in *soc.hierarchy*, particularly *soc.motss* (Members of the Same Sex), *soc.couples,* and *soc.singles.*

Not always chaste chatting

Chats are a big draw to many Internet users: Imagine a cocktail party with 5,000 to 10,000 people! And anything goes — think Spring Break for net nerds. Chat on the Internet is actually done using a system called Internet Relay Chat (URL): You need to get a piece of chat software, like WSIRC for Windows, and Homer on the Mac, both public domain.

Then you find a server (usually your software contains preconfigured servers), and you can start chatting. Chat has channels, and you *join* the channels. Some of the most popular channels include *#hottub, #hotsex,* and *#netsex.* You can also create your own channels with provocative names, and people will come join *you.*

Frenzied file transfers

Everyone is always asking where to find X-rated pictures on the Net: so much so, a whole mythology has grown out of it. If you ask someone in the know, they'll tell you there are no X-rated ftp sites. What's really happening is this: An individual makes available his or her own collection of pictures at an *ftp site,* which is a location on the Net where files can be converted into usable formats and exchanged. They then post a message to one of the *alt.sex* newsgroups, letting people know that it's there. Within hours — no, minutes! — hundreds or thousands of people visit the site, causing so much traffic that the site eventually shuts down. That's the real story.

An easier way to find X-rated photos is to go to Web sites that have them.

X-rated photos

As noted in "Frenzied file transfers" above, words aren't the only things that are exchanged over computers. Pictures are also available, and that's one of the main concerns of those who are looking to censor cyberspace. *Playboy* and *Penthouse* have addresses in cyberspace where their pictures are offered. But some of the pictures that are available go beyond even the XXX variety. Literally millions of pornographic pictures are online, and some depict the ultimate in degradation, like bestiality, child pornography, and other things that even I can't bear to mention.

On top of that, some people take nude pictures of themselves and send them up into cyberspace in the hopes that, if their online prose won't lure somebody to meet them, their naked flesh will. It's not a tactic that I would recommend — even to someone with a perfect body — but, as Shakespeare once said, what fools we mortals be.

The technique for sending and receiving pictures is not the fastest process in the world. If you are being charged by the minute, it can cost a fortune to download a pornographic image. If this is something that you can't stop yourself from doing, at least make sure that you have the fastest possible modem so that you limit the time it takes and the expense. (If you know nothing about modems, pick up a copy of *Modems For Dummies* to fill you in.)

If you really are interested in seeing pictures of naked people on your computer screen, and if you don't need those people to be performing unnatural acts but just looking gorgeous, then you may be better off just purchasing an X-rated CD ROM. Each CD ROM will only be a one-time expense, so that you can be certain of staying within your budget. The CD ROMs come in all sorts of varieties, from the *Playboy*-type to vintage postcards to . . . whatever. Some of these CD ROMs have video games that also appeal to prurient interests. If you're interested in purchasing any of these, simply look in just about any computer magazine and you'll see plenty being offered.

For those of you who don't have a CD-ROM drive in your PC, sexy video games are also available on regular discs. These usually have animated subjects that take up a lot less memory than real pictures do.

Virtual sex

Peering into the future, many are speculating on what virtual sex (or, as some have called it, *teledildonics*) will be like. *Virtual reality* is a computer-generated way of putting you into another dimension instead of just staring at a screen. You put on a special headset that allows you to see only what the computer wants you to see, and, by moving your head and hands, you can actually manipulate the scenery.

Of course, if that scenery includes a gorgeous woman or a hunk of a man, you're going to want to manipulate more than the air, which is why futurists envision some further attachments such as a clinging penis holder or vaginal prod so that you can make the realistic effects an all-over-body experience. I don't know how satisfying that type of sex will be compared to the real thing, but it certainly is safe since the viruses of humans and computers aren't interchangeable.

More for women?

Speaking of the future, I want to add one hope regarding computers and sex, and that has to do with women. To a great degree, cybersex has appealed more to men than to women. The visual images that are floating around up there are mostly aimed at men. Even the naked men that are shown are mostly aimed at gay men.

What form might material aimed at the female market take? How about some cyber-romance novels? Or a serialized sexy soap opera that has a plot to go along with the nudity?

I'm not an expert in computers, so I can't really say exactly what this female-oriented material should consist of, but whatever the final form, it should be longer on plot, filled with fantasy, and loaded with romance. I hope that somebody makes an effort to produce some more material that will make cybersex as much fun for us women as it is for the men.

The 5th Wave By Rich Tennant

"We met on the Internet and I absolutely fell in looove with his syntax."

The Telephone and Sex

Because sex is a form of communication, it is only natural for the telephone to play a part in our sexual activity. In fact, the telephone was a forerunner of cybersex. The anonymity of communicating by phone quickly made it the ideal way of asking someone out for a date. On the telephone, the physical reaction of both the person asking and the person being asked can remain secret, and that makes the process a little easier on everyone.

That anonymity also encourages many people to flirt over the phone (as they do over computer lines). In most cases, that flirtation never goes any further, especially because the two people may be separated by a great distance. And, although some people may "give great phone," you might be sorely disappointed in them if you were to see them in the flesh.

These forms of sexual contact are basically innocent, but Alexander Graham Bell would probably have buried his invention if he'd foreseen some of the other ways that his telephone has been transformed into a sex toy.

Obscene phone calls have long been a problem, although some of the latest innovations, like Caller ID, may soon make them a thing of the past. Some of these calls are merely pranks pulled by rambunctious teens, who are looking more to shock than to actually excite anybody, least of all themselves. But some people do become addicted to making obscene phone calls. Not so long ago, a college president lost his job because of his habit of making such calls.

Pay to play — 900 numbers or 976 . . .

Recently, people have been using the phone lines more and more for conversations that have, as a goal, one or both parties reaching an orgasm. Some people have always "talked dirty" to each other while masturbating. I even recommend such behavior to couples who are separated by long distances and want to keep their sexual relationship going while living apart. But what exploded the use of such behavior was the commercialism that came after the breakup of the Bell telephone system and the deregulation of the industry.

Nowadays, you can find hundreds of phone numbers that are exclusively used for sex (most are 900 numbers or have 976 exchanges). You can call and speak to someone who will fulfill whatever phone fantasy you might have — talking about sex to a woman or a man, ordering a submissive slave on the other end to obey your every command, or being dominated by a cruel master — all accompanied by the masturbation of the callers, who can make the fantasy last, pay the additional costs, or hang up as soon as they find the relief that they were seeking.

Because we are in need of safer sexual outlets, I suppose that these phone sex companies do fill a need, but they do have some drawbacks that disturb me:

- ✔ I don't believe that children are adequately protected. In theory, you have to be 21 or older to call, but do they really check? Even if callers are supposed to use a credit card number, what if a child, even a teenage child, uses a parent's number?

- ✔ Another drawback is the cost. Some people have become addicted to these sex phone lines, and their bills are astronomical. I have to admit that, if these people are adults, they are doing this of their own free will, but it still bothers me.

I just called to say . . .

How about phone sex between two people in a relationship? If they're in a long-distance relationship, sure. But if they live nearby and they regularly have telephone sex as a means of safer sex, I'm just not sure. How realistic is it that two people who go out and date will continue to have sex only when there is a telephone line between them? Eventually, they are going to want to get together, so they had better be prepared for that moment and not rely on phone sex to keep them safe. However, I can't really criticize any couple who does have phone sex because, in this day and age of AIDS, no measure that is taken to remain healthy can be regarded as extreme.

The phone can be a helpful tool to spice up your sex life, even if you're married. When you talk on the phone, you're speaking right into the other person's ear. Whispering "sweet nothings" — or "hot somethings" — into the phone, so that only your lover and you can hear them, can let you get up close and personal at any time of the day or night. You can use these moments as part of your overall strategy for foreplay. And, if the circumstances are right, once in a while you can even have real phone sex, with one or both of you masturbating, just to throw in some variety.

The Radio and Sex

Here is one area in which I can rightfully take my place in history, because I helped to pioneer the concept of *media therapy*. My little radio program, "Sexually Speaking," first aired in New York on WYNY on Sunday nights from 12:15 to 12:30 a.m. It really amazed — maybe the better word would be shocked — people to hear me talk about penises and vaginas and orgasms on the radio. What made it acceptable was that I didn't do it to shock people, but rather to inform them. And I believe that my accent, which some people identify with the psychiatrist Sigmund Freud, also helped.

My show began in 1980, and people still talk about the first time they ever heard it with almost the same awe they have for the first time they ever "did it." Sex still plays a role on radio, but, surprisingly, it is still used mostly to shock. The premier Shock Jock is Howard Stern, who will use whatever word he thinks he can get away with in order to give a jolt to his audience. Even I have been a guest on Howard Stern's show, so it would be hypocritical of me to criticize him and those who follow in his footsteps, but I do regret that there is less information about sex being broadcast these days on radio than there is offensive language.

But radio remains a cool medium, meaning that, although certain words are used more often than they once were, none of it is really sexy. By that I mean that I don't believe that anyone really gets turned on by listening to any of these radio programs.

Sex and Television

Television, being a visual medium, always had the potential to bring sex directly into people's homes; although, in the early days, even married TV couples like the Petries on *The Dick Van Dyke Show* had to sleep in separate beds. Broadcast television in America stayed fairly tame for many years because, like radio, it was available to everyone, children as well as adults. Nudity appeared on European TV long before it did on the American tube, and, apart from a few shows like *NYPD Blue,* both naked bodies and certain words have remained taboo on mainstream TV even up until today. But TV soon branched out way beyond network television, and that's where sex has played a big role, with the public acting as more than simple spectators.

Cable brought television off the public airwaves and out from under the scrutiny of the government. R-rated movies quickly made their appearance, and certain public access shows, especially in big cities, took advantage of the new freedom and began to air both raunchy talk and naked bodies. But the producers of even these shows were always a little worried that they would go too far so that, while the shock value is certainly there, much of the erotic content is missing. You can now see truly erotic movies on pay cable, but even those are tame compared to the type of materials available on videocassette.

Renting films to view alone or together

Although there are certainly X- or NC-17-rated movies in America that I would object to, in general, I am in favor of people renting erotic films. For the single person, erotic films provide an outlet for masturbation that, considering the dangers posed by going to a prostitute or having a string of one-night stands, almost makes the availability of these films a public service. And, for couples, viewing such films can provide both some added spice and maybe even the knowledge of some new positions or techniques to their sexual repertoire. European films are much more sophisticated in this respect, providing truly artistic treatment of sexual subjects.

Starring in your own sex flick

On the heels of the videocassette player came the video camera, which now enables couples to star in their own versions of *Deep Throat*. Again, if filming your sexual escapades adds a fillip to your sex life, then I'm all for it. But I must advise certain precautions:

✔ Don't pressure your lover into doing something that he or she doesn't want to. If one partner wants to film their lovemaking, and the other objects, that's the end of it — no filming.

✔ If you want to keep those tapes, remember that there is always a risk that they'll fall into the wrong hands. My advice is to watch the tapes a few times and then erase them.

Now I know that some people actually take those tapes of themselves and sell them so that others can rent them at their favorite video store. My opinion of that? It's downright stupid. It's almost guaranteed that somebody is going to show those tapes to the one person who shouldn't see them. It could be your kids, your parents, your boss, or your biggest customer. And it might not happen this year or next year, but five years down the road, and then the consequences might be even worse. You may no longer be with the person in the film, and your new partner may not be so open minded.

If you really want the extra thrill that comes from knowing that other people are watching you have sex, then videotape your lovemaking while fantasizing that the camera is connected to NBC and is broadcasting to millions of homes. But don't ever actually let such a tape leave the confines of your house.

Multiple Partners

Before the printing press was around to print pornographic literature, or the camera to take lewd pictures, or motion picture cameras, phones, computers, or any of the modern gadgets that people now use to take sex to where no one had ever gone before, men and women were still finding ways to enjoy elicit pleasures. The most common of these was to have more than one sexual partner. In some cultures, such as parts of the Middle East, this act was given official sanction, as men were allowed to take more than one wife, but that probably took half of the fun out of it.

To some degree, adultery in ancient times was more forgivable than today. Young people were often forced to marry by their parents, and, although many of these marriages worked out fine, many did not. If someone was stuck with a sexually incompatible partner or one whom he or she hated — and especially as divorce was almost unheard of — then it is understandable that some of these people would look for greener pastures.

The lure of adultery

I've read several different accounts as to the number of people who commit adultery today, and the studies are all contradictory. Some say that it is the rare couple who remains faithful throughout a marriage, while others say the opposite. Because no one can seem to agree on the actual numbers, I won't try to give you any percentages, but we don't need statistics to know about something that is taking place under our very noses. Incidences of adultery abound all around us, be they among the rich and famous that we read about in the news, or among our neighbors and co-workers that we hear about through the grapevine.

Cheating comes in all different forms, from the man who goes to a prostitute while on a business trip, to the woman who sees an old boyfriend every Wednesday afternoon, to adulterous couples who see more of each other than they do of their respective spouses. But, whether quickies or lifelong affairs, all cheating affects a marriage in some way or other, because the person cheating is usually forced to lie about what he or she did, and that leads to a string of other lies, all of which begin to tear at the bonds of marriage.

One recent development that has had an impact on this type of behavior is the risk of AIDS. Nowadays, I find that more and more people are trying not to stray. Why? They're trying to patch up their marriages and work things out simply because they are afraid of the health consequences that fooling around on their spouses can bring. To the extent that people are trying to have better sex with their spouses — not to mention build better relationships — I applaud this movement, but I do wish that it had arisen in greater part due to the spread of knowledge about good sexual functioning rather than out of fear.

Wife swapping, swinging, and group sex

Of course, not all sex that married people have outside their marriage involves cheating. Some couples make the conscious decision to have sex with other people.

- ✔ Some couples bring a third person into their bedroom, be it a man or a woman; that's called a *menage á trois*.

- ✔ Sometimes two couples get together, which is called *wife swapping* (and I think that the fact that it's not called husband swapping is significant, but more on that in a minute).

- ✔ Sometimes a larger group of regulars meets in someone's home to exchange partners, which is called *swinging*.

- ✔ And sometimes just a group of strangers get together, usually at a club, and have sex with anyone else who happens to be there, which we label *group sex* and used to be called an *orgy*.

All of these activities grew in popularity in the late 1960s and early 1970s. I believe this was mostly a result of the development of the birth control pill, which allowed people to have sex without the risk of pregnancy. But this type of behavior has been going on for a long time (take, for example, the notorious Roman orgies or the scenes depicted on Angkor Wat, the temple in Cambodia), and it will never totally disappear.

Throughout this book I say that sex becomes better as the couple learns to communicate on a higher level and further their relationship. If that's so, why do people want to have sex with people they barely know? What's the attraction?

- ✔ Inside all of us are a little bit of exhibitionism and a little bit of voyeurism. Some people are appalled at those feelings and do the best they can to hide them, while others enjoy giving into them, and you can certainly do that at an orgy.

- ✔ Another attraction is the promise of strong visual stimulation that comes from watching new partners or other couples engage in a variety of sexual activities.

How fulfilling are these exchanges sexually? For many men, to whom visual stimuli are very strong, these scenes can do a lot for their libidos. On the other hand, many women need to concentrate in order to have an orgasm, and these situations are not conducive to their sexual functioning. And there lies the answer to why it's called *wife swapping* — because it's the men who usually derive the most pleasure from these situations and who push their wives or partners into them.

But, although the men are usually the instigators, I've seen situations where they've also been the ones to most regret having started their wives off on this path.

Betty and Phil

Betty and Phil were married for about five years when Phil was invited by someone he knew at work, I'll call him Gary, to go to a wife-swapping party. He was very eager to go, but Betty wasn't. He kept begging and pleading, and eventually she consented, but she kept to herself the real reason why she had said yes. It turns out that Betty had met Gary at the company Christmas party and found herself attracted to him. She would never have acted upon that attraction, or at least that's what she told me, but when Phil begged her to go, she decided that maybe it was an opportunity not worth passing up.

It turned out that Gary had caught Betty looking at him, and that's why he had asked Phil to join the group. Naturally, when things started getting hot and heavy at the party, Betty and Gary gravitated toward each other and wound up having sex. Phil had sex with someone at the party and then went looking for his wife. When he saw her going at it with Gary, he at first dismissed it, but after a while he started feeling jealous. This jealousy affected his ability to have a second erection, and so he became really upset. On their way home, Phil lashed out at Betty, who fell back on the argument that it had been his idea.

Eventually Phil's jealousy calmed down, and he started fantasizing about the party. When the next one rolled around, he decided that they should go. Betty tried to talk him out of it, but he swore up and down that he wouldn't be jealous, and so they went.

I don't have to tell you the rest of the story, as I'm sure that you can guess the ending. Betty came to me to see whether I could help her repair her marriage, and I did try. But it was really too late. Gary aroused much stronger sexual feelings in her than Phil did, and because she and Phil had no kids, she finally decided that she'd prefer to spend the rest of her life with Gary.

So, while Betty did find the experience of wife swapping pleasurable, her focus all along was really on one man, Gary, and not having sex with a variety of different men. I think that's what happens to a lot of women who enter into this scene. Even if, initially, a woman does have sex with a lot of men, she doesn't necessarily have to be sexually aroused for that to happen. Eventually, however, she fixes her focus on another man, not her husband. And then, when her husband realizes this, the trouble begins.

Of course, couples for whom swinging works out don't go to see a sex therapist like myself, so perhaps this sort of lifestyle works for more people than I know. But I've seen enough people who've had problems with these situations to know that the risks to a marriage are great. You see, the libido is very strong, but it is also easily satisfied. There's no such release as an orgasm for jealousy. Jealousy is the type of emotion that tends to build and fester over time, and that usually spells trouble. The only advice I can give you now is to keep thoughts about group sex as your fantasy and don't try to live them out.

Part V
Maintaining Healthy Sexuality

The 5th Wave
By Rich Tennant

"THEY'RE A VERY PROGRESSIVE COMPANY—IT COMES
WITH MATCHING COLORED CONDOMS."

In this part...

Sex is a bodily function, which is good. That means that it's a part of our very nature. But, like any other aspect of our humanity, things don't always work out exactly as we would want them to. After too much exercise, your muscles might be sore, and after a great meal, you might have gas. I may not be able to help you make the earth move every time, but in this part I do offer you practical advice that may help to bring a little more pleasure into your life.

Chapter 21

What You Can Catch and How to Prevent It

. . . .

In This Chapter

▶ Recognizing a host of sexually transmitted diseases

▶ Evaluating risks for men and women

▶ Fighting the sexual invasion

▶ Maximizing protection

. . . .

*I*n a perfect sexual world, terrific partners would be easy to find, everyone would have great orgasms easily, and no one could get sick from having sex. Of course, we don't live in a perfect world, sexually or any other way, and so one out of four Americans between the ages of 15 and 55 will catch at least one sexually transmitted disease (STD).

"Did she say *at least* one?" Yes. Because there are more than 30 sexually transmitted diseases, oftentimes the people who engage in the behaviors that lead to getting one disease wind up getting more than one. In case you haven't heard it already, the sexual revolution of the previous decades, in which people suddenly felt free to have sex with a number of partners, is over. With so many diseases around, you might say that we're now in the middle of a sexual invasion, with the result that having multiple partners can lead to mucho trouble.

If you have had sex many times with many partners, don't assume that you are disease-free just because you don't have any symptoms:

✔ Many people with STDs don't show any symptoms at all, especially women.

✔ Other people with STDs have only a slight fever, which they don't connect with an STD, and no more symptoms for years. While having an open sore certainly means that you are highly contagious, the fact that you have no symptoms at all does not mean that you can't give someone the disease.

> ✔ Just because your partner has no outward signs of having a sexually transmitted disease doesn't mean that your partner is disease-free; because your partner may never have had any symptoms, he or she could pass something onto you in all innocence.

Did I say something about the sexual revolution being over? If you want to remain healthy, you'd better act as though the sexual revolution is dead and buried.

The Sexual Invasion: Repelling STDs

That the sexual invasion is made up of so many different STDs makes it a complicated one to fight, and since the arrival of AIDS, the consequences of failure are more likely to be deadly. My advice, therefore, is to find yourself one partner, make sure that you are both healthy, use condoms if you have any doubts about your respective health, and practice safer sex.

Because this advice may be too late for some of you, or because accidents happen, no matter how hard you try to prevent them, I'm going to give you a list, in alphabetical order, of some of the diseases that you might run across. Although the figures used in this book are for the United States, which keeps careful statistics, they are generally true throughout the developed world. Third world countries vary widely in the incidence and prevalence of STDs. As they say, to be forewarned is to be forearmed; read this list carefully so you can become as familiar as possible with the enemy.

Before I go into the list itself, a few other words of advice.

Because AIDS, which has grabbed all of the headlines, hit the gay male population first in the United States, it may seem as if men are more likely to suffer from STDs. But taking all of the STDs together, the consequences of this sexual invasion are worse for women than for men. Here's why:

> ✔ Women tend to get STDs more easily than men, probably because they are the recipient of fluids during intercourse.
>
> ✔ Many of these diseases do not show any initial symptoms in women.
>
> ✔ It is often more difficult to treat a woman who has an STD than a man.
>
> ✔ More often than not, it is the woman who suffers the more serious consequences of STDs, such as infertility, ectopic pregnancy, and chronic pelvic pain.

If you do have a sexually transmitted disease, or even think that you have one, see a doctor. This may sound obvious, but too many people don't seek medical advice, probably because of embarrassment. They may be embarrassed because they don't want to reveal their sex life or because they don't want to submit to an exam of their most private parts, or both.

An all-too-common form of treatment adopted by young people is to self-prescribe medication. If a doctor has prescribed a medication for a person, a friend who has similar symptoms just uses that medicine too. Sharing prescriptions is a bad idea. Even doctors sometimes have difficulties diagnosing which STD is which. By taking the wrong medication, you may make your situation worse.

Candidiasis

Often called a yeast infection, *candidiasis* is actually caused by a fungus, candida, that is normally present in the mouths and intestines, as well as the vaginas, of many healthy women. When the body's normal acidity doesn't control the growth of this fungus, an overgrowth can occur. Candidiasis is the result. Its symptoms can include a thick, white vaginal discharge; itching or irritation of the vulva, penis, or testicles; a yeasty odor; and, sometimes, a bloated feeling and change in bowel habits.

- ✔ The fungus, candida, can also appear in the mouth, throat, or tongue; when it does, the disease is called thrush.
- ✔ Candida is not usually spread as an STD, but it can be — more likely through oral sex than intercourse.

Prescriptions for antibacterial creams, ointments, or suppositories are the normal cures.

Chancroid

Chancroid is a sexually transmitted disease caused by the bacterium *Haemophylus ducreyi.*

- ✔ Chancroid usually starts as a small pimple on the penis, labia, or cervix.
- ✔ If untreated, the pimple can grow into painful genital ulcers accompanied by swelling of the lymph glands that drain the ulcer.
- ✔ Chancroid is often accompanied by a fever, and the genital swelling can make walking difficult.

Chancroid symptoms are more often painful in men than in women. Chancroid is easily treated with antibiotics; if it's not treated, however, the ulcer can grow to the point where amputation of the penis is necessary.

Chancroid is common in Africa, but is rarely seen in the U.S. Because anyone having it is much more susceptible to HIV infection, it can have serious consequences.

Chlamydia

Chlamydia is the most common STD in the U.S., affecting four million people every year.

- ✔ Chlamydia often has no symptoms in women; in men, the first symptoms are usually painful urination and pus coming from the urethra.

- ✔ Symptoms may start within a few days after sexual exposure.

- ✔ In women, the disease can cause scarring of the fallopian tubes, sterility, ectopic pregnancy, or chronic pelvic pain.

- ✔ In men, the organism is thought to be responsible for half of the cases of *epididymitis*, an infection of the epididymis, which can cause painful swelling of the testicle.

Although chlamydia can be successfully treated with tetracycline or other antibiotics (a single-dose version is available), the disease is often difficult to diagnose because of the lack of visible symptoms. People who have the disease and who do not take all the medicine prescribed for the full time that it's prescribed often get the disease again. Because chlamydia is often accompanied by gonorrhea, the two are usually treated together.

Cytomegalovirus (CMV)

CMV is a rare disease passed during close personal contact, including sexual intercourse, and through blood transfusion and shared needles.

- ✔ Although the man or woman infected with the disease often has no symptoms, CMV can have severe effects on a newborn infant if the mother is infected with the virus.

- ✔ Not every baby whose mother has CMV will become infected; however, a small number of babies who are infected suffer serious damage to their central nervous systems.

CMV can be diagnosed through a blood test, but there is no known treatment or cure.

Genital warts

Nearly two million people are infected in the U.S. every year with genital warts, which are caused by the *human papilloma virus (HPV)*. Genital warts are spread through vaginal, anal, and oral intercourse. They can also be passed on to infants during childbirth.

- Not always able to be seen, the warts are soft and flat; they grow on the genitals, in the urethra, the inner vagina, the anus, or the throat.

- The warts often itch and, if allowed to grow, can block openings of the vagina, anus, or throat, causing discomfort.

- Because genital warts are often unseen, they can easily be passed onto sexual partners.

Genital warts can be treated in several ways, including topical medical creams. In cases of either large or persistent warts, other treatments may include surgical removal, freezing using liquid nitrogen, or cauterization by electric needles; however, the warts often recur.

Gonorrhea

Although almost two million cases of gonorrhea are reported in the U.S. every year, because it is thought that about 50 percent of women and 10 percent of men with the disease show no symptoms, the true number of cases is much higher — making it the second most common STD. When symptoms do occur, women may have a green or yellow-green discharge from the vagina; frequent, often burning urination; pelvic pain; swelling or tenderness of the vulva; and possibly arthritic-like pain in the shoulder. Men may have pain during urination or a pus-like discharge from the urethra.

- Gonorrhea can be spread through vaginal, anal, or oral intercourse.

- Gonorrhea can cause sterility, arthritis, heart problems, and disorders of the central nervous system.

- In women, gonorrhea can cause pelvic inflammatory disease, which can lead to ectopic pregnancies or sterility.

Penicillin was the treatment of choice for gonorrhea, but, because more recent strains of the disease have become penicillin-resistant, a drug called ceftriaxone is now more commonly used. Gonorrhea is often accompanied by chlamydia, and so they are often treated together.

Hepatitis B

Hepatitis B is the only sexually transmitted disease for which there is a preventive vaccine. Hepatitis B is very contagious, more so than HIV. Hepatitis B can be transmitted through intimate contact as well as sexual contact, so that kissing, sharing the same toothbrush, or sharing needles can transmit the disease. Health-care workers are particularly susceptible and are almost always vaccinated.

- ✔ Hepatitis B can cause severe liver disease or death, but the virus often has no symptoms during its most contagious phases.

- ✔ While reported cases are only in the tens of thousands, it is estimated that one American in 20 has been infected with hepatitis B, which can remain active over a person's lifetime.

No medical treatment exists for hepatitis B, but, in 90 percent of cases, the body's own immunological response causes the disease to fade away. It is particularly important that people with multiple sex partners get vaccinated.

Herpes

Herpes, which is caused by the *Herpes simplex virus* (HSV), is another incurable STD. With half a million new cases reported each year, anywhere from 5 to 20 million Americans have been infected with this disease. Herpes actually has two forms: herpes-1 and herpes-2, although 1 is most often associated with cold sores and fever blisters "above the waist."

The most common symptoms arise from a rash with clusters of white, blistery sores appearing on the vagina, cervix, penis, mouth, anus, or other parts of the body. This rash can cause pain, itching, burning sensations, swollen glands, fever, headache, and a run-down feeling. These symptoms may return at regular intervals, sometimes caused by stress, menstrual periods, or other reasons that are not well understood.

Most people think that herpes is contagious only when the sores are present, but studies have shown that some people may spread the disease even when they have no sores.

- ✔ During pregnancy, herpes may cause miscarriage or stillbirth, and the disease can be passed on to newborns.

- ✔ If the sores are active during childbirth, there are serious health consequences for the babies. To avoid these consequences, cesarean sections are usually performed when active sores are seen during the time of childbirth.

> ✒ If you have herpes, you should always use a condom when having sex, unless your partner already has the disease.

Although you should always use a condom, you should know that condoms can't entirely protect you from herpes. If the man has the disease, and the only sores are on his penis, then a condom can protect the woman. However, because vaginal secretions may leak over the pelvic area not protected by the condom, the condom does not protect men as much.

Herpes can spread beyond genital contact, including to other parts of the already-infected person's body. If you touch a herpes sore, always wash your hands thoroughly before touching anyone else or any other part of your body.

Be aware that oral herpes can be transmitted by kissing, sharing towels, or drinking from the same glass or cup.

Although herpes has no cure, it is important to see a doctor if you suspect that you have the disease. You should see a doctor both to make sure that herpes really is the cause of the symptoms and to learn how to live with herpes and not spread it to others. If you're the infected person, the doctor can give you a set of rules to follow to help keep you from contaminating others or other parts of your body.

Human immunodeficiency virus (HIV) and AIDS

If there's one sexually transmitted disease that you've probably heard of, it's the acquired immunodeficiency syndrome, AIDS, which is linked to infections by the human immunodeficiency virus (HIV). Why is there so much more attention given to this disease than to any other STD? It's quite simple: AIDS is deadly, there's no cure, and there's no vaccine against it.

HIV now infects close to 2 million people in the United States and close to 15 million people worldwide. HIV is most commonly passed on through sexual activity and by shared needles, although it can also be passed through transfusions of contaminated blood products, from a woman to her fetus during pregnancy, and through breastfeeding.

If you think that you are safe from AIDS because you are not a homosexual man, you're wrong. Because anal sex, a form of sex most common among homosexual men, is more likely to allow the transmission of the disease, in the Western world this plague decimated the homosexual community first. But in Africa, where AIDS is most common, it is primarily a heterosexual disease, and the incidence of AIDS is rising faster among heterosexuals in the West than in the homosexual population. A growing number of women are getting the disease as well. AIDS poses a risk to everyone.

✔ HIV infections weaken the body's ability to fight disease, causing acquired immunodeficiency syndrome (AIDS) and other health problems.

✔ A person can be infected by HIV and not show any symptoms for up to ten years.

✔ If AIDS develops, a variety of different ailments may attack the body, leading to death.

There are actually two known human immunodeficiency viruses, HIV-1 and HIV-2. They both cause disease by infecting and destroying blood cells called *lymphocytes* that protect the body against infection. HIV-1 is most common in Western countries; HIV-2 occurs most frequently in Africa, where the disease is thought to have originated.

The first case of AIDS in America was reported in 1981. By 1994, more than 300,000 cases of AIDS had appeared in the U.S., resulting in more than 200,000 deaths.

HIV infection is diagnosed with tests to detect HIV antibodies in the blood (see Chapter 6). These antibodies usually appear in the bloodstream three to eight weeks after infection. Because of this window of time, it is possible to have a negative HIV test and still be able to pass the disease onto others. In addition, the first 60 days after being infected with the virus is a period of high contagion. That's why you should always use a condom: it's impossible to really know if a partner can infect you or not.

Initial symptoms may resemble those of a common nonsexual disease, mononucleosis: high fevers, swollen glands, and night sweats. Following that may be a period, which commonly lasts for years, during which there are no symptoms. Eventually, as the body's immune system weakens from fighting HIV, some *opportunistic* microbe — an organism that the body's immune system would normally dispose of — causes an infection, like pneumonia, that just won't go away. It's usually at this point that a doctor discovers that the person is infected with HIV and diagnoses a case of AIDS. In the U.S., the median life expectancy from the time of infection is about 12 years. Life expectancy is shorter for those infected by transfusions of blood or blood products and for people who do not get good medical care.

There is no vaccine against AIDS as yet, nor is there a cure. There is some evidence, however, that the drug AZT, if given early in the course of the infection, may prolong the life of the patient.

Molluscum contagiosum

The Molluscum contagiosum virus can cause a small, pinkish-white, waxy-looking, polyp-like growth in the genital area or on the thighs. It is spread by sexual intercourse but can also be spread through other intimate contact. It can usually be treated by removing the growths either with chemicals, electric current, or freezing.

Pelvic inflammatory disease (PID)

Pelvic inflammatory disease, or PID, is the term used for a genital infection in a woman that has spread into the deeper organs of her reproductive system, including the uterus, fallopian tubes, or the structures around the ovaries. PID is not really a sexually transmitted disease, per se, but may be a consequence of an STD, usually either gonorrhea or chlamydia. One way PID is spread is if an IUD is inserted into you when you have an undiagnosed STD. It is estimated that a million cases of PID are reported a year in the U.S., with another million going unreported because of minimal or no symptoms.

The symptoms of PID can include fever, nausea, chills, vomiting, pain in the lower abdomen, pain during intercourse, spotting and pain between menstrual periods or during urination, heavy bleeding or discharge or blood clots during menstruation, unusually long or painful periods, and unusual vaginal discharge.

Treatment for PID usually includes antibiotics and bed rest. It is also absolutely essential that you refrain from any sexual activities. Surgery may be required to remove abscesses or scar tissue or to repair or remove damaged reproductive organs.

Whether treated or not, PID can lead to sterility, ectopic pregnancy, and chronic pain. The more often PID strikes a woman, the more likely her chances of becoming sterile.

Pubic lice

Pubic lice, also called *crabs* or *cooties,* can be spread not only by sexual contact but also by coming in contact with infected bedding, clothing, and toilet seats. Their bites cause intense itching,

You can treat pubic lice yourself with over-the-counter medications including Kwell, A-200, and RID. In addition, you should thoroughly wash or dry-clean all bedding and clothing that has come into contact with the lice.

Syphilis

Syphilis was first noticed in Europe in the 15th century, coinciding with the return of Christopher Columbus from the New World. No one knows for sure whether the disease came from America or West Africa, but it did cause a tremendous epidemic with a high fatality rate.

Syphilis is caused by a spiral-shaped, snail-like microscopic organism called *Treponema pallidum*. Because syphilis resembles so many other diseases, it is known as "the great imitator." The disease progresses over a long period of years with different stages along the way.

- ✔ The primary syphilitic lesion is the *chancre:* a circular, painless, and firm sore that appears at the site of the invasion either on the lips, mouth, tongue, nipples, rectum, or genitals anywhere from 9 to 90 days after infection.

   Six to ten weeks later, the chancre heals by itself, followed by a symptomless time (latent period) of anywhere from six weeks to six months before symptoms of secondary syphilis appear.

- ✔ Secondary syphilis is marked by rashes of various types that do not itch and that heal without scars. These rashes indicate that the microbes have traveled through the bloodstream and lymphatic system to every organ and tissue in the body.

   Secondary syphilis is followed by another symptomless period, which can last a lifetime, or the disease can reappear after a number of years.

- ✔ Tertiary syphilis attacks the nervous system and can destroy normal skin, bone, and joints as well as interrupt the blood supply to the brain. Syphilis can be deadly in this last phase.

Syphilis is passed from one person to another during vaginal intercourse, anal intercourse, kissing, and oral/genital contact. The disease is especially contagious while the sores are present in the primary stage.

Treatment with long-acting forms of penicillin is effective for primary, secondary, and latent syphilis; however, the damage caused by tertiary syphilis cannot be reversed by penicillin therapy.

Trichomoniasis

Usually called "trich," trichomoniasis is one of the most common vaginal infections. It causes about one-fourth of all cases of vaginitis. Many women have no symptoms, and men rarely have symptoms. Symptoms that can appear include a frothy, often musty-smelling discharge and itching in the vaginal area. Sometimes there is also an increased urge to urinate.

Trichomoniasis is treatable with antibiotics, and any sexual partners should be treated as well to prevent reinfection.

Vaginitis

If you experience a vaginal discharge or burning or itching in the vaginal area, you are suffering from vaginitis. Vaginitis can be triggered by several different organisms. It is not always spread through sexual contact, but, since a man who carries the organisms may not have any symptoms, it is usually a good idea to treat both partners so that you don't keep passing the infection back and forth. The symptoms include

- A burning or itching of the vulva
- An abnormal vaginal discharge, sometimes tinged with blood
- An unpleasant odor

Most women get some type of vaginitis during their lifetime. Treatment varies according to the cause of the disease.

Let's Get Serious

There's no vaccine against AIDS. There's no cure for herpes. There are STDs that have no symptoms but can later leave you sterile. Are you scared of catching an STD? If you're not, you should be — scared enough to practice safer sex.

I use only the term *safer* sex. Truly *safe* sex means celibacy. Safe sex *can* also mean monogamous sex with an uninfected partner, but, sorry to say, one mistake by one of the partners can lead to both of them becoming infected, so we're really back to *safer* sex.

Certainly the fewer partners you have, the less risk is involved, but it only takes one time with one infected partner.

Remember, when you go to bed with someone, the germs of every partner that this person ever had are climbing under those covers with you.

Condoms give good, not great, protection

And what about condoms? Condoms offer protection — that is absolutely true. But condoms do not offer absolute protection against AIDS or the other STDs.

- ✔ Condoms sometimes break.
- ✔ Condoms can break down in the presence of oil-based products.
- ✔ Condoms sometimes leak when you take them off.
- ✔ People sometimes forget to use condoms.
- ✔ Even people who do use condoms for intercourse often don't use them for oral sex, which, while less risky, is not safe.

So the best preventive measure is a combination of responsible sexual behavior and condom use. Adding spermicide to comdom use is even better, especially for women.

Have a relationship before you have sex

Now I know that it's difficult to find one person to fall in love with when you are young and to stick with that person for the rest of your life. That is the ideal solution — to preventing AIDS and a lot of other social ills — but it is not realistic to assume that everybody can do that. Most people do have multiple partners, and so most people are at risk.

But just because the vast majority of people have more than one partner is not an excuse for you to have as many partners as you can. I believe it is just terrible that there are people out there who still engage in very risky behaviors, especially among the gay population that has been devastated by AIDS.

I don't like to preach because I know it doesn't do any good, but I can't avoid saying one more time to all of my readers — please be careful, your life is at stake.

Don't Be a Silent Partner

In our society, more people are willing to engage in sexual activity together than to talk about it, and a good deal of the blame for sexually transmitted diseases comes from this failure to communicate.

You all know the Golden Rule about doing unto others as you would have them do unto you. If you were going to have sex with someone and they had a sexually transmitted disease, wouldn't you want them to tell you in advance? The same applies to you: If you have a sexually transmitted disease, you have to tell any potential partners. Notice that I said potential, because I won't hide the fact that, if you tell somebody that you have an STD, they may suddenly run in the opposite direction. If you have a disease like herpes, which never goes away, you are going to face not only a lifetime of outbreaks, but difficulty in finding partners. You have to accept that. You cannot go around infecting other people.

By the way, it's not just Dr. Ruth saying that you have to warn prospective partners if you have an STD. Recently a U.S. woman was awarded $750,000 in court from her ex-husband because he gave her herpes, and the legal trend is to make people accountable.

But I don't want you to be up front about your disease merely to keep the law away from your bankbook. I want you to do it because you have sex only with people whom you care about, with whom you have a relationship, and to whom you don't want to pass a sexually transmitted disease.

Some of you out there may want to be honest but are saying to yourselves right now, "How do I do it?"

I say more about this in Chapter 6, but in a nutshell, the answer to your question is very simple: you just do it. If you have the gumption to have sex with somebody, then don't tell me that you can't work up the courage to open this subject. I'm not saying it's easy. I *am* saying it's not impossible, and that you have to do it.

Minimize Your Risks

After reading this list of sexually transmitted diseases, you've probably had the thought that maybe sex isn't worth the risk. The problem with that reaction is that it will fail you when you most need it.

What do I mean by that? At some point, you'll be with somebody that you're very attracted to sexually, and that person is attracted to you. Maybe you'll be in your apartment, or maybe in your partner's. And you'll be kissing, hugging, and stroking each other. Temperatures will start going up. Clothes will start coming off. An erection and a lubricated vagina will be on the loose. A comfortable bed will be nearby. You'll both be absolutely ready to have sex, and there won't be a condom nearby.

In that scenario, will you remember these pages and all these nasty and deadly sexually transmitted diseases? Will you be willing to say no, or to put your clothes back on and go find an all-night drugstore? Or will you say to heck with the risks and jump into bed?

Although some of you may have the fortitude to place caution ahead of passion, many of you won't. That's why you have to be prepared ahead of time. That's why you have to carry a condom in your purse or pocket or glove compartment or bedside table.

You all know my reputation. I don't try to scare people away from having sex. Instead, I want to make sure that you have the best sex possible. But an integral part of great sex is healthy sex, protected sex. Although, in the heat of passion, you might well be willing to take any risk, afterwards, if you catch one of these diseases — especially if it's AIDS — you'll regret that orgasm for the rest of your life.

Have great sex, but be careful. In fact, have terrific sex and be very careful.

Chapter 22
Male Sexual Problems

1 know that many of you men don't believe that your gender suffers from any sexual dysfunction, even if you yourself may be a prime example. This is because, in general, men have a tough-guy image to keep up and so are less likely to seek help for a problem of any sort, especially if it has anything to do with their "John Thomas," or whatever pet name you have for the penis.

But, as reluctant to admit it as you or any man might be, many men do suffer from a sexual problem of one sort or another, at least at certain times of their lives. Sometimes sexual problems can result from disease, such as testicular or prostate cancer. (These problems are covered in Chapter 2.) But, lucky for you, the most common male sexual problem is not a physical problem at all, but a learning disability.

Premature Ejaculation

The subject that I'm asked about most often is premature ejaculation. I get questions from men who suffer from the problem and from their partners, who also suffer as a result of the problem. (I've yet to hear from any family dogs, but I'm sure that even they are suffering from the problem, because ill-tempered masters aren't going to be as generous with their treats.)

First, we have to define *premature ejaculation*. The definition that I use is that a man is a premature ejaculator when he cannot keep himself from ejaculating before he wants to. Notice that I said before *he* wants to, not she. That is an important distinction.

Because not every woman is capable of having an orgasm through sexual intercourse, it's possible for a man to keep his erection all night and still not be able to satisfy the woman he's with, if all the couple does is have intercourse. But, because most women do want to feel the sensations of sexual intercourse, no matter how or if they reach their orgasms, most men should do all they can to learn the techniques that will allow them to last for a certain period of time.

Just how long is the period of time a man should last? Now we have to go back to my definition — it's up to the man. If your partner reaches her orgasm after 20 minutes of intercourse, then that's a good time to aim for. If she doesn't climax through intercourse at all, then maybe all you want is to last for ten minutes. What's important is that you learn how to gain control of when you have your orgasm, so that you can decide when to ejaculate instead of ejaculating due to circumstances beyond your control.

As with many sexual dysfunctions, there are different degrees of premature ejaculation. Some men are so severely afflicted that they cannot last long enough to penetrate a woman for intercourse. Some men even climax in their pants at the very thought that they are going to have sex with a woman. But even a man who can penetrate his partner and last 15 minutes may fall under the umbrella of premature ejaculator if he would like to last five extra minutes and cannot do so.

Does circumcision make a difference?

The penis of a man who has not been circumcised is often more sensitive than a circumcised man's (see Chapter 2). The reason for this is that the glans, or head, of a circumcised penis gets toughened by coming into contact with the man's underpants all day without the protection of the foreskin.

I don't know of any scientific study on the effect of circumcision, but, for most men who are premature ejaculators, the problem is in their heads — not the heads of their penises. So I do not believe that it makes a significant difference whether or not you're circumcised, and most certainly a man who is not circumcised can learn how to prolong his climax just as effectively as a man who is.

The age factor

A young man's *libido,* his sexual drive, is stronger than an older man's, and so premature ejaculation is a problem that sometimes disappears, or at least is less of a problem, with age. Mind you, I said sometimes. I've heard from men in their

80s who've suffered from premature ejaculation all their lives. And when I say that the problem is ameliorated, I've also heard from men who were able to last three minutes instead of two, so how much better is that? My advice is not to wait for age to take care of this problem, but rather to act as soon as possible.

Home remedies

We all know men who refuse to stop and ask for directions when they're lost, so it shouldn't come as a surprise that many men, rather than seek professional help, decide that they can handle the situation by tinkering with their technique. As you might expect, the results are mixed, so, although I don't recommend any of them, here they are:

The "slide" technique

Probably the most common method that men use to control their orgasmic response is to think of something that is not sexy. Woody Allen immortalized this technique in a film where, in the middle of making love, he yelled out "Slide!" What he was doing was thinking about Jackie Robinson running the bases, instead of the woman he was with, in an attempt to delay his orgasm. (By the way, the film is *Everything You Wanted to Know About Sex But Were Afraid to Ask*.)

This technique can work to some degree, but it's not a good way of making love. It makes a chore out of the sex act, rather than something pleasurable, and your partner may feel that wall you're putting between you and the act and think that you're trying to distance yourself from her.

Rubber love

Condoms do cut down on the sensations that a man has, and some men can control their premature ejaculation by using condoms. If one condom doesn't work, they put on two or more.

I certainly recommend that people use condoms — sometimes I sound like a broken record about it — but that's in order to prevent the spread of STDs. It would be a shame to use these same condoms as a crutch, lessening your pleasure, when there is a better way.

Snake oil

There are products on the market which supposedly lessen the sensations in the penis so that the man can last longer. In the first place, I do not know whether these products really work. But, even if they do work, just as with condoms that lessen sensation, why go for the quick fix when there is a permanent cure?

Masturbation: Taking matters into your own hands

A method adopted by some young men is to masturbate prior to going out on a date that may lead to sex. The object here is to decrease the intensity of their desire for sex in the hopes of gaining some control.

Although this method sometimes works, it has several drawbacks:

- ✔ Masturbation may not always be possible. What if the two of you are living together or married? Or what if the woman pays a surprise visit to your dorm room?

- ✔ Another drawback is that of timing. What if you masturbate in anticipation of having sex after the date, but she wants to have sex before you go out, and you can't get an erection?

- ✔ And then there's your enjoyment. The second orgasm may not be as pleasurable as the first, and, with all the worrying about when to masturbate, the sensory experience of sexual intercourse ends up being diminished.

When it comes to curing premature ejaculation, my advice is to keep your hands to yourself and learn some self-control.

Different positions

Some men do say that they have more control over their orgasms in one position or another. The missionary position is probably the one in which men have the most problems, but that's not always the case. I even had one man write to me saying that he could control his climaxes if he was lying on his right side but not his left.

Some researchers have found that greater muscular tension can increase the tendency towards premature ejaculation, which means that the missionary position, in which the man holds himself up with his arms, might accentuate premature ejaculation. But, because I really believe that this condition is a psychological one rather than a physical one, there may be some psychological factors, different for each individual, which also come into play regarding positions.

If you find that you have more control using some positions than others, then sticking to those positions is a possible solution to the problem — but it's not the most satisfactory one. If you limit yourself to that one position, sex may become boring. Why not try to learn how to take control of the situation altogether so that you can engage in any sexual position and still have control?

The real cure: Recognizing the premonitory sensation

The real cure for premature ejaculation is for you to learn to recognize the *premonitory sensation.* What is that, you ask? It's that feeling that a man gets just before he reaches the point of no return, also called the moment of inevitability.

Each man has a certain threshold of pleasure; once it's crossed, there is no stopping his orgasm. A fire engine could go through the bedroom, and he would still have an orgasm and ejaculate. But, right before he reaches that point, if he so desires, he can cool the fires and not ejaculate. And if he wants to abandon his status as premature ejaculator, that is exactly what he must do.

How do you learn to recognize this premonitory sensation? By treating your orgasm with kid gloves and approaching it very carefully. You cannot imitate Beep Beep the Roadrunner, heading for the edge of a cliff at full throttle, and then apply the brakes and stop just before you fall off the edge. With that approach, you're more likely to wind up like Wily Coyote, who is always chasing right after the Roadrunner, but can never seem to stop in time and ends up racing over the cliff and plummeting down into the canyon.

The idea, then, is to learn how to slow down the process before you get too close to the edge. Exactly how you do this depends on several factors, the biggest being whether or not you have a *cooperative* partner, with the accent on cooperative. Someone you've had sex with only a few times, and not very satisfactory sex at that, might not be willing to be as supportive as you need. But if you have someone who loves you, and who wants to make your sex life together better, then you're probably well on your way to curing the problem.

 Although it may be easier to cure premature ejaculation as a couple, it is not impossible to make progress alone. In other words, you can practice recognizing premonitory sensation through masturbation and begin to develop some control. (Not every man can learn this control by himself, because it is the presence of the woman that causes some men to get overexcited in the first place.) It probably takes more effort and more self-control to practice this technique alone, but it certainly is worth trying.

The Masters and Johnson Method

The Masters and Johnson method of controlling premature ejaculation involves learning how to recognize the premonitory sensation and to stop before you get to the point of inevitability. You do this by slowly increasing your level of arousal, stopping, allowing yourself to calm down, and then heading back upwards again. Some people advise assigning a numbered level, from 1 to 10, with 10 being the point of no return. If that helps you, fine. If it distracts you, then just concentrate on the sensations.

When a couple comes to me looking to solve a case of premature ejaculation, I usually forbid them from having intercourse for a set time, as a way of removing the pressure from the situation. That doesn't mean that I want them to remain frustrated, so I allow them to give each other orgasms after their lessons, but not through intercourse.

During a couple's first lessons, the woman uses her hand to arouse the man and stops the motion when he signals her to. Slowly, he begins to exercise more and more control. Eventually, I assign them a new set of exercises in which they practice the same technique using intercourse. Depending on the man, this whole process can take a few weeks or a few months, but it is almost always successful.

Squeeze techniques

If the man is having trouble keeping control, even just with his partner's hand (or with his own), then I might add the squeeze technique. A penis becomes erect when it gets engorged with blood (see Chapter 2). If the penis is squeezed, gently but firmly, at its base, the flow of blood decreases, the erection softens, and the man becomes less aroused. Integrating this squeezing of the penis is usually sufficient to make the exercise successful.

Another useful aid in controlling premature ejaculation can be the *pubococcygeus (PC) muscle,* which, when squeezed, has a similar effect to the woman squeezing the base of the penis. The first thing you have to do is find this muscle. Put a finger behind your testicles. Pretend that you are going to urinate and then stop yourself. You'll feel a muscle tighten, and that's your PC muscle. If you exercise this muscle regularly, by squeezing it in sets of ten (the Kegel exercise of Chapter 13), it will get stronger, and you can then use it to help control your ejaculations.

Is it really that simple?

When I describe the treatment to some men, they look at me and say, "Is it really that simple?" The answer to their question is yes and no. The technique itself is very simple, but there is some discipline involved, and that's not always so simple.

Some men, when they first start doing the exercises, are all gung-ho. They look forward to solving this problem, and, if their partners are equally excited, they apparently make a lot of progress, at least during the initial stage. But then they get impatient. They don't listen to Dr. Ruth, and they decide to try out what they've learned before I give them permission. Sometimes it works, and sometimes it doesn't. When it doesn't work, they get disappointed, and some even give up entirely.

Learning to exercise control is not always easy. Look at all of the people who cannot stop themselves from overeating or smoking cigarettes or what have you. If premature ejaculation is a habit that has become highly ingrained, you cannot assume that you can make it go away without some effort on your part. But, or should I say BUT, if you do put in the necessary time and effort, you *can* gain control over when you ejaculate.

Going for help

This section tells you enough that, if you suffer from premature ejaculation, you could try to cure yourself on your own. As I said before, this process works a lot better if you have a partner who's willing to help you. But, though it's OK to try on your own, that doesn't work for everyone. Some men need the extra guidance provided by a sex therapist. In that case, my advice to you is to go and find one. For more information on how to go about doing that, see Appendix A.

The Other Extreme: Impotence

On the opposite end of the spectrum from men who get overexcited and can't control their ejaculations lies the next most common male problem: impotence.

By *impotence,* I mean a man's inability to have an erection. The causes of impotence can be either psychological or physical, while the degree of impotence can vary from a simple loss of rigidity to a total inability to have an erection. Although impotence can strike at any age, it becomes much more common as men grow older. Among men in their late 70s and beyond, some symptoms of impotence are almost universal.

Because I know how much importance you men out there put into your erections, let me say right away that impotence does not necessarily mean the end of a man's sex life. Depending on the cause of the problem, there are usually several possible solutions, so take heart.

The precursor: loss of instant erection

I can say a lot on the subject of impotence, but the most important point has to do, not with actual impotence, but with its precursor. The reason its precursor is so important is that it affects every man, at least every man who makes it to a certain age in life, so you men should all pay careful attention, as should you women readers.

It sneaks up on you

Young men get erections all the time, often when they least expect it and at times when it can be embarrassing. These erections can be caused by a variety of stimuli — something visual, like the sight of a pretty girl in a short skirt; a fantasy about that girl in the short skirt; or even just by a whiff of perfume that reminds the young man of that girl in the short skirt. This type of erection is called a *psychogenic erection,* meaning it is stimulated by something that triggers the brain to release hormones that cause an erection.

At a certain age — and that age differs with every man, but ranges from his late 40s to early 60s — a man loses his ability to have a psychogenic erection. That ability usually doesn't disappear all at once; he begins to get fewer psychogenic erections and may not even notice at first. But eventually the decrease becomes apparent to him, and, at some point, his psychogenic erections cease altogether.

This change can be a precursor to impotence, but it is not impotence because the men experiencing it can still have erections. All that changes, when a man arrives at this stage in life, is that he needs direct physical stimulation to his penis in order to get an erection. This means that he has to either use his hands or have his partner use her hands or mouth in order to make his penis erect.

Spreading the word

The loss of psychogenic erections wouldn't be much of a problem if it were expected, the way that women expect the hot flashes that accompany the start of menopause. Surprising, at least to me, is that so many people still have no idea that this is part of the natural progression of growing older. It is this lack of knowledge that causes the real problem.

The reaction of many men, when they no longer are getting erections the way they used to, is to think that they must be impotent. Rather than seek help, they begin avoiding sex. When this happens, wives think that their husbands have either stopped being attracted to them or that they are "giving at the office." Some couples fight over this; others withdraw from each other.

This breakdown of a relationship is so sad to me because it's not necessary. All that these couples have to do is include foreplay for the man exactly the way they have been using foreplay for the woman's benefit all along. If they do this, then there is no problem.

I think that one of the reasons the loss of psychogenic erections is not so widely known is that it doesn't really have a name. One could call it a symptom of so-called *male menopause*, but men don't like that phrase because it is really not appropriate, and I don't blame them. We need to coin a catchy phrase for this syndrome; then the media will pick up on it, and a lot of unhappiness will be prevented. I think a good name would be The Male Cooling Off Period. (Why don't you write me in care of IDG Books Worldwide and tell me of any names you can think of. Maybe together we can make some real progress toward removing this cause of a lot of unhappiness.)

Impotence in older men

As a man gets older, his erections begin to get weaker and weaker, and he may need more and more stimulation in order to get an erection. Some older men can get an erection but can't keep it long enough to have intercourse. Sometimes they can get an erection, but it's not stiff enough to allow for penetration.

These are all real, physical problems, but they don't necessarily spell the end of a man's sex life. If they are aware that these problems are caused by age, and if they're willing to take appropriate action, many men can continue to have sexual relations through their 90s.

I was holding regular clinics in the department of geriatrics at New York University Hospital in New York, and many of the men who came to see me had problems with impotence. I remember one man in particular. He was well into his 80s, and he hadn't had sex in about a dozen years. When his erections began to peter out on him, he just gave up.

The only reason this man came to the clinic to see me was that he had started seeing a woman, and she wanted to have sex. When he told her that he couldn't, she told him that he had to at least try, and so, to please her, he sought help from me.

I had him checked out by a urologist and, physically, he was fine. I worked with him for about a month, and one day he came to see me in the clinic beaming. He and his lady friend had had intercourse the night before, and he couldn't have been more happy. I've helped a lot of people over the years, but I have to say that the morning that man reported to me his new found success made me the happiest of any.

The morning cure

For many men, the best solution to their problem with impotence is just to change their sex habits to suit their age. The easiest suggestion I can offer you older men is to have sex in the morning instead of at night. Since you are probably retired and have no children at home, there really is no reason for you to always try to have sex at night, except the force of habit. However, there are good reasons why changing your routine can help you become better lovers:

✔ Older gentlemen are often tired after a long day, and, because getting the blood to flow into the penis is what an erection really is, the more tired you are, the more difficult it is for this process to work correctly. In the morning, you have more energy, and so erections are more easily obtained.

> ✔ Another reason is that the male sex hormone, testosterone, is at its peak level in the morning and at its weakest at night. Because this hormone is instrumental in effecting erections, trying to get an erection in the morning makes a lot of sense.

Now I don't tell you to try having sex first thing in the morning. Since you probably don't have to be on a rigid schedule, I suggest getting up, having a light breakfast, and then taking your partner back to bed for a sexual interlude.

Some older men resist this suggestion at first. For some reason, doing all of that planning doesn't suit them. But, if they do listen to me, many find that the fires which had died down start burning once again (see Chapter 16).

The stuff technique

Now, if there are men who think it strange to have sex after breakfast, you can imagine how hard-headed some men are when it comes to getting them to try to have sex without first having an erection. But sometimes this is exactly the technique that works best.

The *stuff technique* is just what it sounds like. The man, with the help of his partner, stuffs his nonerect penis into her vagina. Sometimes, once a man begins to thrust, the blood flows into his penis, and that elusive erection finally rises to the occasion.

Short-term impotence

Unlike long-term impotence, short-term impotence is almost always psychological in nature. Many, many men, at one time or another, suffer from *impotence* — meaning that they can't have an erection when they want one. In fact, sometimes it's because they want an erection so badly that these men fail.

Susan and Jimmy

Susan was a transfer student, and Jimmy spotted her the very first day he returned to college in his senior year. She had the type of looks he'd always dreamed of, and, to his amazement, when he struck up a conversation with her, she responded.

Jimmy had slept with a few other girls during his years in college, but the thought of actually going to bed with Susan drove him wild. He managed to play it casual for a while, and, after a week went by, he asked her on a date. She accepted, and they had a great time. They had a few more dates, each one advancing further than the last, so that, on his fifth date with her, Jimmy was pretty sure that they were going to have sex.

The anticipation was almost torture to Jimmy, and he had an erection for much of the day. They went to a dance and, with their bodies clinging to one another during all of the slow dances, he felt that he was as ready for sex as he ever had been.

Jimmy had never had problems getting an erection, but as they were walking back towards his dorm, he started having doubts about his ability to please Susan. He was sure that someone as good-looking as Susan had had sex with all kinds of guys, and he began to question whether or not he could stand up to the test. By the time they got back to his room and took off their clothes, Jimmy was in a state of pure panic, and his penis reacted accordingly by staying limp. Jimmy was more embarrassed than he ever thought possible.

Anticipatory anxiety has caused many a Jimmy to experience similar problems. What *anticipatory anxiety* means is that the fear or expectation of a possible failure causes an actual failure. If a man starts worrying about his erection, usually this is enough to prevent him from having one. And the more he worries, the more likely it is that he will fail the next time he tries. There have been men who, because of one failed erection, have suffered through years of misery.

Visit a urologist

Because this problem is more often than not psychological rather than physi-ological, it is usually easily cured with the help of a sex therapist.

If a young man comes to my office with a problem like this, the first thing I do is send him to visit a *urologist,* which is a medical doctor who specializes in the male genitourinary tract.

- One reason I send men who are experiencing impotency to a urologist is to make sure that there is not a physical problem, which, because I am not a medical doctor, I could not handle.

- But the other reason I send them off to have their physical plants checked out is that just getting that clean bill of health is often enough to clear up the problem.

 You see, many of these men have been worrying so much about there being something wrong with them that just hearing from a doctor that they're A-OK is enough to give their penises the psychological lift they need.

Even if the doctor's visit is not sufficient by itself, it is a very good first step.

Build confidence

After sending an impotent client to a urologist, my next job is to build the man's confidence in his penis back up to what it was before he ran into trouble. Sometimes just getting him to masturbate does the trick. Sometimes I have to get him to do certain confidence-building exercises with his partner. This usually involves prohibiting intercourse for a while, but allowing the couple to engage in other sexual activity. The man can usually get an erection when he doesn't have the pressure of needing an erection in order to penetrate the woman. After he gets his erection back, it is usually easy to transfer that confidence to having erections when he is going to have intercourse. In the majority of cases, if he's willing to work at it, I can get him back to his old self.

Study sleep habits

If the man is physically sound but not responding to treatment, the next step is to find out if he is having erections while he's asleep.

During the course of the night, a healthy man gets several erections during REM or "dream" sleep. This does not necessarily mean that he's having an erotic dream or any dream at all, but having erections is definitely part of the male sleep pattern. This phenomenon even has its own name, *nocturnal penile tumescence,* and initials, NPT. Having initials means it's really official.

Because a man usually does not have performance anxiety while he's asleep, a man who is suffering from impotence during his waking hours, but who doesn't have a physical problem, usually has erections while he sleeps.

The simple, at-home test to find out whether you're having erections during your sleep is wrap a coil of stamps around the base of your flaccid penis. If the circle of stamps has been broken when you wake up, probably it is because you had an erection. (Once in a while the tooth fairy goes astray, but usually she's too busy checking children's beds.)

If the coil of stamps doesn't work, and I still suspect night-time erections, a sleep lab is the next step. At a sleep lab, physicians substitute the stamps with plastic strips and Velcro connectors, which — as you might guess if you're as big a fan of the Post Office as I am — are more reliable indicators than postage stamps. And there are even more precise devices, if needed.

If all of this testing doesn't turn up any sign of erections, then I have to send the client back to the medical community, because there's nothing that I can do for him. But, for many men, these tests do uncover some erectile functioning, which probably indicates that the problem is psychological in nature. This is not true 100 percent of the time, but it's certainly worth following up. The basic aim is to build back his confidence to the point where he can have erections while he is awake — and even with a woman around.

When Mother Nature needs a boost

I've now given you all of the techniques that may help to solve impotency problems without any added apparatus. If none of these techniques work, then it may be time to help Mother Nature with medical or mechanical assistance.

Two methods used by urologists that have proven very effective are the implantation of a penile prosthesis and injection therapy.

Penile implants

Penile implants are either hydraulic or non-hydraulic. The *non-hydraulic prostheses* are basically semi-rigid rods that are surgically implanted within the erectile chambers. Although they are reliable, they have one major drawback — after the surgery, the penis is always in a rigid state. You can push your penis down when you're not having sex, but the erection may still be visible, and that can be embarrassing.

The surgery required for the penile implant does leave a soreness in the area, and sex is not allowed for several weeks. But most men report very good results and are quite happy. The only men who seem to complain are those whose hopes were too high, and who expected to have erections as strong as the ones they had in their youth. This will not — and could not — happen because, since the erection is permanent, it needs to be at least somewhat concealable.

The *hydraulic prosthesis* has a fluid reservoir and a mechanical pump that a man uses to fill the prosthesis and create an erection when he wants one. Men report liking the system, but it has been prone to mechanical failure. Like the implant, it requires a surgical procedure.

Injection therapy

Another method that was developed in the 1980s is self-injection therapy. The latest product is Caverject. A man injects himself in the penis with a medication that relaxes the muscles, thus allowing the blood to flow into the penis and cause an erection. Though the thought of injecting yourself in that particular spot may not sound appealing, the penis is an area relatively insensitive to pain, so you can barely feel the injections. Most men who use this system have reported good results. Possible side effects include scarring and, rarely, *priapistic erections,* that is, sustained erections that won't go away without medical treatment. (You can flip ahead in this chapter for more on priapism.)

Vacuum constriction

Another method of relief for impotence is the use of *vacuum-constriction devices.* Basically, a man places a vacuum pump over the penis and, as the air is pumped out, blood flows in, creating an erection. He then places a ring at the base of his penis to hold the blood in place.

Now I do receive letters from men and their wives saying that vacuum pumps work wonders. And at least these devices do not require surgery. But certain side effects have kept vacuum-constriction devices from becoming very popular:

✔ The erections these devices produce are not as rigid as those produced with a prosthesis.

✔ Sometimes mild bruising occurs as a result of using these devices.

✔ Some men have difficulty ejaculating after using these devices.

But vacuum-constriction devices are a possible alternative for someone who doesn't, or can't, undergo surgery, and who doesn't care to stick a needle into his penis every time he wants to have sex.

Retarded Ejaculation

Premature ejaculation and impotence are the two main male problems, but some other problems, such as retarded ejaculation, are more rarely encountered by men. Unlike premature ejaculation, where a man can't stop himself from ejaculating, *retarded ejaculation* is when he can't make himself ejaculate.

Now, although being able to last a long time is something our society puts great value on, retarded ejaculation is definitely a case of too much of a good thing, at least where the male is concerned . . . even if he brags about his lasting powers to cover up the problem. Obviously, a man who cannot ejaculate is going to wind up feeling frustrated and angry and may actually begin to turn off to sex.

Sometimes retarded ejaculation is caused by some medical problem, in which case only a urologist can be of help. Sometimes it's psychological, so that a sex therapist like myself can treat the problem. One factor in the psychological causes can be a relationship problem, so that the man is unconsciously holding back. In that case, fixing the relationship is key to curing the problem.

Priapism — The Case of the Permanent Erection

Like retarded ejaculation, priapism is another one of those too-much-of-a-good-thing diseases. In *priapism,* a man develops a permanent erection. This can be the result of injecting himself with medication because he suffers from impotency, or it can be the result of some disease that thickens the blood, making it impossible for blood to leave the penis after it has entered it. Sickle cell anemia is one such disease.

Although priapism was named after the Greek god of fertility, that fact certainly doesn't make the man afflicted with this problem feel good about his masculinity for very long. Priapism is not only painful, but the man usually ends up in the emergency room. Priapism can now be treated without surgery, but it is still something for which a doctor's care is required.

The Bent Penis

Peyronie's disease inflicts some men with their worst possible nightmare — they go to sleep with a functioning penis and wake up the next morning with a penis that bends so severely when it becomes erect that it is impossible for them to have intercourse (see Figure 22-1).

The cause of Peyronie's disease is unknown; in many instances, it arises as a result of an injury. In early stages of the disease, there is usually pain associated with having an erection. Sometimes that pain begins before the actual curvature starts, so that it can act as an early indicator.

How bad can Peyronie's disease get? Bad enough for doctors to describe severe cases in which the erect penis looks like a corkscrew. On the other end of the

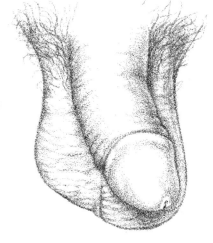

Figure 22-1:
Peyronie's disease throws a curve in men's sex lives.

spectrum, the bend may be very slight, not affect the man's ability to have intercourse, and be no cause for concern. In mild cases of the disease, if there is any pain, it usually goes away on its own; all the doctor has to do is reassure the man that in two to three months all will be well.

Sometimes the curve disappears on its own. Because the disease is basically a scarring process, some men have reported positive results from taking vitamin E, although there is no scientific proof that this works. Surgery can sometimes remove the scarred tissue, but surgery can also result in a loss of the man's ability to have an erection, so that a prosthetic device would then need to be implanted.

The best advice I can pass on to any of my readers who have Peyronie's disease is to visit a urologist who can help you. Some men are so embarrassed by their condition that they won't try to get help, but urologists have helped many men with this problem, so there's no reason to be shy.

I've received letters from men or their wives saying that they've lived with Peyrnie's disease for years, and some have even consulted physicians. So let me add here that, if the first urologist you consult can't offer you any help, look for another one. It's worth the effort.

Lack of Desire

Another problem I'd like to tackle is lack of sexual desire (which can affect women, too; see Chapter 23). One of the most common causes of this problem these days is stress. You come home late every night from work, or you've lost your job or whatever, and sex becomes the last thing on your mind. If your partner is amorous and then starts to complain about being rejected, you become even more tense and want to have sex even less. A vicious cycle builds up, and the couple's sex life can deteriorate down to nothing.

Can you fix a problem like this by yourself? Maybe, but it's not easy. One of the components of this problem is usually a lack of communication. And breaking down the barriers that have been set up can be very hard to do. My recommendation is to visit a sex therapist or marriage counselor (see Appendix A).

Some of the causes of loss of sexual desire are not emotional but physical. A good sex therapist always asks that the man see a medical doctor first in order to be able to rule out any medical problems. (Testicular and prostate cancers, treatment for which can affect the libido, are covered in Chapter 2.)

Show 'em Who's Boss

I hope that, if you have any of the problems mentioned in this chapter, or if you ever develop them, you won't turn your back on them, but instead will take some positive action. Many men act as though their genitals were separate from the rest of their bodies and not totally under their control. But, of course, that's ridiculous. So, if something is bothering you, take charge and get the problem fixed.

Chapter 23
Female Sexual Problems

Although many men believe that the most common female sexual problem is the headache (as in, "Not tonight, dear, I have a headache"), sexuality in women seems to be a more complex proposition than it is in men.

That Elusive Orgasm

The main problem, simply stated, is that many women have difficulties achieving an orgasm. The complexity stems from the broad array of reactions that women have to this problem, ranging from a desparate need to experience orgasms all the way to relief at not having to experience them, with many subcategories of reactions in between.

Banishing the word frigid

I'd like to start off on this topic by banishing a word you may have heard applied to women who have problems with orgasms — *frigid*. In the first place, the connotations of the word are totally mistaken. Using the term "frigid" makes it seem as though the reason a woman may have problems reaching orgasm is that she has a heart made of stone-cold flint. The truth is that the warmest, most loving woman in the world — a woman with the proverbial heart of gold — can have problems experiencing orgasm.

Secondly, most women who do not have orgasms, or who have difficulties obtaining orgasms, are capable of having orgasms; they just don't know how to jump-start their orgasmic engines. For these reasons, I prefer the term *pre-orgasmic,* because it connotes that these women will one day be orgasmic, once they set their minds to it.

An orgasm waiting to happen

It's been widely reported, and my own practice bears this out, that the number of pre-orgasmic women is high. Now, for a small percentage of these women — about 5 percent of all women — there is no cure. Such women usually have a physical problem, like diabetes or alcoholism. But the vast majority of women, 95 percent in fact, can have orgasms, so it's just a question of giving them the right information.

What might cause a woman to be pre-orgasmic? Society at large, for one thing. In the not-too-distant past, it was thought that a woman wasn't supposed to enjoy sex. Sex was only for procreation, and, as long as the woman could become pregnant by having sex with her husband, what more did she want out of sex? Pleasure? What an absurd idea — if not a sinful one.

Lucky for us women, this attitude is changing, particularly in Western cultures. But it has not entirely gone away in the U.S., and, on a worldwide basis, it is far from extinct. Believe it or not, today, at the edge of a new millennium, millions of women, mostly in Africa, are forced to undergo *cliterectomies,* the removal of their clitorises, so that they cannot enjoy sex. This horrible torture continues, not just because it is imposed on these women by the men in their society, but also because so many of the older women who have undergone this "surgery" (which is rarely done by a surgeon) believe that the next generation needs to undergo the same process.

It was probably because an unintended pregnancy was such a dangerous and unpreventable occurrence — along with the fact that it was important to keep track of people's lineage — that society developed these attitudes so long ago. If women weren't supposed to like sex, and if sex didn't bring them pleasure, then they wouldn't stray and have children who were not their husbands'. Although I don't believe that this ever was a valid excuse, there is certainly no reason why such attitudes should continue today. We now have many means of preventing pregnancy, and many women are enjoying terrific sex, so a woman today can be as sexually promiscuous as any man without becoming "with child" (not that I advocate such behavior by either sex, especially because of the risks of sexually transmitted diseases).

In any case, because women have been discouraged from giving full expression to their sexual feelings, and because the orgasmic response is not as "automatic" for women as it is for men, many women end up being pre-orgasmic or, if they are orgasmic, they have difficulties having orgasms regularly.

I have to stop and make an important point here, and that is: A woman should never feel pressured into having an orgasm by society, by the man in her life, or even by reading this book. If there is one thing that I am against, it's pressure — especially because I know that, when it comes to sex, pressure has just the opposite effect . . . even if the person putting the pressure on you is you, yourself. If you're desperate to have an orgasm, that desperation is only going to make it tougher on you. The most important step in becoming orgasmic is learning to relax. And, if you really don't ever want to have an orgasm, then that's OK, too, as long as you're being honest with yourself, and you're not just saying that because you think that you can't learn.

Helping yourself

Because every woman is different, there are no hard-and-fast rules to becoming orgasmic. Learning what gives you an orgasm, followed by what gives you a fabulous orgasm, is part of the overall procedure of becoming orgasmic. But, if you've been having problems, then I recommend one method that is an integral part of a sex therapist's repertoire, and that's masturbation. (Chapter 19 explores this subject in detail.)

Although almost every adolescent boy masturbates, masturbation is not as prevalent among adolescent girls. That's not to say there aren't many girls who do it, just that it's not universal the way it is for boys. In fact, the sex researcher Alfred Kinsey reported that, although most males who are going to masturbate during their lifetime will have done so by the time they reach their late teens, fewer than half of the females who even try masturbation have done so by that age. You can find some possible reasons for this in Chapter 19.

In the not-so-distant past, marriage was something that was arranged — and often at an early age. If a 16-year-old girl was already married and engaging in intercourse with her husband, then masturbation wasn't such a big issue. But today marriage, if not intercourse, is often delayed, and that means that women are more responsible for their own pleasure.

It is not unusual for women to have several sexual partners over the course of their lives, and, luckily for them, men today are much more likely to be concerned with the woman's sexual enjoyment than in olden times. But, if a woman wants to be orgasmic, she has to teach those partners what to do to please her, and, for that to happen, she must discover for herself the things that please her.

Now this doesn't mean that a woman can't use the help of a man to learn what things give her pleasure. In the best of worlds, her first lover would be so good that he would explore her body with her, and together they would find the best ways of bringing her to ecstasy. The problem is that, all too often, a woman's first lovers are only worried about their own orgasms. Having sex in the backseat of a car, worried about whether or not a policeman is going to come by and flash a light on your exposed genitals, is not the best of circumstances for two young lovers. So, although plenty of young women are having sex in their teens, they are not necessarily having orgasms.

Faking it

Are all the young men who are having sex with pre-orgasmic women brutes who don't care whether their partners enjoy sex or not? Some certainly are, but most are not, and they really can't be faulted. These men think that they're doing a great job as lovers because the women they're with are faking orgasms.

Does faking it really work? Are the men really fooled? If you've seen the film *When Harry Met Sally,* then you know the answer to that one. But for those of you who haven't (and you really should go out and rent it), the answer is yes, a woman can fake it so well that no man will be able to tell that she's not having an orgasm.

Now I wouldn't make it a hard-and-fast rule not to fake it. There may well be times in your life when your partner really wants to make love to you and really wants you to enjoy it, such as on your wedding anniversary, and you just aren't in the mood. If you tell him that you don't feel like having an orgasm, even if you're willing to have intercourse with him so he gets his pleasure, then he's probably going to be disappointed. So, if you want to fake it occasionally, then I say go ahead.

But if you are faking it all the time, if you never have an orgasm and are covering this lack by faking it, then that behavior has to change. I don't mean that you have to stop faking it right away, but I do mean that you should make the effort to learn how to have an orgasm. Then you can stop faking it, because you're really having it.

The most important ingredient in learning to have orgasms is a relaxed atmosphere. Having a partner around, even someone you love very much, may not be a situation that is relaxing enough for you to have an orgasm.

Wendy

When Wendy came to see me she was 28. She'd had several boyfriends and even lived with a man for three years, but had never had an orgasm. It wasn't that the men she'd had sex with hadn't tried. The man she lived with had really given it all he had, showing patience and spending long periods trying to make her climax. In the end, it was because he couldn't provide her with sexual pleasure that he left her. Sex became unsatisfying to him as well as to her, so he ended up sleeping with another woman, whom he finally married.

Wendy had tried to masturbate, but it never worked for her. She didn't really like the idea, and, when she tried, she would be all tense. After five minutes of touching her vagina, she would give up.

I told Wendy that she should set aside an hour a night for a week to practice, but that she should not try to have an orgasm. She should touch herself and think pleasant thoughts, but the goal was to learn what made her feel good, not to have an orgasm.

She was an obedient client, and she didn't have an orgasm that first week. But, when she came for her next visit, she told me how excited she had become the night before and that she thought she was ready. I gave her permission and asked her to call me the next day, and was she ever grateful during that phone call.

What Wendy needed was to learn how her body responded without having the pressure to have an orgasm. The world is full of Wendys, and they too need to explore their vaginas and clitorises to see what feels best.

Some women can't stand to have their clitorises touched when they've reached a certain point of excitement. Their clitorises become so sensitive that direct clitoral contact is painful.

Brenda

Brenda was a virgin when she fell in love with Brad. He, on the other hand, had slept with many women and thought of himself as an expert lover. He had learned to give these other women orgasms by using his finger and his tongue, and he had no doubt that he'd be able to do the same for Brenda.

The first time they had sex, Brad spent half an hour rubbing and licking Brenda's clitoris, and all she felt was a tremendous irritation. For several days, she was really sore. When he started to do it again the next time, rather than endure the pain, she faked an orgasm. That made Brad feel great, but it also meant that Brenda would never have an orgasm as long as she was with Brad, because he was certain that he knew exactly how to bring her to orgasm.

When Brenda practiced masturbation after seeing me, she discovered that what gave her the right sensation was to touch *around* her clitoris, not directly on it. By rubbing around her clitoris, she learned to give herself orgasms. Because Brenda was able to teach her next boyfriend exactly what she needed and didn't need, they had a satisfying sex life.

I need more

Some of the women whom I send off to practice masturbation tell me that, no matter what they do, they can't seem to get sufficient stimulation. They report feeling as if they're close to having an orgasm, but they can't get past that point to actually having one.

For women who just can't seem to give themselves orgasms, I usually suggest buying a vibrator. Vibrators can often supply the added stimulation that these women need. Not every woman uses the vibrator directly on her clitoris, because the sensations are too intense; others absolutely need to. Some women who use vibrators also need to have the feeling of something filling their vaginas, and so they might insert a dildo into their vaginas while using the vibrator on their clitorises.

If you want to learn more about vibrators and dildos, or about masturbation, read Chapter 19. After you've learned to give yourself an orgasm with a vibrator, you must then transfer that ability to your partner. Hopefully, the added excitement of having sex with a partner will be enough that he can bring you to orgasm without using a vibrator. You'll show him what you discovered with the vibrator — how and where you need to be touched — and he'll be able to duplicate those movements with his finger or tongue and get the same results. If that doesn't work, then you may want to have him try with a vibrator.

Because vibrators can provide so much more stimulation for the woman, it may take a while to wean yourself off of it. But I believe that most couples would prefer not to have to be dependent on a piece of mechanical equipment like a vibrator. Of course, if you can't learn to have an orgasm without using a vibrator, then that's not the end of the world. No one would ever put you down for taking a car to get around instead of walking, so I wouldn't make a big deal about having to use a vibrator to have an orgasm.

The flat moment

Some women can bring themselves, or have their partners bring them, very close to an orgasm. They have all the physical signs of being about to reach an orgasm, but all of a sudden they reach a *flat moment*. When this happens, these women think that they're not going to have an orgasm. And, as soon as they think that, it becomes a self-fulfilling prophecy, and they don't.

Pat

When Pat came to see me, she was in tears before she got halfway through her story. She so badly wanted to have an orgasm, but she was sure that she was incapable.

The first thing that I do when a new person comes to my office is give a sexual status examination, which means I ask every detail imaginable about his or her sex life. When Pat described to me what sex was like with her husband, I immediately sensed that she might be one of those women who have problems getting through the flat moment.

Her husband could bring her to a high state of arousal, but, after a while, she would suddenly go back down. As soon as that happened, she would become frustrated, stop the lovemaking session, and start to cry. Her husband, needless to say, was becoming as frustrated as she was.

I instructed Pat not to stop her husband when she felt that her sexual excitement was going down, but to let him keep doing whatever it was that had been working up until then. She seemed doubtful, but she agreed to give it a try. Sure enough, after a few minutes more of having her clitoris fondled, Pat's arousal level resumed its steady climb, and she had an orgasm.

The key to overcoming the flat moment is to keep at it. Not every woman goes through this flat moment, but enough do to indicate that it's a fairly common occurrence. But the flat moment is only a momentary thing. If the stimulation keeps up, then a woman will go back upwards on the arousal curve and have her orgasm. So, as far as the flat moment is concerned, persistence is everything.

The missed orgasm

If you've ever misplaced something — like your glasses or the keys to the car — you know how frustrating an experience that can be. Imagine the frustrations of not being able to find your orgasm!

Right about now, those of you not suffering from this condition are probably saying to yourselves, "Dr. Ruth, you're pulling my leg. How can you miss an orgasm?" I know that the partners of women who have missed orgasms don't understand what's going on, because that's what they report to me in their letters or in my office. When a woman tells her spouse or lover that she doesn't know whether she's had an orgasm or not — something that men have absolute certainty about — he just can't believe it.

And the women themselves can't really believe it either. They say to me: "Is it possible? Could I not recognize an orgasm? Isn't it supposed to be a very strong, very intense feeling? How could I not recognize it? How could I miss it?"

Unlike a woman who cannot have an orgasm, a woman who has missed orgasms does have an orgasm, at least physiologically, but the sensations don't register in her brain. What I mean is, her heart rate goes up, her vagina lubricates, she has all of the outward physical signs of an orgasm, but none of the pleasure.

Treating women who have this problem can be a bit tricky. They have to be taught to feel the orgasms that their bodies are undergoing. It is usually helpful to these women to know that they are indeed having orgasms, at least physically. A sex therapist might use any of several different modalities of treatment.

If you have missed orgasms, I definitely recommend seeing a sex therapist, because you probably won't be able to handle this problem on your own. Appendix A discusses visiting a sex therapist.

I can give myself an orgasm, but he can't

Some women are definitely orgasmic, because they can give themselves orgasms through masturbation anytime they want to, but they can't seem to have orgasms with their partners. A variation of this is when a woman is orgasmic with one partner and then anorgasmic with another.

Sometimes the cause of this problem is as simple as not having enough foreplay. Other times, there's a complex reason that requires therapy. But, if this is something that affects you, before you flip ahead to Appendix A, you can try a few things on your own.

The key to making progress here is to learn how to relax with your partner. Since you know that you are orgasmic, that knowledge should give you some of the self-confidence you need to overcome the difficulties you are encountering. In the first place, it gives you a fall-back position. If you don't have an orgasm while with your partner, you know that you can satisfy yourself at some later time. Remembering this might be important to developing the relaxed attitude you need to have an orgasm with a man.

What you're going to have to do in a situation like this is to become a teacher. Think back to your favorite teacher in school. More than likely, it was somebody who was able to make you laugh while he or she was teaching you. In the bedroom, as in the classroom, having a sense of humor is very important. If you adopt a positive but lighthearted attitude, you'll be more likely to succeed.

This instruction session can be a highly erotic moment, if you let it. The first thing you should do is let yourself fantasize about the session for a few days before it actually takes place. Think about what you are going to do with your partner during this show-and-tell session. Maybe you can even masturbate while you're thinking about it. The picture that you have to put into your head is not one full of stress and worry, but instead one that has a warm, loving glow.

There are two basic approaches to showing your partner what you need to reach a climax, and you can choose either one or combine them.

- ✔ One is to show him how you masturbate without allowing him to take part.
- ✔ The other is for you to masturbate yourself using his hand.

To combine these approaches, you can start masturbating yourself and then take his hand and guide it through the right movements. Explain to your partner ahead of time that he's not to take any initiative but just do whatever you tell him to, which might simply be to lie back and watch. Maybe "watch" isn't exactly the right word, because he has to be paying attention. He has to be carefully noting what it is you do to bring yourself to orgasm, and the sequence in which you do it.

Now, when it's his turn, he might not get it right the first time, and that's OK. Remember, you can give yourself an orgasm anytime, so, if you don't have an orgasm during the first couple of sessions with him, don't worry. If I sense my client is very uptight, I'll order her not to have an orgasm just to take the pressure off. This way, she can show him the motions she likes, and he can try them, but orgasm won't be the goal.

Whether or not you have an orgasm from these sessions, I can assure you that they'll be highly erotic to your partner. Watching a woman masturbate herself is a fantasy of many men, as it's often depicted in X-rated movies and in girlie magazines. So, whether or not you get very turned on by this lesson, I can guarantee you that he will, and you shouldn't leave him frustrated. Make sure that he has an orgasm, either by engaging in intercourse, by stimulating him orally or manually, or by letting him stimulate himself; that way, he'll volunteer for as many private lessons as you need.

Ouch! — It's Too Tight in There

Some women get so tense from the thought of having intercourse with a man that their vaginal muscles involuntarily tighten up to the point where penetration by the man's penis is painful or sometimes even impossible. This condition is called *vaginismus*.

If this happens to you the first time you have intercourse, you may believe that it has something to do with the size of your vagina, but that is very, very rarely the case. The cause is almost always that the muscles at the entrance to the vagina have contracted tightly as a result of tension.

Now the first thing that I do when you come to me complaining of painful intercourse is to send you to your gynecologist. Although the size of the vagina is almost never an issue, there could be a separate medical problem, and we have to rule that out anytime there is pain.

Assuming that you get a clean bill of health, then, once again, the treatment involves getting you to relax. What exactly you must do depends on what the other factors are. If you've also never had an orgasm, then learning to give yourself an orgasm through masturbation might be step one. If you're already orgasmic, then my instructions have to do with getting your partner more involved in the orgasm-producing process.

Although vaginismus itself is usually treatable, when untreated, it can be a very serious issue between a couple. This is especially true if the woman is a virgin, gets married, and intends to lose her virginity during the honeymoon (see Chapter 10). She and her new husband are both all set to start their sex life, he tries to penetrate her with his penis, and either she feels too much pain to let him continue or he can't get in at all. This usually results in bad feelings at best, or very often in a fight, followed by tears. If the couple doesn't go to get help, it may even mean the end of the marriage.

Lack of Desire

One of the major reasons a couple gets married is to have sex. True, it is also to have a relationship, share companionship, have children, provide financial and emotional support, and a lot of other things, but sex is definitely a major part of the pact.

Now, if you believe almost every comedian that you see on television, all husbands want sex all the time and almost all wives never want sex. Since life is not a sitcom, the truth is not so cut and dried. I hear from many women who want sex more often than their husbands. But, sadly, a lot of women do have problems with sexual desire.

Some of these women start out with a low sex drive. Others have problems after they've had children. Still others don't begin to have such problems until after menopause. A number of women also have low desire after surgery to remove their ovaries (oophorectomy) or the uterus (hysterectomy).

Low desire needn't mean no sex

For the partner who has a very low or nonexistent desire for sex, be it the woman or the man, the problem is not as acute as it is for the partner who does want to have sex. He or she is left being constantly frustrated, relying on self-pleasuring, or finding another partner. In the first two instances, the marriage often suffers, because the anger from the frustrated partner usually spills over into other areas. The last choice usually spells the end of the marriage.

As you know, I am not in favor of pressuring anybody into having sex. On the other hand, I do take pity on the frustrated partner, so I strongly believe that something needs to be done when one person has a very low desire for sex. Notice I said *very* low. It is rare that two people have exactly the same level of desire for sex, so most couples have to compromise somewhat. But "somewhat" cannot equal sex every other month.

You can treat the problem

The cure for such a lack of desire depends on the cause:

- **Depression:** If a woman is suffering from depression, then she's not going to want to have sex. If she gets help for her depression first, then her libido will probably go up by itself. A woman may also suffer depression after a hysterectomy, equating the loss of her uterus with the loss of youth, feminity, and beauty. If her ovaries are also removed, the woman is thrown in to "early menopause," which brings its own set of problems (see Chapter 3). If you are feeling low and have recently had a total hysterectomy, speak with you doctor and consider counseling (see Appendix B).

- **Childbirth:** New moms sometimes get so emotionally tied up with their babies, not to mention so tired from lack of sleep, that they lose interest in sex. The dads, who may have stopped having sex with their wives during the last month or two of their pregnancy, and who gave her the time she needed to recover from the effects of giving birth, begin to get testy after several months have gone by.

  Although these new mothers may have some very good excuses, in my opinion, it is a mistake to use them. You may have to make a conscious effort to put the spark back into your sex life, and you should do it. Get a grandparent to baby-sit (they'll love it) or hire a baby-sitter and go out with your husband for a romantic evening. If the baby is a light sleeper, or if there are other distractions in the house, rent a motel room. But don't just let sex slide. A new mom without a husband is not a good position to be in.

- **Menopause:** The production of a woman's sex hormones declines during menopause, causing certain side effects that can affect a woman's sex life. But menopause does not have to mean an end to sex. In fact, many women find they have a stronger desire for sex after menopause because they no longer have to worry about becoming pregnant. Plus, this is a time when women and their husbands have more privacy because their kids have grown up and moved out.

  You may have to make some adjustments for menopause, like using a lubricant, but you can still have a satisfactory sex life. For more suggestions, read Chapter 3 and Chapter 16.

Problems with Body Image

I don't know if it's mostly the fault of Madison Avenue (home of the advertising industry), Seventh Avenue (home of the fashion industry), or Lake Shore Drive (home of *Playboy*), but modern women face a lot of pressure when it comes to trying to make up the difference between their bodies and today's "ideal" body type.

Putting away the scales

A quick glance through the history of art, going back to the very first statues made by cavemen, will show that men have always liked the so-called voluptuous woman. As luck would have it for any voluptuous woman living today, our society now puts the skinny waif on a pedestal. Most women would like to lose a few pounds to resemble the women they see on TV and in magazines. But they don't let the fact that their bodies are more suited for Rubens' paintings of voluptuous nudes rather than Hugh Hefner's sleek centerfolds stop them from having sex. Nevertheless, I do get letters from women all the time who say that they're too fat to have sex with their husbands.

Most of these women are not saying that their partners are having any problems. Yet some of these women won't even take off their clothes in front of their husbands, although they've been married for 20 years. Now you can't tell me that their husbands would have stuck around so long if they didn't find their wives sexually attractive. After all, not every man wants to lie on top of a woman who is all skin and bones. But these women believe that they are unattractive, and they let that belief spoil their lives in myriad ways.

Women suffering from a body-image problem don't need a sex therapist so much as a counselor who can help them to overcome their low self-esteem (see Appendix B). Sometimes just getting them to believe that their husbands really do find them attractive is all that it takes. For other women, the task is more difficult. At the extreme end of the spectrum are women who are anorexic or bulimic, so that, even though they are wafer-thin, they still believe that they need to lose weight.

Beautiful at any age

Some women begin to have these same feelings of inadequacy as they grow older. As a woman ages, her body starts to change — certain parts sag, wrinkles appear, and she looks less and less like she did in her wedding picture. Has this woman become less attractive to other men? Probably. Has she become less attractive to her mate? That's another story.

The attraction that a woman's partner feels for her does not stem only from looks. A lifetime of shared memories, including experiences, can more than make up for any changes in appearance — especially when he no longer can fit into the tux he wore on his wedding day, either.

None of us is perfect, but that doesn't mean that we can't enjoy sex just as much as those cover girls and guys, and maybe even more so.

Sex after a Mastectomy

One in nine women in America will be diagnosed with breast cancer, and many of those women will undergo a *mastectomy,* the surgical removal of a breast. Naturally, survival is the first concern but sexual feelings shouldn't be forgotten either.

Because the breast is regarded as a symbol of femininity and attractiveness, and is often a source of sexual arousal in the man, a woman who loses one or both breasts often has a strong fear of rejection. Some women choose to have reconstructive surgery. But, although the new breast looks good under clothes, the look and feel of the breast is altered, and so that fear of rejection still lingers.

Another factor to consider is that many women go for surgery thinking they may only be having a *lumpectomy,* the removal of a lump in the breast, and wake up from surgery having lost their entire breast to a mastectomy. In such cases, postoperative counseling is usually vital. Your doctor or social worker can usually recommend someone to you, and many hospitals have support groups.

What a counselor must do in treating women who've undergone such surgery is regard the return of sexual functioning as matter-of-fact so that the woman receives the message that she is not going to be rejected.

The husband or sexual partner should be part of the counseling process, and plenty of reassurance is called for on his part, especially in the physical form of touching, kissing, and hugging. Because of their fear of rejection, most women won't initiate sex after a mastectomy, and the partner may also hold back, because he's not sure whether she's physically ready.

Good communications are necessary after a mastectomy, and a counselor can help establish this. Some counselors believe that the husband should be included in the physical recovery right from the very beginning, assisting in changing the dressing during the hospital stay as a way of letting his wife know that her new appearance is OK with him.

Support groups composed of other women who have undergone mastectomies can be especially helpful to a woman who doesn't have a partner, but they can also help any woman get through the trauma of losing one or both breasts (see Appendix B).

Some women have similar feelings after a hysterectomy. Discuss these feelings with your doctor. Hormonal therapy may help, or you may need counselling to revitalize you body image. The American Cancer Society has some excellent pamphlets that help you deal with sexual issues after mastectomy or hysterectomy (see Appendix B).

Chapter 24

Sex and the Law

. . . .

In This Chapter

▶ The prying eyes of the law

▶ Society's stake

▶ Protecting children

▶ Legalizing prostitution

▶ Redefining rape

▶ Changing view of illicit sex

▶ Liability for disease

▶ Safeguarding abortion

. . . .

This book is supposed to help you achieve good sexual functioning, right? So why have I included a chapter having to do with sex and the law? One reason might be that there are more than 400,000 lawyers in this country, and I want all of them to buy a copy of this book.

But seriously, my reason for including this chapter is that, despite the fact that having sex is one of the most private things we do in life, these private moments are very much under the rule of law; although, over the last few decades, the laws that govern sex have been severely weakened or, in many cases, removed altogether from the law books. But these hard-won freedoms will only last so long as we realize that we have them and work together to protect them.

Society in the Bedroom

The laws concerning sexual conduct that we currently have on the books, as well as those all through the ages, are based first of all on a moral code. People developed these codes over time as they decided what was the right way to act and what was wrong. Because the human child takes so long to develop to the point where it becomes an adult and can function on its own, it was vital to the survival of humanity that children be born into an environment where they could be nurtured for many years. And because women were needed to take care of the children at home — whether that be a cave, tent, castle, or mud hut — men had to take up the duties of hunting for food and protecting the home from predators, both of the four-legged and the two-legged variety.

For a woman to have a child without a man being around probably meant death to both the woman and the child. Societies couldn't allow that. So they developed codes which insisted that, before men and women had sex and produced children, they had to make a commitment to each other. These commitments were upheld by the society at large, be it through simple tribal justice or the fully developed legal codes we have today.

Those codes held up for thousands of years, and they were certainly still in effect while I was growing up. But in the United States and many other Western countries, those thousands of years of tradition have crumbled. Thanks to the invention of the birth control pill and other forms of contraception, sex has been decoupled from pregnancy, leaving people to make up their own rules. Some of the laws that govern sexual conduct still remain on the books, but most of these go unenforced and are only vestiges of the past.

I do believe that some of the of individual laws are still relevant, and I'd like to examine them because they can teach us some very important lessons when it comes to good sexual functioning.

The Laws against Child Abuse

We may no longer absolutely need both a mother and a father to support a child — witness the millions of children of single mothers who manage to survive, if not thrive, in our present day society — but our children still need to be protected from the damage that adults can inflict upon them. We read about children who are hit and burned and neglected in every way all the time in our newspapers, but one of the most common forms of child abuse remains sexual abuse.

As a mother, I cannot fathom why an adult would want to have sex with a child. I can maybe understand it a little in the case of an adolescent, who is considered a child under the law, but who in fact may be very developed from a sexual point of view (like the fictional Lolita, who exuded such a strong sexual hold over Humbert Humbert, even if she didn't fully understand the consequences of what she was doing).

But even the Lolitas of this world need the protection of the law. And, of course, those even more innocent, the little ones, whose sexual abuse really sickens me, certainly need protection, right? I mean, that goes without saying because, after all, who would ever question such laws?

The North American Man Boy Love Association, that's who. This organization, NAMBLA is its acronym, advocates the removal of such laws so that men can freely have sex with little boys. NAMBLA says that it is only because society says such acts are taboo that makes this sort of behavior bad. They say that the boys themselves like the attention and are not harmed in any way.

To me, this is utter nonsense. But I bring this group up for a reason. There are always those around who say that we have too many laws, and that governments should only perform a few limited tasks, such as defending the nation from intruders and maybe building roads. They definitely reject the idea that government has any role to play when it comes to our sexual behavior. You might instinctively agree with that, until you think about NAMBLA. More than 99 percent of us believe that these men are sick, yet they exist. And so we need laws to protect children even, or maybe especially, from what we do in the privacy of our homes.

The Age of Consent

As I write this book, there is a 33-year-old New York city teacher being sought by the FBI because he ran away with one of his students, who was only 15. Now he broke a number of laws, some because the couple crossed state lines, but the specific law I want to address here is that of *statutory rape*, which is defined as an adult having sex with a minor, even if the minor consents.

The *age of consent* — the age at which people may decide on their own to have sex with someone older than they are — has changed over the years. In England, from the 16th to the 18th centuries, the age of consent was only ten. Then it jumped to 16, where it is now. In the United States, the age of consent is set by each state, and the range goes from 12 to 18.

The age of consent does not mean the age when a young person *should* have sex. It only means the age that is legal for that person to have sex with an adult. Considering that young people mostly have sex with people their own age, the actual ages at which people first have sex vary widely.

The Legal Marriage Age

Separate from the age of consent is the age at which a person can get married without parental consent, which, in the United States, is also set by each state. Some countries, especially in Latin America, Africa, and Asia, encourage early marriages for girls, shortly after puberty.

Through most of human history, it wasn't the child but the parents who chose the spouse, especially in the case of young girls who were married off to older men because of some political or other gain to the parents. Although this custom has been dropped from American society, it is still widely practiced around the world. In fact, I know Camelia Sadat, the daughter of the late president of Egypt, Anwar Sadat. Camelia's father married her off to an older man when she was only 13.

Which is worse, the father forcing his 13-year-old daughter to get married, or the 33-year-old man who falls in love with a 15-year-old girl and runs away with her? I'll let you think about that. But I believe that whatever answer you come up with, you'll find yourself agreeing that society does have a responsibility when it comes to children and sex.

Incest: A Violation of Trust

Another area of the law which also dates back to Biblical times includes laws that forbid incest. Incest occurs when two people who are closely related have sexual intercourse. Here again, these laws are based on experience. It was noted that, when a pregnancy resulted from close relatives having sex, the offspring often had physical or mental disabilities.

Now, although many parents fear sexual abuse from those outside of their family, most sexual abuse occurs within families, and incest is certainly part of the problem. (Other types of child sexual abuse, such as sodomy or just fondling of the child, would not be considered incest as no pregnancy could result.)

When children are molested by family members, the consequences are often more serious than if they are molested by strangers because the natural element of trust between adult protector and child is destroyed. Often other members of the family are either unaware of what is going on, or, at the very least, close their eyes so as not to see, making the child feel even more abandoned.

As adults, we must take responsibility for the welfare of any child that we know. Sexual abuse always has serious effects upon the child that, if not apparent right away, will appear as he or she grows up. Children must be protected. Many people who practice child abuse were abused as children themselves. It's an evil circle, and we all must share in the responsibility of breaking it.

Sex Education: Spreading the Word

If parents have the right to say whether or not their child can get married, do they also have the right to stop that child from being taught in the schools about sex? While there are some people who rank sex education right up there with the three Rs, and I'm one of them, others fear that having their children learn about sex will turn them into sex maniacs.

In European countries where sex education is mandatory, such as Sweden, not only are the children not sex maniacs, but the rates of teenage pregnancy (including illegitimacy and abortion) and sexually transmitted diseases are very much lower than rates in the U.S. Sex education policies vary from country to country. In Sweden, sex education begins when school starts, for children at age 7. In the Philippines, sex education is mandatory at the high-school level. Other countries with mandatory sex education include Germany, France, and China.

In most of the U.S., if parents really object to having their child taught in school about sex, they can request, usually in writing, that their child be excused. My suspicion is that most of the parents who object to sex education don't ask that their children be excused because, if they did, then they themselves would be faced with the task of educating their children about sex — something that I don't think most of these parents want to think about, much less actually do.

On the other hand, I do agree with the courts in Florida that convicted a couple of "lewdness" for answering their 14-year-old son's question about where babies come from by demonstrating for him the method by which he had been created.

I am also in agreement with one argument used by people who oppose sex education because of their religious beliefs. Many of these people object to sex education, not because they don't want their children to know about the birds and the bees, but because they want to see a moral message imparted at the same time. This is something I also feel strongly about — so strongly that I wrote a whole book on the subject, *Sex and Morality*.

Because we are not allowed to promulgate religion in U.S. public schools, most teachers conduct sex education classes in a very straightforward fashion, without talking about right and wrong. I don't think that this approach teaches children all they need to know. We force our children to understand the basic concepts of arithmetic, even though they could perform all of the functions with a calculator. So I think we also need to explain to children how morals fit into good sexual functioning, rather than just give them the mechanics. I believe that schools can impart this general moral message without connecting it to any one religion.

Children are too impressionable to give them the facts about sex without telling them about the risks of sexual activity and the moral framework they need to make good judgments.

Rape: A Growing Concern

The law defines rape as a man having sexual intercourse with a woman, who is not his wife, without her consent. Rapes are often violent acts, but even if no force is used, if the woman consents because she believes that she might be in danger, then she has been raped.

There's no doubt that rape is and should be illegal, and rapists should be prosecuted to the full extent of the law. On this issue, my feelings are with the majority. But on a subdivision of this issue, I part company with many people, and that's date rape.

Naturally, I am not in favor of rape of any sort, or even of people pressuring each other to have sex. But, if a woman gets fully undressed and climbs into bed with a man she knows, she has to be aware of the risks. She may only want to go so far, but unless she knows the man very well, and unless she communicates how far she is willing to go quite explicitly beforehand, the chance for a miscommunication is good — especially if both parties have been drinking.

My advice to any young woman who wants to avoid date rape is to watch your step — stay in control. Don't drink and be sure to give clear signals about how far you want to go before you two come to the stopping point. If you get a man too excited, he may not be able to control himself. That has nothing to do with the law, but rather with human nature.

But, even in criminal cases where the rapist and the victim are strangers, legally defining rape has never been easy. For some time there was a presumption that, if the woman didn't actively fight back against the rapist, there was an element of consent. Today, the U.S. legal system recognizes that to fight back can put the woman in even greater danger. So now a man can be convicted of rape even if the woman does not put up a struggle. But this definition of rape can make it easier for a man to be falsely accused.

And, as if this subject wasn't complicated enough, a new twist has recently been added: *marital rape.* It had always been assumed that there could be no such thing as marital rape because marriage was thought of as blanket consent to all sexual intercourse on the part of the woman. But more and more society is coming to realize that, even in marriage, sex requires the active consent of both partners and that, just as there is spousal abuse, there can also be spousal rape. The laws dealing with spousal rape are different in every state, but we have certainly made tremendous progress in protecting women from abusive husbands.

The Law and Contraception

The reason that I became a sex therapist is that, for a time, I worked for Planned Parenthood. When women starting asking me questions about sex that I didn't know the answers to, I decided that it was time to go and study the subject more in depth. Because of those early years at Planned Parenthood, I have a great respect for the founder of that organization, Margaret Sanger, as well as for all of the other people who fought against the laws that made contraceptives illegal in the U.S.

That's right. Up until 1965, contraceptive devices were illegal in many American states. It was the Supreme Court, in the case of *Griswold v. Connecticut,* which ruled that the Constitution barred states from interfering with a married couple's decisions about childbearing. (Unmarried people were not given the right to get contraceptive services until the Supreme Court's 1972 decision in *Eisenstadt v. Baird.*) Today, you can walk into a drugstore or even some supermarkets and pick a box of condoms or a spermicide right off the shelf (see Chapter 7 for more information about birth control). I consider this tremendous progress, though even today not everyone agrees with me.

Contraception is freely available in most European countries (except for Ireland) and in some Third World Countries, such as India, though the issue in developing countries is still controversial, and many areas still ban contraceptives and even information about them.

The Law against Spreading Diseases

With so many people coming down with sexually transmitted diseases, and with the consequences being so grave, it was only a matter of time before the courts got involved. I've been telling you to practice safer sex in this book, but from a legal point of view, that is no longer enough. The U.S. courts have ruled that if you have an STD, you must inform any potential sex partners so that they can decide for themselves whether or not the risk is worth it. And, in fact, more than half of the states have laws that make it a crime for a person with HIV to have sex at all.

In addition to AIDS, herpes has also been a prime instigator of court cases, and some celebrities have settled multimillion-dollar damage cases for having passed on this disease that has no cure. But don't assume that the courts won't expand the scope of their oversight to other diseases in the future. So if you're a carrier of any STD, you must tell the truth, or what you don't say might be held against you.

The best advice I can give you is to be open and honest. You may lose some sexual partners that way, but at least you'll keep yourself from paying for past mistakes again and again.

Abortion: A Legal Safeguard

Another issue where there is wide disagreement is abortion. An abortion is the artificial ending of a pregnancy before the natural birth of a child. Up until the Supreme Court's 1973 decision in *Roe v. Wade*, abortions were illegal in the United States — although that didn't stop women from having them. The wealthier women went to have their abortions in other countries where they were legal. Some middle-class women found doctors who were willing to perform illegal abortions for a price. And the poor women would go to illegal abortionists, most of whom were not doctors, and many women died as a result.

Now, abortions upset me. As a mother, it goes against my instincts; as a religious woman, it also goes against the rules of my faith. But the situation for women before abortions became legal, with so many women dying, is to me even worse. Now if I had only one wish, it would be that no woman would ever want to have an abortion again. But I know that this wish will probably never come true because we are a long way from having the perfect form of contraception, we are even further away from people perfectly using the methods of contraception we have, and, finally, we may never totally eradicate rape and incest. Because of this imperfect world, I believe that abortion must remain legal.

Having said that, let me tell you a story of what happened on my radio show one night. A woman called me and said that she had already had three abortions. I asked her if she was sexually active, and she said yes. I asked her if she was using a contraceptive of some sort. When she answered no, I hung up on her.

Although I am in favor of having abortion available for cases of contraceptive failure or rape — as I told my radio listeners — I am totally against people using abortion as a method of birth control. Abortion is not something to be taken lightly. It may be a freedom that we should have, but it is definitely not one that we should abuse.

While I am on the subject of abortion and the law, RU486 — a pill invented in France that induces abortion — is still not approved in the U.S. (see Chapter 7). So, you see, Americans have been granted a certain amount of freedom in this area, but not absolute freedom.

The Law and Homosexuality

The men who make up NAMBLA (the organization which asserts that men should have a right to have sex with boys) are *pederasts,* a variation of homosexuals who enjoy seducing young boys more than adult men. Most homosexuals are not pederasts, yet they all seem to share the blame, even if their sexual behavior is only among consenting adults. Is that fair?

Before all you heterosexuals answer that question, I want you to answer a question to yourselves. Should you be blamed for all the heterosexual men who seduce young girls? Or what about all the heterosexual fathers, uncles, and brothers who commit incest with young girls in their family? Does that have anything to do with your having sex with a consenting adult heterosexual? No, right? Then why should the state care what two consenting homosexual men or lesbian women do behind closed doors?

Actually, today's laws were written, not so much against homosexuals themselves, as against their sexual practices. As far as homosexuals are concerned, vaginal intercourse is impossible. The main sexual acts that homosexuals do engage in, oral and anal sex, were labeled *sodomy* and made illegal; although, the way these laws were written, a heterosexual couple partaking of these practices was committing a criminal act just as much as a homosexual couple would be.

But it wasn't the content of the laws that affected homosexuals so much as the way these laws were enforced. If you admitted to being a practicing homosexual, then you were also admitting to breaking the laws against sodomy. And if the police decided to go after you, your bedroom might well prove to be a target for an investigation.

Not every culture has condemned homosexuality. It is well known that homosexuality was a part of the culture of the ancient Greeks, but there have been many other cultures throughout the world and throughout the ages that have also allowed homosexuality to flourish. One could easily say that the United States in the late 20th century is one of those cultures. But, historically, to be a homosexual has also meant risking death for practicing one's sexual orientation — most notably during the Nazi era in Germany.

Prostitution: The Case for Legalization

Prostitution — sex for money — is known as the world's oldest profession. In ancient times, among the Jews, Greeks, and Romans, it literally was a profession, meaning it was a legal way to earn a living. In some European countries, it still is legal, and there are approximately two million prostitutes plying their trade in

America. In addition, illegal prostitution flourishes in many parts of Asia and Eastern Europe. Does it make sense, given the history and widespread use of prostitution, to continue to keep it illegal?

In my opinion, prostitution should be made legal everywhere in the United States, not just in Nevada. I held that opinion before the onset of AIDS, and now I believe in it even more.

Prostitutes can be major spreaders of sexually transmitted diseases. In the days when the big worry was syphilis, which was treatable, that was no big deal. But today, because AIDS has no cure, it is a very big deal. We haven't been able to put a stop to prostitution yet, so there really doesn't seem to be much hope that we'll be able to stop it in the foreseeable future.

So what are our alternatives?

- ✔ Alternative one is to continue the current situation, where prostitution is illegal but continues to flourish and is a major contributor to the spread of AIDS.

- ✔ The other alternative is to legalize prostitution, control it, make sure that the prostitutes are as healthy as possible, try to keep them off of drugs where they might share needles, and make sure that they or their partners use condoms.

A good many prostitutes — females and males — enter the field when they are under age. Often they are tricked into becoming prostitutes, and made to become drug addicts as well. I can't say that this particular aspect of prostitution would disappear if prostitution were legal, but it would certainly be curtailed, and those regulating the houses of prostitution would see that no minors were allowed to be working there.

I admit that, even if prostitution is legalized, every prostitute won't be perfectly healthy, and some illegal prostitutes will still ply their trade — in other words, we won't be able to fully stop the spread of AIDS via the prostitute population. But, although we won't be able to halt the spread of AIDS, what if we cut it in half? Isn't that worth something?

Pornography: Erotic or Obscene

I can't begin to discuss this topic without defining what pornography is, and that's not easy to do because, to some degree, pornography is in the eye of the beholder. To get a handle on the word pornography, I need to bring in two other terms so that I can make a comparison. The first of these is *erotic*. To me, any work of art — a book, poem, painting, photograph, film, or video — that contains an element of sexuality in it is erotic. Now in my book *The Art of*

Arousal, I included some paintings that to me were erotic because of their overall content, but in which all of the subjects were fully clothed. So you see, it's a very broad description.

Now some erotic material is stronger than others: It's more frank, there's a greater element of sexuality, and it was made with the intention to arouse sexual feelings. That's material that I would call pornography. If that material steps over another boundary line, so that it is bizarre, brutal, and really shocking — and thus against the law — then I consider it obscene.

Obviously, there are certain pictures that one person will find only erotic, another will believe to be pornographic, and a third will see as obscene — which is why these terms do not come with hard-and-fast rules. What the U.S. courts have said is that it is up to the community to decide, and that decision has proven to be as difficult for the many as it is for the few.

What I consider to be obscene, and which governments should put a stop to, is any material in which the sex involves violence or children or animals. But I don't think that the government has any business banning a film because it shows two people having intercourse, oral sex, or anal sex.

Let me quickly add that I am talking about having these materials available for adults, and kept out of the hands of children. I don't like seeing all those magazine covers (that clearly show more than they cover) in a newsstand where children passing by can see them. And, if a video store wants to stock X-rated films, I believe it should keep them behind a closed door, not just on one shelf where a young person can still see them.

Some people object to such material altogether, because they believe that it drives men to act out the fantasies that seeing these images creates. I disagree. In countries where pornography is legalized, like Denmark and West Germany, the statistics for rape have not risen — and, because more women began to report rape, its occurrence may well have gone down.

Everyone needs a sexual outlet. In an ideal world, that outlet would come in the form of a spouse. But many people, for whatever reason, cannot find a permanent partner or even a series of irregular partners. That they end up taking their sexual frustrations out on others should not come as too big of a surprise. Given outlets for this sexual energy — and erotica assists greatly for one such outlet, masturbation — these people end up having better control over themselves.

Some feminists believe that, because pornography tends to feature women and make them sex objects, pornography is demeaning to women and devalues their worth. Certain images, be they visual or verbal, do demean women — of that there is no doubt. And I would deem much of them obscene. But I don't think, as a whole, that pornography hurts women in any significant way. One could certainly make the point that this same era, the latter half of the 20th century, has seen both the spread of feminism and the spread of pornography. Although I am not saying that there is a direct correlation, I do believe that if we as a society were to begin repressing one of our freedoms — in this case, the freedom to view pornography — it might well portend a return to the suppression of women as well.

It's true, however, that erotica has its down side:

> ✔ Some of the women who perform in these films or pose for these pictures are being exploited. Maybe they have a drug habit to support, or a child to feed. But, although these women deserve our sympathy, I don't know that, if the sex industry were wiped out tomorrow, they would end up being better off.

> ✔ Some men become addicted to erotica. They abandon their wives in favor of videos, or they never marry in the first place because they can't tear themselves away from their stack of magazines. The question we have to ask ourselves, as a society, is whether we should all have our rights to view such material squelched in order to protect the small percentage of people who abuse these materials.

My opinion is that we should not limit the majority, in this case, to "save" the minority. But if you disagree with me, that's fine. That's what makes this such a great country.

Adultery: Cheating the Law

Adultery occurs when at least one of the two people having sex is married to someone else. Laws have historically banned such practice. In the 19th century, Nathaniel Hawthorne's novel, *The Scarlet Letter*, had banishment and the wearing of a red letter A on the woman's dress as a punishment for adultery. Even today, some states continue to have laws against adultery. Among the reasons for originally banning adultery was that wealth was mostly passed on from generation to generation and playing around with the gene pool by having sexual relations with outsiders was not looked upon kindly.

Whether or not adultery should be a criminal act today, it certainly can have a negative impact on a marriage. Adultery is probably the single most-cited grounds for divorce. I am not one of those people who says that every marriage has to last forever, but it would be preferable if people would decide to end their marriage *before* having sex with other people. You do, after all, take a vow to be faithful. But I also know that adultery is something that will never go away, whether it is against the law or not. People do fall out of love, for whatever reasons, and it is oftentimes easier to cheat than to separate.

Chapter 25

Keeping Children Safe

· ·

In This Chapter

▶ Playing doctor

▶ Answering questions about sex

▶ Understanding the importance of privacy

▶ Keeping your children safe from strangers

▶ Teaching your teenager about sex

▶ Protecting kids against cyberporn and X-rated videos

· ·

*W*hen I was a teenager living in an orphanage in Switzerland, one of my duties was taking care of the younger children. Later on, I worked as a kindergarten teacher in Paris, where I was surrounded by children all day long.

My doctorate is in the study of the family. I am the mother of two children and the grandmother of one. Needless to say, I love children, and making sure that they remain safe is a high priority of mine.

Now, although I could certainly give you some good advice on how to teach children to cross the street so as to minimize their danger or how to tie their shoelaces so they won't trip on them, you didn't buy this book for my expertise in those areas, did you? That's why, in this chapter, I tell you how to help keep children safe from the risks they face from sex.

Stuff That's Not Dangerous

Let me begin with a situation which just about every parent faces, and which many find embarrassing, but which poses little or no risk to the child. Even though children are not capable of having sex, their sexual organs are sources of pleasure to them. Some parents think that, if their child touches his or her own genitals or plays doctor with the kids next door, then the child is doing something harmful. This couldn't be further from the truth.

The reason that children touch themselves is simple — it feels good — just the way it feels good when we touch our own genitals, or someone else does. So it is perfectly natural that children would be curious about these good sensations and would try to duplicate them. This process begins in the womb, where boys have erections and girls' vaginas lubricate, which should prove to you that this is a perfectly natural phenomenon and can do them no harm. And you certainly can't stop children from doing these things while they are inside of their mothers, nor can you say that they are behaving immorally, so there's no reason to stop them after they are born.

Now, because in our society anything to do with sex is kept private, children do have to be told that they shouldn't touch themselves in public. Children can be made to understand this, just the way they learn that they are not allowed to pick their noses when they're out in society. But, in the same breath that you tell your children not to touch themselves in public, you have to reassure them that it is normal to want to touch their own bodies. If you overreact and don't reassure them, your children may think that they are doing something bad, and thinking of themselves or their bodies as bad could lead to sexual problems for your children later on. Chapter 19 discusses this subject in greater detail.

You should always call children's body parts by their real names, so that children learn the appropriate terms instead of family names which, though cute, may confuse them later on when other people use different words.

Teaching Proper Functioning as Well as Proper Etiquette

Remember, although it is important to keep your children safe from sex abuse (a topic I get to later in this chapter), it is also your responsibility as a parent to see that they function well as sexual beings. If your children get all sorts of hang ups passed on to them from you, then it is going to affect their sexual behavior all through their lives.

If your children are ashamed of their bodies, if they feel guilty when they touch themselves, then those same feelings will not suddenly go away. If you weren't raised openly, then it is understandable that it may be difficult for you to be that open with your children. But do make the effort, because it pays off in the long run. You probably have many good traits that you want to pass on to your children, but I hope you agree that making them sexually uptight shouldn't be on that list.

No Prescription Needed to Play Doctor

Although many parents buy children a toy doctor's kit, most don't do it in anticipation of what a doctor's visit really entails. Exposing body parts normally kept clothed and even touching these parts as they play doctor — also known as "I'll show you mine if you show me yours" — are common practices among children.

Basically, this is something that most children do because they are naturally curious about each other's bodies. Under normal circumstances, no harm can come to children this way. If you discover children engaging in this activity, you do have to tell them to stop — not because it is inherently bad, but because you don't want the other parents in the neighborhood to think you're running an illegal sex clinic in your basement. But don't say it in an angry way, as if they had been behaving badly. Just let them know that we have to respect each other's privacy and that they shouldn't engage in that kind of play any more.

Although it's OK for children to experiment with their bodies through games, I do need to give you a few words of caution:

✔ Make sure that an older sibling doesn't take part in this play. That could change the dynamics, especially if the older child is heading towards puberty.

✔ Keep an eye out for how often these games are played. In most cases, this is not a regular habit among children, like playing tag. Sometimes, however, there is one child who tends to lead the others in such games again and again.

Any young child who seems to be obsessed with sexual matters may have a problem. Perhaps some form of sexual abuse is going on in that child's home, or maybe the parents are just overstimulating the child in some way, but you don't want to have it affect your child negatively.

So if you find that the neighborhood children are playing doctor regularly, and especially if there is one child who seems to be the instigator, find a way of stopping it. You may want to talk to the other parents, but certainly try to take your child out of this situation.

✔ One consequence of such games, or of little girls seeing their brothers naked, is that the daughter may feel that she is missing something — namely, a penis. Again, don't make a big issue out of this, but simply explain to her that boys and girls are built differently and that she is not missing anything: rather, she is constructed just the way Mommy is and is perfect just the way she is.

Answering Children's Questions

If you're a parent, or if you hang around kids long enough, at some point you're going to be asked a question pertaining to sex. Many adults panic when confronted with such questions. Right away, they think that they're going to have to explain the whole scenario, and they're just not ready.

My first word of advice is to relax. In all probability, the answer the child is looking for is something very simple. You should answer honestly, but only give one piece of information at a time and see if that satisfies the child. If children are too young, they're not ready to hear the whole explanation of the birds and the bees, so don't rush into it without first ascertaining exactly what kind of answer they are looking for.

Little Jimmy

Little Jimmy was five and had just started school two months ago. One day, he came home and asked his mother this question: "There's this girl in my class, Kim, and she said that she was different from me. How is she different from me?"

Jimmy's Mom jumped to the conclusion that this was one of those questions that she'd always been dreading. She sat Jimmy down and spent ten minutes telling him the differences between boys and girls. When she was finished, she gave a deep sigh, hoping that she had answered his question. She asked him if there was anything else he wanted to know.

"Yes, Mom. Kim said she was Chinese. What does that mean?"

As you can see, Jimmy's mother could have saved herself having to give that particular lesson if she had asked her son some more questions before starting in. And, although it certainly did Jimmy no harm to hear her explanation of what makes boys different from girls, that wasn't his question. He probably didn't pay all that much attention to what she was saying, because he wasn't hearing the information he was seeking.

One day, the question your child asks will be about sex, and then you'll have to be prepared to answer it. One recommendation that I can give you to make this situation a little bit easier is to buy a children's book on sexuality ahead of time and get it out when the time comes. Then you'll be prepared if your child really does want to know, or need to know, the answers to some question having to do with sex.

You may be wondering why I said "need to know." I wasn't referring to something actually having to do with sex, at least not yet. Sometimes your child may be hearing things from other, possibly older children that he or she finds frightening. You have to be ready, in those situations, to give your child a full lesson so that he or she understands that there's nothing to be frightened of.

Having a book to look at together makes teaching your child about sexuality a lot less embarrassing for both of you. You can read the parts that embarrass you, rather than having to stumble around in your own words. And the book will probably have pictures or drawings to help you.

After you've given your lesson, leave the book out so that your child can look at it on his or her own. I wrote a book for 8 to 12-year-olds titled *Dr. Ruth Talks to Kids*. One of the first things I say in that book is that children should be allowed to take it into their rooms, close their doors, and read it in private. Just the way that we need privacy when it comes to sexual matters, so do kids. And you have to respect that privacy.

Personal Privacy

Teaching your children about privacy is critical. Make sure that all of your children understand that, not only are they allowed to maintain their privacy at home, but that they absolutely must maintain it outside of the home, especially when around strangers. Now you don't want to frighten your children, but you do have to make sure that they understand that, unless Mommy or Daddy says it's OK, such as when the child goes to the doctor, no one is allowed to touch their private parts. It's very sad that child molesters are out there, but they do exist, and we have to teach our children to be extra careful.

Now, if you listen to the media, child molestation seems to be rampant. I've read estimates which say that as many as 40 percent of all children are abused sexually in some way. Let me start on this topic by saying *calm down*. Child molestation is certainly out there, and you must do all that you can to protect your children, but common sense and my own experiences as a sex therapist tell me that it does not go on as much as all that.

Because children will try to give answers that they think adults want to hear, I don't know whether we can ever get a scientifically valid survey as to how much child abuse there really is, but I believe that the pendulum has swung too far in the direction of identifying child abuse. These days, things have gone so far that, if a little girl falls down and starts to cry in a playground, the father of another child will hesitate to help the girl because he's frightened that he'll be accused of child abuse. We have to bring back a little sanity to this situation, because paranoia isn't good for our mental health either.

Warning Signs of Possible Sexual Abuse

Although I believe that the percentages are much lower than proclaimed, child abuse certainly does exist and, as a parent or guardian, you have a duty to protect your child. A report issued by the Sexuality Information and Education Council of the United States (SIECUS), on whose board I used to sit, gives certain guidelines that I want to pass on to you. These are behaviors that you should watch for to see if a child under your care is undergoing sexual abuse:

- ✔ The child focuses on sexuality to a greater extent than on other aspects of his or her environment, and/or has more sexual knowledge than similar-aged children with similar backgrounds who live in the same area. A child's sexual interest should be in balance with his or her curiosity about, and explanation of, other aspects of his or her life.

- ✔ The child has an ongoing, compulsive interest in sexual or sexually related activities and/or is more interested in engaging in sexual behaviors than in playing with friends, going to school, and doing other developmentally appropriate activities.

- ✔ The child engages in sexual behaviors with those who are much older or younger. Most school-aged children engage in sexual behaviors with children within a year or so of their age. In general, the wider the age range between children engaging in sexual behavior, the greater the concern.

- ✔ The child continues to ask unfamiliar children, or children who are uninterested, to engage in sexual activities. Healthy and natural sexual play usually occurs between friends and playmates.

- ✔ The child, or a group of children, bribes or emotionally and/or physically forces another child/children of any age into sexual behaviors.

- ✔ The child exhibits confusion or distorted ideas about the rights of others in regard to sexual behaviors. The child may contend: "She wanted it" or "I can touch him if I want to."

- ✔ The child tries to manipulate children or adults into touching his or her genitals or causes physical harm to his or her own or others' genitals.

- ✔ Other children repeatedly complain about the child's sexual behaviors — especially when the child has already been spoken to by an adult.

- ✔ The child continues to behave in sexual ways in front of adults who say "no," or the child does not seem to comprehend admonitions to curtail overt sexual behaviors in public places.

- ✔ The child appears anxious, tense, angry, or fearful when sexual topics arise in his or her everyday life.

- ✔ The child manifests a number of disturbing toileting behaviors: plays with or smears feces, urinates outside of the bathroom, uses excessive amounts of toilet paper, stuffs toilet bowls to overflowing, or sniffs or steals underwear.

> ✔ The child's drawings depict genitals as the predominant feature.
>
> ✔ The child manually stimulates or has oral or genital contact with animals.
>
> ✔ The child has painful and/or continuous erections or vaginal discharge.

If you discover that your child is showing any of the above signs, you should consult with a professional — starting with your pediatrician — to find out whether or not there is a problem. Don't try to confront this situation by yourself. Even an expert may have difficulty trying to learn the truth when dealing with a child, and any efforts on your part may only frighten the child so that you will never learn whether anything is wrong.

The Accidental Voyeur

I don't want you to worry about the accidental time your child catches you making love. This is something that happens to a lot of couples, and, if you don't make a big deal of it, the child will probably not realize what was going on, and there will be no consequences whatsoever.

The danger to children comes not from an accident, but from repeatedly seeing material that is not suited to their age. You certainly know that, if you show a small child a horror movie, that child is going to have nightmares. Well, if you let children watch shows that have a high sexual content, they will have the equivalent to a nightmare, only, instead of scaring them, it will play havoc with their libidos.

It is also important that a child know that Mommy and Daddy love each other. If you and your spouse kiss and hug in front of your child regularly then, if someday your child does catch you having sex, he or she won't connect it with something terrible — even though the noises adults can make while engaged in sex can be frightening to a child.

Again, although no great harm can come to a child from catching you "in the act," a very cheap method of protection is available — the eye-and-hook lock. You can purchase such a device for less than a dollar, and, if you remember to lock it when you are making love, you can save yourself some embarrassment, if nothing else.

Protecting Your Children from the Media

A report issued by the Sexuality Information and Education Council of the United States that issued the warning signs of possible sexual abuse also noted that professionals, meaning counselors and teachers, are finding that children are demonstrating sexual behavior much more frequently than they ever did before. The reason for this is simple: Children today see so much more sex in the media.

Although, as an adult, you may welcome the fact that television has become more open about sexual matters and that you can rent R- and X-rated films to watch in the privacy of your home, seeing this type of material can — change that to *will* — overstimulate your child. Just watching the soap operas with your kids is enough to make them lose the innocence that they deserve. Children do imitate the behavior of adults they see, and, if they see sexual situations, they will try to copy them. Because children do have sexual feelings, some of these behaviors can have direct consequences, so that a child may start to play with his or her genitals on a regular basis because that child has been overstimulated.

By letting children see sexual material regularly, you are also putting them at risk if they do come in contact with someone who is looking to take advantage of them. If a child sees people on TV having sex — and I don't mean anything more than the type of scenes soaps show all the time — then, if some adult proposes that that child do something similar, he or she will not be frightened, but may accept this behavior as normal.

As far as the television and other materials are concerned, you can do several things to protect your child, although the most important thing is to keep a careful eye over what your child is watching.

- ✔ Keep any tapes that might be inappropriate to children out of their reach. Definitely don't leave these videos out along with the rest of the tapes. Do the same with any other erotic material, including magazines and books.

- ✔ When going to the video store to rent movies, be strict about the Motion Picture Association of America (MPAA) ratings. Kids will plead with you, but show them the rating on the box and don't give in, because, once you do, it will be very hard to go backwards.

- ✔ Most cable companies offer ways that you can lock out certain channels that carry material that is not suited to children. Call your cable company and find out what you can do.

- ✔ Children shouldn't watch too much television in the first place, but certainly not late at night when adult programming is on. If you have a child that won't sleep, the last thing you should do is let that child come into your bed and watch TV with you. You'll not only be encouraging your child not to develop proper sleep habits, but you might be overstimulating him or her as well.

- ✔ Try not to let your children watch the news. Oftentimes the news carries stories that are not appropriate to children. And, because the topics switch every few minutes, the inappropriate stories may come on suddenly before you realize it.

✔ If you use baby-sitters, give them specific instructions concerning what shows your child is allowed to watch or not watch. Tell your child these rules, as well, and afterwards, ask your child whether or not he or she watched any of the forbidden shows. Little children are not likely to lie about such things.

✔ If you have children of a broad age range, make sure that the older children don't watch inappropriate shows around their younger siblings. MTV is one channel that you should monitor under such situations.

I know how easy it is to use the television as a baby-sitter, especially in this day and age when both parents work. I'm not saying not to do it, but just take every precaution you can. This is even more important if your children fall into the category of "latch-key kids," that is to say, that they spend the time from when they come home from school to when a parent returns home, alone. If inappropriate material is around, the temptation will be strong to watch it. So, if you have such material in your home, make sure that you take the time to remove it or put it under lock and key.

Protecting Your Children from Cyberporn: Good News and Bad News

Kids are certainly smarter than we are about computers: that's the bad news. The good news is that, recently, all of the major commercial online computer services, many adult bulletin board systems, and now even the Internet, provide tools for parental control. With varying degrees, they let you "surf" for what you want without worrying too much about whether your kids will also find it.

Educate your kids

But, as always, common sense prevails: tell your kids that the same rules they use when walking down a street (see "The Speech about Strangers," later in this chapter) applies when they're surfing the net. The National Center for Missing and Exploited Children (1-800-843-5678) has an excellent pamphlet, *Child Safety on the Information Highway,* which has good rules of thumb:

✔ Set guidelines for how your child uses the computer and discuss those guidelines with your child.

✔ Don't let your child give out personal information, like address, phone number, or school.

✔ Don't let your child arrange for online meetings with a stranger or send his or her photograph.

✔ Tell your children to come to you *immediately* if someone is sending them messages that they don't like.

Control kids' access

Allowing adults access to a wide range of material while protecting it from children has thankfully become a priority for online companies and users. The commercial online services, as well as the Internet, have several ways of protecting curious young minds from inappropriate materials. Two commercial online services, America Online and Prodigy, are trying to provide family-oriented services while still catering to adult interests online. CompuServe has indicated that they will be adding control features in the future.

America Online (AOL)

AOL probably has the best parental control capability, with the "adult" member having separate access from children's subaccounts. This master account can restrict access to instant messages, chat rooms, and Internet news groups (see Chapter 20 for more on computers and sexual materials). AOL is currently adding controls for the World Wide Web.

To implement parental controls, use the AOL keyword function, select Members, and then click on Parental Control.

Prodigy

Prodigy offers parental controls in the form of what is basically an On/Off Function. Each person in the family can be set up with separate access. To set this up, click on jump, then type in **Member Access,** and follow the directions.

CompuServe

As of this writing, CompuServe isn't offering separate accounts for purposes of parental control. However, from the main member account, you can request that particular CompuServe forums be made unavailable. Contact the forum sysop (system operator).

Adult Bulletin Board Systems (BBSs)

Most responsible adult BBSs require proof of age for access. Usually, a driver's license or some other form of ID is required, often via fax to the sysop. These bulletin boards have built-in software, which then restricts access. Contact the BBS systems operators you use for their individual policies.

Internet

New software has recently appeared which allows parents to control their children's access to sexually explicit material on the Internet. Three products are currently available:

- ✔ For parents who want to let their kids surf, yet keep them out of the nasty stuff, *SurfWatch* (SurfWatch Software, Los Altos, CA, 800-458-6600, http://www.surfwatch.com) filters material coming in from the World Wide Web, Internet News Groups, Internet Relay Chat (Chat Groups), and other Internet services. It hides in the background and waits for someone to request inappropriate material; it then blinks a message: "Blocked!" SurfWatch comes ready to block thousands of sites, which is a big advantage for parents who don't have time to look for these sites themselves. The sites are selected and updated monthly by the company. An On/Off switch with password control allows parents to turn SurfWatch off after the kids are asleep. For Windows and Mac computers.

- ✔ For a more disciplinary approach, *NetNanny* (NetNanny, Vancouver, B.C., 604-662-8522) pulls the plug. When a child types in a key phrase such as **sex,** it simply turns off the computer. The parent decides which key phrases cause the shutdown (this can be a lot of work, or a fun word exercise). For DOS computers.

- ✔ Another product that hides adult stuff from the kids is *CyberSitter* (Solid Oak Software, Santa Barbara, CA, 805-967-9853), which can block access to graphically based applications and types of picture files coming into the computer. By identifying all .gif files (graphic interchange files, or picture files) coming in, all visual material (both good and bad) is stopped . Other Internet services are not stopped unless specifically identified. For DOS and Windows computers.

The Speech about Strangers

Parents now have two speeches to give to their children. The first is how to handle strangers and the second is about sex. The tricky part about the first speech is that you want your child to recognize the dangers posed by strangers, but you don't want to scare them so badly that they won't leave your protection.

I suggest that you give the speech about strangers in pieces and repeat it often. Kids don't really comprehend too much new material at one time, and they usually must hear it more than once in order for it to sink in. Also, children can grasp more mature concepts as they get older so that, although saying "Don't accept candy from a stranger" might be enough for a four- or five-year-old, a child who is slightly older has to be told that it isn't just candy that should be turned down, but any favor, including money or a ride home from school.

Tell kids to tell an adult

As important as telling children what they shouldn't do is to tell them what they *should* do if a stranger approaches them improperly, which is to run away and immediately tell an adult. I think the first part, not doing certain things, is easier for a child than the second part, because, if they experience sexual abuse, kids will often put these encounters out of their minds or, if they sense that they may have done something bad, actually try to hide it from you.

Because you want your children to tell you about *anything,* you must be very careful to let them know that they will not be punished if they report that something occurred. It is not easy to pass this reassurance along, and, once again, I think that the best way to do it is to repeat the message several times until you are relatively sure that your child does understand.

If a child ever does report something out of the ordinary to you, it is also important that you don't overreact. The child will sense that something is wrong, and that might shut off communication at a time when you need your child to tell you as much as he or she can. So try to remain as calm and matter-of-fact as you can while you dig for information.

Organize with other parents

It is always better to have a network set up *before* trouble happens than afterwards, which is why I recommend that you organize with other parents and nonparents on your block right now. Again, this is not an issue to get hysterical about — a child abuser is not hiding under every rock — but it is certainly a good idea to be prepared in case one does show up.

The organization you set up can be quite simple. It can consist of one meeting at which everybody agrees to watch out for each other's children, and you put together a list of names and phone numbers. The most important aspect of this organization is that, if any adult on the block sees something going on with your child which he or she thinks might be suspicious, that adult will know, ahead of time, that he or she has your permission to investigate. This might mean that you'll get a few phone calls complaining when the kids are making too much noise playing ball in the street, but it is well worth it if the network you create can stop even a minor incident.

That Other Discussion — Sex Ed and the Older Child

Throughout this chapter, I give you some ideas about how to handle the-birds-and-the-bees discussion with little children, but that heart-to-heart talk gets a lot more complicated with older children. Many parents slough it off and hope for the best, but in this era of AIDS, that is a risky maneuver. Yes, your child will probably be told some things about AIDS and other sex-related topics at school, but will it be enough?

In my opinion, sex is a topic that should be handled by parents and school together, with active participation by both groups. School teachers are better equipped to actually teach the material, because they are professional educators, and you are probably not, but it's up to you to inject the moral message, which is an important component.

I think that schools should notify parents when they are teaching these particular topics and send home some sort of questionnaire for the parents to fill out, sign, and return to the school. This form would require that the parents ask their children certain questions to make sure that they understood the lesson. Part of the process should include a discussion between the parents and the child, during which the parents could add their moral guidance. Both parents should be a part of this discussion, if possible, and they should make a vow ahead of time to keep the tone of the discussion as calm as possible, so that tempers don't flare, which can happen with teenagers.

Knowing doesn't equal doing

The biggest worry that parents have about sex education is that, if they acknowledge to their teens that sex does exist, and if they go over safer sex practices with them, then they will be giving the message that it is OK to have premarital sex. That fear is groundless if you, as a parent, take charge of the situation. If you tell your teen in no uncertain terms that you do not approve of premarital sex, then your teen is not going to get mixed signals.

If you don't buy that idea, think of some other examples. How many fathers have taken their sons aside and taught them how to box, throwing punches while protecting themselves with their other hand? When the father does that, does he expect the child to march next door and get into a fight with the kid who lives there? Of course not, he just wants him to be prepared. Or, if a mother gives her daughter ten dollars before she goes out on a date so that she can take a cab home if the boy gets fresh, does she expect that to happen?

I don't believe in giving percentages, so I won't here, but I do know that many teens engage in sex. Therefore, it's a lot riskier to let your child go out into the world, possibly not sure of what constitutes safer sex, than to avoid telling that child the facts about sex because he or she might think that you're giving the green light.

I don't believe in scare tactics, either, because I know that they don't work. During World War II, the army showed recruits films about venereal diseases that should have scared the pants *on* them, but did it work? No. If a soldier had the chance to visit a prostitute, he never gave those films a thought.

The libido is very strong, and, if two young people fall in love, there's a chance that it will lead to sex. You can slow the process down, but, if it's going to happen, you can't stop it. You can't be there every second. Because of this, your job as a parent includes making sure that your child understands safer sex procedures.

To give or not to give condoms

Some parents take their responsibilities so seriously that they make sure that their teens, particularly boys, know where condoms are kept in the house. Because no parent is going to resist the temptation of counting those condoms from time to time, you better be prepared to accept your child's sexual life if you adopt this policy.

If you know yourself well enough and are sure that you are going to stick your nose into the situation as soon as those condoms start disappearing, then maybe you'd better not play drugstore. Condoms are easy to buy these days, but your child's trust is not. If your child thinks that the only reason you stored those condoms was to catch him or her using them, then you may seriously damage your relationship with that child.

Other Messages You Don't Want to Give

You communicate to your child in many ways, and that communication always has an effect, even if you don't realize it. So watch what you do and say in front of your children. Let me give you some examples:

Daddy and Debbie

When Debbie was a little girl, she was always sitting on her Daddy's lap, giving him hugs and kisses, and he loved it. Then, when she started showing signs of becoming a woman—when her breasts started to develop and the rest of her figure filled out — Daddy suddenly withdrew all these physical signs of affection. He decided that they were inappropriate and began treating Debbie as if she were just another woman and not his little girl.

Debbie felt really hurt when that happened. She didn't understand why Daddy was rejecting her. She felt that she had done something wrong and, to make up for that, she looked for someone else who would make her feel good the way Daddy used to — and she quickly found a boy who satisfied those urges.

Some girls react the way Debbie did if their fathers suddenly pull away from them during puberty. Others think of their new bodies as ugly and unattractive, because Daddy rejected them, and crawl into a shell. Neither reaction is good, and that's why daddies have to be careful how they treat their daughters.

Billy's case shows how some parents may fail to acknowledge their children's individuality.

Dad and Billy

Billy's Dad had never dated much in high school. He ended up marrying the first serious girlfriend he had in college, and she was the only woman he ever had sex with. Although he loved his wife, he often had regrets that he hadn't had more lovers.

Dad and Billy were always close, playing sports together or watching games. When Billy started dating, Dad began to live vicariously through his son. He would admire the girls that Billy brought around, and he would encourage Billy to have sex with them by making various comments like, "Boy, she looks like she's good in bed."

Billy might not have had sex with these early girlfriends, but from the way his father was talking, it appeared as if he was supposed to, and so that's exactly what he did. But he resented his father for it. The closeness that the two shared started to disappear, because Billy didn't want his Dad even to know when he was dating someone, and he especially didn't want to bring those dates around the house.

Parents can make all kinds of mistakes, but they may not realize the seriousness of the mistakes having to do with sex. Try to analyze your behavior around your children from their point of view. If you don't like what you see from their perspective, then try to change your ways. If you have difficulties doing this, but suspect that you may be making some mistakes, go out and get some books that cover the areas where you have some concern.

Remember, although sex makes it easy to become parents, it does not make us experts at parenting. But you can learn how to be a better parent, and it is definitely worthwhile to make the effort.

Part VI
The Part of Tens

The 5th Wave By Rich Tennant

"Oh, wait a minute Arthur! When I said I'd only have safe sex with you, this isn't what I meant!"

In this part...

*1*n the Jewish tradition, the number 18, which stands for life, is considered to be a lucky number. But my good friend, John Kilcullen, at IDG Books, seems to be more attached to the number 10. Maybe it makes him think of Bo Derek. Well, I liked that movie, too, because Dudley Moore is short, like me. So you see, it's all in your outlook. And if there's one thing that I hope you've gotten out of this book, it's to look at the bright side of life. *L'chaim.*

Chapter 26

Ten Dumb Things People Believe about Sex

● ●

In This Chapter

▶ If I haven't had sex by the time I'm 18, I'm a loser

▶ You can wait too long to have sex

▶ The more you score, the more pleasure you'll have

▶ I'm heterosexual, so AIDS can't get me

▶ The grass is always greener in the neighbors' bedroom

▶ Having sex will make everything all right

▶ A good lover has to be an open book

▶ You should always compare partners

▶ I can't become a better lover

▶ Lovers are like Siamese twins

▶ I'm too old to have sex

● ●

*T*he key to good sexual functioning is to be sexually literate, and one important way of earning your master's degree in sexual literacy is to do a little housecleaning upstairs and sweep away any sexual myths that have been hiding in the corners of your brain.

Lots of people still believe some very dumb things about sex, so don't be surprised if you find some of these damaging concepts lurking about your brain cells. And some of these ideas aren't that easy to get rid of, either. So it's not enough to tell yourself only once not to believe any of these falsehoods; you have to maintain a steady vigilance to make sure that they don't come creeping back. You might get used to relying on a crutch belief like "I can't become a better lover," but you have to develop the reflex of throwing that belief away each and every time it pops back into your brain. Anyone can become a better lover. But you have to work at it.

If I Haven't Had Sex by the Time I'm 18, I'm a Loser

When you're 85 years old and you're looking back at your life, the age at which you first had sex will be absolutely irrelevant. You won't care, and neither will anybody else. But for many 18-year-olds, or 22-year-olds, or 25-year-olds who are still virgins, the weight of this sexual status seems to grow heavier by the hour. Somehow, they feel that the fact that they've never had sex is written across their foreheads for all to see, and that everyone is laughing at them.

If you're in this category, please don't put any added pressure on yourself. If you feel sexually frustrated, there is nothing wrong with masturbating. Be grateful that you can give yourself orgasms rather than resenting the fact that someone else isn't doing it for you.

Now, if you don't have a significant other, and you feel lonely, then finding a partner is a goal worth going after. And then, if you do find someone to love, having sex may become a realistic possibility. But you might be just as happy waiting to have sex with that person until you get married. That's up to you.

 Remember, many people start having sex when they're very young, but because the situation isn't right, they never learn to become great lovers and never have terrific sex lives. Rather than rushing into sex just because you're at a certain age, learn to give your feelings time to grow and develop. You're better off if you wait to have sex until the time is right and the person with whom you have sex is right.

The More I Score, the More Pleasure I'll Have

I am not one of those who say that you should absolutely never have a one-night stand. In some instances, the chemistry between two people is very strong, the opportunity is perfect, and it is very hard passing up such a moment. If you are very careful about protecting yourself, and if you are fully aware of the risks you are taking, then a one-night stand may be something that you indulge in once, or maybe twice.

But some people make one-night stands a part of their lifestyles. For these people, variety is the spice of life. They don't want a relationship, but prefer a string of sexual partners. To them, it's not quality but quantity that makes the best sex.

All I can say to you if you're one of those people who think that more sex is better than good sex is that this attitude is dumb, dumb, and dumb.

In the 1990s, with AIDS spreading and other sexually transmitted diseases already rampant, if you multiply the risks by multiplying your partners, you are asking for trouble. There is no such thing as safe sex between two people, only safer sex. This means that, although you might not catch an STD the first time you have a one-night stand, or the second, or maybe even the third, each time you have one, you increase the odds — in particular, because those people with whom you are having these one-night stands are obviously also prone to risky behavior. So, if you have one-night stands again and again, at some point, you're going to come out a loser.

And what if you're a woman and a mistake happens and you wind up pregnant? What kind of support do you think you are going to get from someone you barely know?

Apart from the risks, one-night stands just do not make for the best sex. What makes having sex with another person better than masturbating is the intimacy, the shared feelings, the romance that is attached to the moment. None of these exist during a one-night stand.

And then there's the next morning. Was it the first of a long string of sexual encounters, or a one-time affair? If you would like to see the other party again and they'd rather not, imagine how much worse the feeling of rejection is going to be than if they'd said no in the first place. And if you're the one doing the rejecting, well, how good an experience could it have been if you never want to repeat it?

Putting another notch on your bedpost is not as satisfying as exchanging the full range of emotions that pass between two people who are making love.

Being a Heterosexual Makes Me Immune to AIDS

Because, in the U.S., the AIDS epidemic struck the gay community first, many straight people refuse to admit that they can catch this deadly disease. They think that they can engage in unprotected sex without suffering any consequences. Well, guess what? That's just not true.

In Africa, where AIDS is the most widespread, it is primarily a heterosexual disease. And the fastest growing rate of the disease in Western countries is among heterosexuals, not homosexuals. The pool of heterosexuals who have AIDS grows every day and, therefore, so do the risks to every other heterosexual.

Your sexual preference does not make you immune to this killer disease. At the moment, nothing does. Therefore, you have to protect yourself and always follow safer sex practices. (Chapter 21 discusses sexually transmitted diseases, including AIDS, in detail. If you're guilty of overlooking the threat of AIDS, then I insist you go back and read that chapter!)

Believing that AIDS can only happen to gays is a prejudice that could cost you your life.

The Grass Is Always Greener in the Neighbors' Bedroom

Some people think that they're missing out by staying within the bounds of marriage. When it comes to having an affair, these people believe that the grass is greener in the next pasture. Although sexual boredom is certainly something to watch out for in your own life, maybe you ought to remove those green-colored glasses when looking over the neighbor's fence.

The media are filled with sex these days. On TV and in newspaper and magazine articles, it appears as if you can discover exactly what's going on under everyone else's covers if you believe all of the reports, especially those that draw their conclusions from surveys of one kind or another. And, if the activities in your bedroom don't appear to measure up, then you become dissatisfied with what had been a satisfying sex life.

My advice to you is to take all the information that people are throwing your way with a grain of salt. When people answer all those questionnaires, do you really believe that they are telling the truth? Would you be completely honest, or would you exaggerate a bit?

In my opinion, most people exaggerate. So, when you read how often people are having sex, or how many partners they've had, or any of the other statistics that are floating around, and then look at your own life, yours may seem inadequate. But, if those numbers are all inflated, then you're really not losing out, are you?

Stop paying attention to what everybody else is supposedly doing and concentrate on how to make the best of what you already have. Most people can improve their sex lives, and I am certainly an advocate of that. But, if you try to make those improvements only because you want to keep up with the Joneses, then you'll only be setting yourself up for disappointment. (Besides, the Joneses may be trying to keep up with YOU!)

Having Sex Will Make Everything All Right

Sex is not a cure for a lousy relationship. That may seem obvious to some of you, but many people don't seem to know this, particularly women. A woman may be in a relationship with someone who mistreats her, and, instead of running for the hills, she agrees to go one step further along and have sex with him. Why? She thinks that, because sex is what he seems to want so badly, he'll change into a pussycat after he's had his way with her. In some cases, both partners get some pleasure out of this sex; in others, only one. But sex is not enough to hold together a relationship, no matter how good it feels.

This is a prime example of putting the cart before the horse. You have to work on the relationship — build it up and make it into something worth sharing together — before you add the final ingredient, which is sex.

Sex is like the whipped cream you put on an ice cream sundae. Without the ice cream to hold it up, the whipped cream alone is not satisfying. But, if mixed in with the rest of the ingredients, that whipped cream tastes absolutely delicious.

Sex by itself cannot make up for all the other inadequacies of a relationship, so before you have sex with someone, build the foundation first.

A Good Lover Must be an Open Book

When you first meet somebody, you probably try to sweep parts of yourself under the carpet. If you have pimples, you cover them with a cream. If you have bad breath, you suck on a mint. If you're a slob, hopefully, you put on some nice clothes.

If the two of you hit it off, slowly but surely you begin to peel away the layers and reveal your true selves. Part of that revelation certainly takes place if you have sex together. Other aspects of your personality that you reveal have nothing to do with sex, but are just as important, or more so, as far as letting the other person know who you really are.

This process is wonderful and is vital to building a relationship, but you can also take it too far.

- ✔ If you love the other person, but you think that his nose is too big, there's no point in telling him that again and again, or even once.

- ✔ If, when you're making love, you fantasize that you're actually in the arms of Sharon Stone or Julio Iglesias, don't tell your partner that either. It serves no purpose other than to hurt your partner.

- ✔ And if you've always fancied making love in the center ring of the circus, but your partner is a prude, then don't bother revealing this side of yourself. If you do, it will only lead to your partner thinking less of you.

Yes, you should be as honest as you can with your partner, especially if you are married to him or her. But honesty is not the best policy if all that it accomplishes is to cause pain to the one you love.

I Should Always Compare Sexual Partners

I can understand comparing certain things. If you compare two restaurants, for example, and you decide that you like one more than the other, then the next time you go out, you can go back to the one you prefer. The same goes if you visit different places on vacation, or decide between two pairs of shoes.

But comparing partners, sexually that is, can be a lose/lose situation. Now I'm not talking about comparing two people from whom you intend to choose. I mean when you have developed a relationship with someone, you enjoy each other's company, and you end up becoming lovers. If, at that point, you begin to compare the way this person makes love to the way your previous partner did it, you're asking for trouble.

Although sexual feelings can be so strong, they are at the same time very fragile. For example, if a man worries about whether or not he will get an erection, he probably won't be able to get one. Or if a woman starts to think, "when is my orgasm going to come?," it probably never will.

You see, although you may think that your sexual feelings are centered between your belly and your knees, in fact, they are seated right at the top of your body, between your ears. And it is easy to distract your mind from the business at hand.

So, if you start the comparison process — even if your new lover comes out on top and proves to be the better lover — the fact that you're busy comparing instead of letting your mind go and partaking of the pleasure of the moment, lessens your enjoyment.

So play down those urges to compare lovers and keep your mind focused on what's happening to your body right then and there.

I Can't Become a Better Lover

If you ever read the life story of someone who is at the top of their field — a professional athlete, a famous actor, a great artist — you always find that those individuals worked very hard to get where they are. Sure, natural talent has something to do with how good you are, but it is just as important to seek to improve your skills, because the more effort you put into being good at an art, the better you become.

This is just as true when it comes to sex. Everyone can become a better lover. Some of the most common difficulties that people experience can be easily alleviated. I get asked two questions more than any others:

✔ Men frequently ask me what to do if they are premature ejaculators. I say, because this is only a learning difficulty, any man who puts his mind to it can eradicate this problem. And if he does this in partnership with his significant other, it will be that much easier. (See Chapter 21 for more on the topic of premature ejaculation.)

✔ Among women, the most common problem I see is the inability to have an orgasm. Here again, the vast majority of women suffering from this problem are really only *pre-orgasmic,* which means that they definitely can teach themselves how to have orgasms, and can then pass on that information to their partners. (See Chapter 22, for more on the topic of being pre-orgasmic.)

The old saying, "never say never," applies to sex as well.

Lovers Are like Siamese Twins

He likes chocolate; she likes vanilla. She loves fish; he adores burgers. She loves the opera; he falls asleep in his seat. Yes, you and your lover probably have some tastes in common, but certainly not in everything. And there's no reason that you should.

Naturally, this goes for sex too. Although I'm sure that you both enjoy orgasms, how many you need in a particular period may well vary, as well as your likes and dislikes for the methods you use to have those orgasms.

If you accept that you are different, and if you agree to make compromises, then you shouldn't have any problems adapting to each other. One of the skills you may have to learn is how to satisfy your partner when you're not interested in having an orgasm. But it's not that difficult a skill to learn, and it can help make your relationship a lot better.

It's when you have unrealistic expectations that you can get in trouble. So don't expect your partner to be your Siamese twin. You'll be a lot happier for it.

I'm Too Old to Have Sex

We human beings find that many of our faculties grow weaker as we grow older, but there seems to be none that so many people give up on as easily as sex.

If your eyesight gets weaker, do you give up reading and watching TV, or do you run to the eye doctor to get glasses, or at least a stronger prescription? If your hearing becomes impaired, do you go around saying "What?" all day long, or do you get a hearing aid? If you have trouble walking, you might get your hip replaced, or at least use a cane to get around. So, if your sexual apparatus diminishes, why would you give up on it entirely?

That sexual functioning declines with age is a given, but that it disappears altogether is most definitely not. As you grow older, you go through certain stages, which are different for men and women. Men lose their ability to have psychogenic erections and need their partners to stimulate their penises. Women stop producing natural lubricants and have to apply the store-bought variety. (You can find out more about these changes in Chapter 16.)

If wearing glasses doesn't interfere with your enjoyment of reading a book, then adapting to the necessities of age, when it comes to sex, shouldn't be that big of a deal either, as long as you don't make an issue out of it. And certainly you should never give up on this most enjoyable aspect of life.

Keep having sex as long as you are physically able to, and it will help keep your life worth living.

Chapter 27
Ten Tips for Safer Sex

In This Chapter

▶ Learn to say no

▶ Limit the number of partners you have

▶ Don't rely solely on your instincts

▶ Never dull your senses when you're with strangers

▶ Make the first move toward safer sex

▶ Use condoms

▶ Develop a relationship first

▶ Don't engage in risky behavior

▶ Don't forget about the other STDs

▶ Don't sell the other options short

*T*here are no absolute guarantees when it comes to having safe sex between two people, but you can enjoy *safer* sex if you're careful to follow the guidelines that have been developed by the experts.

If you can't remember the following ten tips, then write them down with a felt marker on your wrist every time you're in a situation where you might have sex. Do this until the time comes that they're indelibly etched in your brain — right next to the spot where the law of always backing up your computer files sits.

Learn to Say No

No one ever died from sexual frustration. That's not something you can say about sexually transmitted diseases.

Just because you haven't had sex in a long time and the opportunity presents itself doesn't mean that you should give in to those urges. The less you know about a person, the greater the likelihood that he or she could infect you with a disease. So learn to say no to casual sex.

Yes, you can try to protect yourself, but there is no 100-percent sure way of doing that. Considering that we're talking about your life here, isn't it worth being cautious?

Limit Your Number of Partners

Have you ever seen the trick that the clowns do in the circus with the little car? The car drives around the main ring, and it seems as if there's barely room for one person inside of it; the next thing you know, 25 clowns, big feet and all, come pouring out. Well, that's exactly the image you have to conjure up when you look at a potential partner. The more sexual partners a person has had, the more trouble that spells for you.

When you go to bed with someone, it's not just the two of you. Hiding under the covers is every partner with whom that person has ever had sex, and the partners of those partners. Although you may not be able to see their large red noses glowing in the dark, you can be sure that any viruses that they may have left behind inside of the warm, naked body that's presently in your bed are making a bee-line for any openings in your body.

To a virus, you're nothing more than a host — the perfect place to reproduce and multiply — and if the process destroys you, well, let's just say their consciences aren't as well developed as their ability to reproduce.

Don't Rely Solely on Your Instincts

Some people have honesty written all over their faces. You just know that if you lend them your car, you'll get it back exactly at the time they say they'll bring it back. But what if they have a split personality, and the half of them that's the thief takes off with your car for parts unknown? You trusted your instincts and you got burned, that's what.

The problem with trusting your instincts when it comes to sexually transmitted diseases is that there are people out there who really believe that they are disease-free when in fact they are not. Some sexually transmitted diseases invade a host's body and cause absolutely no symptoms, so, when these people tell you they've never had any diseases, they give the appearance of being absolutely honest, because they *are* being absolutely honest. The difficulty that your never-failing instincts face in such a situation is that these people's honesty isn't worth a coot. They have a dark side that they are unaware of having. They truly believe that they can't infect you, but in fact they truly can.

When it comes to sexually transmitted diseases, it is much better to be safe than sorry. Instead of trusting your instincts, put your faith in the rules of safer sex. In the long run, you won't regret it.

Never Dull Your Senses When You're with Strangers

I often recommend to people that they have a glass of wine or two to help loosen them up, which can then lead to better sex. But that's only when the two people involved are already a couple. In certain situations, any dulling of the senses caused by alcohol or drugs can be very dangerous.

Many people have wound up having sex because they were high, under circumstances that they would never have said yes to had they been sober. Now, if you're in your local pub with a few friends and you have a few beers too many, the likelihood of it turning into a sexual scene is slight. But, if you get invited to a party at somebody's house and you don't know the host that well, or many of the guests, and you then start to imbibe too much, you may regret the consequences.

If there's a bedroom down the hall, you may well find yourself in it, with your clothes off and somebody doing some very intimate things with you. Under such circumstances, you will not be thinking safer sex, assuming you're capable of thinking at all. And that goes for the person you're with, too.

To practice safer sex you have to be responsible. And to be responsible, you have to have all, or at least most, of your faculties operating. So, if the situation calls for keeping your wits about you, order a soft drink — or one of those nonalcoholic beers, if you don't want anybody to realize that you intend to remain sober.

Make the First Move toward Safer Sex

If you're dating someone and it looks like the relationship is moving forward, don't wait to talk about safer sex. The closer you get to the point where having sex is just on the horizon, the harder it will be to delay going ahead.

Certainly, if you already have your clothes off, it's far too late to be suddenly thinking about safer sex. But I believe that you should have that safer sex discussion long before you reach that point. If you are going to insist that this potential partner be tested for AIDS, then you can expect a six-month waiting period before you can engage in intercourse. That's why the sooner you bring the topic to the table, the sooner you can begin having sex (see Chapter 6).

I'm sure that you find many aspects of a person's character so important that you wouldn't consider getting involved with that person without knowing them, like his sense of honesty or her ability to give of herself. So just add sexual history to that list, and you'll wind up a lot safer.

Use Condoms

Condoms do not offer absolute protection against sexually transmitted diseases. If used improperly, they can leak. Once in a while, they break. And certain viruses, like hepatitis B, can actually pass through the latex. But, compared to having intercourse without a condom, they are like the brick walls the third little piggy used to keep the wolf away.

You have no valid excuse not to use a condom. Men don't lose their ability to have an orgasm because they are wearing a condom. They may like sex better without a condom, I can't deny that, but it is still better to have intercourse using a condom than not to have intercourse at all, and, when it comes to safer sex, there can be no exceptions to that rule.

In order to use condoms, you have to have one with you. Although young men have long stuck one in their wallets for "emergencies," you should know that heat and age do affect condoms, so make sure that any condom you use is fresh. But, in this day and age, it's not just men who should carry condoms. Any woman who is sexually active should be prepared to keep herself safe, not only from an unintended pregnancy, but from sexually transmitted diseases as well.

Develop a Relationship before You Have Sex

Some people get paranoid about safer sex, and I don't blame them for taking every precaution imaginable. But, for many people, it's just not something that is always on their minds. If they're in a special situation, if the stars are shining very brightly, if the chemistry is just perfect, and no condom is available, well, they might give in to the moment. There's no point in scolding someone who does that; let's face it, it's part of human nature. None of us is perfect, and we all give in to temptation now and then, whether it's that of a moonlit night or a container of Häagen-Dazs.

That's why the key to safer sex is to not have sex with anyone until you have developed a relationship with that person. If you get to know someone really well, if you've been dating for a while, if you've had long talks about life and love and know their sexual history — if, after all of that, you really believe that it is reasonably safe for the two of you to have sex (using a condom, of course) then you may decide to go ahead.

Sadly, there are people out there who are liars, and every day they infect innocent people with dreadful diseases. Even a marriage license is no guarantee against sexually transmitted diseases. But there are no absolute guarantees in life, and every day we are faced with choices, the outcome of which we can't know in advance. We can't let the unknown paralyze us entirely. Sometimes you just have to take a leap. However, if you take every possible precaution, the odds of success are a lot higher.

Don't Engage in Risky Behavior

The chance of passing on HIV during anal sex is greater than during other types of sex. Unprotected oral sex is not safer sex. Having sex with someone you meet at a bar or bath house is dangerous. Going to a sex club is far from risk free. Wife swapping does not promote good health. Sharing needles is an invitation to sharing the HIV virus.

Most people don't even think about trying such risky behavior, but then there are those who seem attracted to living on the edge. These people seem to be daring the fates to strike them down, and, more often than not, they do.

At the time that you are engaging in risky behavior, a certain thrill may be attached to the moment. But, when you're lying in a hospital dying, that thrill will not be a happy memory but a nightmare that you'll live through over and over until the end.

 ✔ If you can't keep yourself from going to a gay bar or bathhouse, masturbate while watching others, but don't do anything risky.

 ✔ If seeing what goes on at a sex club is too much of a temptation for you to
   resist, go with a partner and don't have sex with anyone else.

 ✔ If you're a drug addict, go get help right this minute (see Appendix B).

You can find the willpower to avoid risky behavior — I know it. If you can't do it by yourself, then go for help.

Don't Forget about the Other STDs

While AIDS has been grabbing all of the headlines, it is only one of many sexually transmitted diseases. Most of these STDs have been around for hundreds of years (see Chapter 21).

Some think that Columbus may have brought syphilis back to Spain with him from the New World. Whatever the exact method of its spread throughout the world, it's been plaguing mankind for a long time, and it killed many people before a cure was found.

Some forms of syphilis and gonorrhea have become resistant to the normal types and doses of antibiotics, which means that they are no longer illnesses that you can just shrug off. Hepatitis B is much more contagious than most STDs; luckily, you can get a vaccine that prevents you from catching it. There is no vaccine against herpes; nor is there a cure. Usually, the partner of the person who has herpes ends up getting the disease as well. Some STDs, like chlamydia, are raging across the country, and none of the STDs show any sign of fading away on their own.

Although you may be with somebody that you suppose doesn't have AIDS — and you might even be right — that doesn't mean that you are safe from catching an STD. It's a bit of a war zone out there. So be careful. Please.

Don't Sell Your Other Options Short

If the main reason that you're having sex is that you want to have a baby, then intercourse is surely the only way for you to go. But if that's not your aim, if it's pleasure that you seek and not progeny, then you have plenty of other ways to get sexual satisfaction without undertaking the risks of intercourse.

What makes intercourse dangerous is the exchange of bodily fluids, which can contain viruses of various sorts. But orgasms don't depend on an exchange of fluids. You and your partner could both be wearing full rubber body suits, so that not even a drop of sweat would be exchanged, and still give each other orgasms.

Hands and fingers are wonderfully agile and can give a lot of pleasure. (Oral sex, while safer than intercourse, cannot be considered a form of safer sex because bodily fluids are exchanged.) If you want to be creative, you can even substitute your big toe. A man can rub his penis between a woman's breasts, and a vibrator can give fabulous orgasms without passing on a drop of anything liquid.

If you really feel the need for sexual release, but you don't know the person all that well, don't sell these safer-sex practices short. You can get sexual satisfaction without having any regrets later on.

Chapter 28

Ten Things Women Wish Men Knew about Sex

● ●

▶ The age of chivalry isn't dead yet

▶ Appearances do count

▶ You can't hurry love

▶ A clitoris is not just a small penis

▶ Women need to bathe in the afterglow

▶ Kinky sex isn't sexy sex

▶ Wandering eyes mean less sex

▶ Slam bam thank you ma'am doesn't cut the mustard

▶ Changing diapers is sexy

▶ Just because you can't doesn't mean you won't

● ●

*I*t's amazing to me that men are always saying that they want to have sex with women so badly but then so many of them don't put in the effort to find out what it takes to have good sex with a woman. So all of you guys out there who complain that you don't get enough of "it," read the following tips closely. I know how you men often resist asking for directions, but if you've lost that loving feeling, then read on with an open mind and force yourself to accept some guidance on how to get to the Tunnel of Love.

Chivalry Isn't Dead Yet

Apart from a handful of ultra-feminists who get insulted if a man holds the door open for them or takes off his hat in the elevator, I believe most women still enjoy being treated like ladies. Although this also holds true for total strangers, who may only reward you with a wide smile for your efforts, it most definitely applies to the woman with whom you are sharing a relationship, where the rewards can be of far greater consequence.

Bringing a woman flowers or chocolate, taking her out to dinner, calling her during the day, all these little details are important not because of what they cost in terms of money, but because they show that you care, that you are thinking of her, that she matters to you.

Now some of you men have learned to make all of the right moves, but your hearts aren't really in it. You have a goal in mind — getting the woman into bed — and that's it. If you are one of these men, you are not looking for a relationship, but only to put another notch in your gun. Although you may be proud of your conquests, a time will come when you realize what a lonely life you have led.

Empty gestures are not chivalrous, and they won't earn a man his rank of knighthood either. You not only have to show you care, you have to feel it too.

Appearances Do Count

Although many men do worry about their hair (mostly because they know that their relationship with it may be rather fleeting), when it comes to the rest of their appearance, many men are not so careful. Now I understand that, if you have to wear a tie and jacket all day for work, you'll be eager to fling them off the second you walk through the door. Working women are no less eager to remove their heels and confining undergarments. But if you always put on the same ripped T-shirt and paint-stained jeans, that turns women off.

As a man, you are probably very conscious of how the women around you look, whether it's your partner or any other woman. True, you may be more concerned with the length of her hemline than whether or not her shoes match her bag, but you can't get away with saying that you don't pay any attention to the way that women dress. But, although most women take care to look as presentable as possible to their men, many men won't return the favor.

Perhaps you're one of those people who doesn't perceive yourself as being sexy, but you are — especially to your partner — so try to look the part.

If you're the type of person who complains that your wife doesn't make love to you enough, my guess is that you'd have more success in that area if you started dressing more like Casanova than Pigpen.

You Can't Hurry Love

It's a fact that men get turned on a lot faster than do women.

One could speculate on the reasons for this, but the reasons are irrelevant because knowing why won't change anything. Women need time to prepare themselves for sex, and I'm not just talking about the type of foreplay that goes on when you already have your clothes off, and you're in bed (or in the Jacuzzi or on the kitchen floor).

What women wish that men would realize is that, if a man wants to have sex, he has to put romance first. It doesn't have to be anything complicated. Sure, dinner at the best restaurant in town would be great. But so would any opportunity for some quiet conversation, a moment to throw off the worries of the day to let her get in the mood for lovemaking. So, even if you're champing at the bit, you have to learn to be a tad more patient.

Now, if you're like most men, you had no problem giving your partner some of this quality time before you got married or moved in together. You would call ahead of time, make appointments called *dates,* go out to dinner, take her for long walks, and look into each other's eyes. As a result she'd begin to be ready to have sex with you. Now, if she felt the relationship still needed further development, she might well have said no, but that doesn't *necessarily* mean that she wasn't thinking yes. (Some of you men are probably going "Huh, you mean she was ready but she said no anyway?" Yes, but she knew that if she gave in too soon, you'd have been off chasing someone else the next night, so what choice did she have? And the fact that she was ready doesn't mean that she was sure the time was right.)

You men have to learn that those patterns of romantic behavior must continue after you've said "I do" — not necessarily every time, but often enough to show that you really do care.

A Clitoris Is Not Just a Small Penis

Although it should be obvious that men and women are built differently, many men think of a clitoris as just a small penis. These men know that if a woman touches their penis it will get hard, and if she rubs the penis a bit more, the man will have an orgasm. And many men think that the clitoris works just the same. They've grasped the point that the clitoris is the seat of a woman's ability to have an orgasm, but they haven't figured out that a clitoris is a lot more delicate than a penis. Many women can't bear to have the clitoris touched directly because it hurts. They need only to have the area around the clitoris caressed and rubbed in order to give just enough stimulation so that the clitoris doesn't actually hurt. So guys, store this away in your memory banks: just because a clitoris grows bigger when the woman gets excited doesn't make it a penis.

Some of you take the same attitude towards a woman's breasts as you do to the clitoris. You knead them as if it they were dough, forgetting that they're made of tissue, are sensitive, and can even be bruised. Your lover would also appreciate it if you were a little more careful with your knees and elbows, and if you'd make a serious effort not to lean on her hair. You don't want the two of you to be bald, do you?

So, for the vast majority of women, rough sex is a total turn off. If you're concerned with giving your woman an orgasm, work at it gently, and you'll have a lot more success.

Women Need to Bathe in the Afterglow

Women have a lot of different complaints about the way men make love, but if there is one that gets the most votes, it's that men are too quick to go to sleep right after sex. It takes women longer to get aroused than men, and it takes them longer to come down from that aroused state (see Chapter 14). If you roll over and fall asleep (or get up and go home, or go to the basement to watch the end of the ball game), she's going to feel abandoned. And that's not a good way to end a session of lovemaking.

Now I'm not asking you men to spend as long on afterplay as on foreplay but, come on guys, admit it, if right after "doing it" you got a call from a friend with tickets on the fifty-yard line to a game starting in an hour, would you tell him you were too sleepy to go? Of course not. So isn't your wife worth an extra ten minutes of consciousness? (Hint: the answer to that is yes.)

Afterplay has an extra benefit, and that is that if you play your cards right, the afterglow will last right up until the next day and become the start of foreplay for the next session. And don't tell me that you'll be too tired then!

Kinky Sex Isn't Sexy Sex

I receive many categories of letters from people who write to my column, and one category is women asking why it is that men are always asking them to do something kinky. Probably the most frequently asked request is for the husband to watch his wife make love to another woman. Some men just want to watch, while others plan on joining in. Some men don't care if it's a man or a woman, they just want to take part in a threesome. Other men want to join a wife-swapping group or visit a sex club.

Now I'm not saying that there aren't any women out there who instigate this type of behavior, because there are, and sometimes it's their husbands who are the squeamish ones. But, for the most part, it's you men out there who have these unusual sexual appetites.

One thing your wives want to know is why, and I can't give them a good answer. It could be that you men have more active imaginations, or maybe you've been watching too many porno movies. Whatever the reason, most women want no part of these scenes. They're quite content with having sex with their man, without anyone else looking on or joining in.

I am all in favor of fantasies, so I would never tell you men to stop fantasizing. And if you want to ask your wife or girlfriend about a particular fantasy, go ahead. Just don't try to pressure her after she says no. Instead, pretend you are doing whatever it is that turns you on when you are with her. If you don't, if you keep pestering her, all that will happen is that you will turn her off and, rather than getting kinky sex, you'll have no sex at all.

Wandering Eyes Means Less Sex

Men like to look at women, and women usually don't mind being looked at. But there is a time and a place for everything. If you're out on a date, and you see a beautiful woman walk by, and you gawk at her so that your date or wife can see your tongue hanging out, that is not going to sit well with her. She's going to get angry at you, you're going to have a fight, and for the next few hours the odds of the two of you having a sexual encounter are slim to nil.

Women like attention, and, when they're with a man with whom they're having sex, they expect as much of his attention as possible. (Under certain circumstances, such as when you're driving a car or putting the ice tray filled with water back into the freezer, you're excused from this rule.) Women don't find it particularly sexy if they have to fight for your attention, which includes competing against ball games being shown on television, sports cars being driven down your block, and, most of all, pretty women walking by.

Your lover wants to be able to think that you consider her the most desirable woman on earth. Can she really be expected to do that when you're busy staring at the body of another woman? Of course not. So, if you consider yourself a macho stud, don't think that looking at other women needs to be part of this role. Real macho men like to engage in sex, not just fantasize about it, and ogling will not get you where you want to go.

Slam-Bam-Thank-You-Ma'am Doesn't Cut the Mustard

OK, now we're getting down to the real nitty gritty. Obviously, if women need time in order to get themselves sufficiently aroused to have an orgasm, a man who can't "keep it up" (that is, sustain an erection) is going to cause them problems.

Premature ejaculation is the term used in the sexological literature for this particular affliction, but there's really nothing to get worried about if you happen to deserve the label premature ejaculator, because it is nothing more than a learning disability.

If you're wondering whether or not you fall into this category, don't go pulling out a stop-watch. I don't classify a man as a premature ejaculator by some predefined amount of time that he can last before ejaculating. All you need to ask yourself is whether or not you are dissatisfied with your performance. If you would like to last longer and can't, then you need to do the homework assignment I give in Chapter 22. If, on the other hand, you come quick as a jackrabbit, but neither you nor your partner much care because you can do things with your big toe that only a chimp could duplicate, then don't worry about it.

I often get asked why men have this problem, and the answer is we don't know. But as long as we have a cure, it really doesn't matter, does it?

Changing Diapers Is Sexy

How many of you fathers out there do or did change diapers? Whatever your answer, I'm sure that you never thought of it as a sexy experience. Heaven forbid, I'm certainly not suggesting that the sight of a naked baby's bottom should arouse anything more than the urge to thank God for such perfection, *but,* if you never realized how important a role changing a baby's diaper has in your sex life, then you don't deserve the title *terrific lover* yet.

Mommies change a million diapers, but just because they do doesn't make the task any more pleasant. Too many Dads think that, because Mom does it all the time — even if she works at a full-time job outside the home — she likes doing it, but believe me, it's not a job anybody could really like. Oh, sure, babies are fun, but there's still an element to the diaper-changing chore which is offensive to all of us.

So when Dad offers — and that's a key word, *offer,* and with a smile on his face too — that makes Mom feel very good. So good that later that night she'll still remember it, and you, the Daddy, will get your reward.

Now, of course, this applies to any task that always seems to fall on Mom — doing the dishes, folding the laundry, dusting the breakfront. Don't do it just because you expect something; but, if you volunteer for some of the dirty work, I guarantee that you'll earn your reward.

Just Because You Can't Doesn't Mean You Won't

I want to talk to you older gentlemen. I know that you can't always perform the way that you used to. That doesn't mean that it's over yet; it most certainly isn't, but you do need more time to get ready for the next sexual episode. But here's a truism that many of you either don't want to admit or just never realized — you do not need an erection to satisfy your wife.

Very often, if a wife is feeling "in the mood," and the husband is not, he'll either ignore her desires, or he'll try to have an erection. Then, when he can't, he'll give up on the idea of sex altogether. But there's no law that says that you have to have an erection to have sex. You can please your wife in a variety of ways. You can give her fabulous orgasms with your fingers, or your tongue, or a vibrator.

Don't be selfish. Just because you're not in the mood doesn't mean that she has to be frustrated. And remember, no good deed goes unrewarded. So, if at another time you need a little more help on her part obtaining an erection, your helping her during her hour of need will be put in an account that you can then draw on later.

Chapter 29

Ten Things Men Wish Women Knew about Sex

- -

In This Chapter

▶ Try not to give mixed signals

▶ It really does hurt

▶ Sometimes it's OK not to save electricity

▶ The *Playboy* playmate is not a threat

▶ Teamwork is important

▶ The day I stop looking is the day I'm dead

▶ If you really loved me you'd . . .

▶ The way to a man's heart is not through his stomach

▶ To a man, sex is different than love

▶ The older a man gets, the more help he needs

- -

*L*adies, if any of you out there still believe that the way to a man's heart is through his stomach, then you have a lot to learn. Between fast food franchises, pizza, and Chinese take-out, men are quite capable of feeding themselves. But they're not so crazy about taking care of some of their other needs by themselves — and I'm not talking about sewing on buttons.

Now just because a man's apparatus is on view doesn't mean it's all that simple to operate. And while there are auto mechanics to look under the hood of your car, I don't think you want anyone else changing the oil (tinkering with the cylinders, lubricating the ball joint, lifting the valves) of your man, so pay attention to these tips if you want to get the most from your relationship.

Try Not to Give Mixed Signals

It doesn't always take much to turn men on; if you're not careful, you can do it accidentally. Although, as a woman, it takes you a while to get in the mood, a man can have an erection in what seems like milliseconds. And, with those lightning reflexes hard-wired into his brain, it's very easy to confuse a man by some gesture that you aren't even aware you are making.

Imagine that it's a hot day and you've had a tough commute home. When you walk through the door into your apartment, the last thing on your mind is sex. You feel sweaty and confined and, without thinking, you kick off your shoes, hike up your skirt, and pull down your pantyhose. Ahh, relief. Now your partner, who had gotten home a few minutes before you and was just popping the tab off a can of beer, watches all of this. To him, it's not a cooling off gesture, it's a striptease . . . and right in his living room, no less. He may be conditioned to seeing you change in the bedroom and not get excited by it (or maybe he does there, too; you never know), but seeing this sudden exposure of bare flesh where he least expected it will definitely get his blood surging south of the border.

Now he's thinking hot while you're thinking cold, as in shower. He starts sidling over; you see that look in his eyes, think "What is he crazy?" give him a stiff arm, and make a beeline for shower. If you're really in miscommunication mode, once the gushing waters have had their refreshing effect, you'll start thinking about "it," and, after you pat yourself dry, you come out of the shower wearing only a towel to see what reaction you get. But having just been rejected, he figures that, if he reaches out, he'll only get his hand slapped. So instead he plays King Couch Potato and says, "What's for dinner?" which makes you furious.

Mixed signals like this happen to couples all the time. You can't always prevent them, but it helps if you're aware of what type of behavior can trigger them. Is it fair that you can't get undressed in your own living room? I wouldn't worry about losing your freedom. Pretty soon you'll have kids, and you'll be lucky if you can have sex at midnight under the covers.

It Really Does Hurt

The term is *blue balls,* and whether or not a man's testicles actually turn any colors I don't know, but that they can ache from the need for sexual release is absolutely true. Now, it's not so acute a pain that a man can't stand it, and, if no one else is around, then all he has to do is masturbate to bring needed relief. But he's also not putting you on when he says that it hurts.

This is another reason not to give mixed signals. I'm not talking about the type of instant erection a man gets from seeing your anatomy, but one that lasts a longer time and really causes his hormones to stir. If you get a man that excited and then change your mind, he's not going to be pleased. Men really don't like women who tease, because it's not only their egos that suffer, but also their testicles.

While I'm on the subject of pain and testicles, do be careful with the family jewels — even if you don't want them making any part of your family. Testicles are highly sensitive, and if you're too rough on them, or accidentally hit them in some way, then we're talking about real pain. So, unless you're dealing with a rapist — in which case, please be my guest and kick hard where it'll hurt the most— be gentle.

Sometimes It's OK Not to Save Electricity

As demonstrated by the success of magazines like *Playboy*, men get turned on visually. And, although I do urge modesty at those times when the last thing on your mind is a roll in the hay, men would really appreciate it if you would drop those force fields when it's time to make love. I know that you like to cuddle and be cozy, and that a dark room with the covers drawn up to your chin helps you feel safe enough to get aroused, but for the sake of your man, how about leaving the lights on once in a while?

Now I'm not asking you to cover your room with mirrors, not even on the ceiling, because I understand that you have to be able to look your mother-in-law in the eye when she visits. But, as long as the room temperature is warm enough not to cause goose bumps, give your man the visual stimuli he desires.

Teamwork Is Important

So many of you women are sick to death with sports. Having your man spend Sunday afternoon watching some men toss around a football and then hit each other seems like the most boring way imaginable to pass the time. Although I'm not going to suggest that you try to become a sports fanatic — though there are women who have learned to join their men in front of the TV or in the stands and love it — I believe you can learn a lesson from sports regarding sex.

To you, verbal communication is very important. You need to talk to the most important person in your life. Since men, in general, don't talk as much — especially the strong, silent type — it seems as if they are not communicating to each other. But many men would prefer to bond not by talking, but by doing something together, as a team. Having played sports as young men and learned to appreciate the benefits of teamwork, men find that watching sports has a great attraction.

So how does this affect your love life? For one thing, the more teamwork there is in your sex life, the more communication there will be between the two of you, and you'll both be happier. So don't just lie there and expect him to do all the work.

- ✔ The simplest thing you can do is to initiate sex once in a while if that's a task you've tended to leave to him.

- ✔ Buy some sex toys, edible underwear for example, and present them to him one night.

- ✔ Suggest writing up a game plan for the night's sexual activities. Include starting time, which positions, and which room of the house.

- ✔ Buy a team uniform, maybe matching T-shirts, that will be a secret signal between the two of you that — if you're both wearing them — then that night, or that afternoon, is being reserved for sex.

Take an active part in sex and score some points that will put you right at the top of his standings.

The Playboy Playmate Is Not a Threat

I actually do like the articles in *Playboy,* but I know that many women wouldn't care if every issue won a Pulitzer Prize for journalism, they still don't want to see that — or any other magazine that features naked, nubile women — in their homes. Such women feel threatened by these pictures because they themselves are not a "perfect" 36-24-36, they don't get the benefits of an air-brush around their cellulite, and they refuse to shave their pubic hair into a well-shaped vee.

Now I don't want anyone to do anything that's going to make him or her feel threatened, so it's up to you whether these magazines have a place in your bedroom. But this chapter is here to let you women know how your men feel, and I would be remiss to omit this common complaint just to preserve your feelings.

And, you know, in reality, *Playboy* is just the opposite of a threat. Very few men ever get to even meet a centerfold, much less go to bed with one. The man who gets turned on reading — or, if you prefer, ogling — *Playboy* isn't going to rush out of the house looking for Miss October. Instead, he's going to come over to your side of the bed and look for you. He knows you don't look like a centerfold, but he loves you for all of your qualities, one of which might even be that you *don't* look like Miss October, whom he might actually be too scared to go to bed with, fearing he couldn't live up to the moment.

One more thing. Do you ever read romance novels and get turned on? Do you ever get a tingle watching the soaps? Or a Mel Gibson movie? What if your husband told you that he never wanted to see another romance novel on the bedstand, would that be fair? It's true that the sexual content of *Playboy* is more blatant, and you certainly don't want little children peeking between its pages, but if he's discreet about it, I know that your man would really appreciate your tolerance — if not understanding — of his choice of literature.

The Day I Stop Looking Is the Day I'm Dead

In my tips for men, I tell you that women hate it when they're out with a guy and he's gaping at other women. But, although it definitely holds true that men should exercise caution when looking at other women when they're with a partner, that's not the same thing as saying that they shouldn't look.

Men will always look at other women; there's no stopping them. Now, although I suggest discretion on a man's part when he's around you, at the same time, I have to tell you women not to make a big fuss when your man looks, unless he's being obnoxious about it. Remember, if your man stops looking at other women, it probably means he's also stopped looking at you. It may mean that he has lost all interest in sex, and that's certainly not a bonus.

Now we all know that women look at men, although they're much more likely to want to look into a pair of soft eyes than at a passing crotch (though many women report looking below the waist as well as above). And, as far as two partners in a close relationship are concerned, it's definitely not just looks that keep them together, so looking around is really not that much of a big deal. The key to keeping both partners happy is not to force anyone to wear blinders but, instead, to use discretion.

If You Really Loved Me You'd . . .

This is not an open question. I just felt a little prudish about putting what this tip is about right in the title. Most of you ladies can guess what I'm talking about, I'm sure, and certainly many of you do keep your man happy by performing that certain art.

That's right, you guessed it, the topic here is fellatio — oral sex on a man.

Now, although I'm speaking on behalf of men here, I must put my cards down on the table and state categorically that I absolutely do not want any woman to do anything that really repulses her. But, before you go on to the next item, ask yourself this, is it really that repulsive? I'm not saying that you have to necessarily swallow his semen, but is just kissing and licking his penis that big of a deal?

If you're concerned about cleanliness, then go get a wash cloth and clean his penis. He won't object, unless you use cold water.

I really do not believe that men who crave this sex act see it as degrading to women. Rather, they want it because they enjoy the sensations. And maybe you do, too, when he does it to you. Even if this will never become a regular part of your sexual repertoire, you could at least make his birthday special . . . or even use it just to mark the decades.

The Way to a Man's Heart Is Not through His Stomach

I don't know where that saying that the way to a man's heart is through his stomach started, but ask 100 men if they think it's true. Unless all those men are residents of a senior citizens' home, I don't think you'll find the majority in agreement. And I'm not sure that even the seniors would give their vote.

Men like to eat, but, if they have to do something for themselves, they'd prefer to feed themselves. Some women, after a few years, or maybe after they've had a few kids, seem to withdraw from sex. Such a woman might think that, as long as she's putting a good meal down in front of her husband, and maybe ironing his shirts, that's all he really needs from her.

That may work for a while, but then he'll get a new secretary, or go to a convention in Las Vegas, or just look differently at the neighbor's wife, and all of a sudden his attention is permanently drawn elsewhere.

You don't have to be a courtesan, but you definitely shouldn't be disinterested in sex. As a man ages, the urges may come further apart, but they're still there. If, for some reason, you seem to have lost your sexual desire, don't just assume it's because you're a woman. That's nonsense. Loss of sexual appetite is almost always caused by something specific, so find a specialist — a sex therapist or marital therapist — who can help you overcome this problem (see Appendix B).

To a Man, Sex Is Different than Love

I don't want to make any excuses for men who fool around on their wives, especially in these days when he can catch a deadly disease and then infect his innocent wife. But, in general, men and women are different when it comes to sex. Most women need romance to become aroused, which means that their emotions are almost always involved, but most men can have sex without the act triggering an emotional response in them.

This is the reason that prostitutes have always been doing business with men on a quickie basis, while the few *gigolos* (male prostitutes for women) that exist almost always perform for the long term.

The reason it's important for you to know this is that, if you ever catch your man having sex with another women, don't throw away a long-term relationship without doing a careful evaluation. If it really looks like he was only in it for the sex, and if you both love each other, your relationship might be saved. I'm certainly not advocating sticking around with a philanderer, the guy who does it over and over again. But there are instances when you'd be better off forgiving and forgetting (although you can never totally forget).

When it comes to sex, don't assume that he reacts the same way that you do, because you'd be making an error. But if, upon careful consideration, you know that you can't stay with him, even if he only had a casual fling, then I wouldn't discourage you from moving on. Just don't make the decision in a fit of anger.

The Older a Man Gets, the More Help He Needs

Not every man is clued into the fact that, at some point in his life, he loses the ability to have a *psychogenic erection* — that is, an erection that comes by itself, without any physical manipulation — but it's a fact. This does not signal the end of your love life; instead, it means that your partner now needs foreplay as much as you do.

Some of you women may decide that this is the moment to pay him back for all the times that he didn't give you enough foreplay, but I'm telling you not to play those games. When this change first starts to happen to a man, he is pretty upset by it. The first few times he runs across a situation where his penis used to take off for the races by itself and now just lies there, it can be downright scary. So have mercy on him and don't add to his plight.

When a man loses his ability to have erections spontaneously, it is definitely a time when oral sex becomes even more desirable, and if it hasn't been something that you've done before, do consider it. At least one positive change occurs over the years, and that is that your man will probably have gained more control, so he can almost definitely keep from coming to orgasm in your mouth. Many women find that, once that fear has been dealt with, they don't mind performing fellatio.

If your man is experiencing these types of difficulties, definitely read Chapter 22 on male problems to learn as much as you can about what is happening to him and how you can help.

Chapter 30
Ten Tips for Truly Great Lovers

- -

In This Chapter
▶ Don't make love on your first date

▶ Set the mood as far in advance as you can

▶ Find out what your partner needs

▶ Protect yourself and your partner

▶ Don't fall into a rut

▶ Do something about your problems

▶ Use your sense of touch

▶ Become a great kisser

▶ Satisfy your partner even if you don't feel like having sex

▶ Learn to adapt to your circumstances

- -

*A*nybody can teach you how to make love, but I, Dr. Ruth, want you to become not just any kind of lover, but a truly great lover. I want you and your partner to have *terrrrific* sex, and to do that you have to learn how to roll your *Rs* and heed the following tips.

Don't Make Love on Your First Date

Sex feels great, doesn't it?

You may think that, because there's nothing else like it, you want to have sex as often as possible and as soon as possible. But sex isn't a toy to be played with by children; it's a serious act to be shared by responsible adults. A great lover integrates sex into an overall relationship and never has sex with someone he or she barely knows.

Giving into the temptation of having sex before you really know each other can only lead to problems. One of the more serious problems might be that you end up catching a sexually transmitted disease. But even if you do escape with your health intact, you won't be having great sex.

In life, the more time, effort, and intensity you put into an activity, the more you'll get out of it. If you wait until you've developed a relationship with someone you're attracted to, if you devote your energies to learning enough about that someone so that you grow to admire, respect, and love — then, — and only then — can you have great sex.

Set the Mood as Far in Advance as Possible

There's this myth that great sex has to be spontaneous sex — when, in most cases, it's the reverse that's true. Now I'm not saying that spontaneous sex can't be great — it most certainly can — but rarely do two people hit their peak sexual mood at just the same time without some planning.

Part of the reason for this is that women take a longer time to get aroused than men. So the further ahead you set the mood for lovemaking, the more aroused she will become. That's why it's better not to be in such a rush. The more planning and preparation you invest into making the evening (or morning or afternoon) as romantic as possible, the better the sex that will come as a result.

That's also why you should send those flowers ahead of time, instead of bringing them home with you, so that they'll have plenty of time to work on her libido. (If you want to know more about how sending flowers can get your partner in the mood, sneak back to Chapter 11.)

Give your full attention to your partner the moment you walk through the door and don't wait until just before you get into bed. Spend time caressing and massaging the rest of her body before reaching for her clitoris. And start the lovemaking process early enough so that you don't feel as if you have to go right to sleep or head back to your apartment as soon as you've had your orgasm.

And ladies, if you know that you want to have sex with him, don't be coy about it. Let him know that the answer will be yes as soon as you know it yourself. That way he can feel free to give you the best foreplay he is capable of, without worrying about whether or not he's going to have his advances rejected.

So don't stint on foreplay, or afterplay either. By setting the mood as far in advance as possible and taking your time once you're together, you'll be showing off your prowess as a great lover.

Find Out What Your Partner Needs

I hope that you're not under the misapprehension that sex is a selfish act. Just because no one else can feel your orgasm the way you do, doesn't mean that they can't share in your pleasure, or you in theirs. If you want to have the strongest orgasms — the kind that make your heart beat wildly, your breath grow short, and your toes curl up — then you have to work together as partners and give as much of yourselves to each other as you can.

In order to be more giving, you have to know what the other person needs: more foreplay, a certain touch around the anus, the sensations of oral sex, maybe a thousand little kisses. Whatever it is, it is your duty to find out how to please your partner to the best of your ability. And, if your partner does the same, through this teamwork you can have the greatest orgasms and the best lovemaking possible.

To be the best lover you can be, do ask and do tell each other what you would like. You've taken your clothes off, so what's the big deal about stripping away some of that shell that is still covering your psyche? Sex isn't a private act, it's an act of sharing — and the more you share, the more there will be to share.

Protect Yourself and Your Partner

Sex has never been risk free. Having an unintended pregnancy carries serious consequences, both in terms of your health and how society looks upon you. And in this era of AIDS, the risks have multiplied tremendously. If you're not careful, if you don't act responsibly, whether you are a man or a woman, you could actually be putting your life on the line.

If you have the misguided notion that protecting yourself takes away from the pleasure of sex by ruining the spontaneity and placing barriers of latex between you and your partner, then you've been missing out on truly great sex.

The most important sex organ does not reside below your belt, but between your ears — that's where your brain is. If your brain is worrying that, as a result of having sex, an unintended pregnancy may occur or some disease be passed on, then it's not going to allow you to really enjoy yourself. These types of worries actually keep some men from having an erection and some women from having an orgasm, and they can lessen the pleasure for anyone.

Safer sex isn't only less dangerous, it's also more enjoyable. So if you want to be the best lover you can be, always practice safer sex.

Don't Fall into a Rut

The first 10, 20, or maybe even 100 times you have sex with someone, you'll experience a certain excitement that comes from the newness of it all. But after a time, that newness begins to wear off.

For some people, the familiarity brings a certain type of comfort that makes sex more pleasurable, but for others, the sameness of it all makes sex begin to wear thin. Instead of anticipating a certain caress, they begin to dread it. And so, instead of wanting to have sex, they start avoiding it, which can spell not only the end of a couple's sex life, but the end of their entire relationship.

Variety comes in all sorts of packages:

- It can be a different position.
- It can be making love at a different time of day.
- It can be doing it someplace you've never done it before.
- It can be doing it fast when you usually take your time.
- Or it can be making a point of prolonging the act as long as you can possibly stand it.

Even if you find yourself going back to your old ways, because they do bring you a lot of pleasure, force yourself to try something new once in a while. The patterns you and your partner develop can make for great sex, but if you try some new things, you'll appreciate the old ways even more. And perhaps you'll find some new ways of having sex that will make sex better than ever.

Make a point of initiating these changes together. Sometimes surprises are nice, and sometimes they can shock the other person into losing the desire for sex altogether. Talk ahead of time about the different ideas that you might like to try, and have those discussions outside of the bedroom. If you need help coming up with new ideas, look at a book (maybe even this one) together, or watch a tape, and then talk over which of the new positions that you just learned about might be fun to try out. Never put pressure on each other to do something that the other person really doesn't want to do, but also don't be so quick to say no.

Think of your sex life as a building that you're constructing as a team. You couldn't have a building without a solid foundation — but once that foundation's laid, if you want to reach the greatest heights, you'll have to take your chances climbing that ladder.

Do Something about Your Problems

Nobody is born a perfect lover. Everybody needs to practice and work at being the best lover he or she can become . . . even you.

Now you may have a particular problem that's causing you difficulties. Maybe you're a guy who is a premature ejaculator. Or maybe you're a woman who has problems getting sexual satisfaction.

Whatever problems you might have, be they major ones that keep you from enjoying sex altogether, or minor ones that prevent you from reaching your peak sexual performance, don't ignore them, don't expect them to go away by themselves, and don't spend your whole life suffering needlessly. In most cases, help is available (see Appendix A).

For some problems, you can find the answer in this book and work it out by yourself or with the help of your partner. If that's not possible, either because you tried and it's not been working or because the problem is too severe to handle by yourself, make an appointment to see a specialist. And don't dilly-dally. Do it today.

When it comes to most physical problems, be it a toothache or the need for a new eyeglass prescription, you probably don't waste a minute going for help. But if the issue is sexual in nature, you become too embarrassed to talk about it. But take it from me, as someone who's been practicing sex therapy for over 20 years, we sex therapists have heard it all. Sex is what we talk about all day long, and we won't think of you as strange because you have a sexual problem.

And if you're worried that going to a sex therapist is going to bleed you dry, the techniques that we therapists all use are short term. Sometimes even only one or two sessions can work wonders, and would be well worth the investment.

There's no excuse for allowing sexual problems to fester to the point where they not only keep your own sexual pleasure below par, but probably do damage to your partner's enjoyment of sex as well. Thanks to the pioneers in sexual therapy, we have the solutions you need, so pick up a phone and make an appointment.

Use Your Sense of Touch

Researchers have done experiments in which they've left baby monkeys alone in a cage without any other monkeys, and the baby monkeys soon went crazy. Just giving those monkeys a soft cloth doll that they could cuddle up to was sometimes enough to get them through this solitary confinement. You are not a monkey, but you and your partner do have the same need to be touched.

Part of that touching should take place while you're having sex. Remember, though, that the art of arousing your partner through foreplay doesn't mean just touching their genitals. You should pay attention to every square inch of them. Touch them, stroke them, caress them, rub them. You'll both enjoy the tactile sensations.

But this touching has to be a continuous process. You have to touch each other every day, several times a day, without any thought to having sex. You have to hug each other. Hold each other's hands. Rub each other's shoulders. Wash each other. All that touching will bring you closer so that, when the time comes to actually engage in sex, the experience will be heightened for both of you.

Don't limit this touching to your hands. Play footsie and feel how sensitive your feet can be. Lie on top of one another and feel your lover with your whole body. Put your cheeks together — both sets! Don't be afraid to explore. You can build a entire map of each other's bodies, finding out all the places where you like to be touched the most, and then use that information to have the best sex possible (see Chapter 11).

Become a Great Kisser

You may have noticed that, in the preceding section, I didn't mention touching your lips together. That's because the lips deserve a section all to themselves.

The sensations caused by kissing can feel so good, so intense, that some people can kiss each other for hours. Many people have a pleasure zone centered around oral activity. Now, while I despise chewing gum and would never permit it in any classroom over which I presided, I do recognize that humans have special feelings toward oral activities.

Kissing, by the way, is a gentle art. Oh, there are moments when passions are running high, and you may even feel like nibbling on each other, but for the most part being too rough with your kisses will spoil the moment rather than enhance it. Also, although many people enjoy French kissing (that is, deep-mouth kissing), some do not. You shouldn't try to force your way into these people's mouths, because it will only break the mood.

Kissing is an important part of sex and one that should not be neglected, especially since it's something that you can do almost anytime and anywhere. So go for it!

Satisfy Your Partner Even If You Don't Feel Like Sex

You know the saying, "If I've said it once, I've said it a thousand times"? Well, if there's one thing I've said ten thousand times, it's that two people in a relationship are not Siamese twins. Each person has a different sexual appetite, so no couple is perfectly matched. There is always one person who wants more sex than the other. And, as the years go by, those roles may even switch, and then switch back again.

What should you do about this? Help each other out, that's what. You're supposed to be lovers, right? So just because you don't feel in the mood for an orgasm yourself, doesn't mean that you can't help your partner reach sexual satisfaction. There's no law that says both of you have to have an orgasm every time.

Now some women "fake it." Sometimes it's OK if a woman fakes it, as long as she has orgasms at other times. But there's no need to fake it. You can very simply, out of love for your partner, help him or her to have an orgasm in whichever way suits you best. If you're a woman, and you want to just lie back, that's fine. If you're a man and you don't want to have an erection, or can't, you can use your finger, or your tongue, or a vibrator.

The point is, don't force your partner to be sexually frustrated on a regular basis just because your sexual appetites are different. Remember, the Golden Rule applies to sex just as much as to every other aspect of human life.

Learn to Adapt to Your Circumstances

If you put on some weight, do you go around with your pants unbuttoned or do you buy a new pair? If you've reached the limit of how far your arms can hold the newspaper from your eyes, do you stop reading or get reading glasses?

As the years go by, your body changes, and some of those changes are going to affect the way you have sex. You could refuse to adapt; you could say: "If I can't have sex the way I used to, I won't have it at all." And then you'll join the long list of people out there who no longer enjoy one of life's greatest gifts. But that's just as ridiculous as wearing your pants around your knees or giving up reading. You can continue to have good sex, even great sex, up into your 90s, but you will have to make some changes in your sex life.

As they grow older, men lose their ability to have a psychogenic erection, which means they'll no longer have erections just by thinking about something sexy, and instead will need *physical* stimulation. But is it really that bad to have to ask your wife to fondle your penis? Instead of being ashamed, let yourself get carried away by it, learn to enjoy it, and work it into being a pleasant part of foreplay.

Women who've gone through menopause will no longer lubricate the way they used to, and this could cause intercourse to become painful for them. But that's no calamity, because every drugstore sells very good products that can take the place of your natural lubricants and make sex just as enjoyable as it was before.

No matter how well the years treat you, your body will undergo changes. But, rather than let those changes have a negative impact on your sex life, learn to adapt to them and make sure that you continue to enjoy great sex your whole life through.

Appendix A
Step into My Office

Again and again, throughout this book, I recommend that, if you have a problem of a sexual nature which you can't deal with yourself, you should make an appointment to consult with a sex therapist. You don't even need a partner, though if you are part of a couple it works better if you both are counseled.

You probably wonder what visiting a sex therapist entails. We sex therapists know it is this fear of the unknown that keeps many people who have sexual problems from making an appointment with one of us. I hope that, by the end of this chapter, any of you in that situation will know enough about the experience of sex therapy that you'll be able to pick up a phone and make that appointment as soon as possible.

"Baring All" for the Sexual Status Exam

When it comes to the subject of sex, embarrassment is always an issue. Now, if I told you to go to a doctor, you wouldn't be shocked if you had to remove at least some, or maybe even all, of your clothing. It wouldn't really bother you because you know that a doctor has seen lots of naked bodies and that he or she is used to it and doesn't think twice about it.

When you visit a sex therapist, you will never be asked to remove your clothes — certainly not by anybody reputable. If you are, and if that therapist is not also a medical doctor, which very few sex therapists are, then immediately walk out of that office.

But your sex therapist *will* ask a lot of questions dealing with some very private subjects that you may never have spoken about to anyone. Just the way medical doctors are used to seeing naked people, sex therapists are used to hearing about the most intimate details of the lives of the those who consult them. So try not to get all worked up; just accept that you shouldn't hold anything back if you want the therapy to be successful.

These questions form what is called a *sexual status examination,* during which the sex therapist tries to discover exactly what is wrong with you by asking a lot of different questions, including some about your past that you may not find relevant.

To explain to you why these questions are vital to the success of the exam, let me return to the more familiar ground of a doctor's examination. Say you go to the doctor because you are having a particular problem involving one of your body's functions, but it turns out that the doctor determines that your problem is only a symptom of something else that is wrong with you — something that has to be treated first. For example, you may go to the doctor because you are experiencing shortness of breath, but, after finishing the examination, the doctor tells you that your symptom has nothing to do with your lungs. The real problem may be that your arteries are clogged. The same thing happens in sex therapy, which is why the therapist must ask so many questions.

A typical example is the couple who visits me because the man complains that they don't have sex often enough, and they both assume that the problem has to do with the woman having low sexual desire. Very often, I discover that the problem has nothing to do with sex, but rather that she's angry at him for something entirely different, like never helping her with the housework even though they both work full time. Until that problem is fixed, the couple's sex life can't be improved.

I know that it can be embarrassing to answer all of these questions, but you've learned to cope with the embarrassment of removing your clothes for the doctor in order to get better, and so you shouldn't let any such feeling stop you from visiting a sex therapist. Once you get started, you'll find that it's not all that hard to be open and honest because of the relief you'll feel at unburdening yourself in front of someone who can help you fix up your sex life.

Take a ticket; one at a time, please

When a couple comes to see me, I almost always interview them separately first. This way, I get to hear both sides of the story, neither one of which may actually be the whole truth. But, by hearing both sides, I can usually at least begin to spot the real source of the problem.

During this first session, after seeing each partner alone, I then see the couple together. We try to get each partner to understand the concerns of the other one. Some couples, I always see together after that initial visit. With other couples, however, I may have additional separate sessions.

I am not a medical doctor

As you probably know, I answer a lot of people's questions, either on radio or TV or in the newspapers, and one thing that I need to say over and over again is that I am not a medical doctor. That means there are a lot of questions that I can't answer, because they are of a medical nature. However, when a client comes to see me, although I can't answer medical questions myself, I absolutely need to have those questions answered to proceed.

So in addition to the first ethical issue involving sex therapists — keeping your clothes on — here's another: ruling out a physical problem. Any time that the problem is physical in nature, such as a man who cannot obtain an erection or a woman who experiences pain during intercourse, the first thing that the sex therapist must do is send that client to a medical doctor for a check up. Even if I am almost certain that the real problem is psychological in nature, I know that it is my responsibility to make sure that any physical problem be ruled out first.

Why not try to heal the psychological problem first? The main reason is that, if there is an underlying physical problem — say, worst case, a tumor which is affecting sexual functioning — then any delay in treatment could end up being a fatal mistake. The other reason is that I might be wrong in believing that it's all in my client's head, and, if there is a physical problem, why waste everybody's time and energy trying to cure a psychological problem that is not at the root of the situation?

The medical doctor informs me of any physical problems that he or she may have found, as well as any treatment. Once the client gets a clean bill of health, I can then begin to try and help that person by using the techniques of *behavioral therapy*, which is what sex therapy is — changing your behavior.

Sex is natural

A basic, underlying principle of sex therapy is that the sexual response is a natural process, like a sneeze. It's not something that you have to learn. If you are having problems with your sexual functioning, my first assumption is going to be that there is something going on that is keeping you from doing what comes naturally.

By talking with you about your problems, I should be able to find out what that something is, and, once we've identified it, your anxieties about it will lessen. That is an important first step in bringing you back to your natural condition. We sex therapists call it *giving permission,* either to partake in sexual pleasure — by having an orgasm, for example — or not to engage in a particular sexual activity.

Sex Therapists Give the Best Homework

You know what my favorite part of sex therapy is? Giving my clients their homework assignments. After the clients and I have talked about the problems they face and identified the causes, it's time to take some action. Now this action doesn't take place in my office, but in the privacy of their own home.

If I've seen several clients in one day, and given them all homework assignments, later that night I can sit back and picture in my mind what all of them, per my instructions, are doing. And that's one of my favorite parts of my profession — that and the thank yous from people whom I've helped to overcome a sexual problem.

Assignment 1: The start-stop method

Many of the problems that people bring to me have to do with sexual illiteracy. One or both partners just don't know some very basic things about their own sexuality. For example, if a man is having problems with premature ejaculation, he doesn't know how to recognize the *premonitory sensation,* that point of his arousal that if he goes beyond, he cannot stop himself from having an orgasm and ejaculating (see Chapter 22).

To cure himself of his problem, the man has to learn to recognize that moment when, for him, there's no stopping it. And how does he do that? By practicing getting right up to that point and then stopping. If he has a partner, I tell him to go home that night and practice what is called the *stop-start technique,* where she arouses him with her hand or tongue (at this point in their treatment I usually forbid intercourse), he signals to her when he feels that he is getting to the point of orgasm, and she stops. The more the couple practices this, the better he'll be able to recognize the sensations and be able to stop himself. (I describe this process in greater detail in Chapter 22.)

So that you don't think I'm mean, I do let the man have an orgasm after one of these sessions; he's just not allowed to do it through intercourse. The reason is that I don't want him feeling the added pressure of having to perform well at intercourse, which is the problem he came to me with in the first place. By forbidding intercourse, I have removed a certain amount of the pressure from him, and this will help him to discover his point of no return a lot more easily. Eventually, after several practice sessions without intercourse, I'll have the couple try out the man's new-found skills during intercourse.

Assignment 2: Sensate focus exercises

The start-stop method, described in the preceding section, is certainly one of the assignments I give the most. Another is a series of exercises, called *sensate focus,* that teaches couples how to touch each other. Masters and Johnson developed this technique, and it is quite useful because it helps to reduce anxiety and increase communication.

The sensate focus exercises are very simple. The couple gets undressed and touches each other, one at a time. Aha, you say, it's like foreplay? Wrong, it's just the opposite. The person doing the touching is not doing it to please his or her partner, but to please him or herself. The goal is for the toucher to focus on how he or she reacts to the sensations of touching the other person's body. The person being touched remains quiet, unless there is something that causes discomfort, in which case the person is allowed to say, "That tickles," for example.

The partners are not supposed to touch the main erogenous zones, the genitals or the woman's breasts, in the beginning, but graduate to those parts of the body.

Do I need a partner?

You don't need to have a partner in order to visit a sex therapist. Many people come to see me because they have broken up with someone, in part because of a sexual problem, and they don't want the same thing to happen with their next partners. In those cases, my homework assignments may be different, but I can usually still be of help.

I always have these people call me when they do find a new partner. I give them a pep talk and then have them report to me how things went. Sometimes they need to come see me with their new partner, but, because they're prepared — they know their problem, and they don't allow it to drag on — I am able to help many of them with their new relationships.

Using psychosexual therapy

I trained under Dr. Helen Singer Kaplan at New York Hospital-Cornell University Medical School, and her method goes one step further than just the behavioral treatment described in the preceding sections. Some people have more deep-seated problems, and they may literally be stopping themselves from enjoying sex.

In that case, we sex therapists have to delve a little bit further into our clients' backgrounds to see if we can spot the source of what is keeping them from functioning well sexually. It could be something that happened to them as children, including their relationship to their parents, or it may have to do with their relationship to their spouse. Whatever it is, once the client and the sex therapist have identified the problem, we should be able to resolve it. As far as I am concerned, if I feel the trouble is too deep-seated, I often refer that client to a psychologist.

What about sex surrogates?

A sex surrogate is a person trained to help people overcome a sexual problem by actually having sex with them. A sex surrogate would speak with the sex therapist in order to know what the problem was and what they should be doing, and then report back. They were especially useful for helping people without partners. Since sex surrogates get paid to have sex with people, their profession has always been illegal, but because their "hands-on" approach sometimes worked better than merely talking about how to have sex, many sex therapists were willing to overlook this legal aspect.

With the appearance of AIDS, most sex therapists have dropped the use of sex surrogates, because therapists don't want to place their clients into a potentially dangerous environment. Because they have sex with so many partners, sex surrogates are prime targets for disease.

Some people still advertise their services as so-called sex surrogates in papers like *The Village Voice,* but without a referral from a sex therapist, you'd be hard put to tell whether this was really someone out to help you with your sexual problem, or just a prostitute looking for a different way of luring clients. Whatever the case, take my advice and do not have sex with anyone who claims to be a sex surrogate. Having sex with anyone who has multiple partners, whatever their motive, is just too risky. A good sex therapist should be able to help you solve whatever sex problem you may have without resorting to any such dangerous third parties.

Finding a Sex Therapist

Many people assume that, because I am a famous sex therapist, I know every other sex therapist in the country, or at least one in every part of the country. The truth is that, although I do know other sex therapists, I never recommend them unless I know them very well. I am just one person, and I cannot keep track of what every sex therapist is doing. And I don't want to take the responsibility of sending a person to a sex therapist who spoke to me at a convention or lecture but who might not be up to par.

"But if I can't ask Dr. Ruth, then who can I turn to?"

I'm glad you asked. I have two answers that I regularly give:

- ✔ First, call the largest hospital in your area. The best ones are often the teaching hospitals, those associated with a medical school. These hospitals almost always have a referral list of specialists, including sex therapists. At the very least, the people there can tell you whether a particular sex therapist has ever had any complaints lodged against him or her. And, if the hospital recommends many people to sex therapists, you may be able to get even more information about their training, fees, and whether insurance will cover the costs.

- ✔ Another source in your search for a sex therapist is the association of sex therapists, called the American Association of Sex Educators, Counselors, and Therapists (or AASECT). Their address is 435 N. Michigan Avenue, Suite 1717, Chicago, IL 60611-4067. If you write to them, or call them at 312-644-0828, they will recommend some sex therapists in your area who have qualified for AASECT certification. Anyone they recommend will have gone through the proper training.

Choosing a Sex Therapist

If you have several sex therapists from which to choose, I recommend seeing a few of them before making your selection. Each sex therapist has a different style, and you want to find someone who gives you the confidence to talk in a very open manner.

Some therapists specialize in certain disorders. I, for example, do not treat people who are sado-masochists — who like to inflict and receive pain during sex. So, when someone who has difficulties in these areas comes to me, I refer them to someone I know who specializes in this area. But I do handle just about every other sort of sexual disorder, among both heterosexuals and homosexuals.

If you go to a sex therapist, or any therapist or counselor for that matter, and you find that you are not being helped, then feel free to seek out another. The problem isn't necessarily that your therapist isn't good; it may be that your personalities just don't mix properly. Whatever the cause, you shouldn't have to suffer just because you've had a bad experience. Sex therapists have helped millions of people, and you can be helped too — you are no less deserving of sexual happiness than any of the others who've been helped. Just keep working at it.

Appendix B
Terrific Resources

Counseling

American Association for Marriage and Family Therapy, 1100 17th St. NW,
Tenth Floor,Washington, D.C., 20036,202- 452-0109

American Psychiatric Association,1400 K. Street, NW, Washington, D.C., 20005,
202-682-6000

American Psychological Association, 750 1st St. NE, Washington, D.C., 20002,
202-336-5500

Association of Gay and Lesbian Psychiatrists, 24 Olmstead St., Jamaica Plain,
MA, 02130, 617-522-1267

American Association of Pastoral Counselors, 9504A Lee Highway, Fairfax, VA,
22031-2303, 703-385-6967

Sex Therapy

**AASECT (American Association of Sex Educators, Counselors, and Thera-
pists),** 435 N. Michigan Avenue, Suite 1717, Chicago, IL 60611, 312-644-0828

Sexually Transmitted Diseases

Herpes Resource Center, American Social Health Association, PO Box 1327,
Research, Triangle Park, NC 27709, hotline 919-361-2120

National HIV/AIDS Hotline, English 1-800-342-AIDS 24 hours a day; Spanish
1-800-344-7432 from 8 a.m. until 2 a.m. (Eastern)

National STD (Sexually Transmitted Disease) Hotline, 800-227-8922

Sexual Orientation

National Gay and Lesbian Task Force 1734 14th Street, NW, Washington, D.C.
20009-4309, 202-332-6483

Parents and Friends of Lesbians and Gays (PFLAG), 202-638-4200

Gay and Lesbian Information Bureau Computer BBS, BBS# (703-578-4542)

Sexuality and Family Planning

Diocesan Development Program for Natural Family Planning
National Conference of Catholic Bishops
3211 4th Street NE, Washington D.C. 20017, 202-541-3240

Planned Parenthood, 810 Seventh Avenue, New York, NY 10019, 212-541-7800

Sexuality Information and Education Council of the United States (SIECUS), 130 West 42nd Street, Suite 350, New York, NY 10036-7802, 212-819-9770

Sexual Toys

Adam & Eve, 1 Apple Court, P.O. Box 800, Carrboro, NC 27510, 1-800-765-ADAM

Condomania, 1-800-9-CONDOM

Eve's Garden, 119 W. 57th Street, Suite 420, New York, NY 10019, 1-800-848-3837

Good Vibrations, 938 Howard Street, San Francisco, CA, 94103, 1-800-289-8423

The Townsend Institute, P.O. Box 8855, Chapel Hill, NC, 27515, 1-800-888-1900

Romantic Getaways

Club Med, 800-CLUB-MED

Westin Hotels & Resorts, 800-228-3000

American Association For Nude Recreation, 800-TRY-NUDE

Protecting Children

National Center for Missing and Exploited Children, 800-843-5678

National Runaway Switchboard, 800-621-4000

Cancer Support Groups

American Cancer Society, 1-800-ACS-2345

National Cancer Institute's Cancer Information Service, 1-800-4-CANCER

National Self-Help Clearinghouse, (refers to regional self-help groups) 212-642-2944

US-TOO (International Support Network for Prostate Cancer Survivors) 1-800-82-USTOO

Why Me Breast Cancer Hotline, 1-800-221-2141

Index

(continued)

(continued)

• *G* •

• *H* •

• *I* •

(continued)

(continued)

(continued)

IDG BOOKS WORLDWIDE REGISTRATION CARD

RETURN THIS REGISTRATION CARD FOR FREE CATALOG

Title of this book: Sex For Dummies

My overall rating of this book: ❑ Very good [1]   ❑ Good [2]   ❑ Satisfactory [3]   ❑ Fair [4]   ❑ Poor [5]

How I first heard about this book:

❑ Found in bookstore; name: [6]

❑ Advertisement: [8]

❑ Word of mouth; heard about book from friend, co-worker, etc.: [10]

❑ Book review: [7]

❑ Catalog: [9]

❑ Other: [11]

What I liked most about this book:

What I would change, add, delete, etc., in future editions of this book:

Other comments:

Number of computer books I purchase in a year: ❑ 1 [12]   ❑ 2-5 [13]   ❑ 6-10 [14]   ❑ More than 10 [15]

I would characterize my computer skills as: ❑ Beginner [16]   ❑ Intermediate [17]   ❑ Advanced [18]   ❑ Professional [19]

I use ❑ DOS [20]   ❑ Windows [21]   ❑ OS/2 [22]   ❑ Unix [23]   ❑ Macintosh [24]   ❑ Other: [25]_____
(please specify)

I would be interested in new books on the following subjects:
(please check all that apply, and use the spaces provided to identify specific software)

❑ Word processing: [26]

❑ Data bases: [28]

❑ File Utilities: [30]

❑ Networking: [32]

❑ Other: [34]

❑ Spreadsheets: [27]

❑ Desktop publishing: [29]

❑ Money management: [31]

❑ Programming languages: [33]

I use a PC at (please check all that apply): ❑ home [35]   ❑ work [36]   ❑ school [37]   ❑ other: [38] _____

The disks I prefer to use are ❑ 5.25 [39]   ❑ 3.5 [40]   ❑ other: [41]_____

I have a CD ROM: ❑ yes [42]   ❑ no [43]

I plan to buy or upgrade computer hardware this year: ❑ yes [44]   ❑ no [45]

I plan to buy or upgrade computer software this year: ❑ yes [46]   ❑ no [47]

Name: _____   Business title: [48] _____   Type of Business: [49] _____

Address (❑ home [50] ❑ work [51]/Company name: _____)

Street/Suite# _____

City [52]/State [53]/Zipcode [54]: _____   Country [55] _____

❑ **I liked this book!** You may quote me by name in future IDG Books Worldwide promotional materials.

My daytime phone number is _____

IDG BOOKS

THE WORLD OF COMPUTER KNOWLEDGE

☐ **YES!**
Please keep me informed about IDG's World of Computer Knowledge.
Send me the latest IDG Books catalog.

COMPUTER
BOOK SERIES
FROM IDG

BUSINESS REPLY MAIL
FIRST CLASS MAIL   PERMIT NO. 2605   FOSTER CITY, CALIFORNIA

NO POSTAGE
NECESSARY
IF MAILED
IN THE
UNITED STATES

IDG Books Worldwide
919 E Hillsdale Blvd, STE 400
Foster City, CA 94404-9691